URBAN DESIGN
for an URBAN CENTURY
Placemaking for People

by

Lance Jay Brown, FAIA

David Dixon, FAIA

Oliver Gillham, AIA

WILEY

John Wiley & Sons, Inc.

For general information about our other products and services, please contact our Customer Care Department within the United States at (800) 762-2974, outside the United States at (317) 572-3993 or fax (317) 572-4002.

Wiley also publishes its books in a variety of electronic formats. Some content that appears in print may not be available in electronic books. For more information about Wiley products, visit our web site at www.wiley.com.

Library of Congress Cataloging-in-Publication Data:

Brown, Lance Jay, 1943-
 Urban design for an urban century : placemaking for people / by Lance Jay Brown, David Dixon, Oliver Gillham.
        p. cm.
  ISBN 978-0-470-08782-4 (cloth : alk. paper)
 1. City planning—United States. I. Dixon, David, 1947 July 17- II. Gillham, Oliver. III. Title.
  NA9105.B76 2009
  711'.4–dc22

                                2008018992

Printed in the United States of America

10 9 8 7 6 5 4 3 2

Contents

Foreword

At last! Urbanism is in, and urban designers Brown, Dixon, and Gilham offer a focused lens through which to understand it. Combining urban design history and precepts with selected case studies, they generously interlace their text with deeply held convictions about the importance of urban form and place to twenty-first-century quality of life.

Today's urban design bridges disciplines and cultures by entwining shifting demographics, growing social inequities, increasing urbanization, and the overarching need to adapt long-term vision to capture the best use of scarce resources. In response to these challenges, this remarkable compilation offers fresh examples and new ways of thinkging that can enhance the collaborative endeavors of urban designers, public officials, land-use policymakers, and their communities.

In practice as in the pages of this book, amid the bold aspirations of diverse projects such as New York's Penn Station, Shanghai's waterfront, and San Francisco's Mission Bay, urban designers offer engaging visions that define the essential qualities of urbanism for generations to come.

MARILYN JORDAN TAYLOR, FAIA
Dean of the University of Pennsylvania School of Design
Partner at Skidmore, Owing, & Merrill LLP

DEDICATION

Oliver Gillham, AIA, was an architect, planner, author, and friend.
He devoted his professional life to the betterment of the environment
writ large, always writing and speaking with wit, clarity, and a deep
understanding of the issues confronting our urbanizing planet.
He helped communities, developers, and institutions alike confront
the impacts of sprawl, develop saner transportation strategies, and
revitalize urban America.

—LANCE JAY BROWN, FAIA, AND DAVID DIXON, FAIA

Preface

The pace of change in human settlements has been accelerating since humans began to build settlements, but for thousands of years change moved too slowly for people to notice it. Beginning in the Iron Age, however, the pace quickened. People in different places began to take note of the rise and fall of civilizations, and the cities that they created, without thinking that such settlements might be planned in ways that improved on past models. The Romans preferred their cities to those of the civilizations they conquered, but they treated their city-building template as a fixed model, not a work in progress. More than a thousand years into the Common Era, the Italian Renaissance ushered in the concept that human settlement should reflect society's values and aspirations. By this point, change had become a familiar component of human experience, yet its pace remained relatively unhurried and measured in centuries. Prior to the industrial era, concepts of urban form lasted well beyond the span of a human life. These concepts came wrapped as universal truths that reflected human needs and aspirations for community building, ideas that improved on previous (but now outmoded) universal truths.

And why should early concepts of urban form not have seemed universal and ageless? The basic acts of community building they appeared to describe evolved so slowly that they likely felt like constants to each era. Defense, dwelling, commercial exchange, belief—each had its place wherever people built communities. As social animals, people gravitated toward places of communication—the forums, plazas, and squares of their settlements. They walked from place to place unless they were wealthy enough for beasts of burden to pull or carry them. "Fast" meant traveling by water, not land, and rarely covering more than a few miles in an hour. Communities, built with wood and stone, grew or shrank slowly. In *The Guns of August* (New York: Macmillan, 1962), historian Barbara Tuchman noted that until Europe mobilized its armies for World War I, the vast majority of Europeans had never ventured beyond the towns and villages of their birth. Denizens of the wealthiest and most sophisticated societies of their day, they looked to history, not progress, to understand the world around them.

A century later, having passed from the age of industry into the age of technology, we have also entered an age in which the circumstances that guide human settlement evolve constantly in response to the changing needs of society, new economic realities, rapidly changing technologies, and novel means of communication. We can defend ourselves (or attack others) from the earth's orbit, socialize via text messages, and travel thousands of miles for a meeting without batting an eye (even if our suitcase occasionally goes astray). We live in an era in which the pace of change from every perspective quickens continuously. The earth's population—less than 1 billion as recently as 1800—is racing past 7 billion on its way to 12 billion by 2050. The web of a global economy binds every nation more tightly to the others, and within that web technology opens new possibilities for communication, work, transportation, health, and other aspects of life unimagined a decade earlier.

In the United States—the focus of this book—we can add demographics to the list of forces that accelerate change. Maureen McAvey, senior vice president of the Urban Land Institute, has said, "demographics are destiny," and U.S. demographics—and destiny—changed dramatically in the 1990s. For the first time since the Great Depression the demographic underpinnings of suburbia disappeared. With its housing market now dominated by single people, immigrants, younger and older couples, and nontraditional families, the United States turned its gaze back toward cities. After a century of suburbanization, the United States prepared to move into a more urban century.

It may be a Dylanesque cliché, but "the times they are a-changin'." For many, the desire for a large backyard has given way to the desire to grow older in a community that doesn't require a car in order to live independently. Near-universal fear of urban crime has given way, for many, to concerns about the public health hazards of auto-dependent suburbs. A developer recently told one of the authors that he did not need parking to have the most competitive office building in town—he needed environmentally friendly design.

This book serves as a snapshot of a field in the midst of dramatic change. It explores how we arrived here and then surveys outstanding recent urban design in the United States. It attempts to assess what we have done well and sets out principles that could help us do better in the future. It is offered as a text to students, to urbanists, to practitioners in architecture, urban design, landscape design, and urbanism, to city planners and managers, and to elected officials—in short, to all the participants whose hands will shape, over the next decades, our expanding, evolving urban environment.

Acknowledgements

I offer grateful thanks to my family and partners—both personal and professional—for their encouragement, suggestions, and saintly patience. Steve Wolf contributed to the text, edited the manuscript, and supervised the entire process; without his work this book likely would not have seen the light of day. Other Goody Clancy colleagues who made this a better book include Margaret Wommack, Ben Stone, Allan Butler, Kara McLellan, Paul Santos, and Jean Brown.

—David Dixon

I sincerely thank my family and friends for their support throughout this adventure. Irma Ostroff generously read each draft; her comments helped clarify and improve the book at every stage. Robert Geddes, Doug Kelbaugh, and Charles Zucker made themselves readily available and provided wise counsel throughout the process.

—Lance Jay Brown

Together we applaud the colleagues we quote in this book. Their contributions over many years have helped define the field of urban design, expand its reach, and orient it toward a sustainable future.

PART I

Paradigms, Principles, and Process

If you had tagged along with the authors on a typical day during the writing of this book, you would have been hard pressed to describe an urban designer's work. One author began a typical day teaching students about how American cities constantly rebuild their downtowns in response to shifting economic, social, and environmental forces. Later he met with colleagues from across New York City to advance a "green" housing initiative, and he finished the day moderating a seminar on new approaches to creating mixed-income neighborhoods. A second author spent his morning preparing design guidelines for developing more walkable streets in suburban Atlanta; joined two different teams in the afternoon to help prepare plans for new mixed-use urban neighborhoods in Norfolk, Virginia, and Kansas City, Missouri; and finished by hammering out the draft of a talk on the benefits of urban density. The third member of the trio spent much of his day preparing a plan for revitalizing downtown Norwalk, Connecticut, then finished by pursuing research on two topics: the impact of sprawl on American cities and emerging approaches to implementing new policies for managing growth.

A single thread ties these varied activities into a common field of endeavor: the work of finding the right fit between people and place. Through urban design, humans integrate and give physical form to a wide range of cultural, ecological, economic, philosophical, political, social, technological, and other considerations. In the process, they actively shape the environment in which they live.

CHAPTER 1

Urban Design–
A Social and Public Art

Fitting People and Place

The idea of what constitutes place has broadened in stages over the half century since the term *urban design* first surfaced in the early 1950s. Through the mid-1970s, the practice of urban design focused almost exclusively on the "public realm"—streets and other public spaces, particularly in cities—at a time when the flight of people and jobs to suburbs raised questions about the future of cities as a form of human settlement. In the late 1970s and the 1980s, three landmark books—Jane Jacobs's *Death and Life of Great American Cities*, Kevin Lynch's *Image of the City*, and Christopher Alexander's *Pattern Language*[1]—inspired urban designers to broaden their focus to include the quality and character of entire neighborhoods and districts. As urban disinvestment began to slow and then reverse in the 1990s, the field's scope expanded to include planning the revitalization of entire cities. In the early 2000s, growing awareness of the environmental costs of sprawl and automobile dependency widened the field's boundaries again, as urban designers searched for ways that humans can achieve a more balanced fit with nature at a regional level.

As the field's physical scope has expanded, so have the ways in which it touches the human experience. Urban designers initially sought to restore a sense of human scale and activity to cities ravaged by decay and by renewal efforts that focused more on cars than people. Later on, practitioners and others began to view urban revitalization more as a way to address social challenges and to increase economic opportunity. In recent years, urban designers have added addressing sustainability, building community, and protecting human and environmental health to their charge.

Over the past five decades, the numbers and kinds of people with whom urban designers join forces have also grown significantly. When the profession first emerged, urban designers worked chiefly with other architects and design professionals. Today they collaborate with people from many walks of life—with peer professionals and people with little education who are most directly affected by a changing society and economy; with America's wealthiest and most powerful citizens and

3

people who have little control over forces of growth and change; and with people deeply devoted to the quality and character of the built environment and with those who focus on jobs, social equity, and the myriad other issues that shape civic dialogue.

Through these collaborations, urban designers integrate the policies of federal, state, and city officials; the values of advocates for issues such as historic preservation, neighborhood quality of life, and social equity; the technical findings of experts in fields such as transportation, affordable housing, and real estate development; the financial imperatives imposed by those who develop, finance, and insure projects; and the science of ecologists, hydrologists, and others who understand the earth's natural systems. This integration produces the plans, guidelines, and regulations that shape sites, neighborhoods, districts, cities, regions, and, increasingly, the balance between mankind and nature.

Urban design can result in visions and new public policies that establish long-term legacies, offering guidance for shaping growth and change for generations. In accomplishing any of these tasks, urban design can never be a solitary endeavor. Urban designers must constantly reach out to the communities we serve for information and inspiration alike.

William Gilchrist, FAIA, director of planning for Montgomery, Alabama

---

The Evolution of a "Social and Public Art"

Just as architecture predates the earliest modern training programs (France's Académie Royale d'Architecture opened its doors in 1671), urban design stretches back five thousand years to humans' first intentional attempts to shape the environment. Chapters 2, 3, and 4 examine the ways in which people have consciously sited groups of buildings, arranged public spaces, and defined the boundaries between man and nature

---

Urban design *is* an art and not a science or an engineering discipline, but a social and public art rather than a personal or fine art.... Unlike a painter or sculptor, in every aspect of my work I am responsible not only to myself, but to my fellow man and to future generations.

Douglas Kelbaugh, FAIA, dean, Taubman College of Architecture and Urban Planning, University of Michigan, Ann Arbor

---

throughout history. Early human settlements—for example, the villages that sprang up along trade routes—evolved without planning (as some still do today). We can trace a continuous history of places that were visibly designed: Neolithic settlements in western Europe, palace complexes of ancient Mesopotamia, funerary and religious compounds of third-dynasty Egypt, ancient Greek and Roman fora, Aztec city-states, the Forbidden City of Beijing, and the boulevards of nineteenth-century Paris all reflect a human drive to form settlements in ways that expressed their builders' beliefs and responded to nature, economics, and other forces at work around them.

For his book *A World Lit Only by Fire*, historian William Manchester chose a title that dramatically illuminated a central reality of day-to-day life in the Renaissance. His goal was to present modern readers with a late-medieval perspective on the world and help them to see his subject from the perspective of that age, not ours.[2] Any review of the history of urban design requires from the reader an effort to appreciate the vastly different worlds in which humans have designed spaces and settlements. From Mesopotamia onward, urban design has served as a conscious act of mediation among a constellation of influences—economic and social dynamics, religious and cultural beliefs, environmental

---

[U]rban design...all comes down to the management of change[.]

Kevin Lynch, *What Time Is This Place?* (Cambridge, Mass.: MIT Press, 1972)

constraints, and other forces—unique to a community or era. Monarchs, priests, military engineers, and others—the urban designers of their day—only partially saw themselves as creating monuments and adorning their communities. More consciously, they reacted to the needs and aspirations of the gods and societies they served, and they strove to prepare their communities to meet the demands of the world around them. Urban designers pursue the same goals today.

The reconstruction of the Ishtar Gate at Berlin's Pergamon Museum lets modern visitors experience one of history's most stunning gateways—and offers a glimpse into the Babylonian mind of the seventh century BCE. A modern visitor readily interprets the gate's size and majesty as announcing Babylon's significance and the splendor within its walls. Yet, to Babylonians—living in a world where few people traveled beyond the village of their birth, that had no concept of the individual (as our era understands the idea), and that saw history as an endlessly turning wheel of seasons—the Ishtar Gate announced not human splendor but a city of gods as well as humans. For the gate's creators, its roaring lions evoked the protective power of the gods that dwelt inside.

The squares of Greco-Roman cities like ancient Pompeii and Renaissance cities like Siena reflect the

A reconstruction of Babylon's Ishtar Gate, from the seventh century BCE, at the Pergamon Museum, Berlin, Germany, suggests the feelings the gate might have evoked in its creators: awe at the protective power of the gods that dwelt inside the city. Photo © 2006 Chris Wood/ wikimediacommons, http://commons.wikimedia.org/wiki/ Image:Pergamonmuseum_Ishtartor_06.jpg. *See color insert, C-1.*

One remarkable man, the Franciscan friar Roger Bacon, . . . stands on an isolated pinnacle of his own in the Middle Ages . . . . It has been claimed for him that he announced the idea of Progress . . . . His aim was to reform higher education and introduce into the universities a wide, liberal, and scientific programme of secular studies . . . . With great ingenuity and resourcefulness he sought to show that the studies to which he was devoted . . . were indispensable to an intelligent study of theology and Scripture.

John Bagnell Bury, *The Idea of Progress: An Inquiry into Its Origin and Growth* (London: Macmillan and Co., Limited, 1920)

forces that shaped those cultures—and offer striking contrasts to the Ishtar Gate. As gathering places for wealthy, property-owning citizens, Pompeii's forum and Siena's Piazza del Campo both celebrate very human activities and the rise of a comfortable middle class engaged in commerce. Neither served as a setting for public buildings or broad community enjoyment, as modern squares do. Cities shaped during the baroque era and later, like Paris, reflect the influence of monarchal government

Designers working under authoritarian regimes often had the freedom to create monumental spaces and long vistas, as in Paris. Copyright © iStockphoto.com/FotoVoyager.com.

Once the urban transformation had been effected, the city as a whole became a sacred precinct under the protection of its god: the very axis of the universe went…through its temple; while the wall…was both a physical rampart for defense and a spiritual boundary of greater significance.

Lewis Mumford, *The City in History: Its Transformations and Its Prospects* (New York: Harcourt Brace & Company, 1961), 48

and authoritarian rule in great diagonal boulevards, monumental spaces, and long vistas slashing across clustered medieval blocks. The streets of these cities served as models for the grand commercial Main Streets of contemporary American cities.

Considered today an essential element of the public realm, the grid originated to support military efficiency and taxation in Greek and Roman settlements. Its adoption by many American cities was owed largely to a desire to facilitate efficient land distribution and development in a society that believed strongly in the moral benefit of owning real estate. The young United States, with abundant acreage, valued property ownership as an economic prerequisite to democracy—a clear source of distinction from European and other societies. Only in the District of Columbia did Americans pursue the monumental design and diagonal boulevards characteristic of continental Europe—following a plan laid out by a French national.

The recognizable roots of contemporary urban design in the United States lie in efforts to give form to the industrial cities of mid- and late-nineteenth-century Europe and America. The changes unleashed by the Industrial Revolution, beginning with the unprecedented growth of cities, triggered a need to revisit basic assumptions about the form and organization of urban communities. Few cities in human history had attained anything close to the size and complexity of the indus-

What does urban design need most? In a word, collegiality. Urban design is only possible when people from various disciplines and professions, and arts and sciences, agree to work together. In the past, when it was civic design, it focused on the public realm. It was sponsored by civic associations and enriched by civic art…. Today, the field of urban design is unbounded, intellectually and physically…. Architecture extends from room to region.

Robert Geddes, FAIA, dean, Princeton University School of Architecture

trial cities that sprang up across western Europe and in North America after 1850. American industrial cities grew at astonishing rates; the number of U.S. cities with populations greater than 200,000 grew from four in the mid-nineteenth century to more than forty by the early twentieth century. Industrialization alone did not drive this growth; electric streetcars and new building technologies made it possible for cities to grow both horizontally and vertically. Architects and others began to approach cities from an *urban design* perspective that would be familiar today as they wrestled with noise, pollution, and poverty; modern technology; and a new and profound separation between urban residents and nature. They joined European colleagues in advocating sweeping measures under the banner of the City Beautiful movement, introducing the concept of mass rebuilding to restore beauty and nature to cities. Architects and others—to a greater extent in the United States than in Europe—explored ways to escape industrialization's disagreeable side effects through creation of suburban retreats for the rich and, later, the middle class.

Urban design emerged as a distinct profession not as a direct outgrowth of these reactions to urban industrialization but in response to new problems facing American cities in the 1950s. Taking hold even more rapidly than industrialization, these challenges produced a full-blown crisis for American cities, as industry and residents—up to half in some cities—fled to the

▲ As factories multiplied in cities, many residents found the resulting noise, smoke, and soot intolerable. Courtesy of the Library of Congress, FSA-OWI Collection.

▲▲ For the well-to-do, suburban housing offered an escape from crowded industrializing cities. Courtesy of Oliver Gillham.

Highways of the urban renewal era often cut large swaths through dense older neighborhoods. Courtesy of Alex S. MacLean/Landslides—www.landslides.com.

suburbs, taking much of their wealth with them. This dramatic migration arose from the confluence of superficially unrelated factors: the advent of near-universal automobile ownership among middle- and upper-class Americans; construction of a vast national highway system that made suburbs easily accessible; introduction of

> Las Vegas...[was] where we could discover the validity and appreciate the vitality of the commercial strip and of urban sprawl, of the commercial sign whose scale accommodates to the moving car and whose symbolism illuminates an iconography of our time. And where we thereby could acknowledge the elements of symbol and mass culture as vital to architecture, and the genius of the everyday, and the commercial vernacular as inspirational as was the industrial vernacular in the early days of Modernism.
>
> Robert Venturi, FAIA, accepting the 1991 Pritzker Prize (from www.pritzkerprize.com)

mortgage programs that made home ownership far more broadly attainable; a dramatic rise in the number of households with children (and demand for backyards); and the broad diffusion of technologies, including television, that eroded the ties binding people to their urban neighborhoods.

Urban design evolved out of the modernist movement, itself a conscious effort by architects and others to break with familiar design approaches that appeared incapable of responding to economic, social, and technological change. Many of the first generation to identify themselves as urban designers believed that cities could survive only if the concept of the *City Functional* replaced the ideal of the City Beautiful. Borrowing the City Beautiful concept of large-scale reconstruction where necessary, they sought to reshape cities around the automobile, apply aesthetics rooted in contemporary art, and adopt suburban models that suddenly appeared remarkably successful. This approach to city building reached a zenith in the federally financed urban renewal movement of the 1950s and '60s. Noble in intent, the movement sought to restore economic vitality by making downtowns and older, urban neighborhoods more accessible by car. Fragmented landownership and building patterns often required wholesale land takings and demolition of stores and apartments to accommodate the large scale of development geared to automobiles. As a result, urban renewal sometimes removed entire neighborhoods and downtowns built before the car had gained economic and social dominance.

The current approach to urban design began to take form during the 1980s and '90s in reaction to urban renewal and recognition of a need to bridge the gap between planning that restored urban economies and design that restored human scale and vitality to urban communities. Many of the leading urban designers practicing today entered the profession in the waning days of urban renewal. Reaction to the excesses of that program shaped their attitudes and fed a desire to base urban design on human experiences and aspirations rather than the accommodation of automobiles. This approach found strong expression in the New Urbanism movement, advocated most prominently by architects Elizabeth Plater-Zyberk and Andres Duany beginning in the 1980s.

During the same period, four lines of thinking converged to form the foundation for an urban renaissance; they strongly influenced the approach that urban designers brought to their work and the kinds of projects they undertook. Economist Richard Florida's *The Rise of the Creative Class* (New York: Basic Books, 2004) built on Jane Jacobs's message from three decades earlier by demonstrating that vibrant, walkable downtowns and urban neighborhoods attract educated and creative workers who in turn attract investment. At about the same time, housing economist Laurie Volk of Zimmerman Volk, joined by organizations like the Urban Land Institute, identified new demand for urban housing on

> Most civic leaders, however, have failed to understand that what is true for corporations is also true for cities and regions: Places that succeed in attracting and retaining creative class people prosper; those that fail don't.
>
> Richard Florida, *The Washington Monthly,* May 2002

a scale not witnessed since the Depression. This suggested that urban design initiatives intended to enhance neighborhoods and downtowns could attract large numbers of new urban residents, who in turn would want jobs near where they lived.

Beginning in 2000, Dr. Richard Jackson—then working for the Centers for Disease Control and Prevention—coauthored a series of articles and books that documented a growing obesity crisis in the United States and traced it largely to the fact that sprawl discouraged people from walking. Invited to speak at forums such as the Congress for the New Urbanism in 2003, Jackson reinforced from another perspective the need for smart growth and a new generation of mixed-use, walkable, lively urban neighborhoods and downtowns. Finally, in 2004, writer David Owen argued in the *New Yorker* that Manhattan's density enables its residents to use energy far more efficiently—and consequently leave a far smaller "carbon footprint"—than their rural and suburban counterparts. America's largest city, Owen concluded, was its greenest. His provocative article, circulated widely, buttressed a gathering consensus about the role of smart growth in responding to concerns about global warming and environmental health.[3]

> Most Americans, including most New Yorkers, think of New York City as an ecological nightmare, a wasteland of concrete and garbage and diesel fumes and traffic jams, but in comparison with the rest of America it's a model of environmental responsibility. By the most significant measures, New York is the greenest community in the United States, and one of the greenest cities in the world.
>
> David Owen, "NYC is the Greenest City in America," *The New Yorker,* October 18, 2004.

Florida, Volk, Jackson, and Owen were part of an informal movement that arose outside of the architectural profession and, by popularizing research that supported Jane Jacobs's evocative urban vision, contributed to an emerging paradigm for thinking about U.S. settlement patterns. Reflecting shifting demographics, evolving values, and growing environmental awareness, this new view celebrates not simply the value of cities but the joys of urban life. To an extent not imagined since the City Beautiful movement, cities and older suburbs in the United States have begun to prosper by restoring Main Streets, introducing high-quality new housing geared to a wide variety of needs and aspirations, and offering alternatives to automobile dependence. Urban environments that are viewed as vibrant, walkable places with a lively sense of community draw people who can afford to live, work, play—and increasingly, invest—in revitalized communities. In addition to the more visible qualities that make

The incidental exercise that we have eliminated from our daily lives has had major implications, in terms of environmental pollution, in terms of mental health and socialization, but in particular in terms of our own strength, activity levels and obesity levels. While we focus on obesity, the activity level is of equal importance. The estimated difference between people living in sprawling areas versus non-sprawling areas, or more dense areas, is on average, about six to seven pounds. Which, compared to what we've gained, is probably half or a third, but it's still a major contributor.

Dr. Richard Jackson, former director of the National Center for Environmental Health at the Centers for Disease Control and Prevention

these places appealing, some cities have amplified their drawing power with investment in underlying infrastructure by expanding public transit, reopening waterfronts, and rebuilding schools. Urban design plays a central role in identifying, organizing, and showcasing these new sources of strength and helping revitalize cities across the United States after decades of disinvestment.

Integrating Diverse Perspectives and Skills

The University of Pennsylvania and Harvard University established the first U.S. graduate programs in urban design (in 1957 and 1960, respectively), and today there are thirty-six urban design programs in schools of architecture in addition to a larger number of graduate planning-and-landscape-architecture programs that offer an urban design focus. Some urban designers combine a degree in architecture or urban design with training in a field that offers related skills and perspective—such as law, transportation planning, or real estate development—in recognition of the broad range of tools useful in shaping the built environment. Even with such diverse links to other disciplines, however, most urban designers' education begins with a strong foundation in

American attitudes toward cities and older suburbs have shifted dramatically in recent years, with renewed appreciation for the liveliness, walkability, and sense of community urban areas offer. Courtesy of Goody Clancy.

Private investment and public-private partnerships increasingly provide the funding for infrastructure that the public sector once provided—as happened at South Campus Gateway in Columbus, Ohio, whose development was spearheaded by a redevelopment partnership created by Ohio State University. Courtesy of Brad Feinknopf LLC.

design, most often architecture, and many urban design professionals consider themselves architects first.

While urban designers come to the profession from a variety of educational backgrounds and play a broad array of technical roles, they generally share three qualities. The first is a strong interest in the ways physical design can integrate perspectives from a broad array of other disciplines; this often entails a high degree of interdisciplinary collaboration and an interest in transmuting varied perspectives into a physical framework. The second is a strong focus on community involvement and outreach, which often leads urban designers to devote significant time to educating and learning from the communities with which they work. The third quality is a consistent focus on using design and policy to strengthen the quality and character of the public realm that ties together the individual components of the built environment. This often involves advocating the public interest in an era in which private investment and public-private partnerships increasingly finance the infrastructure once provided by the public sector.

Urban design demands much of practitioners: the ability to act as generalists and integrators, to listen and educate, to implement and lead, and to plan and design. These skills are essential to the field's interdisciplinary nature, and they make its practitioners well suited to serve as leaders, partners, and valued contributors in many aspects of shaping the built environment. Urban designers frequently collaborate with a wide range of other professionals—from transportation planners and public officials to environmentalists and lawyers—and with the larger community—from neighborhood leaders and public officials to preservation advocates and business owners.

My job as an urban designer is to collaborate with people in many disciplines to bring creative problem-solving, big-picture perspective, and innovative thinking to the implementation of a wide range of public policies that otherwise might have been guided only by economics or politics.[4]

Rebecca Barnes, FAIA, director of strategic planning for Brown University and former chief planner, city of Boston

The absence of formal certification makes it difficult to determine precisely how many urban designers practice in the United States. The American Institute of Architects (AIA), the American Planning Association, and the American Society of Landscape Architects all have active urban design divisions or practice networks. The Congress for the New Urbanism, which maintains a strong focus on urban design, attracts a highly diverse membership that tilts more toward developers and planners than architects. A rough gauge of urban designers in the United States is the number of the AIA's 81,000 members who affiliate with the group's Regional and Urban Design Committee. Although relatively small—roughly 5,000—this number represents a 360 percent increase over the comparable figure from a decade ago.[5]

The Center for Communities by Design reflects the AIA's increasing commitment to urban design. The center has grown significantly since 2001. Demonstrating the wide range of roles that urban designers play and the varied backgrounds from which they come, the center's current director, David Downey, is a planner whose previous work entailed supporting community revitalization efforts across Michigan. His predecessor, John Ratliff, a lawyer, went on to advise Maryland Governor Martin O'Malley on a wide range of urban issues.

Although twenty years ago most urban designers worked in large cities on the coasts or in the Midwest, the profession today is truly national; urban designers are active in many smaller communities across the United States. The majority work in private practices, often affiliated with larger architecture and landscape architecture firms or, less frequently, with large transportation and environmental engineering firms. Urban designers work for the public sector, often in planning or development agencies at the municipal level, and for smart growth, transportation planning, housing and regional development agencies at the county, state, and federal levels. Urban designers work for and as developers in the private sector and for public-private partnerships and nonprofits that also initiate development projects. Others are academics,

teaching and conducting research or serving as campus planners. Urban designers also work in other settings, including overseeing planning for large institutions like universities and hospitals; in law practices that focus on land use and environmental issues; and in fields that involve mediating between the built environment and the larger forces that shape society, from journalism to executive positions at research institutes such as the Environment Simulation Center in New York City.

The product of all this activity often depends on the goals established at the start, whether there is a clear and agreed-upon planning context, how well the various participating disciplines are coordinated, how much community involvement and public outreach take place, and a host of other factors, including who takes the lead. Because placemaking is a multidisciplinary activity that intersects community involvement, complex permitting processes, and evolving environmental concerns, the job of weaving together multiple strands increasingly falls to the urban designer.

In their various roles, urban designers establish the parameters for fitting people and place. They help erect the frameworks for projects that enhance economic competitiveness, restore community, overcome social fragmentation, repair human impacts on the environment, and in other ways give shape to places that enable other architects to design buildings, developers to begin projects, mayors to revitalize cities, and governors to launch smart-growth and regional-planning initiatives.

Giving Form to a Rapidly Changing Society

Part II of this book details case studies drawn from projects that have received recognition for excellence under the AIA's annual Regional and Urban Design Honor Awards program. Virtually all share the three characteristics noted above: they required designers to collaborate with practitioners from multiple disciplines; they involved significant outreach to a broad spectrum of stakeholders; and they touched directly on enhancing economic opportunity, quality of life, and human and environmental health. This sampling of projects suggests diverse ways in which urban designers—working in private practice, for developers, in academia, as community advocates, and in other venues—shape human environments, and it offers a window into areas of focus within the practice of urban design that have only emerged in the last decade. All of these case studies share a fourth common ingredient: the essential role that community engagement plays in every facet of urban design.

Smart-growth initiatives involve urban designers in reversing the impacts of sprawl and promoting more livable cities. Retrofitting aging downtowns with transit, lively public spaces, and other amenities can restore their appeal as places to live, work, and invest. Initiatives in this area revitalize commercial streets to help them attract new retailers. Channeling growth back into established communities requires innovative approaches to redeveloping brownfield sites and underutilized strip malls or other low-intensity uses.

Smart-Growth Initiatives

- *Envision Utah* (led by Calthorpe Associates, sponsored by the Coalition for Utah's Future) is a smart-growth initiative intended to improve quality of life, promote economic opportunity, and support environmental sustainability for a large region centered on Salt Lake City.

- *Eastward Ho!* (led by architect Dan Williams, sponsored by the South Florida Regional Planning Council) aims to align growth and development in south Florida with the region's fragile environment.

- The *Albemarle County Neighborhood Model* (prepared by Torti Gallas and Partners, sponsored by Albemarle County, Virginia) represents a regional strategy for focusing growth in ways that support mixed-use, walkable neighborhoods.

The Albemarle County Neighborhood Model focuses regional growth in ways that support mixed-use, walkable neighborhoods in Charlottesville, Virginia. Courtesy of Torti Gallas and Partners, Inc./Dodson Associates.

Transportation planning initiatives involve urban designers in creating workable alternatives to automobile dependency and reshaping regions and cities around people rather than the cars. New transit alignments support regional growth, broaden economic opportunity, and improve environmental quality. Introducing mixed-income housing into established communities balances the "gentrifying" impact of transit access at a neighborhood level. Entire new mixed-use (and mixed-income) neighborhood centers ensure more thorough integration of transit into neighborhood life.

Transportation Planning

- *The Boston Transportation Planning Review, or BTPR* (led by urban designer Peter Hopkinson, FAIA; sponsored by the Commonwealth of Massachusetts), a groundbreaking initiative launched in the mid-1970s, created a thirty-year transportation agenda for the Boston region and served as a national model for creating regional strategies that shift the focus from roadways to transit.

- *Boston's Newest Smart Growth Corridor* (prepared by Goody Clancy) was sponsored by a coalition of community development corporations thirty years after BTPR to identify ways in which transit-oriented development (TOD) could serve the needs of low- and moderate-income residents.

- Beginning in 1999, the *New Jersey Department of Transportation and NJ Transit* jointly sponsored an ambitious statewide plan to encourage transit-oriented development along existing rail lines with a package of state incentives and support. The program explicitly cites community revitalization, traffic reduction, and improved air quality among its goals.

- Citywide planning, undertaken by several urban designers and sponsored by the *City of Denver's Community Planning and Development Agency,* integrates new transit lines into the city's neighborhoods.

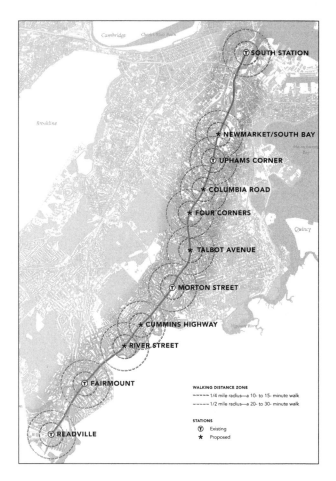

Boston's Newest Smart Growth Corridor identifies ways in which transit-oriented development can serve low- and moderate-income needs. Courtesy Goody Clancy.

Citywide revitalization strategies represent an emerging focus in the field of urban design (so recent, in fact, that few have been submitted to award competitions, and such projects therefore are not represented yet in the AIA's Honor Awards program). These initiatives place urban designers at the center of efforts to capitalize on rebounding urban economies, even in cities that have endured severe disinvestment. Newark, New Jersey, offers a prime example with its Vision for

Newark's Future process, spearheaded by the Regional Plan Association. The process brought together architects, urban designers, and other regional stakeholders in early 2007 for a series of weekend workshops on enhancing quality of life and economic opportunity across the entire city. Preliminary findings identified a need to redevelop vacant lots and abandoned houses with housing at densities sufficient to accommodate a wide variety of new households and to support nearby Main Streets. Social equity required that new development avoid displacing long-term residents and open af-fordable new housing opportunities to them. Newark's reviving neighborhoods will also need a new genera-tion of parks and public spaces to encourage interac-tion between new and long-term residents, helping them build community.

Brownfield and grayfield sites offer opportunities to create entire new districts and neighborhoods, each with a full complement of streets, squares, and parks. Urban designers shape these districts—often involving millions of square feet and relatively tall buildings—and the transitions that tie them into existing, fine-grained neighborhoods and Main Streets. These new districts and neighborhoods also need strategies for addressing such sustainability issues as storm-water handling and urban heat buildup.

Rebuilding public housing and creating new mixed-income urban neighborhoods provides op-portunities to take advantage of renewed interest in urban living and a new willingness by people at all income levels to live in mixed-income communities. These new residents are more diverse by almost every measure—including age, race, income, and house-hold structure—and they require new and more varied forms of housing. Sensitivity to the traditional char-acter of surrounding neighborhoods needs to inform design guidelines for new neighborhoods, and parking requires careful attention to ensure that parking struc-tures remain hidden and that traditional curbside park-ing plays its varied roles.

The Plan for Mission Bay creates a new mixed-use district on a substantial former rail yard site adjacent to downtown San Francisco. Courtesy of Johnson/Fain.

Brownfield and Grayfield Redevelopment

- *Plan for Mission Bay* (Johnson and Fain; sponsored by the San Francisco Redevelopment Authority) to create a new mixed-use district adjacent to downtown.

- *Lake Shore East Master Plan* (Skidmore, Owings & Merrill; sponsored by the City of Chicago) to redevelop former rail yards into a mixed-use, urban neighborhood.

- *Lloyd Crossing Sustainable Urban Design Plan* (Mithun Architects; sponsored by the Portland Development Commission) to create a new thirty-block, mixed-use "urban village."

New Mixed-Income Urban Neighborhoods

- *Park DuValle* (Urban Design Associates, sponsored by the Louisville [Kentucky] Housing Authority) to transform public housing into a mixed-income neighborhood with funding from the federal HOPE (Housing Opportunities for People Everywhere) VI program

- *Martin Luther King HOPE VI Redevelopment* (Torti Gallas, sponsored by the Philadelphia Housing Authority in Pennsylvania) to integrate public housing into a surrounding mixed-income urban neighborhood

- *North Point* (CBT/Childs, Bertman Tseckares, sponsored by Spaulding & Slye Colliers and Guilford Transportation Industries) to transform a decommissioned rail yard into a new mixed-income neighborhood in Cambridge, Massachusetts

Community-based initiatives to transform suburbs into walkable, mixed-use districts. Suburban areas seeking to rectify functional problems by careful redesign constitute another emerging focus in the field of urban design. Atlanta's Emory University launched The Clifton Community Partnership as a forum where the university's neighbors—including institutions like the U.S. Centers for Disease Control, shopping center owners, and home owners—are collaborating on guidelines intended to transform a car-dominated corridor by adding development that introduces rich urban qualities, walkability, and community-building public spaces. A similar need exists across the United States: highway corridors await transformation into walkable streets; suburban development set back from the street needs infill development that lines streets with retail and other pedestrian-friendly activities;

▼ Park DuValle used funds from the federal HOPE VI program to transform public housing into a mixed-income neighborhood in Louisville, Kentucky. Courtesy of Urban Design Associates.

The District of Columbia launched the Anacostia Waterfront Initiative in an effort to stimulate redevelopment in an area bypassed by economic development. Courtesy of Chan Krieger Sieniewicz, © 2003.

and single-use shopping centers need to be redesigned as traditional walkable environments with gridded streets and blocks, stores with housing and other uses overhead, and neighborhood parks.

Waterfront revitalization projects engage urban designers in the task of transforming run-down industrial waterfronts into lively places that enhance neighborhoods and downtowns. Striking a balance between private uses—housing, retail, and jobs-producing activities—and public access and enjoyment of the waterfront is critical. Older downtowns and neighborhoods that have turned their backs on faded industrial waterfronts must be reoriented to embrace new development along the water. New parks and public spaces must be designed and programmed to appeal to people of many ages, incomes, and ethnic backgrounds.

Waterfront Revitalization

- *Anacostia Waterfront Initiative* (Chan Krieger Sieniewicz, sponsored by the Washington Office of Planning) to stimulate redevelopment in an area bypassed by the District of Columbia's economic revival

- *UrbanRiver Visions* (Goody Clancy, sponsored by the Massachusetts Executive Office of Environmental Affairs) to encourage revitalization of key waterfront sites across the state as a strategy for reviving older downtowns

- *West Harlem Waterfront Park* (W Associates, sponsored by West Harlem Environmental Action and Community Board 9 in New York City) to transform a 1-acre parking lot into a waterfront park

Northeastern University's Campus Master Plan extends the university's urban campus while creating connections to surrounding neighborhoods in Boston. Alex S. MacLean/Landslides—www.landslides.com.

Campus-Related Redevelopment

- *East Baltimore Comprehensive Physical Redevelopment Plan* (Urban Design Associates, sponsored by the East Baltimore Development Initiative with Johns Hopkins University Medical Center and the Annie E. Casey Foundation) to revitalize the area around the Johns Hopkins University Medical Center

- *Northeastern University's Campus Master Plan* (William Rawn and Associates, sponsored by Northeastern University) to expand the university's urban campus in Boston and to create a new sense of connection to surrounding neighborhoods

- *Ongoing initiatives by Campus Partners* (supported by Goody Clancy) to revitalize the traditional Main Street and neighborhoods surrounding Ohio State University in Columbus

Campus-related redevelopment illustrates how institutions have enlarged their role in revitalizing urban districts with the help of urban designers. Development that combines mixed-income housing, community-oriented retail, and state-of-the-art research spaces must be designed to fit into existing neighborhoods. Builders of new on-campus housing and academic buildings need to create inviting new connections to surrounding neighborhoods after walling them off for decades. Urban designers need to work with diverse stakeholders—including universities, city governments, and nearby residents—to build a consensus about revitalization.

Mixed-use development integrates the civic and private development undertaken by public-private partnerships, which play an essential role in the cre-

We are charged with revitalization of a community of more than 40,000 people that surrounds The Ohio State University.... The place-making elements associated with good urban design broke through years of deadlock to unlock our ability to achieve long-term success and vitality...and have resulted in more than $100 million in new mixed-use development, including a ground-breaking mixed-use project which will significantly energize the overall revitalization initiative.[6]

Terry Foegler, president, Campus Partners for Community Revitalization, The Ohio State University, Columbus

The Harmonie Park/Madison Avenue Project helped spur revitalization in a Detroit neighborhood plagued by decades of disinvestment. Courtesy of Schervish, Vogel, Merz, P.C.

ation of lively new town centers that neither the public nor private sector could achieve by itself. Complex planning and design are required to unlock the ability of rising urban real estate values to subsidize significant projects, such as construction of a new Penn Station in New York City that recreates the wonder of the original, which was demolished under an urban renewal scheme. Skillfully planned and designed mixed-use development, careful attention to streetscape, and inspiring design of new public spaces can bring new life to depressed commercial districts.

Advocacy planning and design emerged in the 1960s as a term to describe the activities of planners and designers who worked to support neighborhoods in flux. In many respects, advocacy reflected a grassroots response to the wholesale destruction of older neighborhoods under urban renewal. Out of this advocacy base came a series of initiatives intended to institutionalize the concept of community involvement in planning and design. Today, cities and towns across the United States have established formal processes to ensure that residents play a part in planning their neighborhood's future. From advocacy to community boards, it was most often urban designers who introduced, guided, managed, and serviced community-engagement initiatives.

Mixed-Use Development

- *Windsor Town Center* (Merrill, Pastor, and Colgan, sponsored by the City of Vero Beach, Florida) to create a new focus for the community

- *Pennsylvania Station Redevelopment Project* (Skidmore, Owings & Merrill, sponsored by the Pennsylvania Station Redevelopment Corporation) to recreate the grandeur of Manhattan's Penn Station as part of an ambitious mixed-use development

- *Harmonie Park/Madison Avenue Project* (Schervish Vogel Consulting Architects, sponsored by the Harmonie Park/Madison Avenue Development Corporation) to spur revitalization in a Detroit neighborhood plagued by decades of disinvestment

The design for Chicago's Millennium Park, the result of city-wide effort, captured and completed the vision for Grant Park created by Daniel H. Burnham more than a century earlier. © iStockphoto.com/Dilutett72.

Advocacy Planning and Design

- In the late 1970s New York City created community planning boards and formalized resident groups that engage in the planning and urban design of their neighborhoods.

- Working through its Regional/ Urban Design Assistance Team (R/UDAT) program, the AIA assembles teams of architectural professionals to tackle difficult urban design problems at the request of communities looking for added expertise and perspective. The R/UDAT procedure assures formal involvement of the community through extensive public testimony solicited in preparation for each team's assignment.

- During the initial phase of planning for the World Trade Center site after the 9/11 attacks, more than five thousand people took part in deliberations about the future of the 16-acre site and Lower Manhattan in New York City.

Other urban design projects defy easy categorization, such as the plan for Savannah College of Art and Design (by Lee Meyer, AIA). This work involved a downtown-wide development strategy, creation of a plan for the college's urban campus, preservation of historic buildings, and design of lively new streetscapes. Planning and design for Chicago's universally praised Millennium Park (to which more than thirty firms and designers contributed) entailed a design focus on a single site, a downtown-wide perspective, and outreach to a citywide community—and it took place within the context of the vision for Grant Park created by Daniel Burnham more than a century earlier. Other projects exceed traditional measures of scale, such as an emerging vision to use enhanced high-speed rail to stimulate growth along the Northeast Corridor between New York and Boston.

During the era of urban renewal, urban design focused on physical design, but urban designers today employ a much larger tool kit. The array of tools has expanded in part because clients now expect urban designers to embed implementation strategies in their recommendations; community members want to know the impact of urban design concepts on every aspect of quality of life; and urban designers themselves have come increasingly to recognize that their ideas must grow from a comprehensive understanding of the places in which they work. The tools that urban designers employ today include:

Defining context

At every scale—from entire regions to individual sites—urban design begins with an understanding of context, which in turn is defined by factors beyond physical form. For example, values evolve. Americans place a much higher value on environmental sustainability and public health today than they did a decade ago; that and similar shifts fundamentally affect every urban design proposal. Creating economic opportunity is a far greater concern in some communities than others; a city fearful that its youth must leave to find jobs often will—and should—consider far more ambitious proposals than a city more focused on managing the impacts of economic growth. Communities divided by racial tension have a far more difficult time making important urban design decisions, because those decisions are viewed through the lens of race rather than civic value. Of course, the nature of physical context can vary greatly. A historic community in which physical character and cultural heritage are intertwined presents a very different set of issues than a former industrial site or suburban town center.

Planning

Designing the experience of a place requires establishing the essential planning parameters related to transportation, land uses, density patterns, environmental sustainability, and similar issues. For example, in neighborhood projects across the United States today the most important quality people seek is a walkable Main Street. Creating these Main Streets requires planning decisions at every scale. From a regional perspective, Seattle's decision to create a growth boundary concentrated more growth in existing neighborhoods and provided the densities and disposable income essential to resurrecting walkable Main Streets. The city supported this initiative at citywide and neighborhood scales by increasing public transit—making it easier for households to move

Creating successful walkable Main Streets requires planning decisions at every scale. Courtesy of Goody Clancy.

to walkable neighborhoods and to give up one of their cars—and by carefully zoning traditional neighborhood centers to permit higher-density lofts and requiring that they dedicate their street levels to retail space.

Design

While architects may focus on style, urban designers look increasingly at how design can enhance the way people experience a place. Ironically, as urban designers have steadily broadened their purview beyond design, design quality has grown steadily more important to communities and clients. As investment capital grows more mobile, regions and communities turn increasingly to urban design character to distinguish themselves from the pack of locales competing to lure jobs and investment. The concerns of urban designers also include land use and density; building height and massing; the fit of new buildings with their historic or traditional neighbors; the relationships of buildings to the public realm of streets, squares, and parks; the character of places at every scale; and similar issues. Answering these questions helps determine if a region appears to rest lightly on its natural setting

Urban design policies and practice can help to determine whether new development fits gently into its natural setting or overwhelms it with sprawl. Alex S. MacLean/Landslides— www.landslides.com.

or overwhelm it with sprawl. Does a community contain distinctive neighborhoods and vibrant squares that convey a sense of community identity, or is this identity lost in a sea of identical parking lots? Are neighborhood densities sufficient to support the walkable Main Streets so many people seek, or does living in these neighborhoods require driving everywhere?

Across these topic areas and at every scale, changing demographics, values, and technologies create ever-shifting sets of issues. In an era of sprawl, few people in urban neighborhoods feared overdevelopment or *gentrification*. A decade ago an owner of a farm on the edge of a major city could simply wait until sewer lines and roads reached the area and then retire on the proceeds from selling the land to a developer; today environmental regulations would likely preserve the farm, willing owner or not. In an era in which high-rise condominiums can command extraordinary price premiums, the reactions to height differ dramatically. Residents of Boston and Qatar, for example, often see height as a threat to cherished traditional character. Chicago, by contrast, has embraced the prospect of a 2,000-foot tower designed by Santiago Calatrava, and Dubai welcomes a 2,700-foot tower designed by Skidmore, Owings & Merrill.

Measuring Impact

Although hundreds of variables contribute to the success of an urban design project, particular qualities have consistently proved crucial to moving plans into actual implementation.

- **Relevance.** Do the recommendations of the urban design team respond to the problems that spawned the project? Do they map out a convincing path to neighborhood revitalization, for example, or to a more active waterfront? A plan may need to support an agenda that reaches beyond local issues. For example, does it advance sustainability or smart growth? Does it promote transit use? Does it help address district or regional issues like economic competitiveness or preservation of wetlands that protect coastal areas against catastrophic storms?

- **Inspiration.** Successful plans do not simply deliver practical benefits, as important as those are. They also inspire, turning stakeholders into cheerleaders who want to see a plan become reality. Inspiration grows out of a cohesive and compelling vision, rooted in content, but the form in which the plan is presented plays

Helping stakeholders envision the outcome of a plan can turn them into avid supporters who push for implementation long after the planning process ends. Rendering by Dongik Lee, courtesy of Goody Clancy. *See color insert, C-2.*

a part, too. How well does it communicate its ideas graphically? Does it lend itself to promotion? Does it offer clear guidance for moving forward with understandable, realistic steps and a reasonable time frame?

• **Feasibility.** A feasible plan is functional and buildable, and it meets cost, funding, and financial criteria. Feasibility requires someone willing and able to build the plan—either a public agency or a private developer. If the private sector will carry out the plan, as is common today, the plan must meet the added test of market feasibility, and it must build in enough flexibility to allow response to changing markets or to cover a long enough time period to allow market absorption regardless of short-term

fluctuations. Feasibility also assumes that a plan can meet the requirements of all federal, state, and local agencies that will review and issue permits for the project.

• **Phasing.** Because urban design plans often cover long periods of time, most successful plans comprise multiple stages. A plan may specify actions for the earliest one or two phases but simply outline later phases to assure flexibility for responding to a changed environment. Wise phasing sets realistic goals for each phase and calibrates phases to a level the community can reasonably be expected to achieve (or the market to absorb) in a given period. Although all phases should be practical and feasible, more detailed, nearer-term phases should undergo fairly rigorous financial, market, funding, and other testing before completion.

- **Implementation**. Feasibility rests on a realistic implementation strategy that identifies who will do what in order to complete each phase of the plan and establishes when they will do it. As noted previously, the strategy should be more detailed for earlier phases and more generalized for later ones. To the extent possible, near-term phases should identify costs clearly, specify funding sources, assign responsibilities, and incorporate a realistic but flexible schedule.

- **Flexibility.** Flexibility marks most successful urban design schemes. To accommodate long time frames and short market and political cycles, plans often avoid excessive specificity, particularly in detailing later phases. Structuring in some fungibility provides additional resilience. If, for example, the housing market deteriorates while the demand for office space strengthens,

can some office space replace residential uses without upsetting the overall plan? Similarly, if funding sources change, can the order of implementation shift without jeopardizing the whole scheme?

- **Political viability.** In many cases, an urban design team must frame recommendations with an eye toward the needs of stakeholders whose support remains essential for the plan to move forward. Backing from the broader community, for example, cannot make up for insufficient commitment from the elected officials who launched the process and/or who control legislative or legal machinery needed to complete the plan. In urban settings, winning over multiple property holders may hold the key to progress. Persuading other central players—public agency staff members; a major developer; businesses; or environmental, preservation, or other groups with specific agendas—may also prove critical to approval and implementation.

Shaping the Response to a Changing World

At the first American conference on urban design, in 1956, José Luis Sert called urban design the act of "recentralization—a fight to defend core cities against the centrifugal forces of suburbanization."[7] Decentralization, he worried, would leave cities behind to deteriorate. Building new urban *places* of civic engagement would help save cities—and the United States itself.

The job of imagining and designing these new places would fall to urban designers, as it had for thousands of years before the profession acquired a formal name. In effect, Sert had identified the central role urban designers play in helping cities respond to change. That task—finding the fit between people and place—has put urban designers in the United States at the forefront of efforts to respond to cultural, economic, environmental, social, and technological change.

Working with and listening to multiple constituencies, then devising a plan that reflects their concerns, helps build broad support for implementation. Courtesy of Goody Clancy.

PUBLIC POLICY

Public policies significantly influence the design, use, and physical evolution of a given place.

- **Regional and local transportation** policies have some of the most significant impacts on urban design. Are alternatives to the automobile available or will they become available in the future? Does current policy favor automobiles over other modes (such as walking), or does it promote a balanced approach? Does policy link transportation and land use?

- **Land use policy**, whether at the state, county, or regional level, also plays a critical role in shaping urban design. Local zoning expresses municipal land use policies and preferences, which tend to cluster around separating uses, determining lot size, and controlling floor-area ratio (FAR). States and regional authorities may link transportation and land use policies, carve out growth and conservation zones, or establish other broad-scale land use programs. Are there opportunities to provide mixed-use development or greater density? What about clustered development or open-space plans?

- **Choices about infrastructure** can also serve as a policy tool. Historically, many communities have allowed growth to set their planning agendas by extending water service, sewer lines, and roadway capacity wherever development takes place. Some governmental agencies have begun to turn this model on its head by treating infrastructure as a tool for guiding development, prohibiting or severely limiting it in areas without infrastructure and encouraging growth in areas where infrastructure already exists.

- **Preservation and conservation** policies—intended to preserve open space and/or protect the character of historic districts and neighborhoods with unique qualities—shape plans in significant ways. For example, must the entire structure of a historic building be preserved or only its facade? Must new buildings mimic existing historical styles? What criteria govern open-space preservation—environmental concerns, public access, view protection, or other standards?

- **Mixed-income housing** policy, now increasingly common, promotes the preservation of existing mixed-income communities and encourages the use of some profits from market-rate housing to support creation of such communities in high-value real estate markets. In rapidly appreciating urban real estate markets, an acute need for affordable housing has spawned inclusionary ordinances, or regulations that require developers to make a portion (typically 10%–15%) of new housing affordable. The federal government has encouraged this trend, particularly with the HOPE VI program, which funds replacement of distressed public housing with mixed-income developments that are physically integrated into the surrounding neighborhoods. Community development corporations (CDCs) have taken a leading role in incorporating affordable housing into mixed-income projects.

- **Public- and private-sector roles** have shifted as public resources in the United States have shrunk in recent decades and new private and public-private structures have emerged to fill the vacuum. Funded by special assessments on adjoining property owners and tenants, *business improvement districts* (BIDs) have yielded enhanced public-area management in places like Midtown Manhattan. Because a private entity collects taxlike assessments and manages

(continued)

a public space, critics ask pointedly whether such arrangements effectively cede ownership of public spaces to the private sector. Some district organizations plant their feet in both camps, with board members drawn from both sectors. *Conservancies,* which usually focus on open spaces and parks, often mix public and private elements. Under this model, private-sector funds may support work carried out by the public sector with the conservancy's advice and consent. *Community development corporations,* a third public-private model, commonly undertake downtown development projects, attempt to revive or strengthen Main Streets and other commercial districts, and build affordable housing.

- **Special-use districts** take advantage of transit, transfers of development rights (TDRs), special kinds of tax treatment, or other unique resources and are also shaped by policy. *Public transit districts* may offer incentives for mixed-use development, density bonuses, and/or reduced parking requirements. Cities and states increasingly offer incentives to encourage transit-oriented development. *Transfer of development rights districts (TDRs)* offer density bonuses that accrue through the purchase of development rights spun off from other locations where open space is being preserved. Other types of special districts include *tax-increment financing* (TIF) *districts,* which dedicate a defined portion of taxes generated by new development to nearby public improvements that increase the value and market appeal of that development. Improvements might include streetscapes, roadways, parking structures, transit facilities, or other infrastructure a community might not otherwise be able to finance.

- **Growth-management initiatives** can achieve policy objectives. Although complex, such initiatives have enjoyed success in an increasing number of cities and regions, helping to slow the rapid colonization of open landscape for development. Growth management may involve establishing growth boundaries that separate reserves of open land—to remain as farmland or forest—from higher-density areas. Or it may use transit infrastructure to steer growth toward established urban areas while discouraging growth on rural sites. Management techniques include some of the tools already described, such as TDRs, targeted infrastructure investment, and focused transportation policy. Growth-management policies can operate at any scale: local application can preserve the scale of existing neighborhoods and/or their historic resources while directing new growth to brownfield and grayfield sites or to designated transportation corridors.

Urban designers have worked to move the issue of urban sprawl to the top of the national agenda in the United States, educating the architecture profession and the larger community about the importance of healthier and more sustainable patterns of development. Organizing public forums, producing visualizations, and wielding other tools, urban designers help people understand that growth can benefit established communities and bring new life to historic districts. They work with communities to create new forms of development that transform strip malls into lively, walkable communities; commuter parking lots into successful transit-oriented developments; and older housing into higher-density, mixed-use developments that offer more choices in an increasingly diverse marketplace. Urban designers have taken the lead in transforming public housing into mixed-income neighborhoods, in adapting zoning and building codes to support mixed-use and pedestrian-friendly development, and in promoting the reuse of industrial waterfront and factory complexes.

New dynamics shape the kinds of projects on which urban designers work and the visions and plans that they create. Urban designers increasingly focus on transforming outmoded, single-use industrial and office areas into mixed-use districts that offer the amenities to attract the creative workers who staff the growing "industries of the mind." In response to a highly fragmented housing market—the Urban Land Institute describes the United States as a "nation of niches," where, for example, single people occupy a third of all housing units—urban designers create new urban neighborhoods with higher-density development that puts people who want very different types of housing in the same block.

As public budgets shrink, urban designers have responded by creating plans that mix civic and private uses and rely on public-private partnerships to pay for parks, transit, and other public benefits—along with stylish features like winter gardens intended to attract loft buyers and office tenants. In response to steadily increasing diversity, cities ask urban designers to plan parks and public spaces that actively invite shared use by people of varied ages, incomes, races, and backgrounds and encourage the development of new forms of community. Urban designers have worked with other sustainability advocates to develop a neighborhood development track within the Leadership in Energy and Environmental Design pro-

gram (or, commonly, LEED®), creating a set of criteria that measure how well large-scale developments promote environmental health. And in an era in which shifting demographics, rising commuting costs, growing interest in sustainability, and a longing for community fuel an increased interest in urban living, urban designers have signed on to help the United States grapple with one of its toughest challenges: understanding how to build core cities and close-in neighborhoods more densely and in ways that enhance quality of life—helping the country, in a sense, learn to love its cities again.

Changing dynamics will continue to reshape the opportunities and challenges facing communities and thus the kinds of projects that engage urban designers. For example, the wave of housing foreclosures that swept across the United States in 2007 and 2008 unmasked one of these challenges—the overbuilding of many outer-ring suburban markets. In the March 2008 *Atlantic Monthly*, Chris Leinberger reported on research he had conducted for the Brookings Institution and noted that "there will be about 4 million more households with children in 2025 than there were in 2000.... But more than 10 million new single-family homes have already been built since 2000, most of them in the suburbs."[9] This imbalance explains in part why foreclosures have been concentrated in outer-ring suburbs and suggests that suburban revitalization may emerge as an important urban design task. Leinberger continues, "For 60 years Americans have pushed steadily into the suburbs.... But today the pendulum is swinging back toward urban living, and there are many reasons to believe this swing will continue. As it does, many low-density suburbs and McMansion subdivisions...may become what inner cities became in the 1960s and '70s—slums characterized by poverty, crime, and decay."[10] As Americans learn to love cities again, the implications of this shift will touch every aspect of the built and natural environment in the United States.

Public policy, along with public perceptions and misconceptions about the built environment, affect architecture in powerful ways.... Writing and teaching give me an opportunity to educate the general public, developers, and policy makers.[8]

Roger K. Lewis, FAIA, professor, University of Maryland School of Architecture, Planning & Preservation, and *Washington Post* columnist

CHAPTER 2

Roots of Urban Form

This chapter presents a review of key points in the history of human settlements that serve as the origins of American urban design traditions. These origins continue to shape the way urban designers think and work in the United States today.

Early Cities

Whenever archeologists think they have found the oldest human settlement, it seems that a new dig in another part of the world unearths an even older one. Each of these settlements adds to a rich human tradition. Cities exist because humans are social beings, variously tribal, communal, and mutually supportive. From nomadic beginnings—first hunter-gatherers, then herding tribes—came agricultural settlements that eventually clustered for reasons of religion, administration, defense, or economics. With the emergence of surplus economies, hierarchical societies appeared and supported the growth of villages, then towns, and, finally, cities.

In simplified terms, two basic city forms emerged early in Western civilization: the organic and the geometric.[11] Organic cities arose by chance and accretion; they grew willy-nilly. Geometric cities were typically planned,

functional, and rational. Geography, climate, and land apportionment shaped both forms, whether in an administrative center in a Mesopotamian kingdom, a trading settlement on the Silk Road, a Mexican colonial outpost, or a farming community on the Canadian plains.

Likely the more ancient of the two, organic settlements developed around regional crossroads, safe harbors, river crossings, access to mountain passes or other geographic features crucial to trade or defense. Sometimes a decent spread of arable land, reliable access to water, and a good defensive position encouraged settlement. From these beginnings, streets and public ways arose from paths of people and animals traveling according to topography. A variety of factors may have governed land distribution, including original settlement patterns, allotment by rulers, negotiation, and trade. Often the result was a radio-concentric plan as small villages merged and, eventually, spread into a town and then a city. Venice and Siena in Italy fall into this category, as do some newer cities, like Boston in the United States.

The geometric city form represents *design* in some fashion; it dates to at least 2600 BCE and the cities of Mohenjo-Daro and Harappa in the Indus River Valley, two early communities that comprised blocks formed by streets running at right angles.[12] Rectilinear patterns also appear in excavated towns in Babylon and China that date from the seventeenth to fifteenth centuries BCE. The Egyptians also knew geometric planning: Kahun (nineteenth century BCE) and Amarna (fourteenth century BCE) each follow a rigid gridiron plan, as much for religious reasons as for the speed and mechanization such a plan allowed. Lewis Mumford says, "City building under the pharaohs was a swift, one-stage operation: a simple geometric plan was a condition for rapid building.... More organic plans, representing the needs and decisions of many generations, require time to achieve their more subtle and complex richness of form."[13]

Such considerations indicate a more mature society—one that has outgrown purely organic roots. They also suggest more authoritarian rule. Geometric settlements were often planned in advance as central places for religion and commerce, remote outposts for control of regional populations, or colonial encampments designed with defense and control as their priority. The grid offered a practical method for allotting land in colonial settlements and for demarcating land according to use and function.[14]

The Greek city of Miletus in Asia Minor offers one of the best-known early examples of geometric planning. While Greek cities on the mainland tended to develop along topographic contours in an organic pattern, Greek colonial cities in Asia Minor and elsewhere followed a more geometric path.[15] Rebuilt in the fifth century BCE after having been razed during the Persian wars, Miletus spread out on a gridiron around a central, rectangular

agora in a plan often attributed to Hippodamus. This organizing scheme proved so compelling that it took on the city's name—Miletian.

As the Greeks spread westward through the Mediterranean region, they exported the Miletian plan to their outposts in Italy, where the Romans later adopted it. From their rise to power until the demise of their empire in the fifth century CE, the Romans built numerous cities and towns on the Miletian plan throughout the Mediterranean region. These communities, often fortified outposts called *castra*, usually followed the same strict grid pattern around a central forum. Sometimes they were overlaid onto preexisting settlements of other cultures; major cities as distinctive as Cologne, Florence, and London grew from such beginnings. Behind massive sixteenth-century walls, the historical center of Lucca in Tuscany still preserves its original Roman street grid.

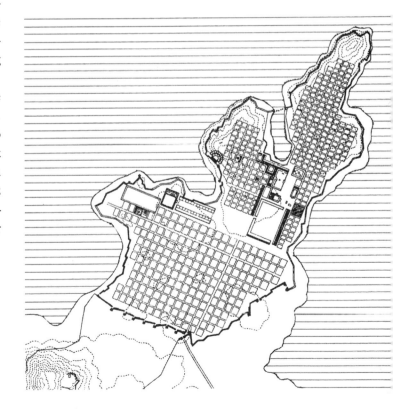

Plan of Miletus (fifth century BCE). Reconstruction of the Greek colony in Asia Minor—carried out after its sacking by the Persians—followed a gridiron plan, with square blocks radiating from a central agora. As they established subsequent colonies around the Mediterranean, the Greeks replicated the Miletian plan. From *The City Shaped* by Spiro Kostof. Copyright © 1991 by Spiro Kostof; compilation copyright © 1991 by Thames and Hudson, Ltd. By permission of Little Brown & Company.

Lucca, Italy. The Romans adopted the Miletian plan and spread the gridiron organization of cities across their empire. The center of modern Lucca retains its original Roman grid behind fortifications built in the sixteenth century. Copyright Compagnia Generale Ripresearee S.p.A.

The classical cities that developed from these two beginnings evolved over hundreds and thousands of years. Rome itself, a city with both organic origins and gridded streets, is today thought to have been rebuilt at least six times, with its original Roman grid absorbed into the successive periods of growth and decay, confounding its clarity.

European Cities in the Middle Ages

Few new European cities arose in the centuries after the fall of Rome, and military considerations strongly shaped those that did: *bastides* in France and *Zähringer* towns in Germany. Inspired by Roman military outposts, these towns were built on a strict Miletian pattern around a central market square. Planned from scratch, they exemplified medieval town planning and urban design.

Bastide towns dotted the Languedoc, Aquitaine, and Gascony during the thirteenth and fourteenth centuries, a time of strife marked by the Hundred Years' War between France and Britain. Bastides were typically planned and built as single units, often by a single lord—for example, Alphonse of Poitiers built several in a bid to consolidate territorial control.[16] Roman influences remained strong in medieval France, and the bastides adopted the plan of the castra that preceded them. Wide streets at right angles crossed a central marketplace, dividing the town plan into super blocks, or *insulae*, which were further divided by narrow lanes. Among other things, the grid plan's modular character facilitated tax collection and record keeping,[17] considerations that would encourage its use in later centuries.

Piazza del Campo (fourteenth century), Siena, Italy. The Piazza del Campo broke with an important medieval city-building tradition. Instead of serving as the setting for a cathedral, the piazza's focus is a secular building, the Palazzo Pubblico, seat of the Sienese republic. The square prefigured the modern idea of secular civic space. Copyright Compagnia Generale Ripresearee S.p.A.

The dukes of Zähringer built fortified towns in Germany's Rhine valley in the twelfth century, seeking, like Alphonse of Poitiers, to tighten control over their domain.[18] Freiburg, Villingen, and Rottweil survive as examples of the form and, as in France, drew heavily on the model of the castra with a Miletian grid plan built out from a central marketplace.

What might be characterized as medieval urban design extends beyond bastides and Zähringer towns, however. Cities during the same period, some dating to antiquity, undertook major renovations and expansions that resulted in some of Europe's most renowned public spaces. From its beginning as a small plaza facing the Basilica di San Marco in Venice, the Piazza San Marco took on its present configuration in the twelfth century, when it was rebuilt to accommodate a historic meeting between Pope Alexander III and the Holy Roman Emperor Frederick I (Barbarossa). The piazza continued to grow incrementally; the doge's palace, the clock tower, and the campanile were added between the fourteenth and the sixteenth centuries.

The Piazza del Campo in Siena sits on gently sloping ground between the three original settlements that make up the present-day city. The piazza we see today dates largely from reconstruction carried out in the thirteenth and fourteenth centuries, when the Palazzo Pubblico was completed. While the piazza may seem like the quintessential medieval space in the quintessential medieval city, it pointed toward a major functional change. Unlike the Piazza San Marco and other medieval public spaces that served as forecourts to Europe's great cathedrals, the Piazza del Campo serves no religious building. It focuses instead on a civic building, the Palazzo Pubblico, prefiguring the Renaissance and the beginnings of modern secular civic space.

Renaissance Forms Reshape Cities

The Renaissance revived interest in Europe in the great civic works of classical Roman architecture, sparked in part by wide distribution of *De architectura*, a rediscovered treatise by the Roman engineer Marcus Vitruvius Pollio (first century CE). The new awareness of classical architecture reflected an emerging humanist worldview that heavily influenced European ideas about cities, as demonstrated in Pienza in Tuscany. Designated a United Nations Educational, Scientific, and Cultural Organization (UNESCO) World Heritage Site in 1996, the diminutive city serves as a prime example of early Renaissance city planning. UNESCO's citation praised the town's "outstanding universal value" as "the first application of the Renaissance Humanist concept of urban design, and as such [it] occupies a seminal position in the development of the concept of the planned 'ideal town' which was to play a significant role in subsequent urban development in Italy and beyond."[19]

Pienza owed its transformation to Pope Pius II, who, in 1459, launched a rebuilding of the center of his native town in conformance with emerging Renaissance principles. To direct the work, he hired Bernardo Rosselino, a follower of Leon Battista Alberti, whose approach to architecture foreshadowed modernity in many ways. In addition to advocating the conscious creation of public places, he and his followers recommended prohibiting noxious and noisy activities, such as tanneries and slaughterhouses, within town precincts, suggesting instead the creation of dedicated districts for craft and industrial use—an early instance of land use zoning. Rosselino brought to Pienza a new vision of urban space that culminated in the creation of Piazza Pio II and its surrounding buildings, including the Piccolomini palace, the Borgia palace, and a pure Renaissance exterior for the medieval cathedral.

In Alberti's wake came a parade of Renaissance theoreticians, from Andrea Palladio to Sir Thomas More, whose writings ranged widely from purely physical design to the philosophical bases for building. Ideal cities such as Palmanova in northeastern Italy and More's literary Utopia, both from the sixteenth century, offered models for centuries of town planning to follow.

While More's *Utopia* imagined an ideal society set in an island nation of reasonable, tolerant, and peaceful people, Palmanova originated in military thinking. Planned from the beginning as a defensive outpost, the town was built to protect Venice's eastern flank from Turkish attacks. Its nine-pointed star plan, with a focal piazza surrounded by radiating streets, grew from the need to serve and command multiple defensive bastions from a central location, and to move troops among multiple bastions quickly and efficiently.[20] Military origins aside, Palmanova's geometry clearly reflected an idealized plan. Its authoritarian pattern, arrow-straight streets, and evident sense of human order overlaid upon nature clearly foreshadow baroque city planning. Those same traits also reflect major advancements in surveying, which allowed the drawing of scaled plans for designing new cities. Ironically, this small military outpost influenced planning for generations. Its pure geometry and containment within a greenbelt of earthworks inspired planners and designers as diverse as Ebenezer Howard and Paolo Soleri.

Architects Vincenzo Scamozzi and Pietro Cataneo also created city schemes that influenced later urban plans. Reviving the classical works of Vitruvius in his *L'Architettura* (1567), Cataneo plotted idealized grid cities peppered with public squares. Even though Cataneo himself saw few of his plans built, they were realized in towns like Charleville in northern France and Avola in Sicily, and they served as models for American cities like Savannah, Georgia, and Philadelphia.[21]

Palmanova, Italy (1593). The strict geometry of the plan for Palmanova—a defensive fort east of Venice—grew out of military necessity, but it influenced town planning for centuries. Its straight, wide boulevards and idealized plan surfaced in baroque-era plans across Europe. Purely geometric inside a broad band of earthen bulwarks, it also inspired designs as varied as English garden cities and twentieth-century visionary projects like Arcosanti in Arizona. Copyright Compagnia Generale Ripresearee S.p.A.

By the seventeenth century, the urban ideas of the Renaissance had matured into those of the baroque and had spread across Europe. The urban plans of the era, like baroque architecture, tended to artifice on a grand scale, with sweeping vistas and long axes slashed through crowded cities. A zeitgeist in which absolute monarchy and the Counter-Reformation figured prominently colored European city building. Rulers and their architects attempted to impose a new sense of order upon the accretive muddle that characterized many European capitals. The new order frequently included an authoritarian preference for straight avenues and clean lines of sight, an inclination reinforced by many planners' backgrounds in military engineering.[22] In some respects, the work of these baroque engineers foreshadowed the impulses of the U.S. urban renewal era more than four hundred years later. It did not seem to bother Italian military engineers of the time, Lewis Mumford writes, that the "encumbrances" they were clearing "were human households, shops, churches, neighborhoods." The fact that this "tissue of habits and social relations" could not be replaced "did not seem important to the early military engineer any more than it seems so to his twentieth-century successors, in charge of 'slum clearance projects' or highway designs."[23]

This unfortunate parallel may hold true, but some of the fundamental concepts of modern urban design also reached maturity in this era: the idea of the street as a spatial element in its own right; the concept of purposely shaped and defined public space, networks of streets, and public spaces organized by visual foci; and the idea of deploying buildings with uniform facades to define streets and other public spaces.[24]

Beyond the development of new concepts, urban conditions required new approaches in the baroque era as the populations of cities swelled dramatically, often overwhelming the functional capacity of medieval street systems. Like planners in later periods, the era's city builders worked to bring public health, light, and air into the city, to clear hopeless gridlock, and to bring order to perceived chaos.

Early in the seventeenth century, Pope Sixtus V worked with his architect Domenico Fontana to devise a new master plan for Rome.[25] It introduced a network of long, straight avenues connecting the Porta del Popolo to a series of churches, monuments, and formal public spaces, among them the basilicas Santa Maria Maggiore (St. Mary Major) and San Giovanni in Laterano (St. John Lateran) and the Colosseum. Sixtus's plan created what Edmund Bacon calls "a controlled sequential experience" out of what is basically a "movement-system design structure."[26] Demarcated by a series of obelisks erected by Sixtus, the system served as the principal framework for city building in Rome for several centuries. Such significant public spaces as the Piazza del Popolo, the Piazza Barberini, and the Spanish Steps were later designed and built around this framework.

Giovanni Lorenzo Bernini's acclaimed Piazza San Pietro, superbly rationalizing the entrance sequence to Basilica di San Pietro in Vaticano (St. Peter's Cathedral), stands as a preeminent example of baroque planning and design. Bernini designed the colonnade and piazza around one of Sixtus's obelisks in another nod to the pope's vision for Rome. Combining an understanding of perspective inherited from the Renaissance with the baroque penchant for illusion and grandeur, Bernini ingeniously blended oval and trapezoidal plans to foreshorten perspective and make the cathedral seem closer to the piazza than it actually is.[27]

Baroque urbanism also broke new paths far beyond Italy. In France an expansion of the Château du Louvre and development of the Tuileries Garden both clearly exhibited baroque preferences. Not satisfied with those projects, Louis XIV built Versailles and relocated his royal residence there toward the end of the sixteenth century, replacing the Louvre as the royal residence. The axial layout of Versailles and the long perspective vistas of André Le Nôtre's gardens rank among the fore-

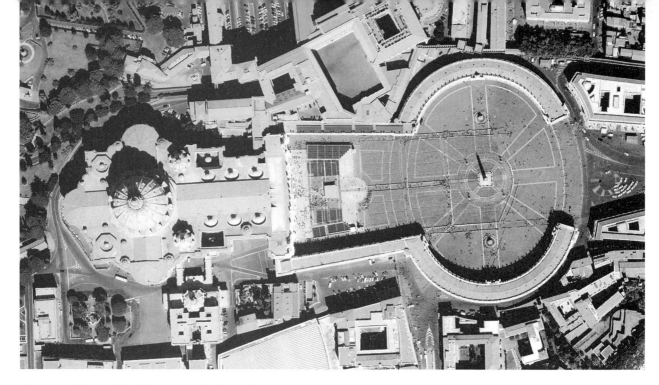

Piazza San Pietro (1656–67), Vatican City. Bernini's quintessential baroque plan for a plaza and colonnade masterfully blends Renaissance knowledge of perspective with the baroque penchant for grandeur and illusion to orchestrate the experience of approaching St. Peter's Basilica. Copyright Compagnia Generale Ripresearee S.p.A.

most examples of urban design and landscape architecture from the baroque period.

In 1660, England's Charles II hired Le Nôtre to plan London's Pall Mall. The Great Fire of 1666 provoked a flurry of proposals for rebuilding the entire city from architects and planners, including Sir Christopher Wren and John Evelyn. None was actually implemented, but most displayed the strong influence of continental designers like Le Nôtre. In submitting his plan to Charles II, John Evelyn invoked three principles for the proposed reconstruction: "beauty, commodiousness, and magnificence." The last principle most clearly reflects the baroque tradition, and Evelyn's plan of gridded streets broken by long, axial diagonal avenues clearly follows contemporary examples from the Continent.

England exported the ideas it had absorbed from the Continent to its possessions abroad. The Regional Plan for the Ulster Plantation was produced in the early seventeenth century as part of the colonization of Ireland.

In a 1614 master plan for the walled city of Derry (now Londonderry), baroque planning principles define the streets and square that make up "the Diamond." The design of space surrounding key public buildings—such as St. Columb's Cathedral and the Bishop's Palace—received careful attention. As buildings (designed in the emerging baroque architectural style) began to fill in the dictated street pattern, they formed collective walls that reinforced the public spaces.[28]

Spain sent baroque European planning ideas to its cities in the New World, as did other colonial powers. In fact, the urban design principles that emerged in the baroque period came to dominate city planning and urban design in both Europe and the New World over the next three centuries. The same ideas of axial public streets and landscaped boulevards; radial and diagonal patterns defined by specific visual focal points; monumental public spaces; and uniform street walls characterized Pierre-Charles L'Enfant's plan for Washington, D.C.,

Baron Georges-Eugène Haussman's plan for Paris, and many other urban plans and expansions in both Europe and the Americas. But baroque planning of another sort, borrowing heavily from the Miletian tradition, ultimately wielded the most influence in North America.

In the Netherlands, the City of Amsterdam in 1607 adopted the Plan of the Three Canals,[29] which called for a quadrupling of the city's area with the construction of three new encircling canals that would also serve as the main streets of new districts. The plan's innovation lay not only in these combined canal streets but also in its incorporation of phased execution over a long period of time: each canal would serve as the outer boundary of the city in successive enlargements. In its long, straight canals and streets, and its radial form, the plan created a spiderweb pattern that drew heavily on the baroque tradition in other parts of Europe. Yet it also relied upon a distorted version of the ancient Miletian grid (borrowing slightly, perhaps, from the earlier plans of Cataneo).

The grid form supported another unique quality of the plan: its joint execution by public and private actors. The municipal government drew up the plan, which

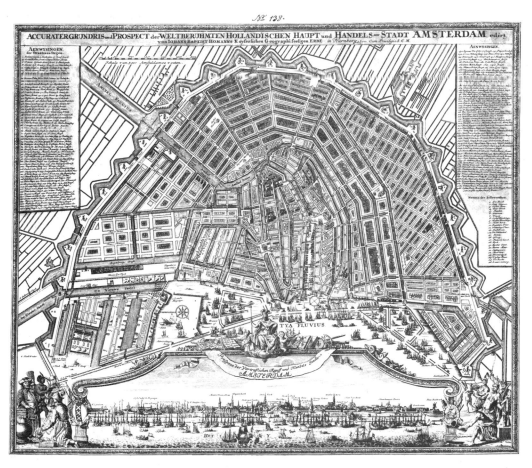

The Plan of the Three Canals (1607), Amsterdam. The Three Canals Plan, adopted by the municipality, introduced a baroque sense of geometry and order into expansions of the medieval city. Amsterdam's novel approach to the plan's execution proved influential in the United States: the municipal government identified the plan area and set guidelines for construction, but it left realization of the plan to private developers. Courtesy of Geography and Map Division, Library of Congress.

parceled out the land in a grid of blocks; established firm guidelines for the use and form of the buildings along the canals; and reserved specific areas of land for churches and marketplaces. That done, the government left build-out largely in private hands—often those of investors working for profit.[30] This approach prefigured the planning of North American cities. Gridded expansion, phased construction, and a combination of public and private enterprise all anticipated the methods that American cities adopted in subsequent centuries.

The New World Turns Toward the Grid

Amsterdam, in fact, served as a model for one of the New World's most important cities. In 1626, less than twenty years after the Plan of the Three Canals, the Dutch West India Company decided to consolidate its scattered North American trading outposts into a single defensive settlement called New Amsterdam at the southern tip of the island of Manhattan.[31] At the time, the Dutch claimed all of the land between Virginia and French Canada as part of their colony of New Netherland, but by the 1640s settlers from New England began planting small towns on Long Island in New York and in Connecticut, moving ever closer to New Amsterdam. Within twenty years the trickle of English settlers into New Netherland had become a flood, and in 1664, after a brief military assault, ownership of the colony passed to the English, who renamed the town in honor of the Duke of York.[32]

New Amsterdam may have started out as an organic, somewhat chaotic settlement, but that changed under Peter Stuyvesant, governor of the colony from 1647 until its handover to the English. By the time the Duke of York's troops arrived, Stuyvesant had transformed the town plan into a miniature version of its namesake city. In a move worthy of baroque European planners, the governor had imposed a lattice of new streets over the "town's confounding jumble of lanes and footpaths."[33] He also built a canal and a dock, repaired the colony's fort and defensive wall to the north, and established rudimentary building and sanitary codes. The result was a curved grid of streets, blocks, and a canal not unlike those laid out in Amsterdam's 1607 plan, albeit much less dense and on a far smaller scale. However primitive, this pattern entered the settlement's DNA, and the English continued the grid pattern, although with distortions. When the city's population exploded in the nineteenth century, the grid devoured the surrounding landscape, taking on the rigidity and uniformity that characterize the city today.

The grid influenced the growth of other English colonies. In 1683, shortly after William Penn received a grant for what became the Colony of Pennsylvania, Thomas Holme published a plan for its urban center—a deliberate grid aligned on an east-west axis, running between the Schuylkill and Delaware rivers. Holme, a surveyor, collaborated with Penn on the plan, which forged the pattern for the city's growth over the centuries to follow. In promoting an orthogonal plan right from the beginning, Penn showed vision far beyond that of the Dutch settlers of New Amsterdam. Indeed, the Philadelphia plan bore the hallmarks of the idealized grid cities of the Renaissance envisioned by Cataneo. The purposeful placement of public squares and axial streets made his simple diagram an almost Utopian vision for Penn's planned community of Quakers.[34]

The grid plan for another early American city, Savannah, Georgia, proved even more sophisticated and visionary. Earlier settlements in the southern English colonies generally avoided use of grids, but Savannah and Charleston, South Carolina, embraced them. Laid out in 1733 by James Oglethorpe, Savannah largely followed Cataneo's plans for ideal grid cities, with a pattern of blocks centered on public squares. Each square anchored a cell of eight blocks, with the east and west ends of the square appointed as sites for churches and other public and commercial buildings. The plan re-

Plan of New Amsterdam (1660). In nearly twenty years as governor, Peter Stuyvesant turned New Amsterdam's jumbled lanes into a gridded pattern that suggested the influence of both the Three Canals plan and baroque planning sensibilities. Courtesy of I. N. Phelps Stokes Collection, Miriam and Ira D. Wallach Division of Art, Prints and Photographs, The New York Public Library, Astor, Lenox and Tilden Foundations.

served other lots for residential use. The Savannah system carried out a political function as well, with each eight-block cell representing a political unit of landowners called a ward. The settlement began with four such wards in the middle of the forest on the banks of the Savannah River. Those four wards fixed the pattern of the city's growth for more than one hundred years.[35]

Not every American settlement started out in such an organized fashion. Boston, settled in 1630, had no planned layout. As a result, it retained a largely accretive character for more than two centuries. Although early maps of the city do suggest a loose and distorted grid pattern, a true and regular orthogonal pattern did not appear in any major way until the filling in of the Back Bay in the mid-nineteenth century. But Boston remains a conspicuous exception; the Miletian approach ultimately dominated in American city building.

Both George Washington and Thomas Jefferson believed that grid geometry represented the democratic principles upon which the new nation was founded, a

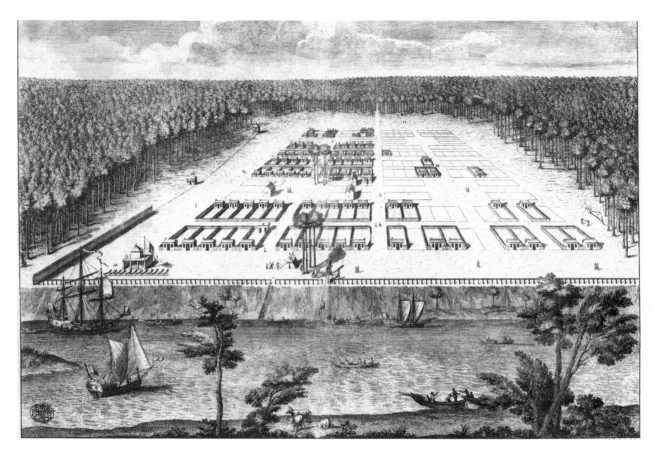

View of Savannah, Georgia (1734). Although not every English settlement in the American colonies adopted the grid, Philadelphia, Charleston, South Carolina, and Savannah embraced it. The visionary plan for Savannah arrayed eight blocks around a central square to form a physical and political unit, with appointed sites for public functions like markets and churches; the rest of the land was reserved for houses. These units (or "wards") remained the building blocks of the town's growth for more than a century. Courtesy of Geography and Map Division, Library of Congress.

belief that reflected the fundamental role real property played in the American idea of democracy. The founding fathers—all men of property—saw holding real estate as a fundamental right of each citizen. They established ownership as a precondition to voting in the early nation, in part because having land seemed likely to assure economic freedom in an agrarian economy. Such freedom remained unattainable in Europe, where only a privileged few owned land. The new democracy encouraged widespread distribution of land—a commodity the United States happened to have in abundance.

Jefferson did much to devise the land-distribution process. He proposed stretching a surveyor's grid of ten-mile squares across the nation's undivided territories; aligning each square with its neighbors would assure that no land was left vacant. In organizing toward these ends, Jefferson saw himself as the designer of a landowning—and hence orderly and self-regulating—democracy. When Congress passed the legislation for disbursing land, it altered Jefferson's original plan by creating "townships of 6 miles square," subdivided into thirty-six sections of one square mile each. The land was to be sold at public auction by section at a price of one dollar per acre, or $640 per section—the smallest parcel that could be bought at the time.[36]

Whether relying on a six- or ten-mile basic unit, the work and theories of Thomas Jefferson guided the parcelization of the United States' vast common realm. Congressional surveyors drew a vast, rectilinear grid across the wilderness—imaginary lines that eventually stretched from the Appalachians to the Pacific Ocean, ignoring topography, geology, water, soils, forests, deserts, wetlands, and wildlife. That grid became the framework for dividing the continent into individual plots of land and placing them in private hands.

Some of the surveyors' work remains visible today. Flying over the flatlands of the West reveals sections clearly defined by property lines and roads. It is even possible to make out the way that surveyors accounted for the convergence of lines of longitude as they move toward the poles. Every so often, roads that run as straight as arrows for miles suddenly make awkward right-angle turns where section lines shift to account for meridional convergence.

That vast geometry inevitably influenced the growth and pattern of American cities. Eventually, Americans applied grids to cities along the eastern seaboard from Savannah to Boston. Western cities, like Chicago, Denver, and San Francisco, grew according to grids imposed almost from the beginning. Although the United States' use of the grid has often been associated with a democratic political attitude—and despite Jefferson's firm belief in it as an instrument of democracy—the grid historically served as much as a method of enforcing power and control as for distributing land. Greek colonial cities, Roman castra, bastides, and many other examples suggest that it took meaning from the way it was applied.[37] Despite Jefferson's lofty aims, in the United States the grid came to symbolize not so much freedom as practicality and speculation.

When railroad companies built cross-continental routes, they financed the enterprise in part by selling off sweeping tracts of public land they had been granted by the U.S. government to encourage construction of the lines. To further their ends, they stamped out hundreds of grid-pattern towns to parcel out the land for quick and easy sale. In 1811, New York City's commissioners created a notorious plan for building out Manhattan: an unrelieved gridiron of regular blocks from 23rd Street to 155th Street. The plan allowed relatively little public open space (no Central Park, for example) or deviation from the grid—Broadway's errant diagonal is nowhere to be seen. The commissioners declared it obvious that "straight-sided and right-angled houses are the most cheap to build, and the most convenient to live in." The commissioners' surveyor, John Randel Jr., added that his plan offered particularly good opportunities for "buying, selling, and improving real estate."[38] In the end, it could be said that the gridded cities of the United States were planned more for the real estate developer than for the designer or the democratic idealist.

The nation's capital, however, proved an exception. When it came to planning the new city, George Washington turned to Major Pierre-Charles L'Enfant, a military engineer in the European baroque tradition. L'Enfant belittled the humble grid plan that Jefferson had sketched out, stating that the plan for the nation's capital should be "proportioned to the greatness which . . . the Capital of a powerful Empire ought to manifest."[39] Scorning grids in general as "tiresome and insipid," L'Enfant proceeded to draw up the plan of starlike squares and diagonal avenues that makes up today's Washington. In its use of long vistas centered on public monuments, this design recalls Sixtus V's plan for Rome. In its pursuit of baroque grandeur, L'Enfant's plan looks beyond democracy to a world in which the new nation might have imperial ambitions. Yet even this bold vision rests upon an ever-practical, ever-convenient, easy-to-use land-apportioning grid that makes up the background of the entire plan.

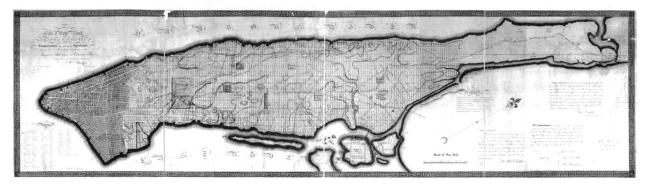

Commissioners' Plan for New York City. The gridiron that signified order and authority to baroque-era rulers in Europe took on a more practical meaning in the United States—it made development easier. This unrelenting grid laid over Manhattan's topography in an 1811 plan provided the basic framework for the city's nineteenth-century expansion. Courtesy of Geography and Map Division, Library of Congress.

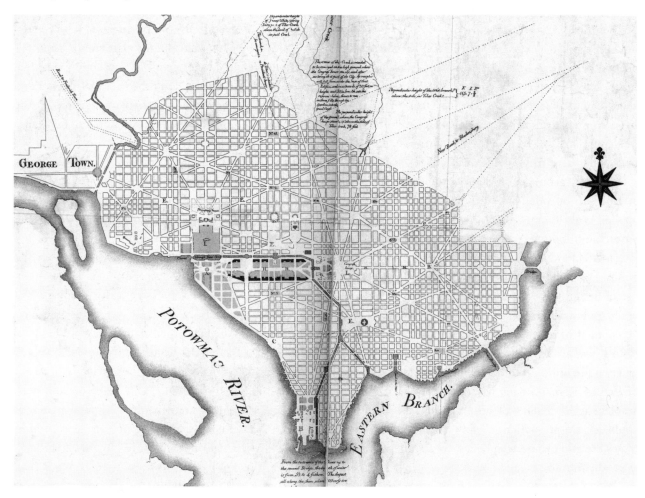

L'Enfant Plan for Washington, D.C. Pierre-Charles L'Enfant scoffed at the simple grid as too humble for a national capital, yet he relied on it as the background pattern for his baroque plan of squares threaded onto a web of avenues radiating from public monuments. Most U.S. cities stuck with a basic grid for ease of design, development, and management. Courtesy of Geography and Map Division, Library of Congress.

In the end, L'Enfant's plan proved an exception to the gridded rule of most U.S. cities (although his ideas would be resurrected in the City Beautiful movement). Ease of design—so easy an office boy could figure it out, said Lewis Mumford—ease of record keeping, and a mass-produced nature made the grid pattern irresistible for a speculative nation in a hurry to grow.[40] It also turned out to be highly suitable for a vast industrial revolution; the grid became emblematic of a whole generation of high-density U.S. industrial cities.

The Industrial Revolution and Reaction

Emergence of the Industrial City

Before the Industrial Revolution, forces such as trade, agriculture, and defense determined the shape of cities in North America and Europe, whether planned or unplanned. How far a person could reasonably walk and the requirements of carts, wagons, and herds of animals heavily influenced the layout and dimensions of city streets regardless of the form the larger city took. Defensive strategy and technology also dictated form, but the resulting walls—and the need to guard them—often gave cities smaller footprints than they might otherwise have produced.

A jumble of uses marked preindustrial cities, where home and workplace were often either combined or located near one another. Because no one wanted to walk great distances, most land uses ended up as close neighbors, even in the most rigid of gridiron plans. No matter how noisy or obnoxious, different activities often existed cheek by jowl and one atop another. Attempts to organize uses—particularly to banish offensive or disruptive ones from residential areas—rarely succeeded. Yet, except for the most jarring juxtapositions—houses next to tanneries, living space over abattoirs, grocery stores next to fulling mills—preindustrial city dwellers generally accepted these conditions. The mix of residential and commercial uses often added to the liveliness, interest, and excitement of a city.

The biggest settlements in the mid-nineteenth-century United States were coastal cities. For the most part, they served as mercantile centers: New York brought goods to market and to harbor from the west through the Erie Canal; Savannah and Charleston functioned as markets and transport hubs for rice, cotton, and other southern agricultural goods. Sailing ships lined wharves. The prime regulator of building height was the number of stairs a person might reasonably climb, which meant that few buildings rose higher than four stories and church steeples stood as the tallest structures on the urban skyline. Noise in the streets came mostly from people, animals, and the wheels of carriages and carts.

The Industrial Revolution redrew this picture from top to bottom, beginning in earnest after the Civil War. To that point, U.S. manufacturers had relied primarily on waterpower—making rivers and streams preferred sites for operations—and favored water for heavy transport. After the war, coal and steam power rose quickly to prominence and with them, railroads. Now factories could locate almost anywhere, as long as they had access to a railroad to deliver coal (for making steam) and to carry away finished goods. But factories also needed labor, and the biggest labor pools were found in mercantile cities, where the markets for goods and the means of cross-oceanic transport were also close at hand. Suddenly, stately urban homes on quiet streets found themselves shadowed by looming, high-decibel factories operating around the clock. Huge new rail-marshaling yards came to dominate many neighborhoods and waterfronts. Lewis Mumford has described the era:

> Large scale factory production transformed the industrial towns into dark hives, busily puffing, clanking and screeching, smoking for twelve and fourteen hours a day, sometimes going around the clock.... Extraordinary changes of scale took place in the masses of buildings and the areas they covered: vast structures were erected almost overnight. Men built in haste, and had hardly time to repent

of their mistakes before they tore down their original structures and built again, just as heedlessly. The newcomers . . . crowded into whatever was offered. It was a period of vast urban improvisation: makeshift hastily piled upon makeshift.[41]

These newcomers represented a vast demographic change wrought by industry. At the beginning of the Industrial Revolution, most Americans lived on farms or in small towns. High factory wages and the opportunities that city life offered gradually drained the countryside. The 1920 census showed that for the first time in U.S. history, more people lived in cities than on farms.[42] A flood of immigrants from abroad joined this rural influx, creating crowding and chaos as cities ballooned. Between 1870 and 1920, New York City's population grew more than sixfold; Chicago's, ninefold.[43] An expanding labor pool attracted more factories, further encouraging overcrowding. As in preindustrial cities, uses remained mixed together, and new housing sprouted next to new factories. There was, at first, no other choice—people needed to get to work, and only the rich could afford to travel by horse-drawn conveyance.

New industry brought new means of travel: first railroads, then streetcars and subways. Both radically altered street design while dramatically extending the distance that people could travel to work and shop. Across the United States, this fueled a rapid expansion of the grid pattern in cities and annexation of adjoining communities to accommodate surging populations and expanding industries. Railroads and transit lines encouraged the development of new, far-flung suburbs, heralding a new era of decentralization. Industrialization itself spurred the trend as workers sought housing and green space removed from the smoke and noise of factories.

To the Horizons: Cities Spawn Suburbs

The first industrial-era American suburbs were leafy enclaves for the rich. In these railroad suburbs, managers and bosses could trade the squalor of cities for a quiet, clean, and uncrowded setting. The onset of industrialization helped promote a new, idealized view of the outdoors. A tremendous volume of literature and sentiment on the subject appeared between 1840 and 1860.[44] During this period Henry David Thoreau published *Walden* (Boston: Ticknor and Fields, 1854), for example, and an increasing flow of publications on suburban cottages and landscaping appeared in architectural circles.[45] Americans began to yearn for a new Eden in the healthful and wholesome countryside—an idyllic paradise of garden cottages far from the soot and din of the industrial city and, ironically, made possible by the era's smoky icon, the railroad.

Railroad Edens

Some early new Edens represented experiments: Llewellyn Park in New Jersey, Riverside outside of Chicago, and Garden City on Long Island. They caught on quickly, however, and railroads soon led to some of America's most celebrated suburbs—from Chestnut Hill and Brookline in Massachusetts to Lake Forest and Oak Park in Illinois. Plans for some of these early suburbs emerged from the offices of such high-profile designers as Frederick Law Olmsted and Calvert Vaux, who drew up plans for New York's Central Park and major urban parks across the nation. True to their design roots, Olmsted and Vaux visualized their new suburbs as "cottages in a park." Generous lots, "English cottage" architecture, and sumptuous landscaping all combined to create the desired effect. Their work shaped a new approach to urban design, closely allied to the English Romantic landscape school and characterized by winding lanes and picturesque views. This approach became the model for later automotive suburbs and for major interventions in the industrial cities themselves.[46]

Middle-Class Suburbs

Suburbs did not remain the preserve of the rich. Complementing the era's emerging forms of transportation, new building methods encouraged an entirely novel class of development, the streetcar suburb. After the middle of the nineteenth century, a new way of framing buildings—using light wooden members joined by industrially produced nails and screws—began to replace more labor-intensive methods. Within a few decades, this new approach had transformed home building from an ancient craft into an industrial process; rapid development of common designs, pattern books, precut housing kits, and manufactured windows, doors, and molding accelerated the transformation. For the first time, housing became mass-produced.

This new building technology and electric railways arrived at the right time for skyrocketing urban populations. While early railroad suburbs had established secluded enclaves far from the city, electrified streetcars, subways, and elevated trains spurred dramatic expansions of the cities themselves. Existing grid patterns marched across the landscape, frequently growing in long ribbons of new construction that shot out from the center of a city along new streetcar lines, with land often developed by the transit operators themselves. The width of the band was partly controlled by walking distance from the rail line and partly by other factors, such as the land acquisitions made by the transit operators.[47]

Over time, the ribbons expanded into what are today the older, inner-ring suburbs of many major cities. These include places like Highland Springs in Richmond, Virginia; Dorchester and Brighton in Boston; Mount Lebanon in Pittsburgh; Shaker Heights in Cleveland; Hyde Park in Chicago; University City in St. Louis; and similar communities. Electrified transit lines created a vast, new urbanized territory that more than tripled the size of many older cities. New York City increased its territory from 27 square miles to more than 300 square miles between 1850 and 1900. During the same fifty years, the radius of urbanized Boston expanded from 3 to 10 miles, and the land inside Chicago's city limits mushroomed from 10 to 185 square miles.[48] These expansions mostly accommodated the working

West Newton Hill, near Boston, Massachusetts. The first American suburbs were leafy enclaves designed for the rich and connected to nearby commercial centers by railroads. Unlike rigidly gridded cities, these suburbs adopted a romantic vocabulary of winding streets, cottage-style architecture, lush landscaping, and picturesque views. In a sense, they represented the anti-grid and introduced a new approach to urban design in the United States. Courtesy of Oliver Gillham.

and middle classes. Electrified transit, combined with wood-frame construction, made land and building cheap enough to realize on a large scale. As Kenneth T. Jackson writes: "For the first time in the history of the world, middle-class families in the late nineteenth century could reasonably expect to buy a detached home on an accessible lot in a safe and sanitary environment."[49]

Streetcar suburbs created an entirely new type of urbanization in the United States: relatively dense, wooden-framed cities of one-, two-, and three-family homes on lots as small as a tenth of an acre. In places like New York City's Brooklyn and the Bronx, with high-volume transit lines, these suburbs became urban neighborhoods in their own right, dense enough to rival any city center. Boston, Chicago, and other cities retained their wooden-frame texture. For all of these communities, a grid layout principally offered a convenient tool for parcelization, development, and land sales. Such pragmatic concerns often left little room for design of the public realm, including streetscapes, public squares, and/or parks.

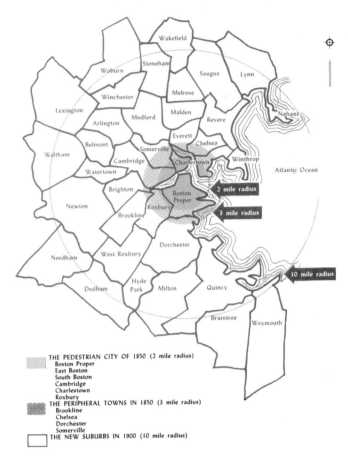

THE PEDESTRIAN CITY OF 1850 (2 mile radius)
   Boston Proper
   East Boston
   South Boston
   Cambridge
   Charlestown
   Roxbury
THE PERIPHERAL TOWNS IN 1850 (3 mile radius)
   Brookline
   Chelsea
   Dorchester
   Somerville
THE NEW SUBURBS IN 1900 (10 mile radius)

Growth of Boston's "streetcar suburbs." The advent of electrified streetcars and new methods for erecting wood-framed buildings supported dramatic expansion of U.S. cities in the last half of the nineteenth century. Development followed the inauguration of new transit lines in an early expression of transit-oriented development. Reprinted by permission from Sam Bass Warner, *Streetcar Suburbs: The Process of Growth in Boston 1870–1900,* 2nd ed. (Cambridge, Mass: Harvard University Press and MIT Press, 1978), 2; copyright © 1962, 1978 by the President and Fellows of Harvard College.

Garden Cities

Europeans in particular looked aghast at such urban patterns, which they saw as the equivalent of late-twentieth-century sprawl. The discontented included Sir Ebenezer Howard, the inspirational planner of England's green-belt towns. In his influential *Garden Cities of Tomorrow*

(London: S. Sonnenschein & Co., Ltd., 1902), Howard set forth a compelling alternative to the uncontrolled suburbanization he saw devouring the English countryside. For haphazard expansion of industrial cities he proposed substituting strings of discrete, mixed-use communities of about 6,000 acres and 30,000 people. Each new city would contain its own employment centers, residential neighborhoods, and shopping districts, together with an ample supply of parks and other public open spaces. He proposed surrounding each community with a permanent belt of agricultural land,[50] in a concept that clearly owed a debt to the baroque military engineers and towns like Palmanova.

Howard's ideas never caught on in America, despite many advocates and more than a century of attempts, but his influence remained powerful. For example, Clarence S. Stein's *Toward New Towns for America* (Liverpool, UK: University Press of Liverpool; Chicago: Public Administration Service, 1951), proposed a series of regional towns based on Howard's model. Walt Disney also drew on the model to develop the plan for Disneyworld's EPCOT Center (built after Disney's death, the project strayed far from the path Disney had mapped out).[51] The greenbelt-community concept enjoyed a brief resurgence in the New Town planning movement of the 1960s and '70s: fragments of Howard's vision appear in the communities of Columbia, Maryland, and Reston, Virginia. More recently, the smart-growth and New Urbanist movements have revived Howard's ideas.[52]

To the Heavens: Skyscrapers

As populations ballooned and new businesses crowded in, cities began growing vertically, too. With the introduction of elevators and steel construction, industrialization broke the height limits that staircases and traditional building techniques imposed. The first true elevators appeared in the 1850s, just as cast iron was making its debut in early industrial-loft buildings.

By the 1880s skyscrapers with all-steel frames began to rise in American cities, particularly in Chicago. To that point, most downtown commercial buildings had relied on masonry walls and interior wood columns and beams (later replaced by iron). Some buildings added cast-iron facades, but masonry walls remained the principal way to support the weight of a building. James Bogardus pioneered the use in America of cast iron for both facades and internal structures in a four-story structure he built in New York in 1848–49.[53] It ranks as one of the first curtain wall buildings built anywhere, and it predated London's Crystal Palace by two years.

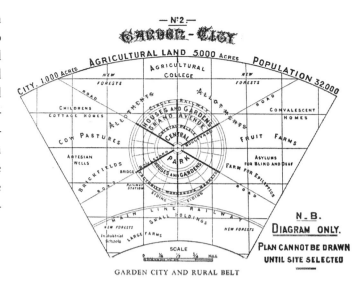

GARDEN CITY AND RURAL BELT

Diagram details for a prototypical Garden City. British reformer Ebenezer Howard advocated an alternative to constant expansion of industrial cities: small, self-contained cities surrounded by permanent greenbelts. His vision, which drew on the plan for Palmanova (among other sources), influenced twentieth-century city planning in the United States, from the first car-oriented suburbs to the thinking behind the New Urbanist movement in the 1980s and '90s. Courtesy of the Town and Country Planning Association (TCPA).

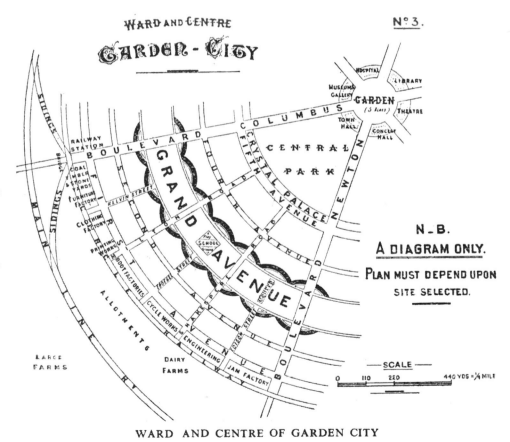

WARD AND CENTRE OF GARDEN CITY

The Singer Building (1908). As New York and Chicago competed to build ever-taller skyscrapers, architect Ernest Flagg argued for setting towers back from the property line once a building reached 10 or 15 stories. He created a model of his approach in his own design for the Singer Building, the world's tallest when it was completed. The idea began to appear in building codes in New York and other large cities in the 1920s. Courtesy of the Library of Congress.

Despite such advances, the first true skyscrapers relied on the tried-and-true technique of masonry bearing walls, using metal for interior structure only. Burnham and Root's sixteen-story Monadnock Building of 1884–92 followed this model in Chicago, but all-steel buildings appeared at about the same time. William Le Baron Jenney's ten-story Home Insurance Building, built in Chicago in 1885, boasted one of the first all-metal skeletons of cast-iron columns and steel beams. Adler and Sullivan soon followed with steel-structure office towers in Chicago, Buffalo, and St. Louis. By 1903, Chicago's D. H. Burnham and Company had completed the twenty-one-story Fuller Building in New York City, which was quickly dubbed the Flatiron Building because of its triangular floor plan. All of these buildings, the Flatiron included, followed the Chicago model for an office tower: a clearly defined base; a straight, vertical shaft that filled the site and rose without interruption; and a differentiated top story.

Within five years Ernest Flagg's forty-one-story Singer Building had overshadowed the Flatiron Building as the tallest in New York. By 1913 the Metropolitan Life Insurance Company Tower reached fifty-two stories, followed by Cass Gilbert's fifty-five-story Woolworth Building.[54] The race was on, as captains of the Industrial Revolution and their armies of managers raised lofty new palaces above the laboring city.

Although U.S. cities had rapidly pushed outward, they remained focused on their core commercial areas. As land values rose, new technology allowed more density and height, which further strengthened land values. For millennia, the design and pattern of cities had been largely confined to the horizontal plane. Now city planners and designers began to think about the vertical implications of their plans in terms of ever-taller buildings filling the space that would frame urban streets and public spaces.

Ernest Flagg himself loathed the shadowed streets and stark canyons produced by the rising crop of skyscrapers. Unable to hold back the tide, the Beaux-Arts-trained Flagg shifted to trying to reform skyscraper design. In a departure from earlier designs like the Flatiron Building, Flagg advocated setting back from the property line the portion of any building devoted to a tower of more than ten or fifteen stories so that the tower itself would occupy only a portion of the entire lot. Doing this, he argued, would open all four sides of the tower element to design and view, and "we should soon have a city of towers instead of a city of dismal ravines."[55] Flagg's Singer Building helped introduce this model. He rebuilt an 1896 structure to serve as the base of a new tower, which rose over 600 feet and was designed in the Beaux-Arts style. The Singer Building and others that followed, including the Woolworth Building, prefigured later building regulations.

Reaction: Regulating the Industrial City

Early in the industrial age, popular prints presented factories as icons of a kind of awe-inspiring beauty. As cities grew more congested and dense during this period, however, such sentiments waned; horizontal and vertical mixing of uses increasingly appeared to pose a threat to public health and an assault on aesthetics. Factories and rail yards in particular made bad neighbors in residential districts, smoking and roaring by day and night, heedless of their impact on light, fresh air, and tranquility. Factory workers lived jammed together in wretched conditions that created serious health and fire hazards. Publication in 1890 of Jacob A. Riis's photographs in *How the Other Half Lives: Studies Among the Tenements of New York* (New York: Charles Scribner's Sons) provided graphic documentation of the squalid living conditions that immigrant factory workers endured, inflaming public opinion and joining a swelling chorus of condemnation in the arts, mass-circulation newspapers and magazines, and the political arena.

In 1916, New York City instituted the first zoning ordinance in the United States, prompted not only by the squalor of industrial slums but also by the encroaching shadows of the skyscrapers that had come to dominate the skyline in a few short years. The new code established specific building and land use districts and spelled out enforceable regulations for building sizes and uses within those districts. Zoning caught on quickly: within ten years, more than 80 percent of U.S. cities had adopted zoning ordinances. As much as public health concerns drove the adoption of these codes, financial concerns also fueled their adoption. Zoning might bring light and air back to city streets and homes, but it also helped stabilize property values by providing some assurances about what might someday be built next door.[56]

One of zoning's major contributions was the separation of land uses into specific districts, or zones. of a city. New factories and rail yards could now be confined to industrial districts and houses and apartments to residential zones; the aim was to separate incompatible uses from one another, so that families would no longer have to share Sunday dinner with the drop forge or hat factory next door.

More finely graduated land use combined with enforced low density as zoning evolved, leading critics to blame it for many things, including suburban sprawl. Jane Jacobs also fingered single-use zoning as the culprit that destroyed the vitality of dense, mixed-use cities in *The Death and Life of Great American Cities*.[57] Despite zoning's flaws and unintended consequences, urban life in the industrial era was undeniably intolerable without it. Only recently has its application to suburbs and postindustrial cities come into question.[58] It is equally undeniable that, from its inception, zoning shaped cities in powerful ways. New York City's art deco "wedding cake" skyscrapers, for example, owe much of their form to the city's early use of zoning regulations that mandated setbacks on new buildings to allow light to reach the street. Following World War II, many cities adopted zoning that took a different approach—allowing construction of taller buildings in exchange for the creation of pedestrian plazas—and produced a strikingly different effect. With the removal of buildings to the center of plazas, sidewalks lost both energy and definition, which diminished the appeal of walking. Throughout its history, zoning has functioned as a powerful urban design tool.

World's Columbian Exposition (1893). The temporary pavilions at the Chicago World's Fair influenced American city-building for a century—most literally in the form of a new interest in classical architectural vocabulary for civic buildings, but more broadly through the City Beautiful movement, which promoted large-scale gestures to improve the appearance of American cities. Courtesy of Chicago History Museum.

Reaction: The City Beautiful Movement

Industry sparked another kind of urban intervention, one that mimicked baroque city-reconstruction plans. Much of this work took place under the banner of the City Beautiful movement, which emerged from the Chicago world's fair of 1893—formally, the World's Columbian Exposition. Under the leadership of Daniel Burnham, a team of America's leading architects and designers— including such luminaries as Frederick Law Olmsted, Charles Follen McKim, and Louis Sullivan—designed a vast, temporary city to house the exposition. Although covered in insubstantial white plaster, the classical vocabulary of the great Beaux-Arts pavilions by Lake Michigan influenced American city building for a century. Visitors to the "White City" returned home to wonder what might be done to bring light, air, and beauty to their own dreary, soot-stained municipalities.

The impulse for beautifying American cities reached back to the 1840s, when writers like Ralph Waldo Emerson, Henry David Thoreau, and Nathaniel Hawthorne began to romanticize the bucolic countryside.[59] In 1853, New York's legislature set aside hundreds of acres of land for a park in Manhattan, partially at the urging of well-known landscape architect Andrew Jackson Downing. In 1857, the city's parks commission selected Frederick Law Olmsted and Calvert Vaux to design what would become Manhattan's Central Park, comprising 843 acres of land.[60] The team drew inspiration from pastoral urban cemeteries like Mount Auburn in Cambridge, Massachusetts, but great European parks like London's Hyde Park and the Bois de Boulogne in Paris provided a more powerful model.

By the time of the Columbian Exposition, several additional European models of urban intervention had emerged, particularly in Paris, where many influential nineteenth-century American architects received their training. In 1853 the French emperor Napoléon III hired Georges-Eugène Haussmann to modernize the city with the aim of improving public health, opening streets to light and air, and enhancing circulation and safety. The City Beautiful movement sought to advance these same goals. Responding to the emperor's political agenda—he specified streets too wide to be blocked by barricades, as the revolutionaries of 1848 had done—Haussmann laid a series of broad diagonal boulevards and starlike squares over the tangled Paris street network. In the grand manner of baroque-period planning, his much-admired scheme showed little regard for the character of medieval streets.

Not everyone liked the results, however. Spiro Kostoff writes that "common people and cultural critics alike looked with increasing distaste and alarm at the new breed of technocrats…who unapologetically gutted historic cores for the sake of circulation. *Eventrement*, evisceration, was the term popular with the most famous 'demolition artist' of the time, Baron Haussmann."[61] In fact, a countermovement arose in Germany headed by followers of Camillo Sitte, whose *City Planning According to Artistic Principles*[62] advocated a more contextual and picturesque approach to street planning. Sitte's followers became dogmatic advocates of curvilinear street patterns, in direct opposition to the more baroque ideas of Haussmann and others.[63] Sitte's ideas and those of his followers eventually influenced American urbanism in profound ways, particularly in the suburbs, but their ideas gained little traction with the principal architect of the White City, Daniel Burnham. He remained a devotee of Haussmann's work.

In the wake of the 1893 fair, Burnham became a chief proponent of the City Beautiful approach, drawing up master plans for Chicago, Cleveland, San Francisco, and Washington, D.C., most of which were modeled in part on Haussmann's plans for Paris. Burnham's plan for Chicago included a series of great diagonals piercing the city's well-known grid, with principal focus on the city's business district and a new civic center. His concerns were both functional and aesthetic; he believed that diagonals saved time and divided traffic but also held beauty. "There is true glory in…vistas longer than the eye can reach," he wrote.[64]

Few of Burnham's plans were fully realized, in part because plans in the "grand manner" needed an authoritarian patron to make them work. France, with a highly centralized government headed by an emperor, differed markedly from the republican United States with stubbornly independent city, state, and federal jurisdictions. Kostoff describes the problem:

> Without the enabling clout of an Haussmann or a Speer, Burnham could not remake Chicago or San Francisco into a City Beautiful. It is not an accident that Washington was the only city to celebrate the Grand Manner unequivocally, when L'Enfant's moribund plan was revived and elaborated by the MacMillan Commission in 1902…. Elsewhere, one could only resort to persuasion and try to advance whatever fragments of the overall plan one could through the tangles of the democratic process. The most appealing fragments were public parks and associated boulevards and parkways, beautifications for waterfront leisure, civic centers, and civic ornaments like approach bridges and entrances.[65]

Fragments or not, the City Beautiful movement left America's cities with significant and treasured improvements. Movement-inspired planning continued into the 1930s and included such iconic works as the National Mall in Washington, D.C.; great parkways like the Merritt in Connecticut; Charles Eliot's parks along the Charles River in Boston; the Chicago lakefront; Kansas City, Missouri's parks and parkway system; the Denver and San Francisco civic centers; and many of the early works of Robert Moses in New York, such as Jones Beach and Riverside Park. In their pursuit of the curvilinear and the picturesque, some of these latter works reflected the ideas of Camillo Sitte and his followers more than those of Haussmann and Burnham.

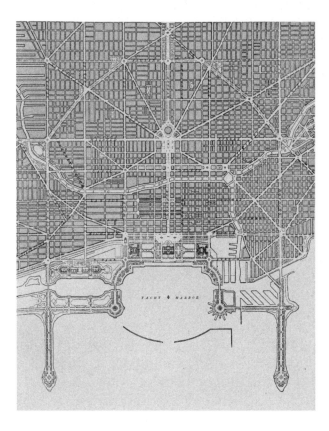

Imagining the Postindustrial City

The year 1939 marked a watershed in American urbanism. The supremely art deco Trylon and Perisphere dominated the world's fair in New York (1939–40), an event that reflected its time while hinting at changes in the offing. The United States had reached the pinnacle of its own special brand of vertical city building: the skyscraper was king, and the urban center was its kingdom.

Cities of Towers

Skyscrapers had evolved from their beginnings in the 1880s to their quintessential American form in the 1920s. In New York—which in 1939 held the largest number of tall structures in the world—the art-deco shapes of the Chrysler and

Empire State buildings pierced the skyline, surrounded by a host of other elegant needles bearing the names of corporate owners like American Radiator, the *New York Daily News*, Cities Service Company, Irving Trust, and Radio Corporation of America. Although the style had originated in Europe, the United States embraced art-deco style and applied it to architecture on a grand scale.

The masterwork of the era, Rockefeller Center, neared completion in 1939. Begun in 1930, the complex comprised fourteen towers designed by Raymond Hood, all clad in Indiana limestone but sliced by vertical stripes of glass and bronze. In many ways Rockefeller Center represents the archetypal work of purely American urban design. Covering three city blocks, its centerpiece is a sunken plaza with a giant sculpture of Prometheus bringing fire to man. Above it rises the knifelike edge of the seventy-story RCA Building (now the General Electric Building), with Zeus wielding a lightning bolt above its entrance. Everything about the complex celebrated twentieth-century industrial modernity, from the towers themselves, with their decorative arts and sculpture celebrating man and industry, to its nickname, Radio City. Sublevel walkways connect all fourteen towers, the city's subway system, and a pedestrian concourse lined by shops and restaurants and ranged around the sunken plaza. The multilevel circulation system prefigured postwar urban design thinking.

Architectural illustrator Hugh Ferriss idealized the style of Hood and his contemporaries, projecting them onto an imaginary cityscape in his 1929 book, *The Metropolis of Tomorrow* (New York: I. Washburn, 1929). His dramatic, bottom-lit aerial perspectives of an archetypal art-deco city, with ziggurat-topped towers rising into the gloom, celebrated a purely American, high-density urbanism. Ferriss's renderings symbolized the age, and by the 1940s skyscrapers in the same art-deco mold dominated the skylines of American cities from New York City to Miami to San Francisco. Boston's John Hancock Building, Detroit's Penobscot Building, Chicago's Board of Trade Building, and the city halls in Buffalo and Los Angeles serve as emblematic examples of the period.

Magic Motorways

If Hugh Ferriss's renderings celebrated height and density, the pavilions at the New York World's Fair (1939–40) suggested different possibilities that in time proved a more accurate rendering of the future of American urbanism. More than five million people climbed the great serpentine ramps leading to the General Motors (GM) pavilion, the most popular exhibit at the fair. Conceived by prominent industrial designer Norman Bel Geddes, GM's Futurama exhibit provided displays and models of future cities served by high-speed, limited-access continental highways. In stunning dioramas, expressways with looping ramps snaked across the countryside. In the "World of 1960," these "magic motorways" sped commuting fathers home to the suburbs at 100 miles per hour. To accommodate

▼ Rockefeller Center, New York (1929–39). Perhaps the crowning achievement of American urban design in the skyscraper era, Rockefeller Center's design celebrated industrial modernity. Among its pioneering features, a web of subterranean walkways connected the complex's fourteen towers and suggested the separated levels of circulation that became a distinguishing feature of many plans in the urban renewal era. Alex S. MacLean/Landslides—www.landslides.com.

▶ Rendering from *The Metropolis of Tomorrow*. Hugh Ferriss's distinctive style of architectural rendering helped romanticize the massing of New York skyscrapers and transform them into models that influenced the shape of urban buildings for decades across the United States. Reprinted by permission from Hugh Ferriss, *The Metropolis of Tomorrow* (Mineola, N.Y.: Dover Publications, Inc., 2005), "Crowding Towers," 63.

an anticipated flood of new cars (the pavilion sponsor did, after all, make them), GM and Bel Geddes redesigned cities, placing vehicles and pedestrians on different levels. Although hardly a new idea—Leonardo da Vinci's fifteenth-century plan for Milan placed service tunnels and canals below grade, reserving surface streets for pedestrians—such plans had typically gone unrealized. Eugène Hénard's "Street of the Future," presented in 1910, and other plans for Paris exhibited similar ideas.[66] Visitors to the fair could actually see the idea already realized at Rockefeller Center in its below-grade pedestrian concourse. General Motors' dramatic vision of grade-separated cities influenced many postwar urban design projects, even though most city streets in the United States remain single-level today.

The pavilion's real vision lay in what it proposed for the open landscape. Hugh Ferriss had posited a vertical urban future in his *Metropolis of Tomorrow*; Futurama unveiled an entirely different vision—a horizontal city rarely breaking three stories and spreading from horizon to horizon. Two decades after the 1939 fair, the United States would be in the midst of just such a building program, laying out a continental infrastructure that would form the underpinnings of a nationwide suburban metropolis.

In fact, GM's auto-dominated future was already taking shape by 1939. An invention of the late nineteenth century, the automobile began as a plaything of the idle wealthy; by 1900 the United States had a modest supply of 8,000.[67] As manufacturing costs came down, and as governments at all levels enlarged the network of paved roads, automobile ownership burgeoned. By 1927 the United States counted 26 million cars, an increase of well over 3,000 percent from 1900. The car was on its way from

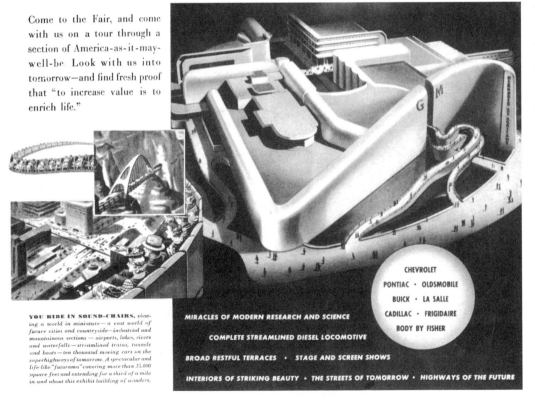

Come to the Fair, and come with us on a tour through a section of America-as-it-may-well-be. Look with us into tomorrow—and find fresh proof that "to increase value is to enrich life."

YOU RIDE IN SOUND-CHAIRS, *viewing a world in miniature—a vast world of future cities and countryside—industrial and mountainous sections—airports, lakes, rivers and waterfalls—streamlined trains, tunnels and boats—ten thousand moving cars on the superhighways of tomorrow. A spectacular and life-like "Futurama" covering more than 35,000 square feet and extending for a third of a mile in and about this exhibit building of wonders.*

MIRACLES OF MODERN RESEARCH AND SCIENCE

COMPLETE STREAMLINED DIESEL LOCOMOTIVE

BROAD RESTFUL TERRACES • STAGE AND SCREEN SHOWS

INTERIORS OF STRIKING BEAUTY • THE STREETS OF TOMORROW • HIGHWAYS OF THE FUTURE

CHEVROLET
PONTIAC • OLDSMOBILE
BUICK • LA SALLE
CADILLAC • FRIGIDAIRE
BODY BY FISHER

Advertisement for the General Motors (GM) pavilion at the New York World's Fair (1939). Among the marvels that GM's popular Futurama exhibit suggested was a vast, auto-oriented suburbia served by a network of superhighways. Within twenty years, the United States was busily making concrete a very similar vision. Advertisement from the *New York Times*, March 5, 1939.

upper-crust toy to middle-class necessity.[68] By 1939, a national highway system was already in place, primarily two- and four-lane arterial roads with traffic lights, roadside retail, and multiple curb cuts. The numbered U.S. roads in the national system began with Route 1 on the East Coast and ended with Route 101 on the West Coast.

By the 1930s, parkways had appeared near cities like New York, Boston, Chicago, and Los Angeles. Often grade separated and with minimal curb cuts, these roads for "pleasure vehicles" often formed part of a park system or had parks as destinations. Considered civic improvements, they were carefully landscaped and incorporated picturesque overpasses that carried intersecting roads to provide for a scenic—and minimally interrupted—ride. Although intended for recreation, the city-centered parkway systems also provided convenient commuting channels from the suburbs. Parkways quickly came to serve primarily as commuter rather than recreational roads.[69]

Suburbs for Automobiles

As early as the 1920s, with a national highway system and new parkways under construction, U.S. cities began to see their first automotive suburbs. Among the most celebrated, Radburn in Fairlawn, New Jersey, gained a national reputation from its 1927 launch as one of the first "towns for the motor age,"[70] with a layout prototypical of suburbs to come. Automotive streets were sized according to the traffic they were intended to support, with large arterial streets carrying the heaviest traffic outside the community, and roads through residential neighborhoods narrowing until they reached cul-de-sacs that each served a cluster of individual residences. The entrances to individual houses turned away from the street to face private gardens, which in turn provided access to pedestrian greenways behind the houses that crossed streets on overpasses and underpasses. Many of Radburn's innovations became standard suburban features across the nation (the parklike greenway system, however, has generally not been one of them).[71]

Radburn represented the crest of a wave of similar developments. During the 1920s, the population of suburbs of America's ninety-six largest cities grew at double the rate of their center cities. The populations in Grosse Pointe, Michigan, and Elmwood Park, Illinois, exploded by more than 700 percent. The population of New York's Nassau County on Long Island tripled during the period, and Los Angeles added more than 3,200 subdivisions with a total of almost 250,000 homes. Much of Kansas City, Missouri's Country Club District dates from the 1920s, as do significant portions of Philadelphia's Main Line. Rail and streetcar service linked some of these new suburbs with downtowns, but the automobile made most of them possible. As early as 1922, almost 135,000 homes in sixty cities could be reached only by motorcar.[72]

The new pattern broke from anything that had preceded it. Walking distance to a fixed transit line no longer constrained these new developments. Because of this, untouched land between rail and streetcar corridors began to fill up. While streetcar suburbs had been relatively dense—thanks to the walking-distance requirement and land prices—automotive subdivisions spread out as increasing access obviated walkable distance and decreased the cost of buildable land by enlarging the supply. The size of an average building lot nearly doubled, while residential densities dropped by half. Garage doors began to replace front porches as houses turned away from the street.[73]

Broadacre City

By 1939, architect Frank Lloyd Wright had formulated plans for a new kind of metropolis (which he fully detailed in his 1958 book, *The Living City*) and built a model of his vision, Broadacre City. He saw dense city centers as a dead end, dominated by machines, choked for air, and shadowed by skyscrapers. Wright pronounced his belief that "the city, as we know it today, is to die."[74] In its place, Wright envisioned a centerless, horizontal city connected by automobiles and advanced telecommunications. "Natural horizontality," he wrote, "is the true line of human freedom on earth." Condemning works like Ferriss's *Metropolis of Tomorrow* as "sterile urban verticality," he wrote that dense American cities were, in truth, nothing more than "pig-pilings" unbecoming to humans.[75] Broadacre City would unroll across the countryside in a carpet of single-family homes, apartments, and office and industrial parks that would stretch farther than the eye could see. In his vision, the houses would be interspersed with farms and forests held "in trust for future generations."[76]

Wright strongly believed that this new city would embody the ultimate expression of Jeffersonian democracy. Decentralization, he felt, was the only way to guarantee individual freedom, and the nascent highway system would deliver that vision. "The great highways are in the process of becoming the decentralized metropolis," he wrote.[77] Wittingly or otherwise, Wright's vision matched GM's—and both came close to describing the United States' postwar urban future.

TOWN PLAN
RADBURN, N.J.

▲ Plan for Radburn, New Jersey (1928–29). As automobile registration burgeoned in the 1920s, Radburn represented one of the first communities designed with the idea that every household would own a car. Many of its features—including a hierarchy of streets geared to handling auto traffic, cul-de-sacs, and houses that turned away from the street and toward private backyards—became staples of suburban planning in the years after World War II. Courtesy of the Regional Plan Association.

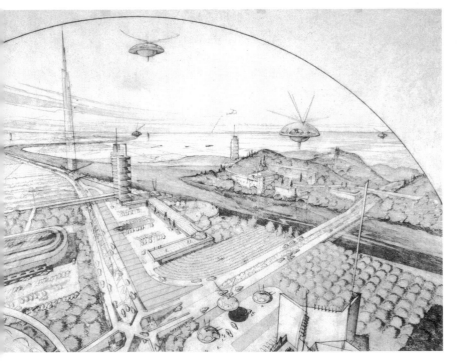

◀ Perspective of Broadacre City. Frank Lloyd Wright's 1939 vision for low-rise, decentralized development matched GM's Futurama ideal—and both predicted the American devotion to suburban development in the post–World War II era. Courtesy of The Frank Lloyd Wright Foundation; copyright 1962, 1998, 2001, The Frank Lloyd Wright Foundation, Scottsdale, Arizona.

CHAPTER 3

Decentralization: The Growth of the Modern City

While General Motors and Frank Lloyd Wright laid the foundations of a suburban vision in America, visionaries in Europe formulated radical ideas for redesigning cities throughout the world based on Western modernist principles that collectively became known as the International Style.

Europe and Modernism

L'Esprit Nouveau

Paris hosted the Exposition Internationale des Arts Décoratifs et Industriels Modernes (International Exposition of Modern Industrial and Decorative Arts) in 1925, an international showcase for the art-deco motifs that would become widely popular in the 1930s in Europe and North America. Yet a modest pavilion designed by an obscure architect and located in an out-of-the-way part of the fairgrounds caused an outsized sensation. Its Swiss-born architect, Charles-Édouard Jeanneret, went by the pseudonym Le Corbusier, meaning "the

crow-like one." His *Pavillon de l'Esprit Nouveau* — the pavilion of the new spirit — was an austere affair in the context of the art-deco-filled exposition: a simple, rigidly geometrical box devoid of any ornamentation. Paintings by Ferdinand Léger and the architect himself — working in the purist style of geometric forms and colors inspired by machines — hung above Michael Thonet bentwood furniture. The fair's art-deco theme was wholly absent; the house, in Le Corbusier's view, was to be a "machine for living," stripped of frivolous decoration.[78]

Even more startling was a glass-encased diorama in the pavilion, where Le Corbusier had unveiled his Plan Voisin for Paris (1925). Named for an automobile company that had helped finance the pavilion, the plan proposed razing almost all of the historic city north of the River Seine. In its place would rise sixty-story glass office towers arrayed in grid formation, each centered on a vast highway interchange and 800 feet from its neighbor. Open parkland and superhighways filled the vast voids between the towers, while titanic linear apartment buildings zigzagged across the fine grain of historic Paris. The

Plan Voisin (1925). Swiss architect Charles-Édouard Jeanneret (better known as Le Corbusier) horrified the French architectural establishment with his plan for razing a large swath of central Paris in order to build massive office towers and apartment buildings set in vast parks and connected by superhighways. His plan reflected a model that swept modernist architectural circles in Europe during the 1920s and ultimately shaped American thinking about urban renewal in the 1940s and '50s. Copyright Artists Rights Society, New York/ADAGP, Paris, FLC.

pavilion's "house," in fact, represented a typical unit in one of the apartment blocks.[79] Compared to intervention on this scale, Haussmann's plan for Paris seemed tame. The diorama so horrified exhibition authorities and the French architectural establishment that they tried, unsuccessfully, to have it fenced off. Instead, it claimed an award from an international jury—or would have, had the French not vetoed the prize.

The Contemporary City

The plan traced back to Paris's 1922 Salon d'Automne, where Le Corbusier had unveiled his Ville Contemporaine, a conceptual city for three million people. As in the Plan Voisin, sixty-story cruciform glass-and-steel skyscrapers formed its main office district. These skyscrapers, containing both the offices and apartments of elite industrialists, sat within large parks framed by the same zigzagging proletarian housing blocks that characterized the Plan Voisin. The plan separated vehicular roadways and pedestrian pathways throughout; at the city's center stood a multilevel transportation center that accommodated buses, trains, a highway interchange, and—on the roof—a landing strip for aircraft.[80]

Like the Plan Voisin, the Ville Contemporaine celebrated the automobile, but both differed significantly from Frank Lloyd Wright's and General Motors' vision of automotive urbanism. These plans deployed high-density structures to free the land from development and allow its use for common-realm activities like parks. The American plans filled the landscape with low-density, private development. In his biography of the architect, Robert Furneaux Jordan described Le Corbusier as believing that "the tall building must at all costs be a liberating thing…to release land for other purposes: recreation, foliage, lakes, schools, crèches, theaters, restaurants, highways and so on."[81]

The Triumph of Industrialism

Le Corbusier's city plans, in turn, reflected the influence of the earlier work of Tony Garnier and his Cité Industrielle, an imagined utopian socialist city, the plan for which Garnier had exhibited in 1904 and published in 1917.[82] Garnier set his city of 35,000 inhabitants on a river bend in southern France. In size it roughly matched one of Ebenezer Howard's garden cities, which may have provided inspiration. Garnier, however, pushed his plan well beyond Howard's diagrams, going so far as to describe both site and complete plan. Anticipating future planners by decades, Garnier zoned his city rigorously, with the industrial quarter clearly separated from residential neighborhoods and hospitals. In a bow to Camillo Sitte, the Cité Industrielle also preserved and incorporated a medieval town within its borders. Garnier's Beaux-Arts training revealed itself in the plan and in some of the city's monumental buildings. But his housing prototypes clearly showed the industrial severity of emergent modernism. First, however, the plan was

Cité Industrielle (published 1918). Tony Garnier's plan for an idealized socialist city in southern France influenced many later plans. Reprinted with permission from Tony Garnier, *Une Cité Industrielle: Étude pour la Construction des Villes* (New York: Princeton Architectural Press, 1989).

a radical vision of a socialist industrial future. "It was above all a socialist city," Kenneth Frampton writes in *Modern Architecture: A Critical History*, "without walls or private property, without church or barracks, without police station or law courts; a city where all the unbuilt surface was public parkland."[83] Garnier's work inspired many plans that emerged after World War I.

In the United States, architects and urban planners reacted to the rise of industry first with suburbs, then with the Beaux-Arts-inspired City Beautiful movement, and then with zoning. Ebenezer Howard and Raymond Unwin typified the European reactions. They hoped to find an antidote to London's sprawling industrial suburbs with their garden cities, imagined in an English country-cottage style. Their efforts represented reactions to industrialism, not its acceptance and embrace. In the same period, prior to World War I, only a handful of vi-

sionary projects like Antonio Sant'Elia's plan for the hypothetical Città Nuova and Garnier's Cité Industrielle actually embraced industry as a new aesthetic force for shaping cities. The world's first fully industrialized war, World War I changed that response, as it reshaped societies in Europe and the Americas. European societies went to war in 1914 in colorful uniforms on horseback but emerged wearing tattered clothes and driving machines. The war's shock waves rumbled through every field of human activity—including architecture and city planning. It accelerated the decline of traditional, crafts-based ways of doing things; speed and industrial production increasingly defined the fabric of European cities.

By the late 1920s, radical plans for city building along the lines of Le Corbusier's proposal had spread across Europe. Germany's Staatliches Bauhaus emerged as a continental headquarters of modernist design during the decade, first under leadership of Walter Gropius and later under Ludwig Mies van der Rohe. (With another Bauhaus faculty member, Marcel Breur, they would significantly influence twentieth-century architecture and urban design.) Radical ideas also spilled out of the newly formed Union of Soviet Socialist Republics (USSR). Konstantin Melnikov's Soviet Pavilion and annex represented the Vkhutemas—the Soviet equivalent of the Bauhaus—at the 1925 Paris Exposition.[84] It offered a stunning representation of the emerging wave of revolutionary architecture and urbanism based on industry.

Throughout the 1920s, the major political battles in Europe—particularly that between Marxism and its opponents—echoed through the world of architecture. Socialists saw industry as a means for achieving socialist revolution; opponents, like the sponsor of Plan Voisin for Paris, Gabriel Voisin, saw it as the province of elite capitalists.[85] Le Corbusier embraced capitalism; he had distinguished residences by class in his Ville Contemporaine. The Soviets, by contrast, aimed for a classless model,[86] a new kind of city that strove to express "the disappearance of the contrasts between center and periphery, between fashionable districts and workers' slums, and even, in the last analysis, between city and country."[87] Imbued with idealism and revolutionary fervor, Soviet architects drew up bold plans for linear cities and crisp, clean housing blocks in parklike settings with plenty of green space, fresh air, and light—all things that the City Beautiful movement had promoted in America but with a drastic revolutionary and industrial twist.

Even in revolutionary Russia conflicting schools of thought emerged. The so-called *urbanists* pushed the communal aspect of the city to the maximum, proposing housing projects that allotted only five square meters of private space to each occupant, with everything else—from bathrooms and kitchens to living areas to all outdoor space—relegated to the common realm.[88] Another group, the so-called *disurbanists*, stressed dispersed settlements of individual detached dwellings organized along transit lines. And Russia, at least for a brief period, actually strove to realize some of these plans, mostly along "disurbanist" lines, in new industrial cities built from scratch, like Magnitogorsk.[89]

Despite their differences, these architects from different countries conspired to bring the world a new *international style* of architecture that adopted the vocabulary of modern industrial buildings and found inspiration in the newly discovered possibilities of steel, reinforced concrete, and elevators. If housing was to become a machine for living, office buildings, too, should lose superfluous detailing; giant towers with walls of glittering glass translated the Industrial Revolution directly into built form. Planning efforts described new

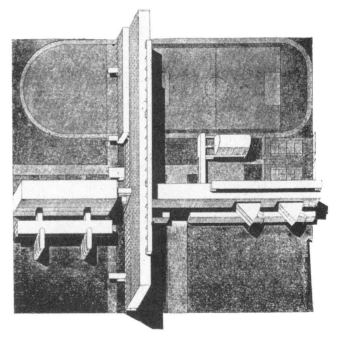

Communal House, by Barshch and Vladimirov (1930). Revolutionary thinking upended traditional approaches to urban planning in Europe after World War I. In the Soviet Union, one school of thinking argued for communal housing that allotted each occupant roughly 55 square feet of personal space, with everything else used and held in common. Reprinted with permission from Anatole Kopp, *Town and Revolution: Soviet Architecture and City Planning 1917–1935* (New York: George Braziller, 1970).

and revolutionary kinds of cities that embraced industry as inspiration while mitigating its impacts with rigorous zoning, better housing for workers, and broad, parklike settings with light and air. It was a logical step for these architects to create an organization for debating, codifying, and executing their ideas.

CIAM and the Birth of Urban Design

Congrès Internationaux d'Architecture Moderne

In the three decades after its founding, and particularly after 1945, the Congrès Internationaux d'Architecture Moderne (International Congress of Modern Architecture), or CIAM, became a significant force in shaping cities in Europe and North America.[90] Le Corbusier and his colleague Sigfried Giedion organized the first congress (known as CIAM 1) and issued a selective set of invitations to avant-garde architects across Europe.[91] Urbanism figured prominently in the CIAM 1 agenda. According to Eric Mumford, author of *The CIAM Discourse on Urbanism, 1928–1960*, Le Corbusier used the conference to restate "the ideas of his Plan Voisin in emphasizing the need for urban 'surgery' to reorganize existing cities." He also "asserted the importance of building at very high densities in the centers of cities while still allowing the maximum of space for greenery and transportation routes."[92] In the end, leftist members, shunning skyscrapers as "the last cry of capitalism," prevented the congress from endorsing these ideas. The congress did, however, support two concepts advocated by Le Corbusier: *centralized land planning* and the *functional city*, based on zoning that separated land uses by function.[93]

The Functional City

Although the rise of totalitarianism in Russia and Germany had muted some voices on the left by 1933, Le Corbusier himself had edged toward that end of the political spectrum in the wake of his involvement in a Soviet competition to plan and design a socialist garden city for 100,000 people. He modified his commentary on the competition into his plan for the Ville Radieuse (or Radiant City), which he presented at CIAM 3 in Brussels. The Ville Radieuse plan at once affirmed and expanded planning ideas embodied in the Ville Contemporaine and the Plan Voisin, and it significantly influenced CIAM thinking and debate. Meanwhile, Walter Gropius had begun to side with Le Corbusier on the subject of tall buildings following a period of sustained opposition to them by German leftists (some of whom continued their antagonism).

Organizers planned to hold CIAM 4 in Moscow, but the Russian political climate and other factors landed it instead on a cruise ship sailing from Marseilles to Athens. Focused on the functional city, CIAM 4 produced little agreement and no formal resolutions, but it did spin off a series of *constatations*, or observations. Edited by Giedion and Le Corbusier, these documents became the defining text for CIAM's urbanism, and Le Corbusier incorporated them into his *Athens Charter* (New York: Grossman Publishers, 1973), originally published in 1943. José Luis Sert (Josep Lluís Sert)—a relatively new supporter of Le Corbusier's ideas from CIAM's Spanish contingent—used those same documents as a model for *Can Our Cities Survive?*[94] which appeared in the United States in 1942, shortly after Giedion's seminal *Space, Time and Architecture* (1941).[95] By this point, Gropius, Giedion, and Sert had all relocated to the United States. All three ended up in key positions at Harvard University's Graduate School of Design, where they spread their ideas and those of Le Corbusier's *Athens Charter* throughout the United States and Canada.

The Athens Charter, ostensibly shaped by CIAM's membership, actually reflected the thinking of Le Corbusier and his close associates Giedion and Sert. The document showed the strong influence of Le Corbusier's Ville Radieuse, his earlier Ville Contemporaine and

Plan Voisin, and Gropius's 1920s housing plans for various German cities.[96] Together, *The Athens Charter, Can Our Cities Survive?* and *Space, Time and Architecture* helped amplify the influence of European modernist doctrine in the United States after World War II. Many of the planning ideas these architects advocated dominated American urbanism well into the 1970s. Some of their thinking has remained consistently influential, while others, once discarded, have enjoyed a renaissance.

CIAM's Urbanism in the United States

Under the banner of CIAM, Le Corbusier, Giedion, Sert, Gropius, and their American followers advanced a series of planning and design principles for cities. First, they posited that cities could be rationally analyzed and described by four functions: *dwelling, work, leisure,* and *circulation*.[97] Although not entirely original, this functional-city idea underlay much of the rest of their thinking. Their second principle excoriated the creeping sprawl of U.S. and European cities and condemned Wright's Broadacre City concept. They endorsed instead preservation of the natural environment from what Le Corbusier described as the "leprous suburbs" of existing cities[98] The solution, they insisted, lay either in wholly new cities, such as those envisioned by Le Corbusier, or in transforming existing cities by what Giedion called "heroic measures." Giedion argued that "the first thing to do is to abolish the *rue corridor* with its rigid lines of buildings and its intermingling of traffic, pedestrians and residences." In other words, the traditional city with blocks of street-defining buildings would have to yield to something new. He echoed Le Corbusier's sentiment that the existing urban street was "no more than a trench, a deep cleft, a narrow passage.... Our hearts are always oppressed by the constriction of its enclosing walls."[99]

Highways—or "parkways" as Giedion called them—would be the new urban corridors, and pedestrians, residences, and vehicles would be clearly separated from one another.[100] Tall buildings housing homes and offices would stand apart from one another to allow sunlight and air to circulate through parklike spaces surrounding them. "In order to achieve the placement of living quarters amidst greenery in densely populated districts, which is imperative," Giedion wrote, "there must be a concentration of groups of high buildings standing in parks or, at any rate, in open spaces. Only by such means can the distances necessary for light and air between buildings be secured."[101] (Despite his noble intent, substituting "open spaces" for parks left the door ajar for parking lots to become the open space of choice in subsequent decades.) This ideal represented the apotheosis of key City Beautiful and zoning-movement goals—maximization of light, air, and green space within the city and full provision of new means of transportation. The automobile would offer the primary means of circulation and the force defining the layout of the cities of the future—just as GM had forecast.

Under their third principle, these architects chose government as the primary mover behind "heroic change." The impediment of private land ownership had been widely debated within CIAM, but most members ultimately agreed on the need for eminent domain to uproot antiquated city patterns in order to realize the necessary changes—a position that helped pave the way for the urban renewal movement.

Dispersion and Firebreaks

At CIAM 3 in Brussels, Belgium, in 1933, Le Corbusier had argued that his towers-in-a-park concept would make residents safer from aerial bombardment and gas attack in war.[102] This argument—advanced when memories of World War I remained fresh—resurfaced in the United States during the Cold War, which gave it new resonance. By 1951 some U.S. planners were arguing that dense, traditional U.S. cities posed a serious civil defense risk in the event of atomic attack. In "Federal Action Toward a National Dispersal Policy," written for

the *Bulletin of the Atomic Scientists*, the chairman of Harvard University's Department of Regional Planning, William L. C. Wheaton, outlined a national policy for dispersing urban centers across the landscape. He recommended "that new construction and urban redevelopment in existing major metropolitan areas be utilized to reduce congestion and excessive concentrations of industry or population." He went on to praise the "programs of urban redevelopment and slum clearance" carried out under the Federal Housing Act of 1949, which were already flattening dense blocks in cities across the nation.[103] In the same issue of the *Bulletin* (devoted entirely to dispersion as a national civil defense policy) a former commissioner of planning for New York City, Goodhue Livingston Jr., recommended creation of urban *firebreaks*. "Such firebreaks," he wrote, "carved out through presently crowded industrial and residential areas, if used as vehicular express highways…will afford a means of escape for thousands who otherwise will be burned or suffocated to death."[104]

It was not only planners who recommended dispersion and decongestion of the United States' urban centers; the newly created civil defense agency actively encouraged dispersal of industry and employment with financial incentives for new plant construction. The National Security Resources Board also produced literature recommending dispersal with such titles as *Is Your Plant a Target?*, some of which carried lurid pictures of atomic blasts. Civil defense considerations such as these, in fact, ultimately helped win passage in 1956 of long-stalled legislation to fund the interstate highway system. The National System of Interstate and Defense Highways opened the floodgates for what was already a steady stream of suburbs-bound migration in the United States, the dream of GM's Futurama and Frank Lloyd Wright's Broadacre City.

Civil defense considerations, along with increasing blight in U.S. cities as they emptied out, helped create a climate receptive to the recommendations of Le Corbusier,

Boston before and during urban renewal. In the second image, taken in the early 1960s, several key urban renewal initiatives are complete or well under way. The elevated Central Artery, not yet ten years old, cuts across the bottom of the photo. Above the highway at right, the low-rise, nineteenth-century buildings of the West End have disappeared; only the Massachusetts General Hospital campus remains in a cluster near the river. The first buildings of Charles River Park—built on a model tracing back to Le Corbusier's Plan Voisin—rise to the right of the hospital. The left edge of the cleared swath of land forms the site for the new Government Center and plaza, still unbuilt. At top center, the framework of the Prudential building rises over former rail yards. From the Malcolm Woronoff Family, Aerial Photos International Collection. Copyright held by the Frances Loeb Library, Harvard Graduate School of Design.

Giedion, Sert, Gropius, and their followers. Yet despite the prevailing emphasis on dispersion, Le Corbusier and his American followers believed strongly in the survival of the city—but only if completely reinvented using Giedion's "heroic measures." The city, Giedion insisted, "cannot continue to exist in its present form." It "must be transformed but need not be destroyed."[105]

Interstate highways abetted this transformation. Construction of the new roadways broke through existing cities, sometimes cutting straight through crowded residential and commercial areas. Supporters used civil defense concerns to justify this destruction to some degree, but more important was the perceived need to modernize older cities in order to compete with a rapidly emerging suburban economy. The new urban unit would be the "superblock," a fusion of multiple city blocks bounded by modern arterial roads and highways. The new "urban corridors" would accommodate cars only, with pedestrians relegated to an independent system on a separate level.

New zoning reinforced federal urban renewal and highway programs in the effort to remake the nation's cities. Modernism soon dominated in neighborhoods and commercial districts razed and rebuilt according to principles laid down by Le Corbusier and his colleagues thirty years earlier. New York City replaced the setback zoning that had defined the art-deco city. Its new zoning transformed the midtown blocks of Sixth Avenue (renamed Avenue of the Americas) into a parade of broad, open plazas, mostly devoid of activity, with slablike towers separated from the street and from their neighbors.[106]

Urban Design Unveiled

In this climate, *urban design* as a profession was born. The followers of CIAM in the United States had for some time believed that there was "no border line" between architecture and city planning and that the architect's ultimate client was society. Le Corbusier and other members of CIAM had arrived at the idea of the "architect-planner" who could "orchestrate" urbanism in the 1930s.[107] As their followers in the United States rose in professional status and recognition, they began to develop the notion further. In *Space, Time and Architecture*, Giedion talks of the "town planner" who would have to think in more than two dimensions.[108] Sert uses the same phrasing in *Can Our Cities Survive?*[109] Yet, as city and regional planning gained widespread recognition as a distinct profession, Sert, Giedion, and their colleagues began to feel the need for something else—neither strictly architecture nor city planning but some combination of the two that could bring about the "heroic measures" necessary to salvage the nation's cities.

In 1953 Sert—now the president of CIAM and dean of the Harvard University Graduate School of Design—gave a lecture entitled "Urban Design" at a conference of the American Institute of Architects (AIA) in Washington, D.C.[110] This is the first widely known instance of the use of that term in an architectural forum. At that conference and subsequently, Sert advocated the "carrying out of large civic complexes: the integration of city-planning, architecture and landscape architecture; the building of a *complete environment*" in urban core areas.[111] In fact, this represented a large-scale evolution of an idea he had first suggested nine years earlier in "The Human Scale in City Planning," an essay in which he argued for countering the American trend toward suburbanization by replanning metropolitan regions based on walkable "neighborhood units" focused on schools and other public facilities.[112] The importance of this, as Eric Mumford later wrote, is that Sert "began to advocate the cultural and political value of urban pedestrian life…right at the moment when many businesses and the Federal government saw the movement of the white middle class to the suburbs as both desirable and inevitable. Out of this combination of the earlier CIAM effort to redesign cities 'in the general interest' with a new focus on pedestrian urban 'cores,' Sert eventually developed the discipline of urban design."[113]

This idea ran counter to thinking within CIAM and in the dispersionist circles of American planning. Influenced in part by a splinter group of younger CIAM members known as Team 10, Sert had broken with CIAM's general deprecation of the density of older cities while hailing the cultural aspect of cities and great urban spaces such as "the Acropolis, the Piazza San Marco, the Place de la Concorde" as models of face-to-face pedestrian interaction.[114] In fact, at the AIA conference in which he first used the term "urban design," Sert presented one side of a debate about the future of American cities. A Tennessee Valley Authority planner, Tracy Augur, championed the other side, arguing that "urban centers make inviting targets" for atomic weapons.[115] Sert disagreed, advocating a renewed focus on city-center redevelopment, albeit with reduced congestion and with new downtown parking facilities and modern roadways (along the lines of earlier CIAM recommendations). In taking this line, Eric Mumford writes, Sert set "the direction of much downtown urban renewal for the next few decades."[116]

Three years later, in 1956, Sert hosted at Harvard what was likely the first conference dedicated solely to urban design. Participation included members of CIAM as well as such luminaries as architect and planner Victor Gruen; head of the Philadelphia City Planning Commission Edmund Bacon; historian and urbanist Lewis Mumford; and writer and activist Jane Jacobs. Many historians agree that the conference gave birth to urban design as a distinct discipline with a specific focus on the renewal of declining core cities. "Urban design," Sert said at the conference, "is that part of city planning which deals with the physical form of the city."[117] Harvard had already introduced a seminar on "Urban Design," describing it as focusing on the "physical expression of city planning" and using the term "urban design" interchangeably with "civic design."[118] Judging from its participants and their comments, the urban design conference represented a sincere attempt to garner a wide diversity of viewpoints

about the future of the city. Nevertheless, Sert's view on the importance of retaining and rebuilding core cities as areas of civic engagement set the framework not only for the conference but for the future of urban design. "The urban designer," Sert said at the conference, "must first of all believe in cities, their importance and their value to human progress and culture." He went on to describe the necessary process as "not one of decentralization, but one of recentralization."[119]

Urban Design in the Urban Renewal Era

How was such recentralization to take place? "After we have so painfully cleared away the old environment, dislocating hundreds of thousands of families, and after we have spent our billion dollars," Edmund Bacon asked the conference, "will the new environment we create be worth the effort?"[120] Indeed, that question troubled many people over the next twenty-five years. Some projects produced during the period won major awards but later fell into considerable disfavor. Others, like Bacon's planning initiatives for Philadelphia, enjoyed alternating periods of favor and disfavor. Still others, like Boston's Government Center, stand at the nexus of continuing controversy today.

Many major urban design undertakings from the 1950s through the 1970s were urban renewal projects heavily subsidized by government. Municipalities used their powers to clear large tracts of inner city and core areas—especially in the industrial cities of the Northeast and Midwest—to introduce new life: the "recentralization" that Sert had called for. Not all of these efforts met the criteria that Sert and other urban designers had laid down. Many of those that did were built around vast civic pedestrian plazas fully separated from vehicular traffic—including the World Trade Center in New York City; Empire State Plaza in Albany, New York; Constitution Plaza in Hartford, Connecticut; Renaissance Center in Detroit; Embarcadero Center in San Francisco; and Prudential and Government centers in Bos-

Empire State Plaza, Albany, New York. Separation of pedestrians and cars—in this case with the civic pedestrian plaza above a highway and parking—became a standard model during the period of urban renewal. Alex S. MacLean/Landslides—www.landslides.com.

ton. In retrospect the underlying model—segregation of pedestrians and vehicles—proved a poor subsitute for the lively streets, squares, and pedestrian networks eliminated to make way for these projects.

Lessons from Suburbia

Even before the interstate highway system began to take shape, the car was fast becoming America's travel mode of choice *and* necessity. Almost every plan from this time period had to find innovative ways of dealing with automobiles. This problem principally involved how to capture the car and store it so that people could walk, shop, and civically engage in a fully pedestrian environment. In a paradigm-setting 1956 plan for Fort Worth, Texas, Victor Gruen proposed building a completely pedestrian urban core surrounded by a ring of parking structures all connected by a loop freeway. For Philadelphia, Louis Kahn proposed a series of parking garage "harbors" served by expressway "rivers."[121] Gruen's plan holds special interest as it essentially recapitulated—on an urban scale—his 1953 plan for a shopping center, Southdale Center, in the Minneapolis suburb of Edina.

Southdale Center opened in 1956 as the first fully enclosed pedestrian shopping mall in the United States. It elaborated on an outdoor mall Gruen had designed earlier, Northland Center, outside of Detroit. Essentially, Gruen designed Southdale as an enclosed downtown shopping street anchored by department stores in the middle of a burgeoning suburb. Unlike a real downtown street, however, the shopping mall arose from scratch and offered ample parking. Moreover, both the public space within and the parking lots outside were privately owned.

Plan for Fort Worth, Texas (1956). Architect Victor Gruen's plan for downtown Fort Worth—a pedestrian core surrounded by garages for cars that arrived on an encircling freeway—recapitulated his earlier plans for suburban shopping centers and established a highly influential paradigm for rebuilding city centers in an auto-oriented age. Courtesy of Gruen Associates (formerly Victor Gruen & Associates).

Gruen was not alone in proposing such an idea, nor was Southdale his first attempt.[122] Other suburban shopping centers preceded it, but Southdale functioned as the prototype for a generation of shopping malls that became the town centers and market squares for countless acres of otherwise centerless suburbia across the United States.

Despite their suburban roots, Southdale and Northland served as the models for Gruen's Fort Worth plan. Like the prototypical mall, Gruen's plan for Fort Worth offered a fully pedestrian environment surrounded by parking, with garages providing the interface between driving and walking. The main differences lay in scale, history, and ownership. Gruen's suburban malls—considerably smaller than downtown Fort Worth—were built de novo, had single owners, and were surrounded by surface parking. The Fort Worth plan covered an entire existing downtown with multiple property owners. Additionally, despite its structured parking, the plan left much of the pedestrianized urban core, of necessity, outdoors. Finally, unlike an all-retail mall, the Fort Worth plan comprised both commercial and civic uses.[123] (Because Texas refused federal urban renewal money, the city could not assemble the funding to buy out the many property owners downtown—one reason the plan was never realized.)

Ironically, Gruen's mall-inspired plan for Fort Worth largely followed the precepts for urban core areas laid out by CIAM at its 1951 congress. Anticipating Sert's call for recentralization, CIAM 8 (entitled "The Heart of the City") recommended that each city have only one core; that the core contain a mix of uses, including retail, office, and civic functions; and that it remain free of vehicular traffic, with cars parked at the periphery. Even in 1951 this was old news: Sert and other architects involved in CIAM (as well as others unaffiliated with the organization) had promoted the idea for nearly a decade. Nevertheless, Gruen's plan for Fort Worth was unique in its clear application of the shopping center model to an entire city, and it followed CIAM 8's

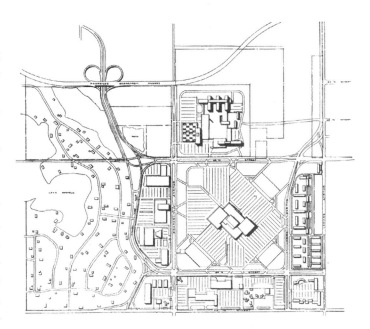

Plan for Southdale Shopping Center (1953). The first enclosed mall in the United States, Southdale opened in 1956. It served as a prototype—albeit on a smaller scale—for many downtown revival plans into the 1980s.

prescription for the urban core, which was no surprise given that the suburban mall followed the model of a downtown shopping street.

Many major downtown and suburban projects have followed Gruen's model of creating parking interceptors as gateways to a pedestrian environment. Today's suburban "lifestyle centers" build on this prototype, as do many downtown mixed-use development projects. In its essential form, Gruen's suburban model for downtown revival led to a wave of fully enclosed downtown malls that became popular across the United States in the 1970s and '80s, from Market Street East in Philadelphia, to St. Louis Centre in Missouri to the Houston Galleria.

Urban Renewal in Boston

Redevelopment of central Boston, which both preceded and continued after the 1956 urban design conference, paralleled the Fort Worth plan while embodying earlier

CIAM notions. Unlike the Fort Worth project, this plan was carried out. Starting in the 1950s, Boston used the Federal Housing Act of 1949 to raze the historic but decrepit West End neighborhood and replace it with a modern housing development called Charles River Park (Victor Gruen served as architect for the development). This attempt to provide housing downtown as an alternative to suburban flight represents CIAM's classic "towers in a park" concept, although one with less room between towers than Le Corbusier would have recommended. It also conformed to modern CIAM-inspired zoning, replacing an older mixed-use neighborhood with a single-use residential district that confined commercial uses to peripheral development along adjoining streets.

At the same time as the West End project, demolition proceeded on a corridor of buildings parallel to Boston's waterfront to make way for an elevated expressway. Planned to provide direct regional automobile access into the city, the Central Artery connected on its northern and southern ends to roads that eventually became part of the interstate highway network. Negative reactions to these two projects, especially demolition of the West End, drove the city's new mayor in 1961 to hire Ed Logue, who had led redevelopment efforts in New Haven, as chief planner.

Under Logue, some projects took on a more mixed-use character, but many tended to follow the Gruen model, with structured parking and exclusive pedestrian zones. In the wake of an award-winning (but unrealized) plan for redeveloping the Boston and Albany Railroad's switching yard, Prudential Insurance Company undertook construction of a monumental office tower on the site, in the city's Back Bay section. Charles Luckman's design for the Prudential Center stands in for an array of similar projects built in the 1960s. Planned as a superblock surrounded by a loop road, the formula followed the by-then-familiar Gruen model, although it placed most parking in a structure beneath the complex rather than next to it. A plinth raised the center's pedestrian level above the surrounding streets. The mixed-use complex centered on the fifty-two-story Prudential Tower and included apartment and hotel towers, secondary office buildings, department stores and shops, and a convention center. Almost all of these components sat atop the parking platform, like so many vacuum tubes plugged into the chassis of an early television set.

Prudential Center, Boston, Massachusetts (1960–65). This redevelopment project incorporated several of the era's common characteristics. It followed Victor Gruen's model of capturing traffic in a parking structure (in this case, below the development); it formed a superblock far larger than the basic unit of the adjacent grid; and it segregated pedestrian and automobile traffic. Alex S. MacLean/Landslides—www. landslides.com. *See color insert, C-3.*

Other projects around the United States—including Constitution Plaza in Hartford, the World Trade Center in New York City, and Embarcadero Center in San Francisco—adopted the platform formula. In a plan for Stamford, Connecticut, an office complex known as the Landmark Center anchored a second-level pedestrian system for the city's entire downtown. The plan was never fully realized, however, leaving parts of downtown with a second-level system—but most without.

In a fourth urban renewal initiative, the City of Boston leveled the delicate tracery of blocks that made up its red-light district, Scollay Square, after declaring it blighted. Use of the "blighted" designation said little about the neighborhood's economic or physical condition but much about decision makers' desire to remove poor people from the heart of the city and signal their own embrace of modernity. Where Scollay Square had stood, the city consolidated federal, state, and municipal offices in modern office buildings, rechristening the area Government Center. The final master plan by I. M. Pei and Partners organized the center around a vast brick-paved plaza modeled on Siena's Piazza del Campo. A long, curving mid-rise office building framed the western edge of the plaza, and a federal office complex designed by Walter Gropius delineated its northern edge. A new city hall, the centerpiece of the project, anchored the plaza's eastern edge, holding the same position as the Palazzo Pubblico in Siena. With the exception of the federal office tower, no building around the space rose higher than ten stories. The city hall itself had been the subject of a much-publicized competition won by the firm of Kallmann and McKinnell. Executed in the concrete brutalist style, the building won wide acclaim as a contemporary masterwork on completion in 1969.[124]

Government Center, Boston, Massachusetts (1962–68). The complex of government buildings replaced an energetic red-light district demolished in the early 1960s. Despite architectural praise for the city hall building, the vast pedestrian plaza has continued to appear desolate in contrast to lively mixed-use streets nearby. Alex S. MacLean/Landslides—www.landslides.com.

Perhaps the quintessential urban design plan of the era, Government Center followed the Forth Worth model. A large adjacent parking garage intercepted cars from the regional traffic system in the hope that the rest of the downtown experience would occur on foot. City Hall Plaza deferred to this notion—its vast brick expanse was intended for public gatherings and to serve as a place of "civic engagement" along the lines Sert had laid out. During the period, similar works appeared throughout the United States, including the Empire State Plaza in Albany, which gathered New York State government functions around a broad pedestrian plaza lifted above a platform of parking with direct highway access. It replaced the Pastures, a "blighted" neighborhood that was actually a stable Italian and Jewish district of Federal and Victorian houses.[125] Borrowing from the Prudential Center model, the Empire State Plaza also stowed parking and services below the platform.

One issue that went unrecognized in the design of Government Center was the extent to which the plaza would actually be used. As soon became clear, adjoining streets were livelier and more interesting than the plaza itself, framed mostly by office buildings. The mix contained no housing to generate activity after 5:00, and what little retail it included sat across a wide street with high traffic volumes. Subsequent decades have produced multiple proposals for redesigning and even eliminating the plaza as a way of solving this problem.

Common Traits

Many projects from the urban renewal period of the 1950s and '60s shared major traits: First, they tended to be unabashedly modernist and monumental. That is, they embraced the aesthetic tradition developed by CIAM in Europe before World War II. Second, most followed CIAM's ideas by setting high-density towers and slab blocks within open space to allow light and air between the buildings. Third, almost all represented attempts to retrofit existing urban patterns to the needs of automobiles by building

car-oriented roadways, creating superblocks, and adding Gruenesque interceptor parking in garages or under platforms. Fourth, most attempted to divide pedestrians and vehicles, creating central pedestrian spaces or networks of pedestrian greenways, often on a level separate from automotive circulation. Fifth, most segregated different uses (usually horizontally), creating distinct zones along the lines of CIAM's functional city recommendations. Sixth, the majority of these projects aimed to stimulate reinvestment in urban areas in an effort to eradicate the urban "blight" that resulted from suburban migration—that is, the goal was to make cities a viable alternative to suburban living in an automotive age. Few defenders of cities questioned these aims at the time, but actual experience soon produced critics who doubted whether such efforts actually met their goals, or ridiculed these approaches for doing more harm than good. At the same time, some architects and planners questioned whether these projects went far enough in meeting the needs of a modernizing world.

Utopianism, Reaction, and Reform

Utopianism

In 1967, more than fifty million people from around the planet flocked to Canada for Expo '67 in Montreal, Quebec. Many found themselves enthralled by one of the fair's iconic structures, Habitat '67, a pile of giant concrete boxes that looked randomly stacked atop one another. The boxes' placement, however, belied the exacting thinking behind their arrangement. Each industrially fabricated housing module joined with one or two others to make a dwelling unit replete with landscaped terraces supported by the roof of the unit below. Habitat was, in fact, a painstakingly planned megastructure, an industrialized casbah, and it won its architect, Moshe Safdie, instant fame. To many, it seemed a revolutionary vision of the future of cities and housing.

Unlike Habitat '67, few such visions were actually built. In the Arizona desert, Paolo Soleri was at work on a utopian megastructure called Arcosanti.[126] In Japan, Kenzo Tange had proposed a megastructural plan for Tokyo Bay, and Arata Isosaki had set out plans for his Joint Core Stem urban system. In Great Britain, three years before Expo '67, Archigram proposed the Plug-in City project—live/work modules that could be moved from one towering infrastructure frame to another and plugged in at the owner's whim. The collaborative generated many unorthodox proposals, including one for a city that moved on great hydraulic legs.[127] In 1968 Paul Rudolph unveiled a proposal that combined 4,000 units of housing with offices, schools, and factories in a single massive structure in Lower Manhattan.

Inspired by the power of industry to manufacture housing for the masses—just as CIAM had been—these designers extended the idea to other urban building types, components, and systems. These projects pushed the idea of the functional city championed by CIAM to its ultimate conclusion, turning transportation and utility systems into organizing spines and cores into which housing and other building types plugged. (CIAM's elegant towers, surrounded by light and air, disappeared in the mazelike nature of some of these projects.) While European countries did complete housing that mimicked these utopian ideas, few such structures broke ground in the United States, where a strong backlash was brewing. Nevertheless, unbuilt utopian projects from this period remained an inspiration for later architects and urban designers.

Reaction

In 1963 the New York City Planning Commission granted a variance allowing demolition of Pennsylvania Station to clear the way for construction of a new Madison Square Garden and an office complex. The commission found no legal basis for denying the variance, because no law then protected historic buildings.[128] The destruction of McKim, Mead and White's masterwork provoked widespread condemnation as a national tragedy, but it

Habitat '67, Montreal, Quebec. Although it looks like a haphazard pile of boxes, Moshe Safdie's Habitat 67 actually was a carefully planned housing development. Built for the 1967 world's fair in Montreal, it stands as one of a handful of 1960s megastructure plans actually realized. Photo by Tim Hursley. *See color insert, C-4.*

Walking City. One of many unbuilt megastructures from the 1960s: Archigram's 1964 plan for a city that moves on massive hydraulic legs. © 1964 by Ron Herron. Courtesy of the Ron Herron Archive.

ignited the historic preservation movement. Originally the preserve of a small group of wealthy Americans, the movement expanded dramatically as preservationists joined forces with community groups to protect endangered neighborhoods from highways and urban renewal projects. Within three years of the Penn Station debacle, New York City had put in place a landmarks preservation law and Congress had passed the National Historic Preservation Act.

Penn Station's demise accelerated a dramatic shift already under way in American thinking about the value of cities. Buildings that architects, planners, and others had once dismissed as blighted now snapped back into focus as valuable historic resources. The delicate network of lively urban streets and blocks appeared to offer an alternative to urban sprawl and modernist superblock planning schemes. The seminal *Death and Life of Great American Cities* had appeared in late 1961, written by Jane Jacobs, a senior editor at *Fortune* magazine.[129] Inspired in part by her experiences working to block the planned Lower Manhattan Expressway in the 1950s, Jacobs advanced the idea that urban renewal destroyed precisely the things that made cities great: the intimate scale and complex social networks found in, say, Greenwich Village, where she lived. She exhorted planners to "go back and look at some of the lively old parts of the city. Notice the tenement with the stoop and sidewalk and how that stoop and sidewalk belong to the people there."[130] "Cities," she said, "need old buildings so badly it is probably impossible for vigorous streets and districts to grow without them."[131] At the same time, she wrote, "the continuity of…movement (which gives the street its safety) depends on an economic foundation of basic mixed uses"[132] that needed to be pretty fine-grained. Small blocks, she said, not vast superblocks, give cities vitality and provide the qualities that make them better and more interesting places to live than suburbs. Prominent academics and intellectuals joined Jacobs—including Lewis Mumford, William H. Whyte, and Ada Louise Huxtable—and a groundswell of opposition soon became a tidal wave as residents in city after city protested the destruction caused by highways and urban renewal.

During this same period a Massachusetts Institute of Technology professor catalogued the elements that make a city work in the minds of its citizens—the constituent parts that contribute to an image people used to navigate through a city. In *The Image of the City* (Cambridge, Mass.: MIT Press, 1960), Kevin Lynch analyzed the features that contributed to what he called the "imageability" of a city. In this and subsequent books, Lynch found that the most "imageable" cities often turned out to be the more historic ones—Venice, San Francisco, and Boston. For one thing, these places tended to contain more "iconic" buildings and features—more memorable structures and places—such as the Piazza San Marco in Venice, the Golden Gate Bridge in San Francisco, the art-deco John Hancock Building in Boston. While some newer plans introduced identifiable markers in certain cities, a growing number of architects and urban designers felt that the mass-produced anonymity of modernist buildings (a logical outgrowth of the machine aesthetic promoted by European modernists and CIAM) lacked this quality of "imageability." Essentially, these new projects might arise anywhere in any city; nothing about them said San Francisco, Denver, or Duluth.

Other factors contributed to cities' distinctiveness independent of the work of architects, planners, or urban designers. Older neighborhoods like Manhattan's Greenwich Village, Boston's South End, San Francisco's North Beach, and Philadelphia's South Street had continued to attract artists, writers, and others who steadfastly refused to move to the suburbs. These people formed the germ of grassroots movements that began to transform entire districts of older cities without government help—and sometimes without government approval.

In the 1960s and '70s, a gradual exodus of garment manufacturing from Lower Manhattan left behind an exemplary collection of nineteenth-century loft buildings. Low rents and large spaces attracted painters, sculptors, photographers, dancers, and other artists who ended up using these buildings as both work and dwelling space.

The City of New York initially tried to discourage this movement, because it violated zoning and appeared to threaten to push other factories—and their well-paying jobs—out of the city. Contrary to the city's desires, the movement exploded in the 1970s, as nonartists began to follow artists into the lofts. By the 1980s SoHo and neighboring Tribeca had become fashionable addresses for many people. Over a twenty-year period, these old industrial buildings were recycled into new, mixed-use residential and commercial neighborhoods that had never existed before, with rehabilitated loft condominiums selling for millions of dollars.[133]

Manhattan offers only one example of the grassroots reinvestment that began in the 1960s. Urban pioneers began fixing up and restoring old buildings in neighborhoods like Charlestown in Boston; College Hill in Providence, Rhode Island; downtown Charleston, South Carolina; South Beach in Miami Beach and Ybor City in Tampa, Florida; Virginia Highlands in Atlanta; Pittsburgh's North Side; lower downtown in Denver; and other neighborhoods in cities across the United States. Although initially antagonistic, most city governments ultimately grew into active supporters of the movement. This change in outlook traces its roots to the work of Jacobs and her political and intellectual allies who had battled the forces of urban renewal and urban highway building.[134]

At about this time, some of the huge public housing projects built in the modernist CIAM tradition (or, more accurately, an often misunderstood and poorly executed version thereof) began to experience major operating problems. Instead of improving the lives of residents, these complexes—with structural deficiencies and social ills contributing in equal measure—made life far worse. The iconic demolition of the troubled Pruitt-Igoe complex in St. Louis in 1972 highlighted this turn and undermined CIAM's notion of the "architect-planner" as an able agent of social improvement. Turning away from CIAM's influence, urban designers across America moved toward the Jacobs camp—and a new idea of urban design began to take form.

Newburyport, Massachusetts. Making a midcourse correction, the city abandoned an urban renewal project, listed its downtown on the National Register of Historic Places, and redirected unused urban renewal funds to restoration. The historic preservation movement emerged in the 1970s as an alternative to urban renewal, offering an approach to downtown revitalization that focused on restoring rather than replacing urban fabric. Courtesy of Oliver Gillham.

Reform

As early as the 1960s, city governments began to modify or abandon their approach to urban redevelopment. Without completely walking away from big housing and redevelopment initiatives, they began to incorporate mixed-use and infill projects that demonstrated more respect for existing urban neighborhoods. The oil price shocks of the 1970s refocused thinking on mass transit as an alternative to highways and parking garages. Cities began to take up what had been a grassroots cause, restoring historic neighborhoods and multiblock downtown areas, often using urban renewal and other federal or state funds to carry out these projects. In the 1970s, Newburyport, a faded seaport north of Boston, reversed course in the middle of demolishing its historic, Federal-style downtown. Instead, the municipality listed the district on the National Register of Historic Places and used the remainder of its federal urban renewal funds to launch restoration. The resulting Market Square Historic District project became one of the first AIA Honor Award winners to encompass historic revitalization of a major portion of an entire downtown.

Faneuil Hall Marketplace, Boston, Massachusetts. The first "festival marketplace" became a national model for urban retail development and adaptive reuse. Photo © 2006 Chris Wood/wikimediacommons. *See color insert, C-5.*

Lowell, Massachusetts, a run-down mill town not far from Newburyport, used National Park Service funding to transform its dying center into a national Urban Cultural Park. Adding federal urban renewal funds, and with the active support of the state, the city sparked the recycling of thousands of square feet of abandoned mill buildings into offices, homes, and museums. Other cities identified and began restoring key parts of their historic downtowns. Philadelphia had already begun work on its Society Hill neighborhood. In Seattle, Pioneer Square became the center of revival efforts; San Diego focused on its Gaslight District; and Providence began refashioning the College and Federal hills neighborhoods.

A major restoration project of the early 1970s became widely influential: Boston's Faneuil Hall Marketplace, created by the Rouse Corporation with Benjamin Thompson as architect. Winner of an AIA Honor Award, the project converted a wholesale food market into the nation's first "festival marketplace" by rehabilitating three vast, 175-year-old buildings and surrounding them with high-quality pedestrian space. Here was a vibrant urban space that made for true civic engagement and enjoyment. Located on Boston's Walk to the Sea, the marketplace created an exciting transition from the

"New Boston" at City Hall Plaza to the city's historic waterfront, where wharf buildings were being rehabilitated for residential use. This lively addition to the city set a national standard for urban retail development and historic building reuse; versions of it can be found in cities across the nation, including the highly successful Harborplace in Baltimore; Jacksonville Landing in Jacksonville, Florida; and Navy Pier in Chicago. As pathbreaking as it was, it is worth noting that Faneuil Hall Marketplace borrowed from the familiar Gruen model—creating a pedestrian shopping zone attached to a large parking garage with near-direct highway access.

By the late 1970s, both cities and small downtowns across the United States were at work restoring historic downtowns and Main Streets with newly available federal funds and tax credits. In 1977 the National Trust for Historic Preservation launched the Main Street program, designed to save the historic commercial architecture of declining downtowns. By 2003, the program had reached sixteen hundred communities in forty-one states.[135]

All these efforts aimed to revive downtowns that had suffered from suburbanization. This work continues nationally as downtowns have established storefront-revitalization programs and signage guidelines and installed new paving, landscaping, and lighting. Revitalization plans have often combined these initiatives with new parking facilities (following the Gruen model) and targeted redevelopment and adaptive reuse of existing downtown buildings.

Postmodernism and Contextualism

Emerging in the late 1970s, *postmodernist* and *contextualist* architectural movements complemented the growing historic-preservation movement. Both movements challenged the dominance of modernism and the industrial aesthetic in architecture, advocating a return to the historic orders, decorative detail, and scale of premodernist architecture—often reinterpreted with contemporary twists. Art-deco reinterpretations became popular alongside a resurgence of nineteenth- and early-twentieth-century styles. More purely historicist buildings, like those of Robert A.M. Stern or Skidmore, Owings & Merrill's One Worldwide Plaza in Manhattan, sometimes reflected architectural styles from the late nineteenth and early twentieth centuries.

In the early 1980s, urban designers shifted their focus to the patterns of historic European and American cities, emphasizing the street and the square, treating buildings as the "background" that helped form public space and reviving interest in planners from previous centuries like Ebenezer Howard, Raymond Unwin, and Claude Nicholas Ledoux. Meanwhile, designers embraced the historic American gridiron pattern of smaller blocks (championed by Jane Jacobs) and turned their backs on the superblock, judged antiurban in its lack of scale and variation. They resurrected the strong diagonals, axial streets, spaces and views, and the use of focal points that characterized baroque and later city planning, including the City Beautiful movement. Parks planners looked to Frederick Law Olmsted and the great parks of the Victorian era and the early twentieth century.

In the vanguard of this new movement were the followers of Colin Rowe at Cornell University and the brothers Robert and Leon Krier, who viewed urban space as essentially "carved out" of a carpet of dense building mass rendered in *poché*. This regime favored background buildings, or at least buildings that borrow their formal vocabulary from their surroundings rather than making bold, individual statements. Shape and form became the governing factor of public space, combined with design guidelines to lend a common look and feel to the architecture that would make up the "walls" of the public space system. In all cases the street wall was to be maintained, not deliberately broken to introduce light, air, and open space as it had been under modernism. The Kriers advocated mixing of uses, along with the density and form of older European and American cities, valuing the vitality that such density and concentra-

tion of mixed uses brought with it—recommendations that aligned well with the work of Jane Jacobs.

Growing distaste for superblock planning and the reviving interest in traditional cities and city blocks coincided with a waning of federal urban renewal funds under the Reagan administration. At the same time, near-completion of the interstate highway system meant that highway funding that had supported urban redevelopment would also disappear. These changes cut the fuel supply that had powered the urban renewal juggernaut. Large-scale land takings and mass redevelopments grew less feasible, especially in the face of now potent anti-urban-renewal sentiment. This gave new prominence to private developers and private finance as agents of urban change—a transformation that favored infill develop-

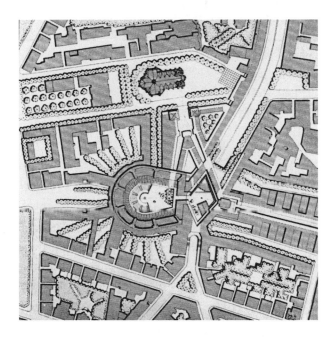

Robert Krier's plan for part of Stuttgart, Germany (1979). In the 1980s, urban designers in the United States began to shift their thinking about public space, treating it as being carved out of a dense background of buildings with harmonious designs and forms. They began to stress the importance of the street wall—the lineup of adjacent buildings—in shaping public spaces. *Urban Space* (New York: Rizzoli, 1979), 126.

ment and small-block planning. In urban areas, the focus shifted to leftover redevelopment parcels and former industrial and military lands or brownfield sites, like the Charlestown Navy Yard in Boston. Its redevelopment as a mixed-use complex entailed rehabilitation of historic naval and industrial buildings; part of the project won an AIA Honor Award in 1994.

Rowes Wharf, a major multiple-use complex on Boston's waterfront completed in the 1980s, exemplifies this period. Also a 1994 AIA Honor Award winner, the project relied entirely on private developers working on public land. The Boston Redevelopment Authority owned the parcel, a remnant of a former industrial redevelopment site, and had "land-banked" it, allowing its use for parking until the market could support its redevelopment. The

complex wraps hotel, offices, and condominiums into a contextual brick package that maintains the street wall of Atlantic Avenue on the west while continuing Boston's line of finger piers along the harbor to the east. A generous archway and rotunda form an iconic gateway from Atlantic Avenue to the waterfront, a water transportation hub, and the city's public HarborWalk. The building complex deploys details and materials from surrounding buildings, making it feel as if it has always stood on the site.

Another major project from this period—Battery Park City in Manhattan—won a *Progressive Architecture* magazine urban design award, and parts of the project earned AIA Honor Awards for urban design in 1996 and 2005. Battery Park City arose on another leftover public site—landfill produced by the 1970s excavation for the World Trade Center. The master plan, devised by the firm of Cooper/Eckstut (now Cooper Robertson and Partners), extended the adjacent street grid through the site to a waterfront promenade and park system, creating a new residential and mixed-use neighborhood of small, pleasantly scaled city blocks. The clearly contextualist pattern followed the recommendations that Jane Jacobs had made more than twenty years earlier. The project architecture borrowed heavily from the vocabulary of New York residential buildings built early in the twentieth century, filling out the postmodernist and historicist details of the plan. In addition to its awards, the plan earned widespread nonprofessional praise.

Other plans of this genre and from this period included the plan for Mission Bay in San Francisco; Boston's Harbor Point; and Mizner Park in Boca Raton, Florida. Mission Bay comprises an entire new district built on a 300-acre former industrial site. Like Battery

Rowes Wharf, Boston, Massachusetts. Diminishing federal funds for urban renewal and highway construction in the 1980s gave new prominence to the role of private developers in shaping urban space. This change accelerated a move from the sweeping urban design plans of the 1960s and '70s toward infill and small-block development. Alex S. MacLean/Landslides—www.landslides.com.

Park City, it extends a contextual pattern of blocks, row houses, neighborhood commercial streets, and parks into a new district; later changes added a new campus for the University of California.[136]

Completed in 1991, the mixed-use Mizner Park development replaced a failed shopping mall with nearly 300 units of housing, a public promenade and park, retail shops and restaurants, office space, cinemas, and a museum. The 29-acre development centers on a tree-lined boulevard of multistory residential buildings with ground-floor retail. The popularity of this model today obscures Mizner Park's singularity at the time it was built: It planted an entirely new "traditional downtown" where none had grown before, and it did so in the heart of a fundamentally suburban community. Its compact building design, vertical mixing of uses, and walkable outdoor environment all recall downtowns of the nineteenth and early twentieth centuries—but instead of growing incrementally, it was built in a single stroke like any suburban shopping center. Older downtowns struggled to accommodate the automobile with sometimes-intrusive parking garages; Mizner Park provided plenty of concealed parking, remarkable for its time, and established a widely followed model for later projects.[137]

Throughout the 1980s, most development left parking exposed in large garages that dominated (or blighted, as critics charged) surrounding streets. Rowes Wharf hid its parking in multiple underground levels, despite having to build essentially underwater. High land costs for an external garage made this sleight-of-hand necessary, and high development returns made it possible. Most projects, especially in less-dense urban and suburban settings, cannot afford to repeat it. Mizner Park pioneered a new ap-

Plan for Battery Park City, New York (1979). This context-sensitive master plan extended the nearby street grid onto landfill and took its architectural vocabulary from familiar New York City building styles. It made concrete many of the principles writer Jane Jacobs had advocated for decades, beginning with her groundbreaking *Death and Life of Great American Cities* (1961). Courtesy Hugh L. Carey Battery Park City Authority.

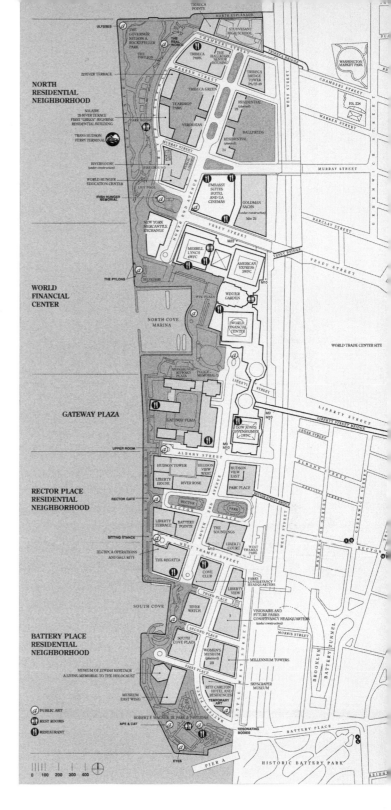

Mizner Park, Boca Raton, Florida (1991). This pioneering 29-acre development introduced a full mix of uses—in essence, a small downtown built from scratch—on the site of a failed shopping mall. Although more sophisticated in execution, it reproduces the basic Victor Gruen paradigm of a highway bringing cars to garages from which pedestrians walk to shopping—and, in this case, to work, home, and other activities. The model has been repeated across the United States. Alex S. MacLean/Landslides—www.landslides.com.

proach, concealing aboveground garages behind residential and retail uses that face sensitive areas (like the main shopping boulevard and surrounding neighborhoods) but leaving them exposed where they face the arterial road that provides access to the complex. In this sense, Mizner Park refined the highly successful Gruen paradigm, with parking, reached by a highway system, surrounding a pedestrian shopping street. Remarkably, though, Mizner Park is neither a traditional shopping mall nor a redeveloped downtown but a totally new development, with all required facilities for contemporary auto-based transportation, built to look like a traditional downtown that has existed for years. Many developments across the nation have followed the Mizner scheme since the 1990s. In some suburban areas these "lifestyle centers" have emerged as alternatives to the traditional enclosed mall.

Redefining Suburbs

Mizner Park broke new ground in the design and planning of suburbs. Its contemporaneous pioneers included entire new communities designed in the postmodernist mode. In 1982 Andres Duany and Elizabeth Plater-Zyberk began planning a community in the Florida Panhandle—Seaside—that came to be seen as the spark for the New Urbanist movement in the United States.

Planners and architects within the New Urbanist movement propose rules for creating compact, "traditional" mixed-use neighborhoods and "towns" at moderate densities suitable for walking and for transit while leaving surrounding green space intact. Pioneering efforts of the movement have included Seaside and Kentlands, Maryland (planned in 1988). Other communities include Windsor and Celebration, both

Celebration, Florida (1994). In the late 1980s and '90s, plans for new "traditional" towns—with denser development that promoted walking, protected open space, and developed a vocabulary of architectural features from older suburbs—helped crystallize the New Urbanist movement. Alex S. MacLean/Landslides—www.landslides.com.

in Florida. Peter Calthorpe joined Duany and Plater-Zyberk early on as founders and leading lights of the New Urbanist movement. At the outset, the movement focused largely on building new communities along traditional lines, reviving qualities that people liked about older suburbs (in contrast to what James Howard Kunstler calls the "nowhere" of contemporary suburbs).[138] These were called traditional neighborhood developments (TNDs). Calthorpe added a focus on transit, working to promote a fundamental change in the auto-dependent suburban pattern by creating transit-oriented developments (TODs) that concentrate pedestrian paths and higher-density development around transit stops.[139]

Since the 1990s, the New Urbanist movement has broadened its agenda significantly to include sustainability and revitalization of existing urbanized areas

before development of greenfield sites in suburban and exurban areas.

Continuing Recentralization

A postmodernist-contextualist tradition, as codified by the Congress for the New Urbanism (CNU), influences much of urban design today. The tradition has won wide public acceptance—arguably much more so than the modernist work that preceded it. Acknowledging the failures of the 1960s and '70s, New Urbanist planning stresses preservation and revival of existing urban neighborhoods over their demolition and reconstruction. Where urban expansion or reconstruction takes place, say New Urbanists, it should take its cue from surrounding street and block patterns. This philosophy has dovetailed with lingering negative feelings about urban

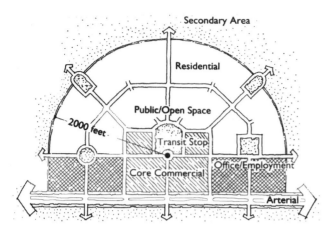

Generic plan for a transit-oriented development. Urban designer Peter Calthorpe helped broaden the New Urbanist movement's focus to include new development around transit connections that reduces auto dependency and urban redevelopment that takes advantage of existing infrastructure while diminishing development pressure on greenfield sites. Reprinted with permission from *The Next American Metropolis: Ecology, Community and the American Dream* (New York: Princeton Architectural Press, 1993).

highways, a body of environmental regulation largely formulated after urban renewal lost favor, and a rising interest in mixed-use, walkable, and transit-friendly urban environments. All of these developments represent reactions to widespread, auto-dependent suburbanization. Working from a different set of principles, urban designers in the United States continue to address many of the same concerns that led José Luis Sert and his colleagues to organize the seminal conference on urban design in 1956: they hope to recentralize the nation.

Reconstruction of industrial waterfronts offers a prime illustration of urban designers' contemporary approach to recentralizing cities. Drawing on the City Beautiful tradition, cities throughout North America have transformed vast acres of waterfront brownfields into parks, high-density housing, cultural districts, and mixed-use neighborhoods. Significant examples appear in Montreal, Boston, Providence (Rhode Island), New York City, Richmond (Virginia), Chattanooga (Tennessee), Pittsburgh, Cleveland, Milwaukee, St. Louis, and San Francisco. Meanwhile, as aftershocks from the urban renewal and highway era have rumbled on, urban designers have become increasingly involved in community outreach, consensus building, and public policy choices.

Opportunities and Challenges

Over the last two decades, a confluence of forces—suburbanization, the disappearance of urban factories, and continuing reaction to urban renewal—has created a new frontier in U.S. cities. The ongoing transition to a postindustrial economy and technology's growing role in shaping life patterns has eroded some traditional limits on cities, such as transportation and economic factors. Other forces, including environmental and social constraints, have emerged as influences on urban development, opening a new chapter in urban design. New voices question past practices, including a reliance on contextualism and history. At a time when many urban designers organize new communities on classical urban grids of blocks, streets, and squares, architectural design has turned back to modernism for inspiration. A new generation of urban designers has appeared in the nation's universities, following the trend in architectural design and taking cues from modernism and the utopian and megastructural ideas of the 1950s and '60s. It remains to be seen whether this movement will become widespread and gain public acceptance in the same way that current practices have.

▶ Early-twentieth-century industrial waterfront and rebuilt riverfront in Providence, Rhode Island. The revitalization of industrial waterfronts offers a prime example of the New Urbanist approach, which advocates reusing and redeveloping abandoned urban industrial sites. Once the focus of commercial activity in many U.S. cities, most waterfronts have lost businesses to suburban locations or other countries. Many cities have begun to reassess how they use their waterfronts, introducing housing, parks, and entertainment uses where industry and shipping once dominated. Providence, for example, turned a neglected riverfront into a defining element of its downtown. Courtesy of Library of Congress, Theodor Horydczack Collection *(top)*; courtesy of Richard Benjamin *(bottom)*.

CHAPTER 4

Recentralization: The City as the Future

Suburbanization, which shaped the United States for more than sixty years, is now widely recognized as unsustainable. Yet it continues to spread, degrading the environment, competing against cities for investment and resources, and undermining public health. In this context, José Luis Sert's call for "recentralization" has become more urgent today than it was fifty years ago. Even so, the last decade has yielded signs of a dramatic change in course. Cities have begun reinventing themselves as centers of the new economy and lodestones for the arts, culture, education, and finance. Former poster children for industrial pollution now win praise as models of sustainability. People and money have begun to flow back to U.S. cities.

Responses to these new forces at work in American cities take place in a context of shifting urban design theory. In the 1970s, sentiment among urban designers began to turn against the "top-down" methods of urban renewal. In the decades that followed, a new paradigm emerged, combining Jane Jacobs's championing of cities' fine-grained qualities, contextualism, and deference to historic building patterns. With groups inside and outside of the profession calling for new ideas, today's orthodoxy may soon give way to something quite different.

Setting the Stage: Fifty Years of Suburbanization

"Detroit," says urban designer Constance Bodurow, "spent the first 50 years of the twentieth century bringing the industrial age to America, and then went to sleep for the next 50 years."[140] She points proudly to revitalization initiatives across her city, but her comments apply to much of urban America. In the late 1940s, mayors and chambers of commerce proclaimed a bright future for U.S. cities—an optimism that frequently proved premature. Instead, a perfect storm of economic, technological, and social forces dramatically refashioned the American landscape after World War II.

Migration to the suburbs mirrored the transition in an economy that no longer needed mills and factories in urban centers. In America's largest manufacturing cities, industrial jobs dropped by more than 40 percent between 1967 and 2001.[141] This shift reflected a fundamental transformation not just of the economy but of social classes. Median income rose sharply after the war, dramatically increasing the number of Americans who considered themselves part of the middle class. With more money to spend on housing, Americans increasingly chose homes in the suburbs. Central cities soon earned a collective reputation as the province of working-class, poor, and black households—people who could not afford the suburbs or who found their paths blocked by discriminatory lending and sales practices. Government housing programs of the late 1940s concentrated low-income housing in urban core areas at the same time that large numbers of Southern blacks trekked northward in search of industrial jobs. These factors aggravated a growing racial and economic gulf between city and suburb.

Rising middle-class wealth joined with high birth rates after the war to drive demand for both home and car ownership. Fueled by government-insured mortgages, this demand spawned tract-housing development on an unprecedented scale. Cities simply did not have the huge quantities of cheap land they needed to compete. By the mid-1950s, heavy funding of the interstate highway system opened another stream of federal subsidy to support suburban development.

As suburban investment rose, urban investment fell. Middle-class and wealthier Americans not only moved out of cities, but they stopped working and shopping there. By 1990, the real value of assessed property in the city of Detroit had dropped to less than a quarter of its 1950 level. Even though the decline elsewhere was less dramatic, almost every American city shifted rapidly from being a center of wealth to a center of poverty. With television providing news and entertainment in the home, some suburban residents took pride in organizing their lives so that they never had to set foot in a downtown or urban neighborhood. By the 1970s, cities and traditional urban forms generally had taken on the air of outmoded relics of an earlier age.

That view has changed since signs of urban fortunes on the rebound first appeared in the late 1990s. Today, interest in urban living has reached levels impossible to imagine in the 1970s, and demographic shifts suggest that this interest will remain strong well into the 2030s. Just as postwar urban decline had its roots in a mix of factors, so does today's urban revival. Since the late 1990s, the United States has experienced a *new* perfect storm of demographic, economic, social, and technological forces that have reshaped housing preferences. For the first time in more than fifty years, the nation's cities have begun to capture a growing share of regional wealth as measured by housing values and household income.

By the1990s the shift from industrial to service economy had largely run its course and the United States found itself making a transition toward "industries of the mind." Economists—most prominently Richard Florida, then at Carnegie Mellon University—argued that regional economic competitiveness depended on a well-educated workforce. Unlike their parents, the "creative class" of well-educated young workers in burgeoning fields demonstrated a growing preference for urban living over suburbs.[142]

As an example, Washington, D.C., virtually bankrupt in the early 1990s, has become the center of what some economic development specialists call the most competitive region in the United States. One element in the shift: by the early 2000s, Washington had come to enjoy the best-educated workforce in the United States, and its government employees, lobbyists, and institutional staff members were choosing to live in the District's large pool of walkable urban neighborhoods rather than in the region's spread-out suburbs.

Cities across the United States—among them Atlanta, Los Angeles, San Diego, and Miami—reflect a similar transition. Fifteen years ago these cities stood as potent symbols of the triumph of suburbia. Working aggressively to direct private investment toward reviving their downtowns and urban neighborhoods, however, paid off quickly, bringing new economic growth visibly spurred by the vitality of downtowns and in-town neighborhoods.

Cities on the Rebound

Although many U.S. cities still suffer from the effects of the postwar suburban boom, evolving demographics, new kinds of housing demand, increasing diversity, and reviving economies have converged to create new demand for opportunities to live, work, and study in cities. Emerging economic, environmental, social, and technological transitions have reinforced this demand.

New Household Types and Housing Demand…

Nuclear families seeking detached single-family housing outside of cities drove twentieth-century suburbanization. Today, childless and single households have increased dramatically, creating a significant demand for multifamily housing in—and bringing generally positive fiscal impacts to—older cities.

Well-educated younger workers are not alone in seeking out urban neighborhoods. From the 1940s through the 1980s, family households headed by people between the ages of 35 and 55 controlled at least 40 percent of U.S. housing dollars; a chart of housing demand showed a dramatic bell curve, with this cohort at its center. In the late 1990s the bell curve began to flatten, and today it approaches a straight line. Now, people of widely different ages command roughly equal shares of the

---

Demographics is destiny. When our demographics change, so does every aspect of how we live and build.

Maureen McAvey, vice president, Urban Land Institute

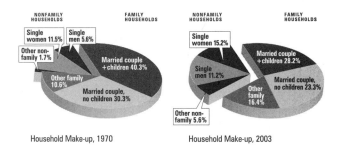

Household Make-up, 1970   Household Make-up, 2003

Source: U.S. Census Bureau, "Current Population Survey," March and Annual Social and Economic Supplements, 1970 to 2003.

Households past and present *Source:* U.S. Census Bureau.

U.S. housing dollar.[143] Just as significantly, while more than 40 percent of households in the housing market in the 1970s included a married man and woman with children, that same figure has dropped to 28 percent. At the same time, the proportion of households in the market that contain only one or two members has reached nearly 55 percent.[144] Younger and older households—and increasingly those with children—are choosing to live in urban neighborhoods.

Aging baby boomers whose children no longer live at home have shown a strong interest in urban living, even in neighborhoods once considered declining and unsafe. As it happens, their children appear to share this feeling. While less affluent on average than their parents, this younger group shows a strong interest in urban living and a greater willingness to seek out neighborhoods from which middle- and upper-income residents fled a few decades ago.[145]

Noting that the average price of a condominium had surpassed that of a single-family house, the *Wall Street Journal* suggested in 2005 that "for many, an urban condo is now more luxurious than a…yard." The article attributed this trend to a fundamental shift in demographics that should last for several decades. Because the households moving into cities are smaller and richer, urban affluence has risen faster than urban population.[146] *USA Today* reported on this phenomenon in 2006, noting significant recent gains in the share of regional wealth (measured by household income and housing values) held by slow-growing central cities. Urban centers such as Pittsburgh, Cleveland, and Boston had registered gains of as much as 10 percent in just five years.[147]

…and the Moneyed Classes' Return

Declining manufacturing in the late twentieth century contributed to unemployment, lower living standards, crime, vandalism, and depression, all of which accelerated population loss in many U.S. cities. Redevelopment and the appearance of new service and information industries have introduced new wealth marked by luxurious housing and mixed-use development.

Although welcome news for cities that endured long periods of decline, these arrivals present new challenges. Returning suburbanites, as already noted, have joined others just starting out in the city—immigrants and the children of the baby boom generation. Erstwhile suburbanites and immigrants in particular compete with residents who have stayed through good times and bad. In cities like New York, the resulting dramatic run-up in housing prices puts enormous pressure on middle- and lower-income groups and on young people just starting out.

Meanwhile, service-sector jobs—in fast-food restaurants, hospitals, or hotels, for example—pay far less than the manufacturing employment that drew many lower-income people to cities in the first half of the twentieth century. This shift in salary structures has placed blue-collar workers on a downward economic path—just as wealthier baby boomers and high-salaried workers in finance and other fields have arrived—and it has produced severe economic fragmentation in some cities. High-paying blue-collar and lower-paying white-collar jobs that once supported a large and stable middle class have become scarce. Even those that remain—teacher and firefighter positions, for example—do not pay enough

to match escalating housing costs, and these workers struggle to remain in the cities where they work.

New York City offers the most acute example of economic fragmentation. Ultra-high-earning professionals in the financial industry have combined with wealthy returning empty nesters and other affluent individuals to drive housing prices to stratospheric levels. Co-op apartments in Manhattan typically sell for millions of dollars. The overheated market has crowded out middle-class housing. The 2007 sale of Stuyvesant Town and Peter Cooper Village offers a case in point. Built with government support in the late 1940s, these projects offered a haven for thousands of lower- and middle-income New Yorkers for sixty years (the two properties have a combined population of more than 25,000). The new owner cannot recoup the properties' purchase price if it continues to charge rents affordable to middle-income residents. This pattern of new construction or gentrification of older neighborhoods has effectively priced middle-income residents out of Manhattan, even as areas of severe poverty remain in Manhattan and other boroughs.

Economic fragmentation raises significant issues—of community stability, housing affordability, and the viability of public education—and it erects barriers to upward mobility. For example, returning empty nesters, their children, and ultra-high earners do not typically use city schools. Empty nesters do not need them, their children often do not have children yet, and high earners opt for private education. This leaves school systems educating primarily low-income students, reinforcing social stratification.

New York, which created the nation's first public housing program, is typical of many U.S. cities. Christine Quinn, speaker of the City Council and a housing activist, said recently: "It used to be when you talked about affordable housing…you meant low- and moderate-income and now you mean low-, moderate-, and middle-income."[148] Lack of affordable housing and economic fragmentation pose special challenges to urban designers in an era of reviving cities. Urban designers across the United States increasingly work to find room for affordable components in housing and mixed-use projects—especially as more cities adopt measures that require this inclusionary approach.

New Melting Pots

America has often been called a *melting pot*, but the ingredients have, in reality, proved difficult to blend. Nevertheless, diversity has taken root in urban neighborhoods. In just ten years between 1990 and 2000, the ethnic diversity of the nation's top one hundred cities increased by more than 20 percent, driven primarily by immigrant groups.[149] Consider Boston: 96 percent white and one of America's poorest major cities in 1960, it had become less than 50 percent white and one of America's wealthiest cities by the 2000 census. As African Americans moved into Irish South Boston, whites moved into African American Roxbury, Hispanics into Italian East Boston, and white-collar families into blue-collar Dorchester. Straight families dot the gay South End, and gay couples with children are putting down roots among

the traditional families of West Roxbury. These rapid increases in cultural and ethnic diversity have generated demand not only for new types of housing but also for a new generation of neighborhoods with public spaces that foster community in the midst of diversity—one of the major challenges facing urban designers today.

For generations America built "one size fits all" neighborhoods for homogeneous markets. Entire neighborhoods arose, for example, to house steelworkers from the same region in Europe. As immigration patterns changed, so did the neighborhoods, but homogeneity remained a constant. For example, as East Boston's population grew from a few thousand before the Civil War to more than 60,000 in the 1920s, waves of immigrants from Ireland, Europe's Jewish ghettos, Italy, South America, and elsewhere flowed through, transforming its ethnic character again and again. After each transition, the area's neighborhoods reemerged as highly homogeneous communities whose residents lived within a web of connection formed by houses of worship, schools, and cultural organizations.

As urban and older suburban neighborhoods become more diverse, neighbors are less likely to share life's everyday activities and the sense of community that such associations foster. Increasingly, neighbors do not worship in nearby churches, do not have kids (or dogs) to take to the local park, and shop at a distant mall or online rather than at the corner store. So, while the icons of older neighborhoods—churches, parks, and Main Streets—remain beloved, these traditional forms have come to represent the body but not the soul of community.

Ironically, the same neighborhoods that for decades symbolized the great social, racial, and cultural divides in American life now demonstrate ways of creating community in the midst of diversity. Working with new and long-time residents, urban designers are mapping out the next generation of development in existing neighborhoods—and, in some cases, entirely new neighborhoods—by exploring concepts that once

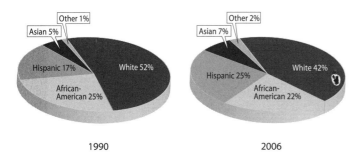

1990   2006

Ethnic composition of the nation's top one hundred cities: 1990 and 2000. *Sources:* 1990 figure from Brookings Institution, *Racial Change in the Nation's Largest Cities: Evidence from the 2000 Census* (Washington, D.C.: Brookings Institution, 2001). 2006 figures from the U.S. Bureau of the Census's American Community Survey, Table C03002, http://www.brookings.edu/projects/living-cities.aspx (accessed August 24, 2008).

seemed unmentionable (density), infeasible (mixed-use development), or unbelievable (mixed-income living).

An Evolving Economic Base

Although industry began moving out of Northern cities as early as the 1920s, serious relocation began after World War II. Trucks and interstate highways freed industry from big urban rail hubs. Air conditioning and refrigeration removed yet another locational restraint. As a result, manufacturing gravitated to the urban fringe, deserting much of the northern United States, particularly its center cities and unionized work force. By 1963, more than half of all the industrial employment in the United States had moved to the suburbs. Less than twenty years later, almost two-thirds of manufacturing was taking place in industrial parks well outside of cities, even as U.S. manufacturers in industries like steel, automobiles, textiles, electronics, and appliances lost market share to overseas competitors. The rise of industry in the developing world has accelerated this process, often aided by U.S. corporations seeking cheap labor and less regulation.

These shifts helped spur a transition to a service economy. In the 1970s and early 1980s, the United States lost 5 million industrial jobs but gained more than 100 million in the service sector.[150] The decentralization and emigration of industry decimated blue-collar employment in older cities like Buffalo, Cleveland, and Camden, New Jersey—cities that still suffer from the loss of these jobs.

While the industrial exodus caused painful and continuing economic and social problems, it improved urban living conditions. With industry gone, the smoke and din that once characterized many U.S. cities diminished significantly. As a steel- and glass-manufacturing center, Pittsburgh endured appalling air pollution for years: smoke-filled skies, poor visibility, and pervasive soot. One estimate suggests that the citizens of pre–World War II Pittsburgh spent $2.3 million every year on extra laundry costs to counter the effects of smoke and soot.[151] At the start of the twenty-first century, however, the largest employer in Pittsburgh was neither a steel company nor a glass fabricator. It was the University of Pittsburgh Medical Center, with 28,000 employees, and Pittsburgh had fewer than half as many unhealthy air-quality days as Atlanta, Houston, or even Fresno, California.[152] An improving urban environment, combined with an increasing reliance on universities, teaching hospitals, banks and similar institutions, has helped cities remake themselves as centers of information technology, health services, and finance.

New Forces Shaping Cities

Resurgent cities cannot rely on the urban design model that shaped the United States before World War II; from demographics to transportation to the environment, cities operate in a strikingly different context today. Suburban growth—which dominated the six decades after World War II—hardly offers a tenable alternative, having degraded the environment, undermined public health, failed to accommodate growing diversity, and overtaxed every aspect of infrastructure in the United States. Creating relevant new urban design models requires a clear understanding of the changing forces shaping urban environments.

The Environment

Announcing an initiative to curb sprawl in 1997, Maryland Governor Paris Glendenning declared that "inner city disinvestment and suburban sprawl are two sides of the same coin.... By curbing sprawl, Maryland can save farmland and forests while simultaneously revitalizing our older suburbs and urban centers."[153] Glendenning ranks among the first U.S. governors to have run for office on a "green" platform, advocating environmental reform and sustainability. (Despite warnings that such an approach would cost him the election, he won two terms.)

Even with initiatives to promote sustainability springing up at local and state levels, and with new training for design students and practice groups for design professionals, suburbanization continues, accelerating climate change and adding to demand for nonrenewable resources. Dense urban centers, once considered the locus of environmental harm, have emerged as the most sustainable pattern of development.

In this context, cities have begun to treat leadership in environmental policy as a competitive advantage. Chicago's Mayor Richard M. Daley has led in this effort, and other cities have followed, rolling out plans to encourage efficient transportation, sustainable building features, and water conservation. Mayor Michael Bloomberg's 2007 congestion-pricing proposal for New York represented a bold initiative along these lines. At the same time, environmental and other regulations have removed many greenfield sites from the marketplace, creating pressure for more intensive use of available land. This trend has helped slow suburban sprawl and turned former industrial properties (brownfields),

failed shopping centers (grayfields), and similar sites into the new development frontier. Demand for sustainable growth has further encouraged recycling of older buildings and increased national focus on older downtowns.

Fossil Fuels

Geopolitical struggles to secure oil supply have disturbed international relations around the globe, and the volatility of U.S. gasoline prices that began in 2005 suggests how vulnerable supplies are to forces beyond our control. Widespread suburban patterns of development generate the majority of problems we face with this finite resource. Driven—literally—by suburban dispersion, automotive traffic accounts for nearly two-thirds of the nation's total petroleum consumption, roughly 132 billion gallons of gasoline. On a worldwide basis the United States consumes more than 33 percent of all transportation energy while accounting for less than 5 percent of the population.[154]

Up to 2008, U.S. demand for highway fuel climbed steadily, despite the most dramatic rise in oil prices since the early 1980s.[155] Then the United States imported less than 40 percent of the oil it used; that figure has grown

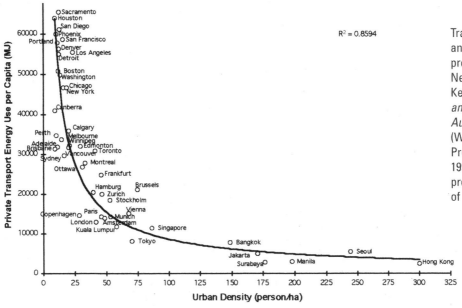

Transportation energy and urban density. Reproduced from Peter Newman and Jeffrey Kenworthy, *Sustainability and Cities: Overcoming Automobile Dependence* (Washington, D.C. Island Press, 1999). Copyright 1999 by the authors. Reproduced by permission of Island Press.

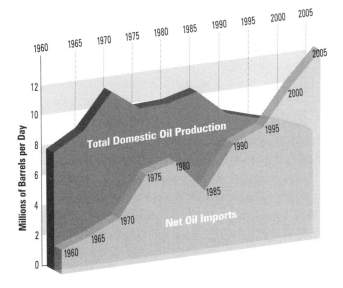

Imported vs. domestic oil. *Sources:* U.S. Department of Transportation (DOT), Bureau of Transportation Statistics, *National Transportation Statistics Report 2000* (Washington, D.C.: DOT, 2007), table 4-7.

to more than 66 percent, and the trend is expected to continue.[156] The run-up in gasoline prices that began in 2007 spotlighted the impact on transportation and housing of an end to inexpensive petroleum. Many U.S. transit systems reported significant year-over-year growth in ridership in 2008, with larger increases coming in systems located in less-dense southern and western cities.[157] In an already-sinking housing market, prices in far suburbs showed steeper and faster declines than properties in center cities and inner-ring suburbs with transit access.[158]

Some experts have issued bleak warnings about global supply. Geologists Colin Campbell and Jean Laherrere believe that 80 percent of the world's oil will be gone by 2050.[159] "There is only so much crude oil in the world," they write, "and the industry has found about 90 percent of it." Campbell and Laherrere predict that world oil production will peak by or before 2010 and then begin to decline. They argue that pinpointing the

precise point at which oil will run out matters minimally. "[W]hat matters is when production begins to taper off. Beyond that point, prices will rise unless demand declines commensurately." As we watch the price of oil rise and as developing countries like China consume an ever-larger share of world oil, it seems reasonable to assume that we have already reached that point.[160]

Automobile-dependent suburbs depend on cheap fuel. As the cost of fuel rises, spread-out development patterns make progressively less sense from an economic point of view. Increasing oil costs will also drive up the price of other support mechanisms for low-density suburbs—petroleum plays a key role, for example, in producing the heat and electricity that serve energy-inefficient detached, single-family homes.[161] Despite these facts, projections suggest that U.S. oil demand will continue to grow in the years beyond 2020, even as global production declines. As rising demand intersects declining supply, alternatives to suburban development will grow increasingly appealing—and, ultimately, essential.

Climate Change

Suburbanization also produces greenhouse gases that warm the planet, melt polar ice, raise sea levels, and unleash powerful storms. The Intergovernmental Panel on Climate Change estimates that rising temperatures will raise global sea levels 0.6 to 2.0 feet by 2095, but other researchers project increases of up to 5.0 feet.[162] Hurricanes from Andrew to Katrina to Ike have highlighted issues facing coastal communities on the Atlantic and Gulf coasts. Three years after Hurricane Katrina, in fact, Gulf Coast communities continue to wrestle with recovery efforts. Meanwhile, insurance companies have raised rates or eliminated coverage for areas most susceptible to storm damage.

The United States generates a disproportionately high volume of greenhouse gases, much of which comes from the cars and trucks that serve a suburbanized society. It produces as well more carbon dioxide

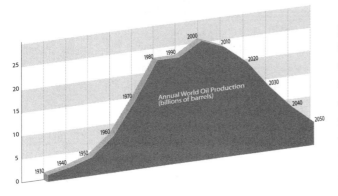

Projected global oil production. Graph based on Colin J. Campbell and Jean H. Laherrerre, "The End of Cheap Oil," *Scientific American*, March 1998. See also Peter Newman and Jeffrey Kenworthy, *Sustainability and Cities: Overcoming Automobile Dependence* (Washington, D.C.: Island Press, 1999), 51. Steven Andrews and Randy Udall examined the difficulties of peak-oil estimating in "Oil Prophets: Looking at World Oil Studies over Time," a presentation to the Association for the Study of Peak Oil & Gas, Paris, May 27, 2003. The presentation included a compilation of more than one hundred estimates, made over sixty years, of peak oil timing and of worldwide recoverable oil supplies. See www.peakoil.net/iwood2003/paper/AndrewsPaper.doc (accessed August 22, 2008). In an analysis of uncertainty about the amount of oil remaining to be pumped from the ground and about the pattern of production, Robert K. Kaufmann and Laura D. Shiers suggest that the peak of world oil production could occur as early as 2009 or as late as 2047. Most likely, they conclude, the peak will fall in the period 2013–2031. See "Alternatives to Conventional Crude Oil: When, How Quickly, and Market Driven?" *Ecological Economics* (2008), http://dx.doi.org/10.1016/j.ecolecon.2007.12.023.

Global warming could disrupt climate and rainfall patterns worldwide, bringing unpredictable changes to regional ecosystems, and the farms, forests, fisheries, and societies within them. Other effects may include species extinctions, agricultural damage, and an increasing incidence of cancer in humans. Because of these dangers, national governments, global institutions, and multinational companies have begun to take climate change seriously. It should come as no surprise that concern over climate change has raised additional questions about continuing auto dependency across the United States.

Traffic

A principal reason that downtowns have become standard bearers for sustainability lies in their access to multiple transportation choices. Older downtowns (and areas with similar development patterns) support transit, bicycling, and walking because they are typically denser and feature a mix of uses. Low-density suburban development deliberately separates uses, forcing residents to

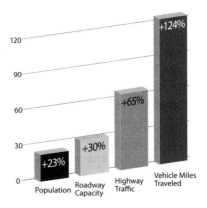

Population, traffic, and roadway capacity. *Sources:* U.S. Department of Transportation (DOT), Bureau of Transportation Statistics, *1995 Nationwide Personal Transportation Survey* (Washington, D.C.: DOT, 1995); and Robert T. Dunphy et al., *Moving Beyond Gridlock: Traffic and Development* (Washington, D.C.: Urban Land Institute, 1997). Reprinted with permission from Oliver Gillham, *The Limitless City: A Primer on the Urban Sprawl Debate* (Washington, D.C.: Island Press, 2002).

from cars and trucks than any other nation on the planet (with, as noted, less than 5 percent of the world's population). This output represents a third of all mobile-source carbon dioxide in the atmosphere, according to a U.S. Department of Transportation report from the 1990s. A 2006 report by the advocacy organization Environmental Defense placed the figure at nearly half the total global carbon load from cars and trucks.[163]

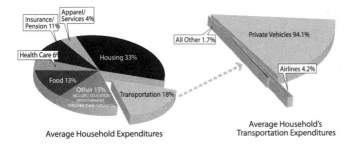

Household transportation expenditures. *Source:* U.S. Department of Transportation (DOT), Bureau of Transportation Statistics, *Pocket Guide to Transportation 2008* (Washington, D.C.: DOT, 2008), 33. Reprinted with permission from Oliver Gillham, *The Limitless City: A Primer on the Urban Sprawl Debate* (Washington, D.C.: Island Press, 2002).

drive everywhere. As a result, nearly 90 percent of all daily trips in the United States are made by car; walking or travel by bicycle, transit, or rail make up the other 10 percent.[164] In a highly suburbanized society, most of those trips can be made no other way, a condition that generates traffic congestion, wastes money, and assures an unquenchable national thirst for gasoline.

As the twentieth century drew to a close, average rush-hour congestion levels rose by more than 25 percent in U.S. metropolitan areas. The average annual delay experienced by drivers across the country rose more than threefold, and drivers burned almost 7 billion gallons of gasoline while idling in traffic jams.[165] Total vehicle miles traveled in the United States continue to grow faster than population.

Although the car remains at the center of the transportation mix in the United States, attitudes about driving have grown ambivalent. "The American love affair with the car is over," a community activist in one city announced at a public meeting a few years ago, "but we haven't yet finished the divorce."[166] While the first part of his statement is only partly true—many in the United States still treasure their cars for the freedom they appear to offer—large numbers of Americans have developed conflicting feelings about the role cars play in their lives.

Some of the most widespread and bitter complaints about suburbanization in the United States swirl around cars and traffic congestion. According to the Heritage Foundation, surveys have shown that 79 percent of those polled identified traffic congestion as one of the worst aspects of metropolitan living, worse even than crime.[167] Polls by Smart Growth America found similar results, with respondents ranking traffic congestion and crime as the most serious issues facing their communities.[168] Time squandered stuck on a highway is palpable to everyone. The average American spends about 477 hours annually behind the wheel of a car—the equivalent of fifty-nine workdays.[169] Estimates of the economic cost of time wasted in traffic run as high as $168 billion per year.[170]

The spiraling costs of owning and operating the multiple cars necessary for suburbanized life represent a growing burden. At the turn of the century, the cost of car ownership surpassed 22 percent of household budgets in some metropolitan areas. Using 2008 figures, the American Public Transportation Association estimated that eliminating one car in a household and substituting travel by public transit—a choice unavailable in most car-dependent suburbs—would save an average user more than $8,000 a year. Redirected, that $650-plus monthly savings could support an extra $100,000 in housing investment.[171]

Growing ambivalence about the car may signal a sea change. From 1995 through 2006, U.S. public transportation ridership increased by 30 percent—greater than both the 12 percent increase in population and the 24 percent growth in highway usage over the same period.[172] Meanwhile, in 2006 alone, voters in thirteen states and regions approved close to two-dozen transit-related ballot initiatives, authorizing expenditures of nearly $40 billion.[173]

Desire for proximity to transit has turned into a powerful market force. In 2004, the Federal Transportation Administration estimated that forty-two regions with rail or light-rail transit would need to double the amount of housing located within a half mile of transit stations to meet market demand by 2025—and then find ways to continue to expand the supply after that.[174] Both housing values and commercial rents are significantly higher across the Washington, D.C. region in mixed-use districts that offer opportunities to walk to work, to lunch, and to shop, and the pattern is especially pronounced where transit access is also within walking distance.[175] Increasing interest in mass transit has added to the attraction of older downtowns while stimulating interest in more *urban* suburban development. As a result, urban designers increasingly focus on the interconnecting issues of land use, density, and transportation in a quest to find ways to get people out of cars and onto their feet.

Transit

In response to growing congestion, high fuel prices, shifting centers of employment, and other pressures, new mass transit systems have begun to reshape metropolitan America. As the mutually reinforcing connections among transportation, land use, and environmental quality have received wider attention, a clear conclusion has emerged: public transportation requires concentrated land uses arranged in nodal patterns—like those found in older urban areas.

In 1977 the District of Columbia inaugurated a new subway/rail system. Designed to help Washington cope with auto congestion and strong economic growth, Metro quickly became a high-profile example of how transit could come to the rescue of a modern U.S. city. A few cities—San Diego among them—had already begun to invest in rail, but the real rush to embrace rail transit began in the 1980s. After dismantling an extensive trolley system in the 1950s, Los Angeles has built a subway, a light-rail system, and an innovative bus rapid transit (BRT) system. Portland (Oregon), San Jose, Minneapolis, and St. Louis have all created heavily used, well integrated, and growing rail systems. Washington has extended the Metro system several times, most recently to a commuter transit corridor in suburban Tyson's Cor-

ner, Virginia. Seattle replaced its BRT with a light-rail line to handle growing passenger volumes. Boston has added a BRT line and dramatically expanded its regional commuter rail; a regional study continues for a new circumferential light-rail line that would intersect all the lines of its current hub-and-spoke system. Atlanta, Buffalo, Salt Lake City, Denver, and others have also made significant investments in rail and BRT systems. Philadelphia went to great expense to through-connect commuter rail systems, making it possible to travel by rail throughout the region (including to and from the airport) with at most one in-station transfer downtown. New York, home to nearly one-third of the nation's regular transit riders, cannot get enough transit: in addition to starting work on a new Second Avenue subway, the city has begun design on BRT routes for each of its five boroughs and construction has commenced on new commuter rail connections from Long Island and Queens to Grand Central Station.

Public transit, urban design, and urban development offer mutually reinforcing benefits. Investing in transit raises nearby property values by making those properties more accessible, and it opens new development opportunities (in tandem with high-density zoning around transit stops). As transit displaces auto usage, it spins off additional benefits—improved air quality, greater access to jobs, and new development that delivers new fiscal resources to host cities.

Nonetheless, public transit, urban form, and ridership rarely maintain alignment. More than half of the U.S. population now lives in suburban areas characterized by high auto use. As convenient as transit can be, most suburban drivers find it difficult to leave their cars because of widely dispersed suburban origins and destinations. Such conditions mean that transit's longer travel times and interline transfers in suburbs militate against its becoming the mode of choice in these areas unless development patterns change. Luring drivers into transit has become a challenge in itself. Buffalo, Seattle, and Portland, Oregon, maintain free-fare zones in their business districts

Federal, state and local transportation policy must respond to the growing crises of global warming and diminishing supplies of oil. Public transit is one small but critical component of new urban strategies that allow the 21st-century planner to readjust land use, energy use, and environmental sensitivity to create a new model for quality of life.

Robert Passwell, former director of Chicago's Metropolitan Transit Authority and director of the Urban Transportation Research Center, CUNY

to make the choice more appealing—at least downtown. Even New York wrestles with this issue. PlaNYC 2030, the city's twenty-five-year environmental blueprint, promotes BRT routes to reach sections of its five boroughs poorly served by subways, but it acknowledges the need to cut travel times to attract new riders.

The approach to transit planning in the United States can be piecemeal. Transit and land use planners—often working for independent agencies—commonly pursue separate, uncoordinated agendas. Other countries have adopted regional or national approaches, in part because they understand the central role that good public transport plays in fostering economic growth. From Shanghai to London, establishing a high-speed transit link between a central city and its airports has become an essential tactic in this competition.

The U.S. approach may be changing, however, as agencies at all levels recognize the importance of combining land use and transportation planning. San Diego adopted transit-oriented development (TOD) and design guidelines in the 1990s. Implemented through revisions of the zoning code, street-design standards, and the city's general plan, the guidelines focus on creating high-density TOD nodes along the city's principal transit corridors. Since the guidelines were implemented in the early 1990s, regional transit ridership—in a notoriously auto-loving region—has risen by about 28 percent.[176]

Oregon promulgated planning rules in the 1990s that required local governments to amend zoning to encourage higher-density, mixed-use development near transit lines. Subsequent growth plans called for developing regional town centers around light-rail stops to balance jobs, housing, and services while reducing auto trips. Since opening its MAX light-rail system in 1978, Portland has continued to invest in transit, opening new lines in 1998, 2001, and 2004, with further extensions under construction and in the planning phase.[177]

Other cities and states have also taken up this idea. The Commonwealth of Massachusetts is working to establish TOD zones around transit stations in the Boston region. Under New Jersey's Transit Village Initiative, nine state agencies coordinate policy and provide financial support to encourage the development of "transit villages" around NJ Transit stops. The program had designated 19 villages as of 2008.[178]

Public Health

Cars produce other harmful emissions besides greenhouse gases, including about one-third of the nearly 5 million tons of toxic pollutants the United States releases into the air yearly.[179] The Harvard School of Public Health and the American Cancer Society have both found strong links between a rise in death rates and pollutants such as benzene, formaldehyde, toluene, acetaldehyde, xylene, 1,3-butadiene, sulfur compounds, and particulate matter.[180] Meanwhile, the EPA estimates that cars and trucks account for about half of all cancers attributed to outdoor air sources of toxics.[181]

Public health threats from suburbanized development take other forms. Obesity, diabetes, and other illnesses attributable to auto dependency have made public health nearly as vital an issue in planning policy as it was a century ago when tuberculosis and other urban diseases helped spur the introduction of zoning.

Among those deeply concerned about the issue is the Centers for Disease Control and Prevention

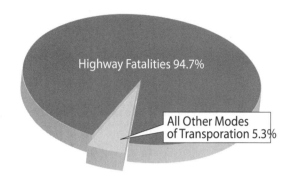

Highway Fatalities 94.7%

All Other Modes of Transporation 5.3%

U.S. transportation fatalities. *Source:* National Transportation Safety Board, October 4, 2007, "Transportation Fatalities Drop in 2006: Largest Single Category Increase in Motorcycle Deaths," SB-07-49. http://www.ntsb.gov/Pressrel/2007/071004.htm (accessed February 20, 2008).

(CDC), operated by the U.S. Department of Health and Human Services. In a 2001 working paper titled *How Land Use and Transportation Systems Affect Public Health*, the CDC pointed to improper diet and inactivity patterns as "the root cause of some 300,000 deaths in the United States in 1990, second only to tobacco."[182] The CDC attributes this situation largely to the design of the suburban environment, which favors auto trips and discourages walking. The CDC concludes that higher densities, mixed land uses, and pedestrian-friendly street design would all promote increased walking and biking and, hence, better public health. In fact, it argues that such changes would be more effective in reducing obesity than structured activities like aerobics classes.[183]

Other public health issues arise from too much driving. In 2004 the United States recorded nearly 43,000 traffic fatalities—roughly the population of a small city such as Charlottesville, Virginia; Jefferson City, Missouri; or Olympia, Washington—and 2.8 million automotive injuries.[184] By contrast, fewer than 2,000 fatalities occurred in all other transportation modes combined, including aviation and recreational boating. According to the U.S. Department of Transportation, motor vehi-cle crashes account for about half of all U.S. accident-related deaths annually and 60 percent of years of life lost from all accidents before age sixty-five.[185]

Privatization of the Public Realm

Democratic societies depend on the ability of citizens to meet on common ground. The earliest American settlements grew up around shared central fields known as commons, where livestock grazed, people socialized, and militias trained. The paths for foot and animal-drawn traffic that bounded these common areas became street networks, another element of the public realm, and served communities in multiple ways. Up to the middle of the last century, children typically played safely in the streets that organized their communities and travelers moved easily from city to scenic open countryside, itself a vital part of the nation's shared heritage.

The spread of automobile-centered suburbia has changed this, as has the declining fiscal fortunes of state and local governments that a nation of suburbs has engendered. Suburbs have replaced millions of acres of scenic open space in the last half century, almost all of it privately owned. Much of the open land that remains is privately owned and susceptible to development. The nation can count itself as fortunate that control of about 37 percent of U.S. land resides with federal, state, and local governments,[186] but most of this acreage lies far from metropolitan areas, and much supports forestry, mining, or other harvesting activities that restrict access under lease agreements.

For centuries, the costs of land and access dictated that only farming or forestry made economic sense as uses for most land. Land served the common good as both a scenic and economic resource. Automobiles and roads dramatically improved access and reduced its cost, making developable land cheap and leading to an explosion of development across the landscape. According to the U.S. Department of Agriculture's Natural Resources Conservation Service, development consumes nearly 2 million acres of land per year on average.[187] Despite its image as a tapestry of farms, quaint villages, and mill towns, New England surrenders 1,200 acres of new land each week to suburban development—a rate that far exceeds population growth, which has remained almost static.[188] That pattern holds fairly steady across the United States; land consumption has grown by up to 60 percent, while population has grown at most just over 30 percent.[189]

New development puts streets and common spaces, once open to the public, off-limits. Gated communities in particular interrupt the continuous web of public ways and common infrastructure present throughout the nation's history. What is true of suburban streets has become true of urban and regional resources long in public hands. Dwindling public funds have combined with mushrooming private wealth to open the door to privatization of public spaces, roads, and even expressways. Who controls these spaces, who may use them, and how they may be used have emerged as significant issues.

The American public has grown increasingly conscious of the value of a shared, common realm of land, natural resources, air and water, public space, and infrastructure. From the formation of land trusts and the use of conservation easements to state acquisition of land forced by ballot measures, strong signals have appeared of a growing movement to preserve public and open space across entire metropolitan regions. Urban design has become a vital part of this movement: increasing density, mixing uses within developments, and redeveloping brownfield sites in urban areas all help preserve scenic open space, forest, and farmland for future generations.

Security

Protecting against possible terrorist attacks has preoccupied the United States in recent years; the underlying impulse traces back at least to the Cold War, when some federal programs encouraged dispersing populations as a defensive response to the threat of nuclear attack. The attacks of September 11, 2001, provoked similar calls for dispersion that have not materialized to date.

Since 9/11, urban designers have devoted substantial effort to helping corporate and government clients find unobtrusive ways to enhance security. They have rethought airport layouts, hardened building entrances, developed roadway barriers, and reconfigured Washington, D.C.'s administrative core to increase the difficulty of staging a car- or truck-bomb attack. Urban design firms have received commissions to redesign everything from Pennsylvania Avenue to the streets around the New York Stock Exchange. Finding elegant solutions to these problems will remain a significant goal for urban designers in the years ahead.

Technology

The rapid spread of television after World War II changed the built environment in profound ways. Commentators worried that the television-centered home could displace the familiar public square, and, indeed, when urban designers produced spaces intended for "civic engagement," like Boston's City Hall Plaza, they remained empty as Americans retired to the comfort of their family rooms.

In the 1990s developers of new mixed-use projects counted on movie theaters to help support stores, restaurants, and bars. Even this strategy faltered before the power of television, as DVDs, on-demand programming, and HDTV ate away at movies' market share. Today the Internet and wireless communications threaten to claim television's dominant position in the distribution of news, entertainment, and information. Digital technology, in fact, has transformed the way we communicate, manage, and manufacture, touching virtually everything in the developed world.

How this revolution will ultimately affect the form of the built environment remains unknown. One vein of speculation holds that highly mobile information technology networks will simply disperse society further: shifting the workplace into cyberspace, this view holds, will further encourage suburban growth. Between 1990 and 2000 alone, the number of people working at home mushroomed from 4 million to nearly 24 million.[190] As more people choose to work from home, the thinking has gone, home offices will remain mostly in suburbs and in exurbs.

Despite such striking statistics, a different scenario seems equally likely to play out. Younger members of the "creative class" described above—generally a more technologically adroit group—have helped boost demand for urban housing. Explanations for this unexpected development vary and will require more research, but anecdotal evidence suggests, first, that the lack of a shared workplace may stimulate stronger interest in finding community elsewhere; second, that urban neighborhoods with access to public transit better serve the need to visit or receive clients for those who work at home; and third, that the kinds of people who prefer to work independently also tend to favor urban lifestyles.

While a suburban home traditionally provided refuge from the teeming workplace, a crowded city may provide relief from the isolation of work at home. Many people who choose cities cite their wish to live among people, art, culture, and food in a world of increasing isolation. In *The New Geography*, Joel Kotkin argues that American urban life will continue to revive because informational industries are "dependent on the sorts of individuals who prefer to live in cities."[191]

Kotkin believes that at least some U.S. cities will regain their preindustrial prominence as centers of commerce and exchange because home-based workers will want easy access to the sort of privileged information that comes only through close personal networks in an urban setting. Thomas Horan echoes some of these ideas in *Digital Places*, asserting that "real life is still the best high-bandwidth experience" and that "digital settings cannot fully replace the traditional sensory experience of place."[192] In fact, Horan argues, the "communities of interest" represented by the Internet must intersect successfully with "communities of place" represented by streets, cafes, public places, and public interactions of the physical communities in which people live.[193] Horan locates home workplaces primarily in urban lofts and townhouses—in other words, in cities and in places like them, because they still function as centers of culture and education.

The Lure of Culture and Education

In 1982 the National Endowment for the Arts organized a conference in Pittsburgh around a simple premise: cities that incorporated culture into their fabric saw far greater economic success than those that did not. Numerous case studies presented at The Arts Edge conference supported the idea, and as a city with a strong tradition of arts and culture that had successfully navigated deindustrialization, Pittsburgh provided an emblematic setting. In *The Rise of the Creative Class*, Richard Florida argued that keeping creative professionals in the city represents a necessary component of innovation and economic development. Culture and creativity reinforce each other reciprocally.[194] Pittsburgh's example bears him out, and today many other cities have built their economic policies on this model.

Prior to the 1978 founding of Savannah College of Art and Design in Georgia, the small city seemed mired in permanent economic decline. The college helped change the city's trajectory by buying up buildings as retailers and office tenants vacated them. The college gave downtown a lively new arts presence that attracted new residents, new employers, stores, jobs, and restaurants. As one new resident put it, the college created "downtown's new sense of cool." During the same period Emerson College scuttled plans to leave Boston and began to redefine itself as an urban college, shifting its campus closer to downtown and investing there. Education represents a growth industry that has offset or helped to stem declines in cities like New Haven, Connecticut; Philadelphia, Chicago, and St. Louis.

Older American cities that have retained their status as centers of culture or education have enjoyed renewed growth, becoming magnets for old-line corporations and emerging industries alike. These cities hold special attraction for financial, information technology, medicine, and other knowledge-sector industries.

Changing Development Assumptions

Developers and financial backers have become more familiar with alternative development patterns. Prodded by rising energy prices and the preservation movement that began in the 1970s, builders have begun looking for more creative ways of accommodating change. This has cast older structures in the center city in a new light: Buildings that developers might once have demolished instead undergo preservation in order to capitalize on the energy and investment embedded in them. Office-to-residential and industrial-to-residential conversions across the United States reflect a growing appreciation of the value of existing buildings.

New attitudes toward sustainability reinforce the adaptive reuse movement. Some practitioners have even begun to advocate designing all buildings like the lofts of New York City's SoHo—structural frames that can be put to multiple uses rather than custom structures useful only once. The adaptive-reuse movement also highlighted weaknesses in single-use zoning. As industry left center cities and residential communities began to colonize the buildings left behind, restrictions on use underwent reevaluation. As a result, taller buildings have even been rezoned vertically, sometimes with retail at ground level and combinations of office, hotel, and housing use above. Changes in household diversity and type, described above, have also reshaped the marketplace. This shift has launched a new period of neighborhood building that looks very different from the past. The United States no longer has the mass housing market that encouraged creation of one-size-fits-all neighborhoods. As diverse households sink money into urban neighborhoods, they bring a far wider range of housing needs and aspirations than previous, more homogeneous residents. This demand for more varied multifamily units near transit has contributed significant momentum to strong housing growth in downtowns and inner suburbs. This even held true in the housing downturn that began in 2007. For example, the District of Columbia's Office of Planning found that housing prices rose in areas of Washington served by transit while prices in distant suburbs outside the district (and unserved by transit) declined by double-digit percentages or more.[195]

The reversal of fortune for Baltimore's Uplands development tells this story at a neighborhood level. Developed in the 1950s as a middle-class community of more than 900 garden apartments, the 52-acre development had gone bankrupt by the 1990s, a victim of middle-class flight that cut the city's overall population by a third. After taking ownership, the city set to work with surrounding neighborhoods to devise a master plan for a new mixed-income neighborhood on the site. During the process, city planners and neighborhood leaders alike were stunned to discover that demand existed for more than 1,000 housing units in the area at price levels three to five times greater than prevailing prices for nearby houses. Even more surprising for a city of homogeneous neighborhoods, this demand came from people identified as black and white, young and old, gay and straight, white- and blue-collar workers. These people sought everything from single-family houses in a range of sizes to row houses, apartments, and lofts. The common denominator among this diverse population: everyone wanted to live in the same new neighborhood.

Where huge tracts of look-alike single-family houses once prevailed, developers now build an array of different unit types for diverse households, many of which do not include children. Where single-use development, easy auto access, and surface parking once dominated, walkable, mixed-use projects in downtown areas accessible to transit have emerged as a significant portion of the housing market.

New Currents in Urban Design

For the first time in six decades, urban designers do not have to swim against the full force of a suburban tide. The flow has turned toward cities and places that feel like cities—dense, mixed-use, walkable, and transit-friendly. Meanwhile, new and sometimes controversial theories about the nature of urban design have begun to appear. Some urban designers argue that the range of forces acting on cities calls for decisive large-scale action in a climate too often marked by lengthy public deliberation. Other critics charge that urban designers have distorted the work of Jane Jacobs and her followers, trivializing urbanism by dressing up auto-dependent suburbs to look like older downtowns. Still others appear to advocate a return to the modernist and utopian thinking of the twentieth century.

In the midst of change and debate, the problems created by suburban development remain. Many cities continue to suffer from reduced investment and population decline, and new suburban development continues to roll across the landscape at a rapid pace. Significantly altering U.S. development patterns will require a continuing and sustained effort.

Urban Revitalization and Historic Preservation

Although the days of urban renewal have passed—along with the federal funds that drove them—efforts to revitalize cities continue. Preserving and restoring historic neighborhoods and Main Streets has become a key focus, although such approaches cannot prevent a continuing loss of manufacturing jobs, can lead to gentrification, and do occasionally fall victim to formulaic solutions. In response, critics have disparaged some revitalization efforts as "lifestyle" or "cappuccino" urbanism.[196]

Some of that critique has merit. Many initiatives in the 1980s and '90s focused exclusively on commercial-area revitalization without regard to issues of gentrification, job creation, or housing affordability. The desperate straits of many downtowns, competing against suburbs that attracted both shopping traffic and offices, often seemed to justify such efforts. Once stores, businesses, and tourism returned downtown, the thinking went, everything else would follow. In many cases, it did, with an unforeseen result: new market-rate housing priced out long-time residents, and new service-sector jobs rarely matched the wages of previous manufacturing employment. In other cases, commercial-area revitalization alone proved a failure.

Today, the emphasis has changed. Affordable housing has emerged as a key component of many downtown programs, often mandated through inclusionary zoning. More projects aim to reverse the decline of public housing, sometimes replanning it as mixed-use and mixed-income neighborhoods. Many contemporary downtown-revitalization efforts rely on new job centers in health care, education, and high technology that make cities stronger competitors with suburbs.

A New Role for Waterfronts

Departing factories opened up the nations' urban waterfronts. For nearly four hundred years, waterfronts provided the backbone of the economy in America's coastal cities—beginning with the export of timber, tobacco, fur, and other raw materials in the seventeenth century. By the mid-twentieth century, American waterfronts bristled with factories, wharves, coal bunkers, cranes, storage tanks, shipyards, and railyards. Worldwide changes in freight handling in the second half of the twentieth century undercut the importance of waterfronts. Huge container ships required new landings far from the increasingly administrative and business core of many cities. At the same time, air freight and long-distance trucking began to draw larger shares of high-value goods from both rail and water transport.

Obsolete and abandoned transportation and industrial facilities became ubiquitous as industrial waterfronts declined, but empty waterfronts opened up new possibilities. Boston, New York, and Baltimore produced famous early waterfront turnarounds as new housing transformed wharves, and crumbling wholesale buildings reemerged as festival marketplaces.

From San Diego to St. Paul, Minnesota, to St. Petersburg, Florida, cities with coastlines and riverfronts have launched dramatic reclamations. To "daylight" its river, Providence, Rhode Island, ripped up a vast parking lot built in the 1960s to help its downtown compete with suburban malls. Restoration of long-buried streets and introduction of bridges and landscaped riverside walks created one of America's premier urban waterfronts, where no waterfront had existed. The same phenomenon has taken root around the world, as cities like Barcelona, Sydney, and London reclaim once-industrial rivers, harbors, and bays.

In the United States, stricter environmental controls, beginning in the 1970s, helped transform attitudes toward waterfronts. The Clean Water Act of 1972 imposed federal water-quality standards—sometimes against the will of both states and cities but with visible results. Legal action also forced dramatic waterfront cleanups, most famously in Boston Harbor. The combination of legislation and court orders set the stage for transforming polluted factory and mill sites on urban waterfronts into vibrant new centers for recreation and mixed-use development across the United States. Even as luxury housing, hotels, office buildings, and festival marketplaces have sprung up on urban waterfronts, industrial

uses continue in some ports. New York, Baltimore, Los Angeles, and Seattle all have major, active container ports. The busiest maintain rail-freight links and some have hopes of expanding. Some small cities, like Biloxi, Mississippi, sustain sizeable fishing fleets and fish-processing facilities, and those industries remain guarded about displacement from the waterfront by other uses. And almost all waterfront cities have both wastewater treatment facilities and oil-and-gas storage and transfer complexes. Boston, Philadelphia, Washington, San Diego, San Francisco, and other coastal cities devote significant parts of the waterfront to major airports with attendant highways and support facilities. Uses like these will remain and even expand.

Urban planners and urban designers in waterfront cities continue to struggle to find the right balance between revitalization and the needs of working waterfronts. Not only do many surviving waterfront industrial uses remain vital to the regional and national economies, but they also provide a significant share of what industrial employment remains at a time when such jobs have grown scarce. At the same time, reclaimed waterfronts raise new issues of public access and ownership. With most industrial users gone, ownership of and access to the water's edge have become contentious issues in many U.S. cities. Urban designers have increasingly joined this debate.

Consensus Building

The road building and urban renewal projects of the 1950s and early 1960s ultimately created a backlash against top-down planning. By the 1980s, top-down planning and urban reconstruction had ended, and communities became part of the city-building process across the United States. The concepts of public participation and consensus building are today firmly ingrained in the urban planning process. In the months after 9/11, for example, more than five thousand New Yorkers came together to review, discuss, and comment on initial concepts for rebuilding the World Trade Center site. These public meetings also signaled a recognition that nothing would get built on the site without ample community input. Unless those who will be affected—members of the general public, neighbors, residents—are invited into the decision-making process, major projects falter.

Urban designers have assumed an increasing role in promoting civic engagement and consensus building. They typically build successful plans from the bottom up by engaging community members, working with them to articulate a vision of where they want to go, and helping them to figure out how to get there. Broad-based community consensus can give a plan significant momentum and help it weather unpredictable politics, funding, and economic cycles.

Sustainability and Smart Growth

The popularity of former vice president Al Gore's film *An Inconvenient Truth*—including its Academy Award—suggests how seriously the American public takes environmental issues and sustainability. The larger issue of environmental survivability has subsumed concerns about energy consumption, born in the 1970s oil crisis. Designers and planners are being asked to think about the environmental impact of every plan and about ways to advance sustainability by conserving energy, land, and natural resources in their work.

Interest in sustainability has propelled the "smart growth" movement to new prominence. In the words of former Maryland governor Paris Glendenning, smart growth is "not no growth or even slow growth. Rather, the goal is sensible growth that balances our need for jobs and economic development with our desire to save our natural environment."[197] At the invitation of Maryland's smart growth program in 1997, a study produced by the U.S. Environmental Protection Agency (EPA) showed that the state had consumed more land in mere decades than it had in more than three hundred years

> We're rediscovering that we can create buildings and neighborhoods that respond to their environment, just as a living system would. Indigenous people have used this approach for centuries. If our designs are informed by and embrace the climate, solar exposure, earth, water, and landscape, the resulting buildings and neighborhoods will be responsive and dynamic living systems.
>
> Bob Berkebile, FAIA, principal, BNIM Architects, Kansas City, and nationally known proponent of sustainable design[198]

since its founding, devouring in the process hundreds of thousands of acres of forests and farmland. The EPA went on to point out that urban sprawl not only consumes land, it also depopulates older urban centers and strains state finances. Between 1970 and 1990, the EPA noted, one Maryland county closed more than sixty school buildings while building another sixty-plus new ones—at a cost of more than $500 million.[199]

Smart-growth advocates argue for optimizing existing infrastructure before building anew; concentrating development instead of spreading it over farmland and forest; reducing traffic; and emphasizing affordability and sustainability in housing. Many of these goals can be achieved simply by reversing urban decay and revitalizing older suburbs and urban centers by choosing to redevelop brownfield (former industrial) and grayfield (strip-mall) sites over building on greenfields (previously undeveloped land). Many urban designers have aligned themselves with this approach, which is helping to refocus the nation's energies on its older cities while creating an entirely new class of sustainable developments in suburban and exurban areas.

Transit-Oriented Development

Transit-oriented development (TOD)—sometimes also called "transit villages"—reflects a clear understanding of the strong connection between transportation and land use. Such development offers an alternative to auto-dependent suburbanization: higher-density, mixed-use communities—often higher-density nodes within existing suburban areas—specifically planned to make transit use convenient and walking both easy and inviting. A typical TOD sets a higher-density, mixed-use core at the heart of the planned community, usually less than half a mile (the optimal walking range) from a transit station. This gives the developments a striking resemblance to older railroad suburbs like Forest Hills Gardens in New York or Evanston in suburban Chicago.

Like railroad and streetcar suburbs, TODs by definition sit either directly on the trunk line of a regional transit system or on a bus line no more than a ten-minute ride from the transit line.[200] They are usually geared toward fitting into a larger, regional strategy of similarly planned transit nodes.

Residential densities in these nodes vary widely but generally range from 7 to 60 dwelling units per acre. These densities do not mean high-rise development: More typically, they blend row houses (about 36 units per acre) and mid-rise apartments (which can reach 160 units per acre).[201] The transit station and mixed-use, relatively high-density development, however, defines the heart of the village. Michael Bernick and Robert Cervero provide a succinct description in *Transit Villages in the 21st Century*: "[A] compact, mixed-use community, centered around the transit station that, by design, invites residents, workers, and shoppers to drive their cars less and ride mass transit more…. The centerpiece of the transit village is the transit station itself and the civic and public spaces that surround it. The transit station is what connects village residents and workers to the rest of the region."[202]

Urban Villages and TNDs

Urban villages—compact, walkable, mixed-use neighborhoods or towns—may be developed either as higher-density nodes in suburbs or as neighborhoods in a city. At their best, they incorporate by design a highly diverse community that offers a wide range of housing types clustered around a shared Main Street, market square, or neighborhood park. By mixing uses and housing types they encourage walking, which cuts down on auto trips. In their most sustainable incarnation, they may also function as TODs.

A subset of urban villages comprises traditional neighborhood developments (TNDs). Typically new construction, often built on greenfield sites, TNDs are more compact than the usual subdivision, favor walking over driving, mix uses where possible, and provide narrower roads, few or no cul-de-sacs, and common greens and squares. A TND is almost invariably suburban; an urban village may be suburban but is just as likely to exist downtown or in an inner-ring location, and it can rise on a variety of sites. Like TOD, the term "urban village" describes functional qualities, suggesting nothing of architectural style. Most TNDs, by contrast, strive to create a "traditional" village neighborhood flavor, emphasizing pre–World War II housing styles and placing neohistorical houses on small lots like those found in older village centers and streetcar suburbs.

The differences between the two terms, ultimately, are relatively minor, and urban villages on nongreenfield sites have grown in popularity as a solution to the centerless qualities of contemporary suburbia. Urban villages, in the words of the Congress for the New Urbanism, "are places where everything you need is within walking distance (shops, restaurants, movies, services), including nice public squares to relax in and meet people."[203]

New Urbanism

Both the TND and the TOD are concepts associated with New Urbanism, a widely used term that describes the application of traditional planning and design strategies as an antidote to suburban sprawl. Since its inception, the Congress for the New Urbanism, the champion of this approach, has drawn both praise and resistance. Whatever their viewpoint, few planners or designers question the sweeping changes New Urbanism has brought to planning and urban design, particularly in suburban areas.

Grounded in the work of planners like Ebenezer Howard, Raymond Unwin, and Clarence Stein, New Urbanism originally gained notice for such communities as Kentlands, Maryland, and Seaside and Celebration in Florida. Although these pioneering communities won praise as alternatives to sprawl, critics derided them as socially uniform places that offered few answers to the perplexing problems of suburbs and cities. Some critics accused the movement of simply promoting a different kind of suburbanization, putting "a smiley face on sprawl." In the years since its founding, CNU has significantly broadened its agenda to encompass both compact developments on greenfield sites and infill development on urban brownfields.

Today, CNU strongly advocates development of existing urban resources before moving out into open land. Its *Canons of Sustainable Architecture and Urbanism*, a set of principles developed as a supplement to the organization's charter, declare that "siting of new development shall prefer already urbanized land." The document also stipulates protection of "virgin forests, native habitats and prime farmlands," wetlands, and watersheds.[204] In fact, both paradigms have a role to play in reshaping twentieth-century patterns of suburbanization.[205] Today, CNU's principles reflect a broadened mission that extends to promoting walkability, connectivity, mixed uses, mixed-income housing, diversity, higher density, smart transportation, and sustainability.[206]

As CNU has evolved, it has systematized many of the rules that have emerged in urban design in the last two decades. Standard professional reference works like *Architectural Graphic Standards* now incorporate CNU's planning standards, replacing more suburban-focused, site-planning principles.[207] In developing these standards, CNU also codified many of Jane Jacobs's principles about higher density, mixed uses, short blocks, and older (or older-seeming) buildings. The organization has, in many ways, become the Congrès Internationaux d'Architecture Moderne (CIAM) of contemporary urban design. And, like CIAM, it has become the focus of criticism from those who believe that urban design needs to move beyond the formulas that have governed it for much of the past twenty years.

Neomodernism and Posturbanism

Within the last decade, as architects have returned to modernism for aesthetic inspiration, critics have begun to criticize formerly praised works of urban design like Battery Park City in Lower Manhattan. Meanwhile, such respected voices as Nicolai Ouroussoff, the architecture critic for the *New York Times*, and marquee architect Rem Koolhaas have essentially pronounced Jane Jacobs an anachronism.[208] When Jacobs died in 2006, Ouroussoff wrote that "her death may…give us permission to move on, to let go of the obsessive belief that Ms. Jacobs held the answer to every evil that faces the contemporary city."[209]

Koolhaas has advocated a return to large-scale, top-down planning, which he calls "Bigness."[210] Michael Sorkin and Douglas Kelbaugh, among others, have labeled this reaffirmation of urban renewal practices "post urbanism," applying it by extension to some of the recent work of architects like Zaha Hadid, Peter Eisenmann, Frank Gehry, and Thom Mayne.[211] Critics like architect and urban designer Tim Love have described the urban design efforts of architects like these as basically works of superscale architecture that recall the utopian urban megastructure projects of the 1960s and 1970s.[212]

Emerging ideas about urbanism championed by Koolhaas and others parallel the revival of the modernist aesthetic, or "neomodernism," in architectural design. Although they do not constitute a formal movement, per se, modernist-influenced architects, urbanists, and critics decry the relentless grid patterns and stress on context espoused by urban designers over the past twenty years. They want something new, refreshing, and different—

Orenco Station, Portland, Oregon. A transit-oriented development puts housing and commercial activity within a short walk of a light-rail station. Reproduced with permission from *Getting There: Metro's Regional Plan in Brief* (Portland, Oregon: Metro, 1999).

something that may, perhaps, be found in the works of the modernist era. In the words of Ouroussoff, "an endless grid of brick towers…is dehumanizing.…The plaza at Lincoln Center—or even at the old World Trade Center—can be a welcome contrast in scale."[213] In his search for contrast, Ouroussoff evokes the superblock models of the past, places like Albany, New York's Empire State Mall, or the Prudential Center in Boston.

Where this new impulse will lead remains unclear. In part it represents a reaction to projects that focused on historicism and appearance without addressing the knotty problems of twenty-first-century urbanization. Suburban projects like Seaside, Kentlands, and Celebration might fall into this category. Ouroussoff and others place urban projects like Battery Park City in this group for its emphasis on contextualism and grid-block patterns.

Yet what are the alternatives? Michael Sorkin saw few in a 2006 article "The End(s) of Urban Design," in which he says, "'New' Urbanism and Koolhaasian 'Post'-urbanism represent a Hobson's choice, a Manichean dystopianism that leaves us trapped between *The Truman Show* and *Blade Runner*."[214] Although extreme, this characterization does suggest some of the issues at hand. If, however, a major shift in thinking lies ahead, it seems unlikely that ideas about grid and context will totally disappear from urban design. If cities became collections of super-scale objects all clamoring for attention, they would look more like suburbs.

Large, sculptural architectural projects, like Koolhaas's library in Seattle, need context in order to stand out. Frank Lloyd Wright's iconic Guggenheim Museum in New York would make a far less dramatic statement without its gridded backdrop of brick and limestone. It may turn out that cities need plenty of background buildings and an easily understood organization in order to work well. Nor does it seem likely that a return to top-down planning lies just around the corner. Public participation may yield frustrating delays, but it helps to ensure a democratic process.

Conclusion

The current controversy is primarily aesthetic in nature, and while aesthetic considerations play a key role in planning, other issues—sustainability, social equity, and the health of the common realm—rank as overriding concerns. The real issues boil down to the kind of urban pattern we will build in the twenty-first century and the opportunities inherent in recentralization. The problems of twentieth-century suburbanization have become abundantly clear. Whether modernist or historicist in look and feel, new city-building projects must address the continuing problems caused by dispersed development. To make the right choices, urban designers must continue to engage the public while working with the tools and principles at their disposal.

CHAPTER **5**

Principles for an Urban Century

The United States stands on the cusp of an urban renaissance. Changing demographics and values will continue to build demand for housing and jobs in cities. Diversity has begun to move from slogan to marketplace reality. Concern for the planet's health now regularly finds expression in zoning that encourages environmentally benign development. Americans increasingly report in surveys that they value community. These changes promise to unlock an era of extraordinary promise over the next several decades.

How will cities benefit in this new era? To begin with, they can use renewed affluence to help pay for the infra-

structure of livability: affordable housing, schools, libraries, and parks. They can also use new wealth to transform islands of poverty, often racially based, into mixed-income neighborhoods that welcome rather than displace longtime residents. They can encourage even more environmentally friendly regulation that stimulates compact development to promote rather than diminish personal—and planetary—health. Compact communities can in turn support new options for transit, walkability, housing, recreation, and other key elements that define urban quality of life. The list of opportunities is long and enticing, and they will not be confined to cities like Seattle, Chicago, and Atlanta, which make a consistent effort to lead in this area. Communities like Roswell, Georgia; Rochester, New York; and Tyler, Texas, have undertaken some of the most exciting smart-growth and downtown-revitalization initiatives of recent years. They represent the larger picture of communities around the country discovering new possibilities for growth and change.

To take full advantage of these opportunities, however, Americans need to develop a new and shared vision of

---

Cities can be designed. There are many individual examples of fine streets, attractive parks, active public spaces, and successful neighborhoods that, if brought together in one city, would create a magnificent urban place. The challenge today is to achieve consistent high design quality everywhere in every city.

Jonathan Barnett, FAIA, FAICP, professor of city and regional planning and director of the Urban Design Program, University of Pennsylvania

---

what community building can achieve. The experience of a planning director in Alexandria, Virginia, highlights what happens when we lack a shared vision. Few communities in the United States are better poised for renaissance than Alexandria. Beneficary of a strong regional economy, endowed with miles of waterfront, and served by one of the country's best transit systems, Alexandria is in a position to build a generation of transit-oriented development (TOD) that creates lively new neighborhood squares and parks, transforms public housing into mixed-income communities (without federal assistance), pays for better schools, and underwrites other improvements that enhance quality of life.

Yet when Faroll Hamer set out to create the first neighborhood plan on her watch—a plan that could yield this impressive list of benefits—she encountered fierce resistance from neighborhood leaders who associated change with loss of community character. Her response was to halt the planning process and engage residents in an intensive education and visioning process. Six months later she had achieved a remarkable turnaround: support from many in the community and unanimous backing from Alexandria's city council for an urban design plan that preserved historic blocks while placing significant density next to a Metro station. Under the plan, that density will pay for a new park, help underwrite the cost of turning public housing into mixed-income housing, and provide both the market support and setting for a new square animated by neighborhood-oriented retail.

Urban designers have misled as well as led when the profession loses sight of the full complement of forces that shape peoples' lives. When a blinkered focus on one set of concerns, no matter how important, has dominated urban design thinking, the results have often proved disastrous:

- Modernist urban design visions of the 1950s and 1960s often drew more inspiration from modern art than from human experience. The windswept plazas and sterile environments they produced led many Americans to fear any kind of change in their built environment.

- In the 1960s and 1970s, the urban renewal movement focused narrowly on making cities more economically competitive but ignored walkability and other key qualities that people value in urban environments—ultimately accelerating the decline of many cities.

- In the aftermath of the oil-price shocks of the 1970s, a focus on reducing energy consumption often trumped every other concern in architecture and urban design (among many fields). Millions of people learned to loathe the hostile, windowless buildings that resulted.

- The rush to fortify cities after September 11, 2001—again, at the expense of other urban qualities—walled buildings off from surrounding streets rather than finding more subtle ways to protect people, undermining the ability of our most important public spaces to foster a greater sense of community.

- Even today, single-focus agendas can pose a threat to broader attempts to enhance the quality and character of urban spaces. An unquestioning reliance on the private sector to animate public spaces by adding retail and entertainment, for example, can create public spaces that are vibrant—but no longer truly public in spirit.

The questions skeptical Alexandria residents raised suggest the need for urban design principles that speak directly to the opportunities and challenges U.S. communities face in this new, more urban century. The suburban American dream remains alive—millions of Americans still yearn for a single-family house with a yard and are willing to endure long commutes in return. The past fifty years have provided a clear set of guidelines for how to create the kind of community that they seek. Millions of Americans, however, prefer a home that enables them to take transit to work, meet friends in a neighborhood square, walk with their kids to a neighborhood park, and shape their lives in ways that promote sustainability. There are no clear guidelines for communities like that, because America has not *built* communities like that in more than fifty years. When Alexandria residents asked, in essence, "How do we know whether higher density is good or bad for our neighborhood?" they gave voice to genuine uncertainty. With no clear model to look to, their qualms should come as no surprise. Urban design principles that respond to urban needs today could help answer their question—and could guide a new generation of community building.

The authors did not set out to create such principles. Yet, as we reviewed the case studies for recent AIA Regional and Urban Design Honor Awards, we realized that they presented a unique overview of successful answers to the question being asked in Alexandria and elsewhere. The more we looked, the more convinced we became: the themes that emerged consistently from these projects—stretching from Hawaii to Texas to Massachusetts (and on to Europe and Asia)—looked very much like principles that communities could use to translate growth and change into powerful tools for building livable communities.

Experience is teaching that prescriptive templates do not hold up well when market forces, changing programs, and new needs come into play. What are needed instead are flexible frameworks that allow for innovation, hybridization, organic growth, change, and surprise. [The] inherent pragmatism [of this approach] has the potential to liberate design and harness many kinds of creativity coming from others. Urban design becomes more like improvisational jazz. In Stuart Brand's terminology, we are learning "how cities learn." Rather than producing finite products, urban design is increasingly about the anticipation and guidance of long-term transformations without fixed destinations, mediating between values, goals, and actual outcomes.

Ken Greenberg, architect and urban designer, principal, Greenberg Consultants, Toronto, Canada

Our hope for these principles is that they can inspire the next generation of work by urban designers and serve as a yardstick by which any community can measure the value of any urban design proposal. By virtue of scale, context, and other qualities, many urban design proposals will address some principles more directly than others. No project, however, should ever compromise a community's ability to pursue any of these principles— and the best projects will advance them all.

1. **Build community in an increasingly diverse society.** Diversity and economic fragmentation tend to undercut community, which needs to be built and nurtured consciously. As the population of the United States grows more diverse, the country requires new elements to take the role of shared churches, social clubs, and other traditional community-building institutions that once served homogeneous neighborhoods. Critical elements include:

- **Create places that draw people together.** In a diverse society, achieving the experience of community entails a concerted effort to plan and design public parks and squares, new housing, entire new neighborhoods and major projects that draw people of widely differing backgrounds and aspirations together. The United States built most of its neighborhoods for homogeneous groups of people who shared the same faith—and churches, schools, and often employers. Redlining, suburbanization, and single-use zoning reinforced the concept of building one-size-fits-all communities.

- **Support social equity.** Sometimes by intent but often by inattention, many U.S. communities have choked off access to jobs, health care, open space, and other elements central to pursuit of the American dream. Through much of the twentieth century decision makers located highways, power plants, and other uses that damaged public health in the middle of poor and minority communities and located public housing in out-of-the-way places adjacent to rail lines and active industry. While not discussed as often as other elements of building community, it is essential to assure that the benefits of an urban renaissance flow to all members of the community and that new urban wealth is spent in part on righting old wrongs.

- **Emphasize the public realm.** In an era of growing cultural and economic diversity, streets, squares, parks, and other public spaces represent the core building blocks of community. Once, these were so natural that they went almost unnoticed; their essential role in drawing together people of different ages, incomes, races, and backgrounds came into sharp focus when suburban shopping malls began to siphon activity out of public Main Streets. Promoting the public realm does not mean simply defending public spaces against private atriums that drain away their life. It also means using development to frame streets and public spaces, to enliven them with retail and other uses that engage passersby, and to enrich them with animated programming and public art that draws people together for shared enjoyment and endeavors. At a time of scarce public resources, new private and public development projects should be judged in part on their ability to contribute to and enhance the public realm—and this ability should include their capacity to tap rising urban real estate values as a new source of financial support for creating the public realm.

The measure of a society's humanity is not the magnificent office towers or the state-of-the-art laboratories it builds, but the care and attention it pays to its public realm of landscaped streets, lively urban squares, and beautiful parks that belong to everyone no matter how rich or poor, young or old, black or white.

Joseph P. Riley, mayor, Charleston, South Carolina

- **Forge stronger connections.** While old divisions of race and ethnic background have receded in many communities, the physical and social barriers that once divided neighborhoods often remain. This phenomenon is visible in the reshaping of public housing developments into mixed-income neighborhoods, the transformation of rail yards and strip malls into mixed-use districts, and the metamorphosis that turns industrial sites into riverfront parks. In many cases, extending local streets to form a new gridded connection breaks down barriers. In other cases, where rail lines, six-lane arterial roads, and highways still form barriers, social connections—formed by an exciting new park, interactive fountain, or other public destinations—take the place of physical connections. For communities in transition, it is sometimes essential to create places that honor and acknowledge the many histories that people of different backgrounds bring to the same neighborhood. The Haitian Cultural Center in rapidly changing Miami, African American Heritage Trail on Boston's gentrified Beacon Hill, and other places across the United States that celebrate diverse histories help Americans find community in the midst of diversity.

2. **Advance sustainability at every level.** While growing concern over carbon-fueled climate change has generated broad support for encouraging green design and materials in planning, these qualities only begin to define the ways in which urban design should promote sustainability. Critical elements include:

- **Foster smarter growth.** Encouraging more compact development is the single most effective step the United States can take to achieve greater environmental benefits in terms of reduced energy use, aquifer recharge, and a host of other measures of environmental health. For example, compact communities, particularly those close to the urban core, can reduce energy consumption per household to one-third the level of houses in sprawling suburbs. At a regional level, fostering smart growth requires increased regional collaboration and policies that favor compact development. In older suburbs and urban neighborhoods, it can mean designing attractive infill development and transforming grayfields, like older shopping centers, into vibrant mixed-use developments where people can live, work, and shop, and where densities support public transportation. In downtowns it can mean designing handsome higher-density housing, lively mixed-use environments, and vibrant public spaces that invite people to enjoy urban life.

- **Address the economic, social, and cultural underpinnings of sustainability.** Every project can contribute to building a better foundation for sustainability. A community that does not offer economic opportunity, is divided by racial tension, cannot educate its youth, or suffers from other deep-rooted problems will find its ability to promote sustainability severely limited. Chattanooga, Tennessee, dismissed dirty air and water as the price of jobs until it adopted a plan to create new jobs by creating an amenity-rich downtown that attracted people to live, work, visit, and shop. Atlanta could not begin to build a regional transit system until its black and white communities came to see themselves as partners in the city's growing prosperity. Many U.S. cit-

ies cannot support more compact regional development until they generate the financial resources to improve the quality of their school systems.

3. **Expand individual choices.** For most of the twentieth century, the United States pursued development patterns that assumed a narrowly defined "American dream" and presented people with a diminishing set of choices about how to live. Conditions are in place to reverse this trajectory and to expand individual choice. Critical elements include:

- **Build densities that support greater choice.** The noise, grime, and crowding of mature industrial cities produced a backlash against density and mixed-use environments. However, areas of low-density housing or other exclusive uses can only function if everyone wants to drive, shares the same housing preferences, is satisfied with a limited range of recreation options, and shares other common needs and aspirations. Greater density creates more choice. Well-planned and well-designed density helps broaden the pool of customers needed to support walkable Main Streets. It introduces a mix of uses that make walking to work a possibility; builds the market for a wider range of housing options to accommodate people of different ages, incomes, and backgrounds; assures the critical mass of riders needed to support public transportation; generates the activity that makes parks safe and enticing; adds development value that can subsidize new libraries, schools, and similar building blocks of quality of life; and, at a regional scale, yields more compact development that preserves access to the natural environment.

- **Build interconnected transportation networks.** We have reached the end of an era in which the needs of the automobile dictated the urban design agenda and made walking impossible. As the economic, social, and environmental costs of an automobile-dependent culture have grown more apparent, Americans have made it clear that they want greater transportation choice. The definition of urban design has widened to incorporate basic responsibility for creating environments that give people access to a range of transportation options: street grids that promote walkable and bicycle-friendly communities; streets and public spaces designed to accommodate pedestrians, joggers, bicycles, people with limited mobility, and others; development patterns that support retail and other destinations that invite people to explore their communities on foot; concentrated areas of development that support public transportation; neighborhood-scale transportation—for example, trolleys, jitneys, or local buses—that connects to regional-scale transit; and other similar services.

- **Provide choices that enhance quality of life.** The rising proportion of younger and older households in the housing market—most of which do not include children—represents far more than a demographic fact. These households do not fit easily into many of America's one-size-fits-all urban and suburban neighborhoods. Young adults who want to remain in the neighborhoods where they grew up, and other residents who wish to move into those same neighborhoods and grow old there, represent the most visible portion of those who want to see a broader range of housing choices in existing and new neighborhoods. And these people constitute only part of the new mosaic; many people looking for housing come from other cultures, belong to nontraditional families, or represent other aspects of diversity. At the same time, growing diversity means that people also desire a broader range of recreational opportunities, shopping, culture, and other core elements of life—ideally, within walking distance. The need for new and more choices extends to other aspects of life; increasingly, em-

We are discovering new ways to build places for human beings that at the most fundamental level "do no harm," but that also steward the regeneration of the city, the earth, connective layers of the environment, and of the human spirit itself. We are on the threshold of the new: Economic thinking is rapidly converging with environmental reality, and the sustainable city will emerge from landscape-urbanism–inspired design.

Joe Brown, FASLA, chief executive officer, EDAW, San Francisco

ployers report that many employees want to walk to work, which requires more mixed-use development in more places; expensive urban land adds pressure for more mixed-income housing; and people ask for new approaches to neighborhood schools, libraries, and other basic services. Every project can suggest new opportunities for personal choice.

4. **Enhance personal health.** Regulations that encouraged suburban and single-use development pushed millions of Americans into patterns of living that produced significant public health impacts. The much more positive public health data associated with denser communities that support walkability and reduce reliance on driving underlie an important new mission for urban design. Critical elements include:

- **Promote public health.** Americans who walk more and drive less are more likely to lead healthier lives. Walking improves health, and spending less time in an automobile significantly reduces the chance of being killed or injured in an auto-related accident—one of America's most significant public health hazards. However, beyond fostering walkability and transportation choices, urban designers can do much more to promote public health. People who live in concentrated poverty suffer from much higher rates of depression, have far less access to health care, and are less likely to move out of poverty than people with the same incomes who live in mixed-income settings. Failing to revive neighborhood Main Streets compounds the challenges of making healthy food readily accessible to urban neighborhoods. Encouraging sprawl—particularly by locating work far from housing and requiring multiple automobile trips for different activities—seriously hampers efforts to clean polluted air. Breaking down the barriers between campuses and the communities around them increases opportunities for lifelong learning and opportunities for enhanced economic opportunity and understanding of health issues. Projects at every scale should be assessed in terms of their ability to promote health.

- **Increase personal safety.** The reality and perception of personal safety are both critical to enhanced personal health. The reality of safety involves many aspects of design that are well understood—providing adequate lighting, avoiding creation of hiding places, making sure there are "eyes on the street" (in Jane Jacobs's expression), and similar techniques. Programming and other aspects of design also make a difference. A well-used corner café does more to make a street safe than a twenty-story office building at night. Multiple doorways on to a residential street (provided, for example, by locating row-house units at the base of a multifamily residential building), instill a naturally stronger sense of responsibility in residents for the safety of passersby and make it far more likely that people nearby will respond to a call for help. A perception of safety is essential to overcoming the doubts that many people still harbor about all kinds of urban environments (despite more than a decade of largely positive news about reduced urban crime). Densities that support lively, populated environments attract people to communities in which they can walk more and drive less.

5. **Make places for people.** Following these principles means little unless people love the places that result. A quick survey of the United States' most admired spaces and communities quickly suggests that what people love is tied largely to context. People love Rockefeller Center in New York City for the excitement its tall buildings generate and symbolize. They love squares of Savannah, Georgia, for the consistent sense of history and the human scale its buildings convey. Providence, Rhode Island, residents love the way that tall, new buildings bump up against the Woonasquatucket River at Waterplace Park, framing it with bustling bars and restaurants, and their neighbors forty-five minutes away in Boston love the city's handsome HarborWalk because legal restrictions keep adjacent buildings far enough away to confer a sense of openness. New Orleans residents love the French Quarter for its quiet streets of nineteenth-century houses in unbroken rows near the Marigny—and for the delightful cacophony of bars, music, shops, and apartments a block away. People in Chicago and Atlanta extol the virtues of new buildings for their height, while residents of San Francisco and Washington, D.C., take pride in preventing buildings from growing taller. In the end, making great places that people love begins with understanding both the people and the place. Critical elements include:

- **Respond to the human senses.** Urban design succeeds at placemaking when it retains full consciousness of the qualities that engender human delight—design and activities that engage people as they pass. Stores along a street, nature in an urban setting, and fountains in a public square are loved because they delight the senses. If the market will not support retail facing a public space, building facades offer opportunities to tell the community's stories by showcasing live-work space for artists or others, providing a glimpse of people working or conducting research, or offering other opportunities to engage passersby. There is little delight in garages that display the latest structural technology, blank walls (no matter how beautifully detailed), or elegant but empty lobbies, and these places do not garner affection as a result. A towering skyscraper can create human scale if it meets the street with details and activities that delight, and a two-story building can lack human scale if it offers only a monotonous facade. A visible bow to context can have the same effect. Many public squares surrounded by ordinary buildings are beloved if the buildings' ground floors form a continuous ensemble of vibrant shops and cafés. A very tall building whose design does not respond to the character of a financial district on one side and the different quality of a historic neighborhood a block away can generate powerful resentment. An equally tall building that visibly steps down and acknowledges its historic neighbor can be loved.

- **Integrate history, nature, and innovation.** One of the most critical tasks that stronger urban economies pose for urban designers and the communities with whom they work is finding the ways in which preserving historic environments; protecting and enjoying nature; and introducing dramatic new places to live, work, shop, and play can reinforce and enhance each other.

- **Emphasize identity.** Whether rehabilitating a historic building or creating a new urban neighborhood, every project offers opportunities to capture

the unique qualities of a place. While design plays an important role—creating gateway buildings, using local materials, incorporating treasured signs or other memorabilia, reflecting predominant scale and building character, and using similar steps—programming can be just as important. Is there an opportunity to include neighborhood-based retailers? To provide a storefront for a prominent community organization? Subsidize a new neighborhood library or other civic use?

- **Celebrate history.** Many of the densest—and best loved—buildings, spaces, and neighborhoods are those where U.S. history remains visible. Historic neighborhoods became the breeding grounds of urban revitalization following the rapid disinvestment that plagued most American cities after World War II—ironically, despite the billions of dollars invested in urban renewal. Spurred by a philosophical commitment to preserving historic legacies and by recognition of the tangible value of preservation, strong preservation movements took hold in cities across the United States and won wide support for pubic financial incentives and protections for historic resources. The rush of investment to cities and renewed interest in living in urban neighborhoods, particularly those in or near walkable historic districts rich in character, are creating a new era of opportunities and challenges for preservation. At one end of the spectrum, developers have proposed inappropriately scaled developments in the midst of historic districts in cities with insufficient protections. At the other end, preservationists fight major developments near historic districts that bring welcome vitality, diversity, and fiscal benefits without undermining a community's connections to its past. Urban designers should work closely with the preservation community to make sure that an urban renaissance enhances the integrity, stories, and amenity of historic buildings, spaces, and neighborhoods.

I grew up in the preservation movement and I love it. We fought a war against urban renewal and won. I think it is entirely fair to say that in the process we saved America's cities. But times have changed and the task of preservation today is not to fight change but to embrace it and own it. We won the war to save history, now we need to launch a grand collaboration with community activists, developers, mayors, planners, urban designers, and others to make sure that this history inspires rather than constrains the future.

Mary C. Means, founder of the National Trust for Historic Preservation's Main Streets Center

---

- **Respect and engage nature.** As the United States reclaims its industrial landscapes and moves to protect the streams and ravines that course through suburbs, there are new opportunities to reestablish a balanced ecology that embraces natural systems along with human-built landscapes. Communities across the United States are discovering ways to protect and restore damaged natural areas while creating entire new recreational systems nearby. Salt Lake City opened a nature trail that begins downtown, adjacent to the state capitol; Manhattan's Waterfront Greenway allows continuous access to the city's rivers and harbor; Boston's Emerald Necklace and Charles River Esplanade provide continuous riverfront greenways that draw more than three million people annually to walk, bike, and jog through many urban neighborhoods. St. Paul, Minnesota, is restoring portions of its Mississippi River frontage to a natural state while increasing access and launching a river music festival. All of these initiatives are funded by stronger urban economies, reassert the role of nature in the city, and enhance livability.

- **Introduce innovation.** Channel growth and change to places where development enhances community quality and character—away from valuable natural areas, historic districts, and traditional neighborhoods. Few communities question the concept of preserving what they love about the past; accepting significant growth, however, often proves challenging. Rapidly evolving demographics and economics present communities with dramatic choices, and the degree to which benefits outweigh costs can be unfamiliar. Suburbs can transform strip retail malls with acres of surface parking into blocks of new, mixed-use, walkable town centers. Downtowns can come to life at night—and hum with activity during the day—as thousands of new residents seek downtown living. After decades of decline, a Main Street can blossom with new shops and cafés when the construction of condominiums nearby enlarges the market that supports local businesses. People who have always depended on their car to go anywhere can live within a short walk of train service, as transit-oriented development replaces commuter parking lots and warehouses along commuter-rail corridors. In the initial reaction to urban renewal, many urban designers took pride in protecting communities from large-scale development that undermined local character. Today's threats are harder to identify. Well-planned and well-designed development—which respects and preserves historic resources, parks, and a long list of other features—increasingly delivers vitality, the dollars to build new parks and schools, new housing options for aging baby boomers and their children just entering the work force, and other new features of civic value.

Process Should Support the Principles

The case studies that yielded these principles also offer important perspective on how process can and should support principles.

Engage the community

Virtually every award-winning project described in Part II of this book took shape within the framework of a community-based process. In each case, urban planners repeatedly redrew the map for moving toward a vision and plan as different participants weighed in. Layering on different community perspectives yielded richer and more nuanced plans. This iterative process of drawing out community needs and aspirations and testing the concepts that emerged from them against a broad range of criteria enabled stakeholders and urban designers to collaborate in creating inspiring, relevant, and achievable visions.

> The people who live where place improvement is happening must be involved; the disciplines whose work shows up in the process must coordinate; and the public-private partnerships that drive design and development in the public realm must work more aggressively to include the community voice.
>
> Mike Dobbins, urban designer and professor, College of Architecture, Georgia Institute of Technology

These urban design processes began by identifying the kinds of participants to be included and laying out an approach intended to draw them into the process. Common mechanisms included community task forces, workshops, regular public meetings, charrettes, or some combination of all of them. This phase of the program addressed ways of attracting diverse stakeholders and encouraging them to work together to resolve difficult issues such as race, class, and cultural differences; put aside political turf disputes; beat legislative deadlines; or ignore election cycles. Most of the plans incorporated active community participation at every stage, offering opportunities for community members to respond to and shape each plan element. Many projects shifted gears in later stages, with community participants focusing on building support—political and otherwise—for project implementation.

Understand potential implementation strategies from the start

Some mix of funding, environmental strategies, political support, and related strategies informed every aspect of the case studies. In contrast to an era when public funding served as a primary implementation tool, the reality of reduced public resources today means that most of these projects required complex public, private, and institutional partnerships to fund and manage implementation. The projects embraced this complexity at every stage, drawing inspiration from the many actors and perspectives it introduced. At project inception, potential strategies helped define program elements that would shape the project (for example, real estate uses that would be essential to creating the value needed to fund affordable housing, public space, or other civic benefits) and stakeholders who would shape the process (such as funding agencies or key political constituencies). In turn, implementation strategies strongly influenced each step in the urban design process.

Identify and understand the context

Project context often presented opportunities and challenges that shaped the urban design plan. How did the region, district, or site relate to adjacent areas—physically, socially, economically, and culturally? What broader social, economic, or environmental goals might be achieved? Was there an opportunity to establish a neighborhood identity, for example, or to promote green building and site planning? What technical, political, or other challenges had blocked progress previously? What options held the most realistic potential for implementation? Asking such questions at the outset and keeping them in mind at each stage of a project played a critical role in ensuring that the final recommendations were achievable.

Identify and analyze key opportunities and challenges

Beyond immediately obvious concerns of design, social impact, and historic preservation, the urban designers for these projects frequently addressed less evident issues, such as community values, cultural traditions, and other subjective points throughout the process. An urban planner typically educates and is educated by key stakeholders and community members in an iterative fashion, leaving open the possibility of altering or modifying the framework of issues as the process of urban design progresses.

Articulate a vision

Context, community involvement, and issues identification all helped to set the goals and direction needed to shape the final version of these plans. Involving a broad range of stakeholders in framing a vision helped embed inspiration, relevance, and political feasibility in the plans' DNA. In many instances, conflicting agendas and constraints (financial, political, or environmental) required planners to help stakeholders negotiate trade-offs that accommodated a wide range of values but helped keep the vision from veering off into wishful fantasy.

Develop a plan

After an initial vision had been sketched out and vetted through the community process, planners followed a variety of paths to produce a series of alternative options for accomplishing the vision. Options underwent a preliminary evaluation by the urban design team for presentation to the client and community stakeholders. Evaluation criteria may have included cost, ability to satisfy stated goals and objectives, environmental issues, implementation considerations, and other factors. (It is sometimes best to postpone making recommendations until all the options have been presented and evaluated in a community forum in which a preferred choice can be identified.)

Communicate the plan

Communication techniques played a vital role throughout these urban design processes, from diagramming of goals and objectives, to mapping of site and analysis data, to communicating and promoting the final plan. Communication techniques included verbal and data presentations and graphic and written materials. Along the way, many of the processes entailed reports, design studies, site plans, models, renderings or other graphics, Web-based tools, and computer-generated animations.

PART II

Putting Urban Design into Practice

Case Studies in Urban Design

Like communities in the United States, urban design is in the midst of a period of rapid transition. We chose to include case studies from the past ten years to provide a window onto that transition. By examining real projects—shaped by the on-the-ground realities of local aspirations, political debates, economic and social transitions, histories, and shifting values—we hope to show how urban design can help communities manage growth and change. Perhaps the most common message in all of these case studies is that they left no community unchanged, but in some way enhanced each of the communities they touched.

We chose to use the seventy winners over ten years of the American Institute of Architects' (AIA) Honor Award in Regional and Urban Design for three reasons:

- The case studies showcase a remarkable sampling of the United States' best urban designers, working in a broad cross section of American communities.

- While other notable awards programs could provide a useful pool of case studies—notably the Congress for the New Urbanism's Charter Awards program and the Urban Land Institute's Awards for Excellence—the AIA Honor Awards represent the only program that focuses on excellence in urban design without also advocating a particular perspective.

- The time frame provides an opportunity to chart changes in theory and practice while drawing all of the case studies from the period of urban recentralization described in Chapter 4.

We organized the case studies around six themes, each of which defines a specific cluster of opportunities and challenges. This organizing structure was at some level arbitrary, as many of these projects could have fit comfortably into several of our categories. We urge the reader to review all of the case studies because each

offers lessons of value across the spectrum. The chapters group the case studies in these areas:

- Guiding Regional Growth and Change
- Rediscovering Downtown and Main Street
- Reinventing Older Neighborhoods
- Inventing New Neighborhoods
- Reclaiming the Waterfront
- Creating the Public Realm
- Transforming Campus into Community

Background: AIA's Regional and Urban Design Committee

Roughly four decades after Harvard's Dean José Luis Sert introduced the now-common term "urban design," the AIA established a national Regional and Urban Design Committee (RUDC), signifying the larger field's embrace of a discipline that focused on designing places as well as individual or groups of buildings. One of the AIA's core knowledge communities today, the RUDC works with the Institute and local AIA chapters on a wide range of programs. Although most of the organization's national committees represent architects practicing in a specialized area—such as the design of health-care facilities or public buildings—RUDC welcomes practitioners from outside the architectural profession who share an interdisciplinary interest in community building.

Beginning in 2003, the RUDC began working with the AIA's Center for Communities by Design (CCD) to promote public education and advocacy on behalf of enhanced livability and civic engagement by architects. This collaboration has produced a number of programs that address changing communities. In 2005 CCD helped sponsor a national symposium, "Reinventing the Urban Village," that focused on ways to introduce denser new

Major past and current activities sponsored entirely or in part by the Regional and Urban Design Committee, and open to participation by architects and colleagues interested in urban design, include:

- **The Regional and Urban Design Assistance Team (R/UDAT)** is a program through which the AIA provides pro bono interdisciplinary advisors who assist communities in responding to a wide range of revitalization, growth-management, and development issues.

- **Sustainability Design Assistance Teams (SDATs).** The AIA established the SDAT program in 2005, based on the R/UDAT model. In contrast to the R/UDAT program, which offers its clients "specific design solutions, the SDAT program provides broad assessments to help frame future policies or design solutions in the context of sustainability and helps communities plan the first steps of implementation."[215] With the help of former Honolulu mayor Jeremy Harris—a trained biologist and member of the AIA board of directors—the Institute designed a program whose broad definition of "sustainability" includes environmental, social, economic, and cultural concerns. By mid-2008, the SDAT program had sent teams of architects, planners, economists, and environmentalists to three dozen communities across the United States.

- **Livability Conferences.** Building on an AIA tradition of national urban design meetings focused on specific topics, the RUDC launched an annual conference in 2002 that now draws several hundred participants to address the changing issues that shape livability. The program began in Des Moines, Iowa. Subsequent conferences have included Boston in 2003 (Density: Myth and Reality), New York City in 2004 (Learning from Lower Manhattan), Washington, D.C., in 2005 (Communities on the Line: Transit-Oriented Development), and Seattle in 2006 (Livable Communities: Walking, Working, Water). In 2007 and 2008, the RUDC shifted its format to a national webcast on sustainability and urban design. For 2010 the RUDC is working with the AIA's Center for Communities by Design to hold a conference focused on architects' roles as civic leaders, in Kansas City, Missouri.

- **Spring Roundtables.** Each year urban designers from around the country gather to discuss common issues, address areas of emerging practice, and suggest agenda items for RUDC. In 2006 the RUDC shifted the roundtables from Washington, D.C., to cities such as New Orleans and Providence, Rhode Island, to highlight core opportunities and challenges.

- RUDC periodically issues **reports** intended to assist urban designers and other architects working with communities to address significant issues.

housing and mixed-use development into older urban neighborhoods to promote revitalization. Later that year the RUDC helped CCD organize the national Governor's Conference on Recovery and Rebuilding, which brought hundreds of people to New Orleans to begin creating a recovery agenda two months after Hurricane Katrina. In subsequent years, the RUDC has worked with CCD to hold a series of Roundtables on Sustainability that have brought more than fifty organizations together to create *Livability 101*, a handbook published in 2005, to help guide the growth and change of communities.

[I]t is no coincidence that in 1857 many of the founders of the American Institute of Architects in New York (Richard Upjohn, Leopold Eidlitz, Edward Gardner, Richard Morris Hunt, Jacob Mould, and Calvert Vaux), also advanced theories on infrastructure, transportation, park planning, and the role of public buildings and spaces, as a means of improving the quality of life within our cities. It was that same spirit that sought to create an architecture organization that would "promote the scientific and practical perfection of its members" that was also brought to bear in the advocacy of a better society for all Americans.... [Today] we can't provide grand visions of what a place may be without fully interacting with the public. This is how architects made a difference in the past, and this is how we will make design matter for future generations.

Mark E. Strauss, FAIA, AICP, principal, FXFOWLE Architects, New York

The Regional and Urban Design Honor Awards Program

Responding in 1994 to growing interest in urban design, the AIA folded a recently established award for urban design into its established program for recognizing architecture and interior design. The AIA Honor Awards recognize outstanding work by urban designers from around the world, but their primary objective is to support the RUDC's mission "to improve the quality of the regional and urban environment by promoting excellence in design, planning, and public policy in the built environment."[216]

The increasingly influential awards showcase emerging best practices in urban design—including in recent years sustainability, mixed-use development, mixed-income housing, smart growth, transit-oriented development, and similar issues—and have helped confer credibility on approaches widely deemed radical or unworkable as recently as the mid-1990s.

Each year's jury for the RUDC awards includes nationally respected urban designers—often award winners from previous years—as well as architects, landscape architects, planners, and others with a strong interest in urban design. Over the period surveyed in this book, 70 submissions (out of more than 1,000) received awards. Primarily produced by urban designers working for private firms, the projects also included work by educators, urban designers working in the public sector, planners, landscape architects, and others.

The awards have recognized the work of both marquee urban designers and those in small or individual practices who toil far from the limelight. The case study projects have touched the full spectrum of communities in the United States—elite universities and small community colleges; affluent suburbs and Native American reservations; state-of-the-art research facilities and traditional rural settlements; exciting new urban neighborhoods; and beleaguered public housing developments. The clients who commissioned this work represented a similarly broad range: public agencies constituted the largest single group of clients, but the list also includes private developers, community development corporations and other nonprofits, foundations, universities, and other institutions. Together, these clients constitute a cross section of the kinds of organizations that sponsor the projects that shape growth and change in the United States.

To learn more about the RUDC and the awards program, visit the AIA Web site: http://www.aia.org/rudc and www.aia.org/awards.

Case Study Chapters

Each of the next six chapters opens with a brief overview of the category under discussion, followed by a description of each case study in that category. Each chapter concludes with a discussion of the lessons that the case studies offer, collectively, for applying the urban design principles laid out in Chapter 5.

CHAPTER **6**

Guiding Regional Growth and Change

Introducing his 1999 award submission for the South Dade Watershed Project, Dan Williams, FAIA, notes that without appropriate regional guidelines, South Florida risks draining away its last drop of clean water. "The 'design of regions,'" he writes, "may well be the future challenge for architects" if America's urban areas are to find a sustainable balance with nature. This approach, only rarely discussed at the time, now appears prophetic: Urban designers increasingly follow Williams's admonition, adopting a perspective with regional sweep that integrates a rich mix of social, economic, environmental, design, and other elements.

Smart-growth planning constitutes another area that was virtually unknown even as recently as the late 1990s. Today, sponsors from the Environmental Protection Agency to foundations to civic coalitions have launched initiatives to curb sprawl, direct growth and investment into developed areas, and preserve the natural environment. Some, like Envision Utah, focus on entire states. Regional initiatives under way in Washington, D.C., Chicago, and other metropolitan areas focus on reversing patterns of sprawl. Smaller communities such as Concord, New Hampshire, have launched projects intended to preserve traditional community character.

Roots

Today's regional initiatives extend a planning tradition with roots in the late nineteenth century, when rapidly expanding U.S. cities began to grapple with complex regional problems. In 1896 Charles Eliot proposed an interconnected system of parks and natural corridors for the Boston region in an attempt to mitigate the impacts of industrialization on urban residents. Eliot's plan, which continues to serve as a visible framework for the region's development, exemplified a new approach to park planning that continued well into the twentieth century under the City Beautiful banner. Frederick Law Olmsted drew up similar plans for extended park and parkway systems in Buffalo, New York; Milwaukee; and parts of the Atlanta region. Daniel Burnham's 1909 Chicago Plan, discussed in Chapter 3, represents another kind of large-scale planning

Because of the depletion of world resources, Americans during the 21st century will wish to collect, once again, into compact settlements—villages, towns, cities—that will be less resource-consumptive than the thinned-out suburban growth of recent decades. With the help of urban design, these re-concentrations will support a more richly varied, more socially communal, and more sustainable civic life.

Robert Campbell, Architecture critic for *The Boston Globe*

effort inspired by the City Beautiful movement. Burnham intended the plan to function as a growth-management strategy designed to overcome the noise and grime of a booming industrial city by structuring growth around a network of handsome parks and boulevards.

The Great Depression and World War II put most large-scale regional planning on hold (with significant exceptions like the Tennessee Valley Authority and a handful of other federal projects). In the years after the war, however, many states established regional planning authorities. But even when these agencies drew up plans, most lacked the control over funding or the power to compel compliance, vitiating their ability to plan on a large scale. Regional authorities in the Pacific Northwest, the exceptions to this generalization, laid the groundwork for ambitious growth-management strategies that steered development back to the centers of Portland, Oregon, and Seattle in the 1990s, resulting in a surge of investment in their core neighborhoods. Mired in economic stagnation as recently as the early 1980s, both cities have since outpaced their American peers in population growth. By 2000, for example, Seattle had regained its 1960 population of 600,000. (Interestingly, because of smaller household sizes, the city needed 35 percent more housing units than it had in 1960 to accommodate the same number of residents.)

During the 1970s, many regions undertook broad transportation planning, among them Atlanta, Boston, and Washington, D.C. In some cases, spurred by re-gional planning agencies and backed by billions of dollars in federal transportation funding, these programs had a profound impact on the shape and character of their regions. The most dramatic example took place in Washington, where the Urban Land Institute calculates that by 2006 more than $25 billion in transit-oriented development had taken place within a fifteen-minute walk of stations on the regional Metrorail system.[217] Chris Leinberger, a planner and developer now leading a study of Metro's impact for the Brookings Institution, reported in 2007 that office, retail, and housing values reached substantially higher levels in areas with "walkable, mixed-use environments, most of which are served by Metro."[218] In Atlanta, which invested heavily in roadways, the impact of this planning is now visible in two forms—a surge in investment around more urban stations along the MARTA rail system downtown and in nearby cities like Decatur, and a clamor from areas not served by the system for expanded service.

Smart growth emerged as a regional movement in the 1990s. Initially advanced by advocates of refocusing investment and growth back into core communities to address economic and social challenges there, the movement quickly embraced a broader range of environmental objectives. Unlike the growth-management plans of previous decades, which often lacked real influence, smart-growth plans have increasingly focused on effective implementation mechanisms, from statewide legislation to rewriting zoning codes to introducing creative incentives for developers. Smart growth has reached far beyond the previous generation of transportation planning and has attracted a much broader array of advocates; sponsors of smart-growth projects have included the EPA, state and local governments, public-private partnerships, nonprofits such as the Urban Land Institute, and a wide variety of other organizations.

No formal definition of smart growth exists, but common themes among the definitions offered by its advocates include reversing the dynamic of ever-expanding sprawl around American cities and redirecting a greater share of growth and investment back into regional cores. Reinforced by increasing demand for environmental sustainability, smart growth has inspired an unprecedented interest in regional-scale urban design.

Approaches Today

Smart Growth America, a national education and advocacy coalition, describes its mission as helping Americans achieve "fewer hours in traffic and more opportunities to enjoy green space; housing that is both affordable and close to jobs and activities; healthy cities, towns and suburbs; air and water of the highest quality; and a landscape our children can be proud to inherit." The organization defines smart growth in terms of desirable outcomes:

1. **Neighborhood livability,** achieved by focusing planning and other resources on ensuring that all neighborhoods are "safe, convenient, attractive, and affordable," a task made far more challenging when growth and investment flow to new neighborhoods far from the urban core.

2. **Better access, less traffic,** achieved by mixing land uses and providing people with more opportunities to live near where they work, shop, study, and play.

3. **Thriving cities, suburbs, and towns,** achieved by "putting the needs of existing communities first" when investing in transportation, schools, libraries, and other public services.

4. **Shared benefits,** achieved by ensuring that "basic needs such as jobs, education and health care" are available on an equitable basis and that all residents share in the benefits of growing regional prosperity.

5. **Lower costs and lower taxes,** achieved by avoiding the significant expense of new roads, utilities, and other infrastructure required to support low-density sprawl.

Central Avenue, Albany, New York. Reviving a commercial corridor that serves the region. Courtesy of Goody Clancy.

6. **Keeping open space open,** achieved "by focusing development in already built-up areas," enabling us to "pass on to our children the landscapes we love."[219]

Case Studies

These projects set out a broad range of explicit goals, from smart growth to environmental protection to preserving cherished cultural and social qualities. An equally important lesson to draw from them is the insight they provide into how communities can harness growth and change for their benefit.

South Dade Watershed Project

LOCATION: Dade County, Florida

URBAN DESIGNER: Daniel Williams, FAIA, director, Miami Education and Research Center, University of Florida

CLIENT: Miami-Dade County; South Florida Regional Planning Council

STUDY AREA AND PROGRAM: Growth management plan for a 500-square-mile area in Dade County corresponding roughly to the path of Hurricane Andrew

YEAR OF AWARD: 1999

STATUS: Adopted as the county watershed plan.

Critical issues

Like most growing regions with no unified authority charged with assuring adequate water supplies, South Florida has expanded without regard for protecting the sources of its drinking water. "In the aftermath of Hurricane Andrew in 1992," Daniel Williams, FAIA, wrote in his submission, "South Florida stood in the precarious position of rebuilding yet more sprawl and paving over the last 100 square miles of the regional recharge area for drinking water."

Key urban design concepts

The plan underscores the unavoidable connections between water resource management and the spread of development. It analyzed such factors as population growth, development characteristics, annual rainfall, storm-water runoff and recharge, tidal flow, and hurricane patterns in an effort to develop guidelines for future growth. Three-dimensional analysis helped to create a vision of proposed urban patterns that could help guide the region toward a sustainable future. In outlining the steps needed for the region to add 700,000 more people over the subsequent decade, Williams suggests a series of approaches that could be applied nationwide to enhance quality of life and promote environmental health:

- Take responsibility for environmental stewardship.
- Establish smart-growth boundaries.
- Promote livable communities.
- Create systems of *hydric* parks—greenways and wetland-conservation areas that double as flood-storage and water-treatment areas.
- Expand sewage reclamation.
- Implement policies that support energy-conscious urban planning and design.
- Focus on transit-oriented development.

Jury Comments

"An architect's involvement in regional planning has aptly anticipated the spatial, physical, and natural consequences of factors like population growth, climate, water recharge, and the tides. Rigorous in analysis and three-dimensional in vision, this plan rationalizes competing needs and interest into a unified 'biourbanism' for guiding one region's future."

South Dade Watershed Project, Florida. The plan recommends creation of "hydric parks," heavily planted waterways that serve recreational and water-recharge functions and help define neighborhood boundaries. Development is concentrated along the coastal ridge, flanked by reclaimed farmland toward the Everglades and a reclaimed coastal zone that provides protection against flooding from hurricanes and improves water quality in Biscayne Bay. Courtesy of Dan Williams, FAIA.

▶ Proposed development patterns would avoid flood plains and leave land open for aquifer recharge from storm water. Courtesy of Dan Williams, FAIA.

▶▶ Existing development patterns on the southern edge of Miami threaten open land needed for aquifer recharge and spill over into areas vulnerable to flooding. Dark lines show engineered Everglades drainage canals; white line indicates US Route 1. Courtesy of Dan Williams, FAIA.

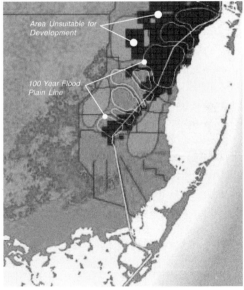

The plan focuses on the threat that sprawl poses to an adequate supply of clean water in Florida's heavily developed Dade County. Its recommendations grow from careful analysis of topography and hydrology and represent the vanguard of a wave of urban plans that respond to growing environmental concerns. Dan Williams, FAIA, lays out steps that Miami-Dade County could take to enhance quality of life in older neighborhoods with the aim of attracting growth back toward the core and preserving undeveloped areas that recharge the South Dade aquifer.

Eastward Ho!—A Regional Vision for Southeast Florida

LOCATION: Dade, Broward, Palm Beach, St. Lucie, and Martin counties, Florida

URBAN DESIGNER: Daniel Williams, FAIA, director, Miami Education and Research Center, University of Florida

CLIENT: Florida Department of Community Affairs

STUDY AREA AND PROGRAM: A 120-mile section of the coast, varying from 5 to 20 miles inland from the coast. Study area covers 70 municipalities with more than 4.5 million residents and corresponds roughly to the geohydrological system of the southeast Florida coast.

YEAR OF AWARD: 2000

STATUS: Adopted by gubernatorial mandate

Critical issues

The Governor's Commission for a Sustainable South Florida had identified sprawl "as a major impediment to a healthy economy, a healthy environment and healthy human communities." The commission adopted the term "Eastward Ho!" to underscore the need to reverse a decades-long pattern of development at the western edge of urbanized South Florida—a threat to the Everglades and critical agricultural areas west of Miami and other cities—and to refocus growth back toward established communities along the coast.

▶ Eastward Ho! A Regional Vision for Southeast Florida. Daniel Williams, FAIA, builds on his earlier South Dade Watershed study by proposing a smart-growth boundary that spans five counties and would reverse a decades-long pattern of encroachment on the Everglades and critical agricultural areas. Eastward Ho! focuses intently on the costs of sprawl—still relatively unknown at the time of the study—and pairs that analysis with proposals for open space, affordable housing, and neighborhood revitalization initiatives that make infill development a more attractive alternative to sprawl. Illustration by John G. Ellis, 2004. Courtesy of Dan Williams, FAIA. *See color insert, C-6.*

Key urban design concepts

"Designing an alternative to sprawl is the leading issue in urban and regional planning," Daniel Williams, FAIA, wrote, describing the core mission of this project as "analyzing the 'true cost of sprawl' and 'designing' the urban and regional patterns that work within the sustainable resources base while creating livable communities." Focusing on a region that already includes 4.5 million people across five counties, and looking ahead to 2040, the plan establishes a smart-growth boundary for southeast Florida that cuts across municipalities. Based on ecologically derived criteria, the boundary preserves agricultural land while creating guidelines for livable communities and preserving urban heritage. By focusing on the costs of sprawl and alternative smart-growth solutions, Williams

makes the case that his smart-growth plan would save taxpayers billions of dollars because preserving the area's natural water supply "will be accomplished at less of a price than typical…engineered solutions."

Jury Comments

"A multijurisdictional, multisector movement for regional conservation and development in southeast Florida….The architect implemented a plan to protect local agriculture and urban heritage, to provide sustainable sources of clean, potable water, and to develop communities that connect to renewable resources."

The plan used ecological data to define an urban growth boundary for five counties along Florida's southeast coast. The boundary would redirect growth back toward developed areas on the coastal ridge and return lower elevations to use for agriculture, recreation, and recharge of the region's aquifer. Illustration by John G. Ellis, 2004. Courtesy of Dan Williams, FAIA.

The Neighborhood Model: Development Area Initiatives Study

LOCATION: Albemarle County, Virginia
URBAN DESIGNER: Torti Gallas and Partners; CHK Architects & Planners
CLIENT: Department of Planning and Community Development
STUDY AREA AND PROGRAM: Comparison of projected conventional development pattern and potential smart-growth patterns in two suburban test areas of roughly 69 and 21 square miles
YEAR OF AWARD: 2002
STATUS: Adopted as a model for the county to use in preparing master plans

---

Critical issues

Like many communities, Charlottesville lacked the design tools to manage rapid growth on its outskirts in ways that reinforce the community's highly valued traditional character and preserve equally important natural areas outside the city. The city engaged the consultant to create guidelines that could be applied across the community

The Neighborhood Model, Albemarle County, Virginia. Torti Gallas's new *neighborhood model* for growth on the edges of Charlottesville, Virginia, calls for a greater variety of housing options and densities, replaces single-use development with mixed uses, sets buildings along a grid of public streets, and locates uses close to each other to promote walking. Projected growth under the model *(at right)* conserves large amounts of open space and employs developed land far more efficiently than development without the model *(at left)*. Courtesy of Torti Gallas and Partners, Inc./Dodson Associates.

to improve the quality of new development and to test the guidelines on likely growth sites. The urban design team's assessment of conventional proposals found that they generally separated housing, retail, office, and other land uses in a manner that discouraged walking but encouraged maximum land absorption. This decentralized approach to development, the urban design team noted, exacerbated economic and social fragmentation by segregating housing according to size and price.

Key urban design concepts

A persuasive neighborhood model for suburban growth on Charlottesville, Virginia's edges could easily serve many regions searching for workable alternatives to

sprawl. The plan calls for housing and other development at a variety of densities; it sets buildings along a grid of public streets and locates uses close to each other to promote walkability and other alternatives to auto dependence. The resulting higher densities enable developers to mix housing of different sizes and prices, ensuring a critical mass of residents to support commercial centers in new developments. More compact development enables the city to preserve natural open space while accommodating growth.

Jury Comments

"It is not only a plan for property, but a sourcebook of guiding principles on what kind of new development is most in the public interest."

The Confluence: A Conservation, Heritage, and Recreation Corridor

LOCATION: St. Louis, Missouri

URBAN DESIGNER: HOK Planning Group

CLIENT: A partnership of five nonprofits representing open-space and cultural resource conservation, social services, greenway and trail development, and educational and interpretation interests; state and federal departments of natural, historical, and cultural resource conservation; and museums and universities

STUDY AREA AND PROGRAM: A master plan for a 40-mile-long interconnected conservation, heritage, and recreation corridor at the confluence of the Missouri and Mississippi rivers. The site incorporates distinctive and unique landscapes such as the Illinois and Missouri limestone bluffs and the nationally significant North American Flyway for migratory birds; significant historic cultural features beyond the area's historically important cities such as St. Louis, including the ancient Cahokia Mounds (a UNESCO World Heritage site) and Missouri's only designated Underground Railroad site; many examples of nineteenth- and early-twentieth-century industrial architecture and engineering; and the many features of a working river.

YEAR OF AWARD: 2004

STATUS: The plan was adopted.

The Confluence, St. Louis, Missouri. HOK Planning Group worked with an alliance of advocates, cultural institutions, universities, and others to frame a new sense of regional identity around creation of a regional park at the confluence of the Missouri and Mississippi rivers. The park incorporates natural and urban areas and creates opportunities to celebrate the region's ecology and history, promote economic development, and improve quality of life. Courtesy of HOK Planning Group and the Confluence Greenway.

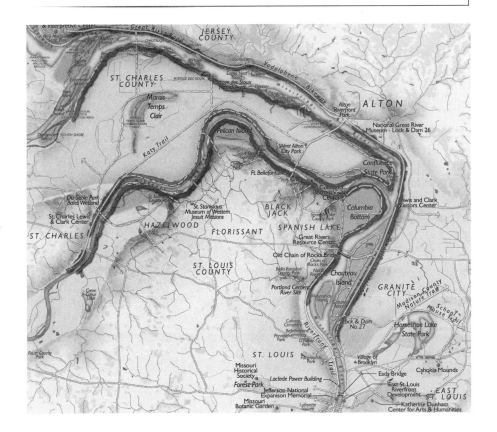

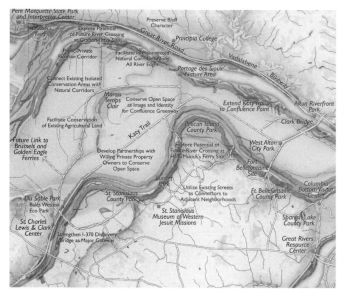

River Bend District focus area northwest of St. Louis. Courtesy of HOK Planning Group and the Confluence Greenway.

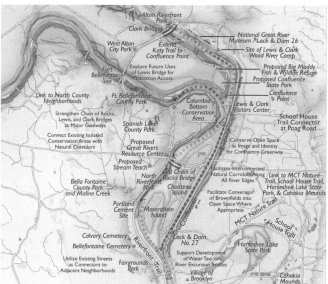

Island District focus area north of St. Louis. Courtesy of HOK Planning Group and the Confluence Greenway.

The Mississippi River at Pere Marquette State Park in Illinois. Missouri lies in the distance, across the river. Courtesy of HOK Planning Group and the Confluence Greenway.

Critical issues

Although inextricably tied to the two rivers, communities of the St. Louis region have become "physically isolated and psychologically disconnected" from the waterways and each other. No regional plan for the rivers exists and some communities offer scant protection for sensitive natural and cultural features. This master plan outlined three core goals:

- "[R]aise the status of the Confluence as a national treasure."

- "[I]ncrease the importance and role of the Confluence in the daily lives of the citizens and visitors of the metropolitan area" to enhance quality of life and build "a new industry of sustainable eco-tourism."

- "[D]evelop a community-supported comprehensive vision for a system of riverfront parks and trails."

Key urban design concepts

The plan "celebrates the meeting of the Great Rivers as the symbolic, physical, and environmental heart of the St. Louis region.... It is an ambitious plan that raises the status of the Confluence to [a] national [level,]...a sustainable plan that promotes environmental sensitivity, conservation, and stewardship [, and]...a unifying plan that connects the people and communities of the region, encourages tourism and economic development, and improves the quality of life." The plan pursues these goals by integrating a series of greenway and conservation proposals that create access to the area's dramatic nature and protect sensitive areas. It "acknowledges that there are appropriate levels of intensity.... While some urban centers offer opportunities to draw thousands...to the river's edge, other sites...are environmentally sensitive and need protection." In addition, the plan lays out a strategy for telling the region's story to visitors by linking a series of historical sites that begin with the region's first human settlement and move chronologically through the Civil War era and the industrial age into the present.

Jury Comments

"A nationally significant park will serve as a lasting legacy to the region and to Lewis and Clark."

Getting it Right: Preventing Sprawl in the Coyote Valley

Location: San Jose, California

Urban designer: WRT/Solomon E.T.C.

Client: Greenbelt Alliance

Study area and program: 6,800 acres of prime farmland and watershed targeted by the city to accommodate roughly 17 million square feet of development and 80,000 new residents and jobs

Year of award: 2004

Status: The plan was adopted.

Critical issues

The Bay Area environmental advocacy group that led this effort accepted the city's growth projections for the last expanse of undeveloped land within San Jose. It worried, however, that the city's urban design model—a series of segregated high-tech campuses and "walled residential subdivisions"—did little to build a sense of community and, as a result, would never achieve long-term economic vitality. The city's low density requirements encouraged dispersed development that would force residents and employees to drive to reach any destination, consume a disproportionate share of the landscape, and degrade groundwater supplies.

Getting It Right: Preventing Sprawl in the Coyote Valley, near San Jose, California. An environmental advocacy group engaged WRT/Solomon to prepare this plan, which offers an alternative vision for managing growth in one of the last tracts of undeveloped land near San Jose. Without losing the ability to add 80,000 new residents and jobs, which an earlier approach would have accommodated in office parks and gated subdivisions, the plan establishes a series of distinct mixed-use neighborhoods developed at densities that can support public transportation, and it preserves two-thirds of the land as parks and open space. Courtesy of WRT/Solomon E.T.C.

Two Growth Scenarios for Coyote Valley

This illustration shows how the principal physical elements of the Valley would relate to each other under the sprawl and Smart Growth scenarios.

Coyote Valley as Sprawl

Land Use
Segregated Uses
Single-use districts (housing, shopping, employment, etc.) that are isolated and unrelated to each other, and provide little or no flexibility for future changes. An automobile is necessary for everyday activities.

Circulation
Automobile Oriented
A network of expressways and distributor streets creates a series of isolated enclaves. Discontinuous local streets and cul-de-sacs funnel traffic onto a few key distributor roads, resulting in larger and busier streets with more congestion and pollution.

Open Space
Isolated Parks with Open Space Fragments
Parks and open space are fragmented and isolated as residual elements between the different land uses.

Hydrology
Engineered Solutions
Flood management is seen as an engineering problem to be solved with large, single-use structures. Creeks are turned into drainage channels. Stormwater runoff is sent off-site as quickly as possible.

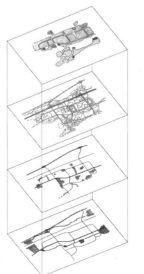
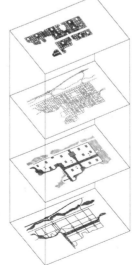

Coyote Valley as a Town

Land Use
Mixed-Use Neighborhoods
A structured and coherent block pattern can accommodate a mixture of land uses in proximity to one another, and provide the flexibility over time to create a compact, pedestrian-friendly, transit-oriented community.

Circulation
Walkable, Bikeable Streets
A hierarchy of interconnected streets and boulevards disperses traffic and creates a network of alternative routes for travel throughout the town. Different modes of travel are safely accommodated, including pedestrians, bicycles, public transit, and the automobile.

Open Space
Network of Parks
Parks and open spaces form an integrated framework that defines neighborhoods and provides for a network of paths linking residential areas to key community destinations. Agricultural lands surround the town, providing an open space buffer and amenity within the context of a working landscape.

Hydrology
Integrated Open Space Solution
Flood management is embraced as natural landscape function and is incorporated into the open space network, maintaining as much of the natural function as possible and integrating improvements as part of a continuous riparian corridor through the town.

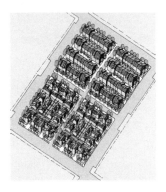

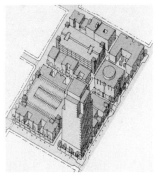

Low-density residential district (10–15 dwelling units per acre). Courtesy of WRT/Solomon E.T.C.

A mixed-use district with ground-level retail beneath residential or commercial space. Active uses line the street level of parking garages to keep streets pedestrian-friendly. Courtesy of WRT/Solomon E.T.C.

Mid- to high-density residential district (32 dwelling units per acre) requires parking in podiums at the base of buildings. Courtesy of WRT/Solomon E.T.C.

Employment-oriented district with a floor-area ratio of 3:1. Courtesy of WRT/Solomon E.T.C.

Key urban design concepts

The plan developed by WRT/Solomon E.T.C. focused on four key objectives applicable to many regional-scale development initiatives:

- **"Harness growth to build a sustainable community"** in a series of distinct mixed-use neighborhoods developed at densities sufficient to support public transportation. The plan establishes a new town center, accessible by transit, that hosts a mix of commercial and civic uses.

- **"Protect the environment and agriculture"** by developing at densities that enable the city to carve out 2,100 acres of parkland, accessible by bike, foot, and transit, and to reserve permanently another 2,300 acres for agriculture. The plan captures some of the high value of development to fund restoration of damaged creek beds and create a natural system to absorb storm water during heavy rains.

◀ A comparison of land use, circulation systems, open space, and hydrology under the original plan and the smart-growth proposal. Courtesy of WRT/Solomon E.T.C. *See color insert, C-7.*

- **"Ensure social equity"** by making 20 percent of the housing affordable to people of low and moderate incomes, providing convenient transit connections between housing and jobs, and setting aside funds to promote workforce readiness.

- **"Promote economic vitality"** by applying higher-density, mixed-use development models that reduce the cost of roads, utilities, and other infrastructure. In contrast to large single-use "campuses," the mixed-use model supports private developers by giving them the flexibility to respond to changing market conditions. Densities that support transit reduce the need for households to own multiple vehicles, which can translate into significant savings for individuals.

Jury Comments

"They took a complex problem, disassembled it, and then reassembled it with great results."

Chongming Island Master Plan, Shanghai, China. Chosen in an invited competition, Skidmore, Owings & Merrill devised a smart-growth framework for reversing sprawl-form development and transforming Chongming Island, north of Shanghai, into an ecologically sensitive community for 800,000 people. Working with Chongming's topography and ecosystems, the plan establishes organic farms that fan out from a network of villages, which themselves are linked to eight urban centers and organized around a system of restored lakes. Courtesy of Skidmore, Owings & Merrill LLP. *See color insert, C-8.*

Chongming Island Master Plan

LOCATION: Shanghai, China

URBAN DESIGNER: Skidmore, Owings & Merrill

CLIENT: Shanghai Planning Bureau

STUDY AREA AND PROGRAM: A regional-scale planning and urban design strategy to guide settlement and growth for 800,000 people while preserving farmlands, establishing wilderness areas, and introducing public transportation on a 750-square-mile island on the Yangtze River in the city of Shanghai.

YEAR OF AWARD: 2005

STATUS: This plan won an invited competition. The Shanghai city government recommended it to the national government, which subsequently approved it.

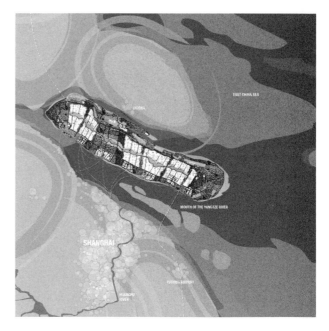

Regional context. Courtesy of Skidmore, Owings & Merrill LLP.

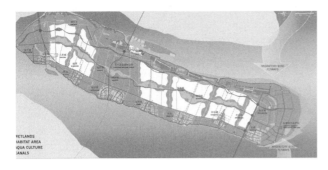

Wilderness areas and ecosystems under the plan. Courtesy of Skidmore, Owings & Merrill LLP.

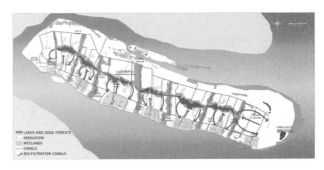

Green systems. Courtesy of Skidmore, Owings & Merrill LLP.

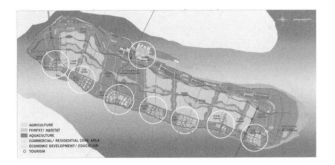

Compact coastal cities. Courtesy of Skidmore, Owings & Merrill LLP.

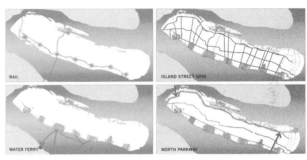

Transportation systems. Courtesy of Skidmore, Owings & Merrill LLP.

Critical issues

The island had been identified by the Shanghai Planning Bureau as a key element in Shanghai's continued growth. Through an international competition, the planning bureau sought to identify a vision for long-term development of the island that would at the same time create "an international environmental showcase through the incorporation of sustainable concepts." Critical issues included:

- Heading off sprawling, single-use development patterns that have appeared elsewhere in Shanghai

- Accommodating tourism

- Minimizing the introduction of overscaled highways and car-oriented development

- Keeping development in balance with nature

- Maintaining existing farming on the island

- Organizing compact, transit-oriented settlement patterns to accommodate growth

Key urban design concepts

The plan's concepts apply to the entire island and to specific development of cities and villages. Both island-wide and in specific communities, the plan focuses on "six key sustainable concepts":

- **Restore the island's wilderness and natural ecosystems,** which form important natural habitats.

- **Maintain farming as a core business,** shifting its focus to organic products and higher-value direct sales to Shanghai restaurants.

- Tie all new communities on the island to a "green," island-wide lake system.
- Create a network of finely scaled roads between communities and avoid creating a network of freeways.
- Organize forty farm villages around the new system of lakes.
- Create eight new cities linked by rail to central Shanghai.

The plan lays out a blueprint for development that will occupy less than 20 percent of the island's land mass.

Jury Comments

"This master plan is remarkable on multiple levels. At the scale of the island, care is taken to preserve the natural attributes and connections to the water, which attracts one to this special place. The spacing between and the scale of the villages and cities are appropriate with their boundaries and edges well defined."

The Arc: A Formal Structure for a Palestinian State

LOCATION: West Bank and Gaza, Palestine
URBAN DESIGNER: Suisman Urban Design
CLIENT: RAND Corporation
STUDY AREA AND PROGRAM: Transportation-infrastructure plan and growth-management model to accommodate significant population growth (to 6.6 million by 2020) and spur economic development
YEAR OF AWARD: 2006
STATUS: This plan was accepted by the client.

Critical issues

A potential Palestinian state needs a plan to guide significant construction to replace crumbling urban-transportation infrastructure—roads, railroad, airport, and seaport. Poor transportation has constrained eco-

nomic development, an issue of growing concern in light of rapid population growth in both Gaza and the West Bank. The Palestinian governing authorities face a variety of pressures to build infrastructure in ways that threaten the historic character of ancient West Bank cities and to replace traditional patterns of compact, walkable—and sustainable—communities with sprawl that follows new highway routes.

Key urban design concepts

This urban design framework demonstrates how growth can reinforce and enrich traditional community character. At the same time, the framework demonstrates how transportation improvements can redefine growth patterns in ways that create a stronger sense of regional character and form. The "arc" from which the plan takes its name is a continuous road-and-rail transportation corridor that would form a new "national Main Street" for Palestinians. The corridor would link direct-

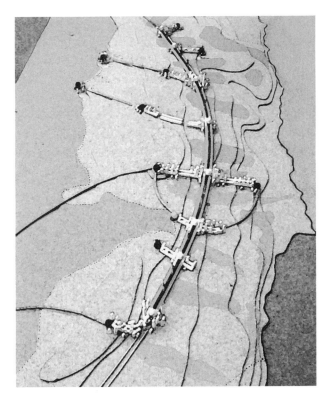

◀ The Arc: A Formal Structure for a Palestinian State, West Bank and Gaza, Palestine. The plan by Suisman Urban Design ties together the major Palestinian communities in Gaza and the West Bank with road and rail connections, demonstrating how new infrastructure and growth can serve as an organizing template while reinforcing traditional community character. The proposed road and rail corridor constitutes a new "national Main Street" that connects directly to the principal streets of each major West Bank community. The plan recommends that these cities employ traditional settlement patterns to accommodate growth in higher-density new development built within walking distance of new rail stations. Courtesy of Suisman Urban Design / RAND Corporation.

◥ A model shows the Arc's route through the West Bank. Cities grow perpendicular to the road and rail corridor. Aerial view of the Arc circa 2005. Courtesy of Suisman Urban Design / RAND Corporation. *See color insert, C-9.*

▶ The plan connects Gaza (left) and the West Bank. Courtesy of Suisman Urban Design / RAND Corporation.

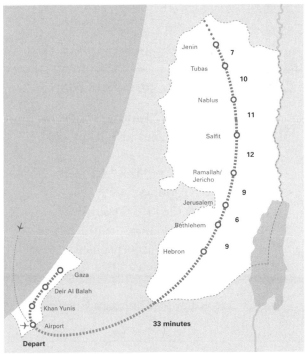

ly to the principal streets of each major West Bank city and proposed new communities, and it would tie the entire West Bank to a new seaport, to seaside tourism development, and to a new national airport in Gaza. The plan would accommodate the majority of growth in higher-density development that lies within walking distance of rail stations in existing cities and new communities alike. To avoid sprawl, it discourages development outside of existing urbanized areas along the corridor.

Jury Comments

"Clear and compelling framework plan for thoughtfully shaping expansion of the newly created Palestinian nation.... The necessity to create public transit to support the huge expansion of population was proposed through the development of a transportation spine, settlement areas[,] and intertwining environmentally sensitive areas, which were conveyed with extraordinary sensitivity.... Visionary plan built on logical approach to infrastructure creating immeasurable hope for a nation."

Chippewa Cree Reservation Plan

LOCATION: Box Elder, Montana

URBAN DESIGNER: Ferdinand S. Johns with Allison Orr

CLIENT: Chippewa Cree Tribal Council

STUDY AREA AND PROGRAM: A fifty-year master plan for the 130,000-acre Rocky Boy's Reservation in northern Montana to accommodate anticipated population growth from 3,000 to roughly 19,000

YEAR OF AWARD: 2006

STATUS: Adopted by the Chippewa Cree Tribal Council

Critical issues

Concerned about preserving extraordinary natural beauty while overcoming decades of extreme poverty and poor social and physical health, the reservation's tribal council asked Johns and Orr to work with the entire Rocky Boy's community to create a plan that encouraged compact growth and preserved the natural environment at the same time that it promoted tourism and other forms of economic development. As in many lower-income communities in the United States, decades of failed promises inclined residents toward skepticism, and they initially ignored the process. Securing participation and widespread community "ownership" of the plan recommendations became a significant issue.

Key urban design concepts

The urban designers built trust and encouraged participation by reaching out to residents, spending long hours listening to their concerns, demonstrating a sensitivity to the community's culture, and using photomontages to help residents visualize each urban design concept. The recommendation to replace the reservation's decentralized "sprawl" with a traditional "higher-density" village approach offers a model for many rural communities, even those that lack the reservation's distinctive environmental, cultural, social, and economic characteristics. Similarly, the design team's patience in engaging the community can serve as a model for processes in other communities. Their work earned them a level of credibility that led to widespread support for—and implementation of—the plan recommendations.

Jury Comments

"The architect thoughtfully integrated nature and culture with ideas of economic, ecologic and social sustainability which are an ongoing issue for any community.... Proposal was respectful of the historical context of the Indian reservation.... This plan worked though a difficult situation because of reticent participation."

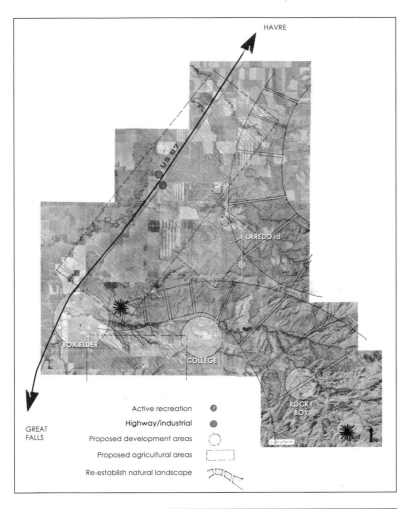

HAVRE

US 87

LAREDO rd

BOX ELDER

COLLEGE

ROCKY
BOY

GREAT
FALLS

Active recreation	⬤
Highway/industrial	⬤
Proposed development areas	
Proposed agricultural areas	
Re-establish natural landscape	

N

◀ Chippewa Cree Reservation Plan, Box Elder, Montana. Ferdinand S. Johns and Allison Orr worked with the Chippewa Cree Tribal Council to create a sustainable plan for the Rocky Boy's Reservation. The plan accommodates rapid growth, preserves "extraordinary natural beauty" and traditional culture, and promotes badly needed economic opportunity by replacing the reservation's decentralized development with traditional higher-density villages that accommodate investment without degrading nature.

Box Elder
Abandon unsightly existing entry to reservation, which routes traffic through school parking area
Create heavily landscaped boulevard and mixed-use village center as new entry from highway
Extend/connect existing street grid to new street grid, heavily modified by natural features
Create community greenway along creekbed, connected to continuous network of green spaces
Infill and rehabilitate to create urbane "village" fabric linked to the greater landscape beyond

All art on this page courtesy of Ferdinand S. Johns, AIA / Allison Orr.

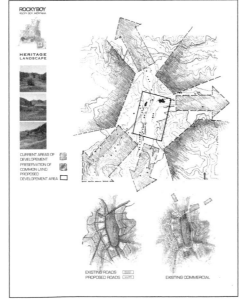

Tribal Center and central green space

Boston's Newest Smart Growth Corridor

LOCATION: Boston, Massachusetts

URBAN DESIGNER: Goody Clancy

CLIENT: The Fairmount/Indigo Line CDC Collaborative

STUDY AREA AND PROGRAM: Four neighborhood community development corporations (CDCs) collaborated to advocate increased transit service for one of the poorest sections of Boston—neighborhoods in which nine out of ten residents are people of color, almost half of the households are carless, and there is no direct bus service to downtown. The CDCs sought to create a vision, framework, and strategy for mixed-use, mixed-income development—including up to 5,000 new houses and more than 200,000 square feet of new commercial space—along a 9.2-mile commuter-rail corridor that runs through some of the Boston region's poorest neighborhoods to the city's core.

YEAR OF AWARD: 2007

STATUS: The four CDCs have received more than $5 million in state funding to pursue projects identified in the plan.

▶ Boston's Newest Smart Growth Corridor. Goody Clancy worked with an alliance of nonprofit community development corporations to create a plan for building more than 5,000 units of affordable housing around new stations along a 9.2-mile commuter-rail corridor that will connect some of the Boston region's poorest neighborhoods to downtown. The vision for a series of higher-density, walkable urban villages has already resulted in plans for more than 1,500 units of affordable housing and helped support revitalization along nearby neighborhood Main Streets. Courtesy of Goody Clancy.

Critical issues

More than 60 percent of the national demand for transit-oriented housing—located within a reasonable walking distance of a transit station—is also demand for affordable housing. Three factors have driven this demand in Boston:

- A steep increase in housing costs over the last decade has forced moderate-income families to move further from the core in search of affordable housing;

- Commuting in metropolitan Boston has grown increasingly difficult—during the 1990s alone, hours spent commuting rose more than 50 percent as the region ran out of land and funds to increase highway capacity; and

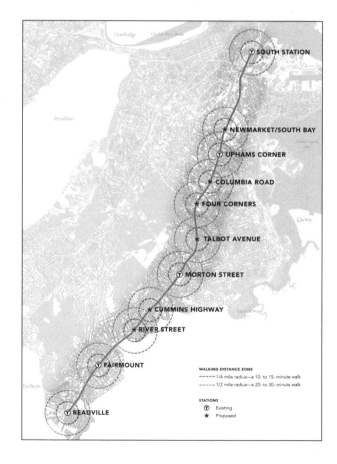

• The cost of commuting by automobile, already high before the run-up in gasoline prices began in 2006, has become prohibitive to many moderate-income households. The Transit Oriented Development Institute reports that households with access to transit spend significantly less on transportation—50 percent less, for example, in a study conducted in Minneapolis and St. Paul, Minnesota.

These CDCs sought to make affordable housing creation a critical ingredient in planning for new transit. They also wanted a strategy to help make their case to foundations and public agencies for funding and other assistance in acquiring sites and laying the groundwork for affordable housing near possible new stations.

Key urban design concepts

The plan illustrates how transit-oriented development can produce higher-density walkable urban villages, not just high-end development. It recommends ways to capture the significant new value created by transit and use some of it to support mixed-income housing and other community benefits. The urban designers helped the CDCs draw largely lower-income residents into the planning process, generate interest in the planning process among elected officials, and build broad support for the plan.

Jury Comments

"There was an impressive collaboration between the CDCs and disadvantaged neighborhoods to affect regional systems and then laying out a vision of how the condition of these stations would affect the neighborhoods.... It focused on access to employment and public services to low-income communities through transit, giving them the ability to move around the city.... Powerful grassroots vision to improve people's lives.... It lays the groundwork for a lot of future events to happen on a solid infrastructure."

Potential development at Readville. Courtesy of Goody Clancy.

Potential development at Morton Street. Courtesy of Goody Clancy.

Potential development at Upham's Corner. Courtesy of Goody Clancy. *See color insert, C-10.*

How the Projects Illustrate the Principles

1. **Build community in an increasingly diverse society.** The concept of harnessing growth and change to foster an enhanced sense of community for existing neighborhoods and encourage its development in new neighborhoods lies at the heart of all these case studies. Each project sets the achievement of vibrant, diverse neighborhoods as an important goal—and a critical element in implementing larger smart-growth objectives. The Charlottesville and Coyote Valley plans stress that new neighborhoods should grow around a system of public streets, squares, and parks, and both plans explicitly label research parks, gated communities, and similar privatized environments as unhealthy frameworks for growth. The Chippewa Cree Reservation Plan and Boston Smart Growth Corridor stress the importance of community in very different contexts, asserting that development enriches and is enriched by shared public streets and spaces as opposed to sprawl (on a Montana reservation) or isolated developments (in Boston neighborhoods).

   Most of the case studies address social equity directly. The South Florida and Charlottesville cases note that existing development patterns have magnified economic and social fragmentation. The Coyote Valley plan makes an explicit argument for creation of a series of mixed-income neighborhood. The Chippewa Cree Reservation Plan approaches this issue from a different angle, relying on growth to broaden economic opportunity. Launched expressly to promote social equity, Boston's Newest Smart Growth Corridor focuses on ways to avoid past patterns of gentrification by using the economic value of new rail access to support affordable housing, better access to jobs, and other community-wide benefits. All of the case studies focus in various ways on the importance of connections to a larger community and among communities created by new growth. The Confluence, South Florida, and Coyote Valley plans emphasize the importance of better access to new and existing park systems that celebrate each region's natural context. Boston's Newest Smart Growth Corridor underlines the importance of designing new rail stations in ways that not only make them highly accessible to the community but also create new connections in areas long divided by the rail right of way.

2. **Advance environmental sustainability.** The South Florida projects, the Arc, Chongming Island, and The Confluence make clear that the natural environment represents a common realm for which the entire community serves as stewards. In varying ways, all of these plans assert that compact development—in tandem with enhancing walkability and providing alternatives to the automobile—plays an essential role in building more sustainable patterns of living. The plans all concern themselves with moving toward a more sustainable equilibrium under which air and water quality, carbon footprints, and other measures of sustainability actually improve after years of decline. The South Florida plan lays out a strategy for restoring the balance between the built and natural environments. The plan for Coyote Valley outlines ways to design new development to get that balance right from the start. The Arc, Chippewa Cree, and Coyote Valley plans all note, in very different contexts, the connections between preserving the natural environment and cultural heritage. The Chongming Island plan sets environmental equilibrium as an explicit goal in the creation of an entire community from scratch.

3. **Expand individual choices.** All nine plans advocate concentrated development that requires increased densities, and all rely heavily on mixing uses. The Albemarle Country, Arc, Coyote Creek, Chippewa

Cree, and Boston plans explicitly connect higher densities and mixed-use development to creating more vibrant neighborhoods and supporting expanded transportation choice. To a degree that makes clear the paramount importance of providing alternatives to the automobile, all nine plans—despite very different settings—make a strong case for public transportation and for provision of varied transportation choices. Even on the rural Rocky Boy's Reservation in Montana, providing bus and other transportation choices plays a central role in achieving plan goals.

4. **Enhance personal health.** The case studies suggest the understanding that has emerged in recent years of the importance of walking as a key to public health. (Awareness of the responsibility to promote improved public health, however, has only begun to shape many urban design plans.) All but The Confluence make clear that fostering walkability must begin at a regional level, and all reflect a growing recognition that air and water pollution represent major causes of public health problems and are best addressed at a regional level. The Confluence explicitly treats the issue at the regional level, with its prescription for viewing, managing, and protecting cultural, historical, and environmental resources and for public health as a unified network.

5. **Make places for people.** All nine case studies advocate regional patterns designed to create communities that are more walkable, support more vibrant town centers and traditional Main Streets, and provide for more direct human contact with nature. Interestingly, all of them—whether addressing the plains of Palestine or the hills of Montana—recommend higher densities and more compact development as tools for achieving these goals. To a degree that may seem counterintuitive in plans that cover large areas, all nine plans place strong emphasis on the importance of reinforcing or restoring local identity and character—qualities that enrich the human experience of built places.

Rediscovering Downtown and Main Street

Renewed interest in city living and increased investment in urban cores have galvanized the dramatic revival of many downtowns and Main Streets throughout the United States. As cities rebounded during the late 1990s, elected officials, community leaders, and developers called for bold initiatives that conveyed a sense of renewed confidence in downtowns and Main Streets. Rather than working merely to save the urban fabric of downtown, urban designers expanded their ambitions and looked for new ways to celebrate cities.

Daniel H. Burnham's City Beautiful vision—and his legendary exhortation to "make no little plans"—inspired a new wave of city building sponsored by municipalities, business improvement districts, developers, business- and property-owner associations, foundations, and other groups with a stake in the future of their downtowns. Study areas might range from a single key block targeted for redevelopment to an area of ten or twelve downtown blocks or even an entire commercial corridor like Central Avenue in Albany, New York, that extends

for miles and serves as the Main Street for multiple neighborhoods. Larger projects usually involve plans to attract a wide range of retail, housing, institutions, and new businesses to older commercial areas.

Large revitalization programs for Main Streets often raise significant questions about historic preservation. In many older communities, such as the predominantly African American neighborhoods along New Orleans' historic Oretha Castle Hailey Boulevard, a revitalized Main Street plays a critical role in attracting people back to nearby residential areas. Urban designers also prepare plans and designs to manage growth in resurgent downtowns and for new mixed-use, walkable districts—projects frequently sponsored by the private sector—that resemble traditional Main Streets and form the heart of new communities such as Celebration or Seaside, in Florida.

In an era of ambitious urban redevelopment, urban designers who work on plans for downtowns and Main Streets increasingly subscribe to Burnham's bold vision of big plans that can "stir men's blood." Likewise, investors and developers often prefer to invest time and resources in large-scale projects that can capture the attention of a busy mayor or city manager. Moreover, the long hours that mayors and their senior staffs must spend responding to the political and other issues raised by redevelopment projects of any size also favor large-scale endeavors. Finally, with urban real estate values rising at a pace not seen since the 1920s, both private and public decision makers favor projects that can achieve significant economic value and lasting civic benefit.

Roots

The sweep of the current urban rebound, and attendant economic and social transformations, draws some of its drama by contrast with the general loss of faith in downtowns that followed World War II. An enormous gap in both incomes and real estate values opened in the decades following the war, dividing cities and suburbs. This gap, along with a mutually reinforcing exodus of Main Street retail to the suburbs, led to a precipitous decline among U.S. downtowns. It also fueled a wide dismissal of traditional urban forms. For example, no one questioned Ed Logue's 1960 urban renewal plan for Boston. The director of the Boston Redevelopment Authority proposed wiping away dense acres of nineteenth-century townhouses that the city had deemed blighted and replacing them with modern towers in a parklike setting (shades of Le Corbusier). The Charles

---

To create positive change in a downtown is immensely complex.... It requires creating vision, motivating the property owners, collaborating with community groups, getting governmental support, securing funding, jumping through regulatory hoops, working with the press, overseeing design.... Leadership is required every step of the way, and in every step a different leader may emerge.

Martha Lampkin Welborne, FAIA, managing director, Grand Avenue Committee, Inc., Los Angeles

---

West 25th Street, Cleveland. Redevelopment of a near-downtown public housing site helps strengthen a neighborhood Main Street. Courtesy of Goody Clancy.

River Park project essentially obliterated the otherwise healthy West End, and this infamous miscalculation ultimately became the poster child for urban renewal's failures in the United States. (Logue also achieved some remarkable successes, blocking an urban renewal plan that would have leveled another historic neighborhood, the South End, and playing midwife to some of the city's most notable modernist architecture and urban design, including the striking—and still controversial—Boston City Hall.)

In the 1950s and 1960s, the urban renewal mindset—and associated dismissal of traditional urban form—swept cities around the nation. In 1956 a front-page article in Cleveland's *Plain Dealer* praised the Cuyahoga Metropolitan Housing Authority for demolishing a nineteenth-century working-class neighborhood on the city's West Side to make room for Riverview, a barrackslike public housing project, that the newspaper suggested residents would value for its "institutional character."

Against this tide, a small group of urbanists, including Jane Jacobs, predicated the stultifying ramifications of urban renewal and its threat to urban life. Many cities ultimately abandoned urban renewal thinking and sought both to reurbanize downtowns and reimagine failed public housing—itself often built along the "towers in a park" model developed by the modernists. In 1996, for example, the Cuyahoga Metropolitan Housing Authority authorized demolition of most of the Riverview project under the federal HOPE VI program, an initiative intended to revive troubled public housing developments by rebuilding them as mixed-income communities using traditional street patterns and architectural forms. Hunter Morrison, director of the Cleveland City Planning Commission from 1981 to 2003, insisted that "Riverview will be reborn as an urban neighborhood whose form and character celebrate urban community." Morrison's faith in the city's downtown and Main Streets and his advocacy of traditional urban form laid the groundwork for a revival of the city's downtown and urban neighborhoods that began in the 1990s.

Jane Jacobs and academics and critics helped inspire a renewed respect for traditional urban character among many urban designers. Later, the remarkable resurgence of urban economies in the 1990s motivated a broader group of city shapers, from public officials to community activists to newspapers to business leaders, to commit to rebuilding downtown cores as the lively, urbane, mixed-use centers they had once been. Many motives fed this revived commitment to downtowns, but rising real estate values certainly explained much of the new enthusiasm. In a March 2008 article in the *Atlantic Monthly*, Chris Leinberger—director of the graduate Real Estate Development Program at the University of Michigan—noted that while "[t]wenty years ago, urban housing was a bargain in most cities…, today, it carries an enormous premium," more than 200 percent in some regions.

Approaches Today

A 2004 conference organized jointly by the American Institute of Architect's (AIA) Regional and Urban Design Committee (RUDC) and the New York chapter of the AIA examined proposals for rebuilding Lower Manhattan. Although the seven principles that emerged from the New York/New Visions conference were intended to guide rebuilding after the attacks of September 11, 2001, they include key goals that urban designers have advocated for downtowns and Main Streets across the United States.

1. **Encourage a mixed-use future for Lower Manhattan.** Intensify and encourage increased diversity of programmatic uses. Capitalize on the cultural, historic, and geographic assets of the district as generators of growth. Develop a true 24-hour community within a pedestrian realm. Promote complementary and productive adjacencies to improve security and develop the regional tax base.

2. **Become a transportation crossroads for the city and region.** Focus on improving accessibility by mass transit; it is the single most important investment in the future health of Lower Manhattan. Magnify public and economic benefits of investment by linking existing and new transportation centers and integrating them with pedestrian flows and open space.

3. **Enhance the reciprocal relationship between Lower Manhattan and the region.** Implement a balanced growth strategy that reflects the reciprocal relationship of Lower Manhattan and the region. Coordinate decisions about the restructuring of the World Trade Center site with development in the rest of Manhattan, the other city boroughs, and key communities in Long Island, Westchester County, and New Jersey.

4. **Become a center for design excellence and sustainability.** Demand design excellence with an emphasis on sustainability to create economic and social value. Create the highest-quality urban patterns and architecture. Require decreased life-cycle costs and energy use. Promote long-term flexibility.

The conference report emphasized the importance of community-based planning at each stage in Lower Manhattan's recovery and noted that redevelopment should respond to the needs and aspirations of "a wide variety of stakeholders."

Case Studies

While the focus of individual projects differs, all of these case studies reflect ways in which cities are reinventing their most public districts to take advantage of resurgent investment in urban neighborhoods and to translate it into enhanced vitality. They share the scope and ambition of an earlier era's urban renewal initiatives but temper them with far greater concern for human scale. Clearly informed by contemporary social and environmental values, they nevertheless draw inspiration from a sense of civic pride and celebration of urban life that underlay the City Beautiful movement. All of these projects evince a new faith in urban living and confidence in the future of U.S. cities.

Jamaica Market, Queens, New York. James McCullar & Associates' design turns a farmers' market into a lively "town square" that mixes food, music, street fairs, and other attractions designed to attract people of different ages, races, and cultural backgrounds, restoring a sense of community as much as it spurs reinvestment. Courtesy of James McCullar & Associates.

Jamaica Market

LOCATION: Queens, New York

URBAN DESIGNER: James McCullar & Associates

CLIENT: Greater Jamaica Development Corporation

STUDY AREA AND PROGRAM: A 26,000-square-foot building that accommodates a farmers' market, food court, and community spaces as part of a larger redevelopment program for downtown Jamaica, Queens

YEAR OF AWARD: 1998

STATUS: Construction completed in 1992

Critical issues

This increasingly diverse urban community lacked public spaces that offered the kind of amenities and attractions that would draw people of different ages, races, and backgrounds together. Years of disinvestment and increasing strip-retail competition had robbed a once-bustling urban Main Street of its vitality, and the Jamaica

By offering prepared foods and dining options in addition to produce, the market draws area residents, shoppers, and people who work in the neighborhood. Courtesy of James McCullar & Associates.

Market was intended to spark revitalization in a manner that would restore a sense of community as much as it spurred reinvestment.

Key urban design concepts

The market was designed to provide a retail center for fresh and prepared foods within a soaring glass space, with a dining area for a growing daytime population of office workers and shoppers from the surrounding commercial district. The design lays claim to the space's importance as a new social and civic landmark. By incorporating performance and community meeting spaces, the market can be programmed with activities that draw the diverse community together. By the time of the award submission, the market had hosted musical events with a Caribbean-American flavor, jazz festivals, street fairs, a 5K run, and a gospel series. Through its planning, design, and programming, the market has helped transform Jamaica's revitalizing commercial core into a twenty-first-century Main Street that serves a far more diverse population than earlier Main Streets designed for much more homogeneous communities. Within five years of its opening, "the market [had taken its place as]…an unofficial town center which it remains today."

Jury Comments

"Responding to the social act of place making, this market is a community force and a community resource … a beautifully executed civic space. The Jamaica Market proves that such a huge urban design success must rely on a marriage of design, policy, and an involved community."

State Street Renovation Project

LOCATION: Chicago, Illinois

URBAN DESIGNER: Skidmore, Owings & Merrill

CLIENT: City of Chicago, Department of Transportation, Chicago Department of Planning and Development, Greater State Street Council, and the State Street Commission

STUDY AREA AND PROGRAM: Reconstruction of State Street to reintroduce traffic and create a new pedestrian realm for nine blocks within the downtown Loop

YEAR OF AWARD: 1998

STATUS: Construction completed in 1996

Critical issues

"Historically the focal point of the city's retail…in 1979 the street was transformed into a pedestrian mall in order to compete with suburban shopping centers. However…the absence of auto traffic…isolated State Street…from an otherwise vibrant and expanding downtown district." In place of an identity once based

▲ State Street Renovation Project. Skidmore, Owings & Merrill's plan bolsters the prominence of Chicago's premier downtown retail street by using the reintroducton of vehicular traffic, removed in the late 1970s, as an opportunity to create a pedestrian-friendly street that celebrates the city's history and its contemporary vitality. The plan melds historic fixtures, such as lighting and subway kiosks, with innovative elements, such as a culture walk that marks the arrival on the street of major educational and cultural institutions. Photo by James Steinkamp, courtesy of Skidmore, Owings & Merrill LLP. *See color insert, C-11.*

▶ Historic subway entrance design. Photo by James Steinkamp, courtesy of Skidmore, Owings & Merrill LLP.

◀ Pedestrian-friendly elements include broad, landscaped tree wells and improved sidewalks. Photo by James Steinkamp, courtesy of Skidmore, Owings & Merrill LLP.

solely on the presence of stores, in particular the flagship Marshall Field & Company department store, this urban design initiative builds a broader identity for the street, based on the presence of educational institutions and entertainment uses in addition to retail.

Key urban design concepts

The urban design plan included five key elements that celebrate State Street's emerging role in the life of the Loop:

- **Restoration of historic sidewalk widths,** which concentrated pedestrians closer to stores and other activities and created "a greater sense of movement and energy on the street."

- **New paving** that visually integrated State Street back into the Loop.

- **Installation of historically inspired and human-scaled lighting and subway kiosks,** demonstrating respect for the street's historic architecture and restoring a sense of dignity and importance.

- **Creation of a "culture walk"** that interprets and honors the street's rich past and historic architecture.

- **Reinvigoration of a program for managing and marketing State Street** as a notable destination that draws a cross section of Chicagoans and visitors downtown for a wide range of reasons.

Jury Comments

"SOM's plan weaves State Street back into a resurgent downtown, returning it to its place as an economically and architecturally important part of Chicago's downtown Loop."

42nd Street Now!

LOCATION: New York, New York
URBAN DESIGNER: Robert A.M. Stern
CLIENT: 42nd Street Development Corporation (a partnership of city and state agencies)
STUDY AREA AND PROGRAM: Interim urban design strategy and guidelines, including streetscape, signage, and facades for both sides of 42nd Street between Seventh and Eighth avenues, the heart of Times Square
YEAR OF AWARD: 1998
STATUS: The guidelines were accepted in 1993 and over the subsequent four years helped inspire revitalization of the block, including rehabilitation of historic theaters and a wide variety of new businesses

---

Critical issues

In the late 1980s and early 1990s, much of Times Square showed tangible signs of decline: theaters in need of restoration, vacant storefronts and low-quality stores, and a paucity of restaurants and other businesses that supported the theater industry. Years of disinvestment had dimmed the visual vitality essential to the area's unique identity and to attracting people to the Theater District. (Ironically, as the design phase of the plan ended, Disney Corporation announced plans to develop a major new theater on 42nd Street, pointing the way toward resurgence.)

Key urban design concepts

The urban design team developed design guidelines to ensure that the cumulative impact of multiple efforts to improve buildings and sidewalks would reenergize the block in ways that evoked Times Square's past but also recognized the need to appeal to contemporary

42nd Street Now! New York City. Responding to years of disinvestment that had dimmed Broadway's appeal, Robert A.M. Stern's urban design strategy introduced a palette of energetic lighting, public art, signage, and related elements "to override its crime-ridden and pornographic nature and return it to its historic role as a center for first-class entertainment." Copyright 1997 Peter Aaron/Esto.

▲ Existing conditions in 1991. Copyright 1991 Robert A.M. Stern Architects.

▶ A view of 42nd Street under the plan guidelines. Copyright 1991 Robert A.M. Stern Architects.

"audiences." The guidelines laid out six principles for individual actors, among them building owners, retail tenants, theater owners, the city, and others:

- **Layering.** "[E]ncouraging the juxtaposition of the old and the new, the high-brow with the low-brow, the low-rise with the high-rise." This principle applies particularly to signage and intermixes retail signs, storefronts, and rooftop displays.

- **Unplanning.** "[P]rohibiting any uniform or coordinated system among adjacent storefronts and signage," in part to discourage "simplistic 'theming' of 42nd Street."

- **Contradiction and surprise.** "[W]e envision a situation where small, local entrepreneurs co-exist with national retail chains" to foster an environment in which businesses "champion individual expression" and maintain "a continued diversity of light levels, types of signage and materials."

- **Pedestrian experience.** Encouraging frequent entrances, visibility into stores, signs that are visible from a distance and attractive to passersby, nighttime illumination to promote personal safety, and similar design elements to provide "a rich pedestrian experience" from many perspectives.

- **Visual anchors.** Locating a series of elements that "draw people towards specific areas...anything from a large illuminated sign to an all-night diner." These anchors are "essentially democratic" and "draw people irrespective of their social and economic backgrounds...from surrounding neighborhoods."

- **Aesthetics as attractions.** "[D]esigns that capitalize on the entertainment value of shopping and eating, making tourism a governing factor in the placement of establishments and signage."

Harmonie Park/Madison Avenue Development Project

LOCATION: Detroit, Michigan

URBAN DESIGNER: Schervish, Vogel, Merz

CLIENT: Detroit Renaissance Foundation; SVM Development Corporation

STUDY AREA AND PROGRAM: The Harmonie Park/Madison Avenue district in downtown Detroit maintains much of its historic character and includes a strong arts community. This project focused on transforming the area into a lively, mixed-use center for entertainment and the arts that connects Greektown—an adjacent, successful downtown entertainment district—to the reviving theater district. The redevelopment program included adaptive reuse of nine historic buildings and new construction to create an active mix of shopping, restaurants, lofts, a hotel, and office space together with new public spaces. When the city's continuing economic weakness blocked the plan's implementation by Detroit Renaissance, the architects themselves undertook the redevelopment over a ten-year period.

YEAR OF AWARD: 2000

STATUS: Construction completed and all buildings 100 percent leased

Critical issues

Few U.S. cities were laid as low by the decline of industrial employment and "white flight" as was Detroit. The city's loss of half of its population between 1950 and 2000 is well documented, but the economic and urbanistic toll the decline took is less widely understood. By 1990, total assessed property value within the city had dropped below one-quarter of its 1950 level (measured in constant dollars), and more than half of downtown office space was vacant. This initiative took on the challenge of reversing decline in a near-downtown neighborhood by bringing "an active, dynamic pedestrian environment" back to an abandoned and largely vacant area. In particular, three daunting challenges posed obstacles:

Harmonie Park /Madison Avenue, Detroit, Michigan. Schervish, Vogel, Merz became developers themselves when initial revitalization efforts foundered in this historic section of downtown Detroit. Copyright 2000 Schervish, Vogel, Merz, P.C.

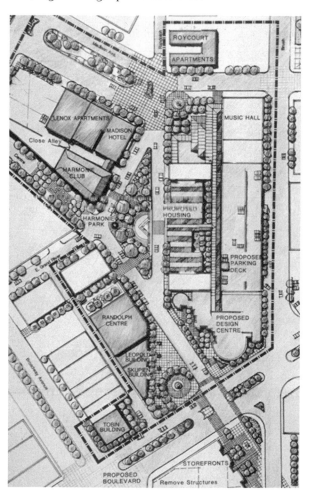

Site plan. Copyright 1985 Schervish, Vogel, Merz, P.C.

Three mutually reinforcing elements undergird the plan: a focus on restaurants and entertainment to bring life back to the area's streets; creation of lofts to attract urban pioneers (drawn in part by resurgent street life); and an emphasis on preservation to showcase the district's distinctive character and add historic tax credits to the financing mix. Copyright 1995 Schervish, Vogel, Merz, P.C.

- In an area where passersby were essential for retail success, sidewalks were largely empty.

- Although attracting people to live in the area was critical to successful redevelopment, vacant and demolished buildings gave the area a desolate, even menacing feeling.

- Despite Harmonie Park's evocative history, much of its fabric had been lost.

Key urban design concepts

The plan addressed revitalization from several perspectives, each of which reinforced the ability to pursue others. To restore street life—and make visiting the district and patronizing its businesses inviting—the plan incorporated a mix of stores, restaurants, bars, and entertainment. Many of these uses benefited from the reemergence of a downtown entertainment scene in nearby Greektown, which drew people to the area at night. Wherever possible, lofts and other upper-floor uses were included to take advantage of the appeal of new restaurants and bars. The plan treated the remaining intact historic buildings as neighborhood landmarks, which functioned as a critical tool in reestablishing the area's appeal. Of particular importance, the plan focused on rehabilitating a suite of historic theaters—one of which became the Detroit Opera House—to draw large numbers of new visitors to the area and burnish its cachet as a place to play, shop, and live. The urban design team won a historic district designation for the area, which unlocked historic tax credits. The credits proved a valuable supplement to an Urban Development Action Grant (federal funding for urban revitalization) and other financing that helped underwrite the ten-year rehabilitation and rebuilding program.

Jury Comments

"A small but strategic seed of urban revival in downtown Detroit."

Pennsylvania Convention Center

LOCATION: Philadelphia, Pennsylvania
URBAN DESIGNER: Thompson, Ventulett, Stainback & Associates
CLIENT: Pennsylvania Convention Center Authority
STUDY AREA AND PROGRAM: New downtown convention center that combines a new exhibition hall and rehabilitation of historic Reading Terminal train shed to create a facility with more than 1,200,000 square feet within two blocks of City Hall, the center of downtown
YEAR OF AWARD: 2000
STATUS: Construction completed

Critical issues

"The primary goal was to successfully place this 1.2 million square foot program into the fabric of the historic city." Like many older cities, Philadelphia has faced significant challenges in adapting a historic downtown to economic roles never envisioned by its builders. A need to protect the integrity and character of historic fabric complicates the challenge.

The easiest and most common solution to this problem simply sets a convention center—or other large facility like a sports stadium or museum—outside of the historic core. Cities that make this choice, however, lose hundreds of thousands of visitors whose patronage could support restaurants and other businesses that make downtown a more inviting place to live, work, and shop. Unless transit access to hotels and cultural attractions (often downtown) is easy, such facilities become automobile-dependent generators of traffic congestion.

Choosing to build such a large facility downtown poses its own challenges, particularly in a historic city like Philadelphia: surrounding streets must remain pedestrian-

The plan kept the historic Reading Terminal Market open during construction of the convention center in light of its "fragile economic viability." Photo courtesy of Brian Gassel/TVS.

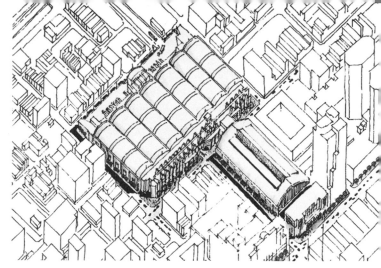

friendly in order to tie the facility in to its surroundings; massing and scale must fit the context; and a facility must be able to accommodate cars and meet other access requirements without overwhelming local streets.

A long period of disinvestment in the blocks east of Philadelphia City Hall and slowing sales in the nearby Gallery East shopping mall prompted a conscious decision to use the convention center as a spur to economic development. The city hoped to extend revitalization from other parts of downtown into this area without repeating the mistakes of earlier urban renewal efforts: wholesale demolition of large areas followed by reconstruction that ignored the city's historic, walkable character.

Key urban design concepts

In contrast to earlier projects that focused on replacing sections of downtown Philadelphia, this massive set of buildings works to reinforce and enrich the traditional downtown. The convention center covers six city blocks, including the historic Reading Terminal, but it has maintained the existing street network by connecting its upper levels on bridges over streets and creating pedestrian-friendly facades at ground level. Despite its

▲▲ Pennsylvania Convention Center, Philadelphia. Thompson, Ventulett, Stainback & Associates rethink the conventional big-box convention center plopped at the edge of an historic city. Their design configures the building as a series of connected structures that fill six central downtown blocks; incorporates the historic Reading Terminal Market, a popular Center City destination; and lines the convention facility's street level with shops, restaurants, and other active uses that encourage more vitality in a faded area of downtown. Courtesy of TVS (Thompson, Ventulett, Stainback & Associates).

▲ Facade materials and design elements echo adjacent historic buildings. Photo courtesy of Brian Gassel/TVS.

vast scale, the structure reflects a careful response to varying conditions on different sides by including shops that face the adjacent Chinatown neighborhood, creating lively tree-lined sidewalks, and incorporating historic architectural elements. The center ties directly to high-speed commuter rail and transit service that offer connections to Amtrak and the airport.

Jury Comments

"An exemplary insertion of a very large convention center into the urban fabric of a challenged redevelopment area."

▼ Pennsylvania Station Redevelopment Project, New York City. The Skidmore, Owings & Merrill design plan for the Farley Post Office Building—a dignified, neoclassical McKim, Mead and White design built to complement the original Pennsylvania Station, which was also the firm's work—responds to a widespread yearning to recapture the urban qualities lost during the urban renewal era and subsequent years of disinvestment. Courtesy of Skidmore, Owings & Merrill LLP.

Pennsylvania Station Redevelopment Project

LOCATION: New York, New York
URBAN DESIGNER: Skidmore, Owings & Merrill
CLIENT: Pennsylvania Station Redevelopment Corporation, United States Postal Service
STUDY AREA AND PROGRAM: Redevelopment of the neoclassical Farley Post Office Building— designed by McKim, Mead and White as a complement to the firm's Pennsylvania Station, which it faced across Eighth Avenue—provides a grand terminal to serve the current 550,000 daily passengers and accommodate new regional service.
YEAR OF AWARD: 2000
STATUS: The plan has been approved and is proceeding through detailed development planning.

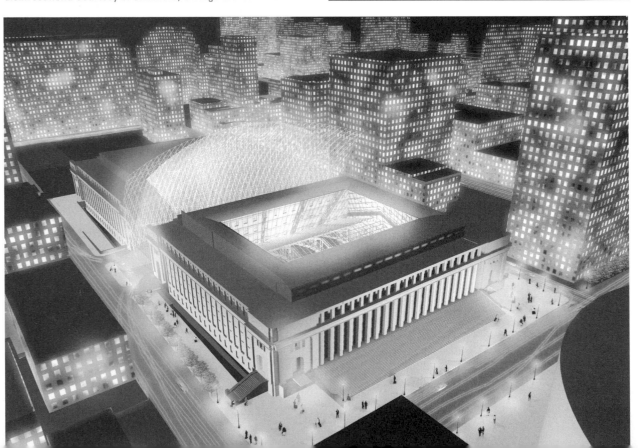

A glass-and-steel ceiling turns a courtyard into a dramatic new train hall. Courtesy of Skidmore, Owings & Merrill LLP.

The firm grafts a glass superstructure onto the building to define a striking arrival area, in the process creating a memorable new transit-oriented entry to New York. Courtesy of Skidmore, Owings & Merrill LLP. *See color insert, C-12.*

A section through the station. The current facility is located underneath Madison Square Garden, to the right. Courtesy of Skidmore, Owings & Merrill LLP.

Critical issues

The new Penn Station is intended to recreate the grand gateway to New York City that the original Beaux-Arts terminal building provided before its demolition in 1963. The initiative would move the current station one block to the west, relocate Madison Square Garden (now directly atop the current station) to a new structure on the Farley parcel, and allow several million square feet of new commercial construction on the current Madison Square Garden parcel. The existing underground train station would continue to serve some commuter rail lines. A goal of the plan is to accelerate revitalization in nearby areas now dominated by declining light industry.

Key urban design concepts

The plan takes full advantage of the vast spaces in the Farley building to provide New York with a railroad gateway that conveys the city's vitality and pride. The station design infuses the Neoclassical building with contemporary information, circulation, and wayfinding systems, and it creates two grand public spaces with contemporary trussed-glass roofs—an entry ticketing area and a train hall. The initiative symbolically acknowledges New York City's renewed confidence and aspiration after years of economic stagnation and the city's recognition that its future will depend heavily on improving the quality of transit service and connections.

Jury Comments

"A celebration of rail transit and a reaffirmation of the central role that it has played in the American metropolis."

The Downtown Racine Development Plan

LOCATION: Racine, Wisconsin

URBAN DESIGNER: Crandall Arambula PC

CLIENT: Downtown Racine Corporation

STUDY AREA AND PROGRAM: Revitalization strategy that identified a series of development opportunities together with new public spaces and approaches to downtown parking

YEAR OF AWARD: 2001

STATUS: Adopted by the Racine Common Council

Critical issues

Following years of disinvestment and spreading retail and office vacancies, the city and private sector jointly created the Downtown Racine Corporation to undertake an urban renewal–scale revitalization that would maintain sensitivity to the downtown's historic character and shoreline. The urban design plan faced many of the thorny challenges commonly found in older downtowns. Multiple earlier attempts to recycle unused department store buildings had failed. Surface parking lots and poorly designed garages visibly undermined the area's historic character. Because industrial uses had traditionally lined the lake frontage—a situation common to most older industrial cities on a river or lake—Racine lacked strong pedestrian and visual connections from downtown to the lake or to the Root River. While downtown had begun to add restaurants and other amenities that would support lofts and other urban housing, a proposal for new housing took the form of a lakefront enclave with minimal connection to the downtown around it. Perhaps most troubling, the community had largely lost confidence

Downtown Racine Development Plan, Racine, Wisconsin. Crandall Arambula's strategy for reversing the flight of stores and offices from downtown Racine focused on raising the area's amenity level. The plan links downtown to the nearby lakefront with a new boulevard and park (above, looking toward Lake Michigan), interpolates a new generation of housing among historic buildings, and replaces acres of surface lots with parking structures hidden behind retail and housing that face pedestrian-friendly streets. Courtesy of Crandall Arambula. *See color insert, C-13.*

The plan transformed three blocks of surface parking lots in the heart of downtown Racine. Courtesy of Crandall Arambula.

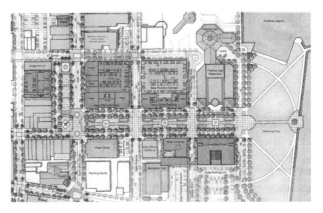

A landscaped boulevard flanked by new housing terminates in a lakefront park. Courtesy of Crandall Arambula.

in the possibility of reviving downtown, even though it continued to see downtown vitality as important to quality of life across the community.

Key urban design concepts

The centerpiece of the plan is a grand boulevard and lakefront park, built on former surface parking lots, that serve as the focus for a series of new mixed-use developments. The plan relocated the discordant parking facilities—including a large lakefront lot—into central structures wrapped with offices and housing and facing the park and the lakefront beyond. A series of target redevelopment initiatives at key locations along the new boulevard create connections to the Root River and adjacent neighborhoods. To confront widespread skepticism about downtown's future, build political support, and gain more detailed understanding of citizen perspectives, the urban design team undertook a community-wide visioning program that ultimately involved more than three thousand people and included a series of "listening sessions" intended to update residents on the plan's progress.

Jury Comments

"Prior to the plan, people said, 'why not just bulldoze downtown and be done with it?' But now the local government, businesses, and the citizens enthusiastically endorse it.... A very thoughtful planning process has achieved a clear, flexible, and realistic vision and has generated a high level of public confidence that will allow the plan to overcome any difficulties in the implementation. The plan incorporates the lake and river to reflect their historic and visual worth, as well as their potential for public use. Integrating residential uses into Racine's historic core will bring an important and much needed dimension back the area.... Community residents and business leaders rolled up their sleeves and worked hard to bring Racine back from the brink."

Santa Monica Boulevard Master Plan

Location: West Hollywood, California

Urban designer: Zimmer Gunsul Frasca (ZGF) Partnership and Patricia Smith ASLA, AICP, in partnership with the city's planning division urban design staff

Client: City of West Hollywood

Study area and program: Transform a 2.7-mile stretch of Santa Monica Boulevard—a major thoroughfare that connects Hollywood to West Hollywood, Beverly Hills, Santa Monica, and the Pacific Ocean—into a pedestrian-friendly boulevard that provides community-oriented public spaces while continuing to carry heavy vehicular traffic

Year of award: 2001

Status: Plan adopted by the city; portions of the boulevard have been rebuilt.

Critical issues

Streets, the urban design team noted in its award submission, "are public environments that reflect social values." This assertion reflects a new attitude toward major streets: communities across the United States have begun to question the balance they strike between serving automobiles and pedestrians. "West Hollywood is a relatively small city with limited open spaces," the team explained. "Residents and visitors depend on the Boulevard for the social, recreational and cultural activities associated with daily life, and major civic events."

As in many communities, residents and businesses worried that enhancing the boulevard's walkability might increase traffic congestion, diminish retail sales, or erode property values. The city addressed these concerns through thorough community outreach that included a forty-two-person steering committee and that

Santa Monica Boulevard Development Plan, Santa Monica, California. Zimmer Gunsul Frasca Partnership and Patricia Smith collaborated with the City of Santa Monica's urban design staff to transform a 2.7-mile stretch of Santa Monica Boulevard. From car-clogged thoroughfare designed primarily to move traffic, the street emerges as a walkable boulevard that strikes a pedestrian-friendly balance between cars and people. The plan reworks the right-of-way to widen sidewalks, add trees and landscaping, introduce public art, and create a string of small community parks and places for neighborhood festivals—a dramatic makeover that reflects "the changing social values of public spaces in Los Angeles." Courtesy of Zimmer Gunsul Frasca Architects LLP.

focused on the issues identified by businesses, property owners, and residents. The city also sought to capitalize much more effectively on Santa Monica Boulevard's dual role as the primary public face for the entire city and for individual neighborhoods.

Key urban design concepts

The submission calls the Santa Monica Boulevard Master Plan a reflection of "the changing social values of public spaces in Los Angeles." To achieve a vision of a major boulevard that serves as an important public space as well as a major roadway, the design team pursued four core objectives:

- **"Balancing big and little ideas"** by introducing dramatic modifications where possible and paying careful attention to design details everywhere. For exam-

ple, the 130-foot width of the boulevard right-of-way on the west side of the city enabled the team to widen sidewalks dramatically, add bike lanes, and enlarge bus stops. (At 80 feet, the much narrower right-of-way on the east side required the planners to maintain existing sidewalk widths.) The plan added more than 1,000 new trees and pedestrian-scale light fixtures to enhance the entire 2.7-mile project area.

- **"Unifying an entire boulevard while enforcing neighborhood identity."** The plan relied on plantings of a single tree species, the Drake elm, throughout the city, to give the boulevard visual continuity. "[A] rhythm of open spaces punctuates this large scale reading," with "boulevard gardens" designed as small parks, public art, and carefully detailed bus stops that reflect the character of and serve individual neighborhoods. "[D]

▲ An old streetcar right-of-way provided enough width to widen sidewalks and introduce medians along part of the boulevard. Courtesy of Zimmer Gunsul Frasca Architects LLP.

▶ Detail of widened sidewalks with new street trees. Courtesy of Zimmer Gunsul Frasca Architects LLP. *See color insert, C-14.*

ramatic landscaping and lighting" highlight gateways to Beverly Hills on the west and to Hollywood on the east.

- **"Creating one street out of two."** By removing an abandoned streetcar median that ran down the western portion of the boulevard, the urban design gained 40 feet of sidewalk space for outdoor dining and sidewalk retailing, both of which greatly enhance the boulevard's appeal to pedestrians and the city's image to passing motorists. The widened sidewalks have become the location of choice for community events such as parades and holiday celebrations.

- **"A framework for collaboration."** The urban design team and the city invited a wide variety of landscape architects, lighting designers, artists, and others to help design individual boulevard gardens and to help create an Art Walk. The street median hosts changing public art displays.

Jury Comments

"The jury applauds the simple and effective recommendations of the urban design, which will improve the everyday lives of people who live and work along the length of the highway.... This is a prototypical corridor project—a wonderful model for other cities. The jury hopes that other communities will feel emboldened by its success and will be inspired to 'take back their streets' too. The procedure underlying the urban design was...indicative of very good public process."

Lakeshore East Master Plan

LOCATION: Chicago, Illinois

URBAN DESIGNER: Skidmore, Owings & Merrill

CLIENT: Magellan Development Group, Ltd., and Near North Properties, Inc.

STUDY AREA AND PROGRAM: Plan for close to 10 million square feet of mixed-use development, including roughly 5,000 housing units and a 6-acre public park, on 28 acres immediately north of the Loop at the point where the Chicago River joins Lake Michigan

YEAR OF AWARD: 2002

STATUS: Plan adopted by the developer team and approved by the Chicago Plan Commission in 2001. Six buildings (of sixteen) had been completed before 2008, with another three under construction.

Critical issues

Although sponsored by a private developer, a project of this size and with such dramatic visibility raised issues that were as much civic as economic. Like many sizable undeveloped sites in cities across the United States, this one had eluded redevelopment through a combination of high costs and the opposition of neighbors who worried that changes would diminish the quality of their community by blocking views, generating excessive traffic, and occupying the last possible location for a new neighborhood park and elementary school. A three-level roadway ringing the site added to redevelopment costs and served to reinforce the site's isolation from the river and lake. Neighboring blocks had been developed by erecting buildings atop parking structures, an approach that established a "ground level" at the same height as the roadway's top level.

Lakeshore East Master Plan, Chicago. Skidmore, Owings & Merrill prepared this plan for a private developer to guide nearly 10 million square feet of mixed-use development a short walk from Chicago's Loop. What might have become, in essence, a large gated community has instead taken form as a mixed-use neighborhood that combines a grid of traditionally scaled blocks with a public park to create a lively public realm animated by the activities that high-density development supports and connected to the lakefront and surrounding neighborhoods. Courtesy of Skidmore, Owings & Merrill LLP. *See color insert, C-15.*

The city threw up considerable barriers to development. It acknowledged that towers already defined the area (and did not want to forgo the opportunity to add considerable high-quality housing, hotels, and other

A public park draws people from adjacent buildings and nearby blocks to create an active public realm. Photographer Doug Fogelson. Courtesy of Skidmore, Owings & Merrill LLP.

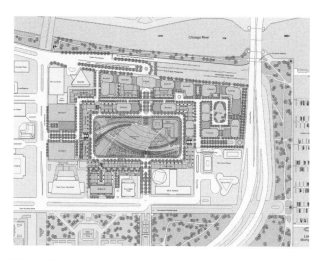

The site includes pedestrian links to the lakefront. Courtesy of Skidmore, Owings & Merrill LLP.

uses made possible by the site's impressive views). Nevertheless, the city expressed concern about increased traffic from the development. It also insisted on design guidelines to ensure that all development would achieve an extremely high level of urban design and architectural quality.

Key urban design concepts

The planning team responded to the goal, expressed both by the city and surrounding neighbors, of creating a mixed-use urban neighborhood, not a large-scale privatized development. It divided the site into a matrix of traditional urban blocks lined with individual buildings that reflect the scale and character of surrounding blocks and ensure multiple points of entry for cars and pedestrians. Blocks along the edges of the site were raised to the height of the elevated roadway, with structured parking below. New development steps down to a six-acre park in the center of the site that will contain a new elementary school. By locating the park on terra firma rather than using air rights, the planning team not only reduced development costs but assured that trees and other vegetation could thrive. Housing surrounds the park and creates connections to adjacent development; those buildings, in turn, screen the structured parking at the base of the perimeter buildings from public view. The plan establishes landscaped pedestrian connections from the park to the river and lake.

Even though the client was a private development team, the planning team conducted ambitious community outreach that reflected the civic importance of a development of this scale. Working closely with neighbors (cumulative attendance at three public meetings approached 1,500); collaborating with five city agencies; and reaching out to advocacy groups and resident associations enabled the planners to create a high-density, extremely urban plan and to demonstrate that well-designed and -sited urban towers can create a genuine sense of community and improve the quality of downtown life across a broad range of interests.

Jury Comments

"A deceptively simple plan surrounding a 6-acre rectangular central park.... [The] plan boldly extends Chicago's density and tradition of towers in creating a mixed-use downtown neighborhood."

Charlottesville Commercial Corridor Plan

LOCATION: Charlottesville, Virginia

URBAN DESIGNER: Torti Gallas and Partners; CHK Inc.

CLIENT: City of Charlottesville Office of Economic Development

STUDY AREA AND PROGRAM: Revitalization of fifteen diverse commercial corridors

"consistent with the physical demands of vibrant civic life." The anticipated potential development opportunities for a variety of land uses include 530,000 square feet for office, 720,000 square feet for high tech and research, 240,000 square feet for industrial, 200,000 square feet for retail, 400–700 hotel rooms, and roughly 1,000 housing units.

YEAR OF AWARD: 2003

STATUS: Plan adopted by the city

Charlottesville Commercial Corridor Plan, Charlottesville, Virginia. Torti Gallas and Partners' plan to pull development back to Charlottesville's downtown and older commercial districts began with a series of neighborhood-specific visions for growth and translated these into models for higher-density, mixed-use development that fit into an urban context. Rendering by Chris Johnson. Courtesy of Torti Gallas and Partners, Inc.

Higher-density commercial infill. Rendering by Chris Johnson. Courtesy of Torti Gallas and Partners, Inc. *See color insert, C-16.*

Neighborhood infill. Rendering by Chris Johnson. Courtesy of Torti Gallas and Partners, Inc.

Critical issues

Like American cities of all sizes, and in every region, Charlottesville faced significant challenges during the twenty years leading up to the plan, including employment loss, declining share of regional retail sales, and flight of affluent households to high-growth suburban locations. With this initiative, the city aimed to identify sites and create new models for the next generation of urban development and build public support for reinvigorating older commercial corridors. In the process, the city also identified the need to address public housing and other redevelopment opportunities in ways that would enhance quality of life for all residents—and thus attract more people to work and live (or remain) in the city.

Key urban design concepts

Starting from the premise "that the neighborhood is the fundamental building block of urbanism," the plan produced a suite of neighborhood-specific visions for growth. These visions combined to yield a new picture of the city's potential to accommodate a higher-density, mixed-use development in older commercial districts and corridors, public housing sites, and other areas. The plan included detailed design guidelines, based on extensive community outreach, to ensure that new development reinforced the character of surrounding neighborhoods. The plan also included a strong social equity component to insure that all residents benefited from a new generation of growth. In aggregate, these studies constituted a vision for how a mature, smaller city can introduce extensive new growth and reassert its role as the region's commercial and retail center.

Jury Comments

"This project illustrated ideas for areas of the city long forgotten and long abandoned, and opened the eyes of residents and officials to a number of new possibilities.... This much-needed plan helps integrate the university-to-town context. The various plans make each mall and corridor more humane and friendly."

Chicago Central Area Plan

LOCATION: Chicago, Illinois

URBAN DESIGNER: Skidmore, Owings & Merrill

CLIENT: City of Chicago

STUDY AREA AND PROGRAM: A plan to accommodate signficant growth for Chicago's central core, a six-square-mile area that comprises the city's downtown and less densely developed areas immediately to the south and west

YEAR OF AWARD: 2004

STATUS: Plan approved by Chicago Plan Commission in 2003

Critical issues

After years of disinvestment, Chicago's central area rode a wave of new growth during the early 1990s; employment, housing, retail, and other development all grew signifi-cantly. Although this growth brought new vitality to the city's streets, it also generated more traffic, larger-scale redevelopment in traditional close-in neighborhoods, and other impacts that provoked a strong community reaction. Rather than working to contain growth—the path some cities had taken in response to strong growth in same period—the city government wanted to encour-age more. It commissioned the Central Area Plan with

▼ Chicago Central Area Plan, Illinois. Skidmore, Owings & Merrill responded to concerns that new development had undermined quality of life in downtown Chicago neighborhoods with strategies to help the city manage growth in ways that yield public benefits. The plan locates significant height and massing away from existing residential areas and requires design that reinforces neighborhood character. Other strategies include linking density to transit access; identifying public benefits like parks and schools; emphasizing sustainable design and operation; locating new housing where it can strengthen neighborhood commercial centers; and ensuring that new construction promotes walkability. Courtesy of Skidmore, Owings & Merrill LLP. *See color insert, C-17.*

The plan makes existing streets more inviting to pedestrians. Courtesy of Skidmore, Owings & Merrill LLP.

Sustainability features and strong neighborhood character. Courtesy of Skidmore, Owings & Merrill LLP.

the twin goals of guiding growth for greater public benefit and establishing a new community understanding of where—and how—higher-density development could enhance quality of life. The plan focused on a series of fundamental questions:

- How should the next generation of buildings be located, scaled, and designed?

- How could the city ensure active street environments in every district?

- What standards would the city assert for streets, plazas, transit facilities, and other public assets?

- How could the city balance the charm and quality of historic design with the city's need to build for the future?

Benefits of development include support for the creation of new parks. Courtesy of Skidmore, Owings & Merrill LLP.

- How could new development remove barriers between districts, neighborhoods, and open spaces?

- How could the city transform the Chicago River into a publicly accessible development and recreation corridor?

- How could the city go about creating livable neighborhoods in downtown?

Key urban design concepts

The plan drew inspiration from the "make no little plans" spirit of Burnham's Plan for the City of Chicago, prepared almost a century before. "The Chicago Central Area Plan is a vision for urban greatness, as measured by the pride, prosperity and quality of life of Chicago's people. It is a plan to expand downtown's economic engine. It is a green plan to enhance a fast-growing residential community and the region's shared cultural resources—identifying as its clear goals economic success, physical growth and environmental sustainability." The plan establishes a framework for growth based on a high-density core, mixed-use corridors, and neighborhoods in between. The plan identifies three key urban design principles as central to achieving this framework:

- **Promote development and diversity** by expanding the Loop's high-density office district into the West Loop around transit stations; developing higher-intensity, mixed-use corridors outside the expanded Loop; supporting the distinctive character of diverse neighborhoods and special places; maintaining a commitment to acclaimed urban design and architecture; preserving Chicago's historically significant buildings, places, and infrastructure; and supporting economic and social diversity in all development.

- **Expand public transportation and access** by making transit the first choice for people coming to and moving around the Central Area (and increasing transit's mode share to 80 percent of all trips by 2020); focusing new development near transit; reducing barriers faced by pedestrians and people with limited mobility; improving the quality of the pedestrian environment; encouraging alternative transportation modes such as bicycles and water taxis; and creating high-quality landscaped streets and highways.

- **Enhance the role of waterfronts and open spaces** by treating the entire waterfront, Chicago River, and lake edge, as a great public place; creating a continuous public riverwalk along the Chicago River; completing the development of the Chicago River Corridor with new neighborhoods, civic institutions, and places for business; creating the next generation of urban and neighborhood parks to support the anticipated growth in the area's population; and completing the Central Area's framework of richly landscaped streets and boulevards.

Jury Comments

"This plan takes a complex problem and explains it with understandable themes and graphics that communicate well. It illustrates an understanding of the city as a growing organism, recognizing the past so it keeps the historic character but adapts and develops in a bigger way."

How the Projects Illustrate the Principles

1. **Build community in an increasingly diverse society.** All of these plans—which range in scale from the 28,000-square-foot Jamaica Market to the expansive downtown of the Chicago Central Area Plan—aspire to build a sense of community by creating places and amenities that draw people together. In recognizing submittals that focus strongly on creating a more inviting public realm—adding vitality to major shopping streets, inserting landscaped public spaces in auto-focused corridors, supporting restaurants and other amenity businesses, and building new districts around parks—the awards juries collectively have sent a strong message about what matters most in shaping downtowns and Main Streets. The projects in these case studies also make a consistent effort to enliven adjacent streets and public spaces. This emphasis stands out most clearly in the Pennsylvania Convention Center plan, which goes to extraordinary lengths to incorporate cafés and other uses that animate the streets around it—a particularly challenging design problem for this kind of structure. Historically, such projects have rarely focused on the design of fine-grained uses to enliven surrounding urban streets. The Arc also explicitly relies on new transportation infrastructure to knit together communities in two noncontiguous territories and to create focal points for community and growth.

2. **Advance environmental sustainability.** All of these projects make a key point about smart growth: even urban districts that appear fully developed can support significant new activity. The State Street, 42nd Street, Charlottesville, and Santa Monica Boulevard cases focus largely on expanding the role these areas already play as centers for shopping, culture, tourism, and socializing. To this assumption, Pennsyslvania Convention Center, Racine, Harmonie Park, Chicago Central Area Plan, and Lakeshore East add physical planning and design concepts for introducing major new construction into urbanized areas—development that will play an essential role in helping these areas contribute to sustainable regional growth. The Chicago Central Area Plan makes the case that increased density in the core plays a critical role in any citywide green strategy, in part because it will shift a greater share of trips to transit ridership.

3. **Expand individual choices.** The programming, planning, and design in each of these case studies is more complex than what took place for previous generations of major downtown projects ("improvements" that very often leached away activity and character). Each of these projects adds major new choices for a neigh-

borhood, a district, and, in some cases, an entire region. They create places that recapture the excitement of downtown Main Streets and theater districts (State Street, 42nd Street); reverse decades of decline in neighborhood commercial districts and big-city downtowns alike (Jamaica Market, Harmonie Park, Pennsylvania Convention Center, and Chicago Central); introduce the opportunity to stroll and meet friends along a major boulevard (Santa Monica, Charlottesville) and recreate it in an older commercial district (Jamaica Market); and add livable new neighborhoods in the heart of older downtowns (Lakeshore East, Racine, and Chicago Central Area). At the same time, each makes a strong case for well-designed density and uses density as an essential tool to support community goals—economic development in Philadelphia and Racine, retrofitting a stretch of car-dominated Los Angeles, intensifying the urban hustle of downtown Chicago, and similar goals.

4. **Enhance personal health.** Although planning for many of these projects predated current understanding of the strong connections among density, walking, and public health, in every case the urban designers took care to ensure that each project would promote walkability. This effort combines two reciprocal elements: creation of a handsome public realm and assurance of its active, lively character by incorporating retail and other uses that attract and engage pedestrians. The Jamaica Market adds an important element—making fresh produce and food that has undergone limited processing more accessible to residents of an area where such options are limited.

5. **Make places for people.** One lesson these projects teach is that architectural style is subsidiary to the goal of creating a great place. Lakeshore East and Jamaica Market use bold modern forms and design to declare their vitality, but the Pennsylvania Convention Center does so by carefully blending new construction into the life in its surrounding nineteenth- and early-twentieth-century context. Even purposefully funky elements that owe more to Las Vegas and theme parks than to the traditional vocabulary of historic cities can contribute to a great place, as 42nd Street Now demonstrates. At a programmatic level, Jamaica Market mixes food, live music, and the buzz of activity to create much of its appeal. Collectively, these projects make the case that rather than style, taking care to understand and work within context most directly augurs success. Each not only enlivens its context but also strengthens the sense of district identity around it. In contrast to many urban redevelopment efforts of previous decades, all of these initiatives represent efforts to enhance an existing district or to create a new one, rather than call attention to individual spaces and buildings. They conjure up bold and innovative places that were mostly unimagined even ten years earlier yet fit elegantly into their respective settings.

CHAPTER 8

Reinventing Older Neighborhoods

When Marilyn Jordan Taylor, FAIA, at the time chair of the Urban Land Institute and an urban designer and principal at SOM, addressed the 2006 Congress for the New Urbanism conference, she described an America that would increasingly engage in retrofitting its cities in pursuit of sustainability, diversity, and a stronger sense of community. She argued that the United States must embrace a future that celebrates "density and mixed use—two qualities that are essential to the future livability of America's cities."

The public sector led a rediscovery of urban neighborhoods and their development potential in the 1980s and 1990s. After years of trying to slow suburban flight and abandonment in older neighborhoods, U.S. cities began to see renewed investment in them. Across the country, municipalities, public housing authorities, community-based nonprofits, universities, and other entities launched ambitious neighborhood-revitalization projects. These public and nonprofit entities sometimes teamed up with seasoned residential developers like St.

Louis–based McCormick Baron Salazar and Cleveland's Forest City Enterprises.

The federal HOPE VI program added momentum to this new wave of investment and provided further incentive for public and private entities to team up on revitalization projects in neglected neighborhoods. The program funded transformation of nearly 240 ailing public housing projects into new mixed-income neighborhoods. More recently, growing demand for housing at every income level has spurred significant collaboration between cities and private developers. The common goal is to build significant amounts of mixed-income housing and reinvest in existing housing stock in older neighborhoods, along with the development of new parks and reinvigoration of commercial districts. Urban universities have spearheaded public and private neighborhood-revitalization projects adjacent to their campuses in cities such as New Haven, Connecticut; New York, Philadelphia, Baltimore, Cincinnati, Columbus, Ohio; Chicago, and Denver.

> The city is like jazz … and the job of urban designers is to repair the broken melody, enhance the rhythm, and make it easier for our fellow musicians to arrive on the stage and play new, more entrancing riffs.
>
> Brenda Case Scheer, dean, College of Architecture + Planning, University of Utah

Roots

Charles Dickens used "suburb" to describe poorer districts at the edge of London whose distance from the amenities and jobs in the heart of the city made them less desirable. Evolving transportation systems broke the link between proximity and access in the last half of the nineteenth century, allowing people—those who could afford to—to leave cities and move to suburbs in search of relief from a deteriorating quality of life brought on by industrialization. After more than a century, the value of proximity to the center of cities has clearly risen: people are leaving suburbs and returning to neighborhoods close to downtown.

The emergence of heterogeneous urban neighborhoods in the United States—where residents come from diverse backgrounds and, frequently, from different economic circumstances—is a recent phenomenon. America's early urban neighborhoods, typically defined by race, religion, ethnicity, economic class, and other shared characteristics, were built for homogeneous populations that readily formed tight communal bonds.

America's oldest neighborhoods—still visible in East Coast ports like Salem, Massachusetts, and Charleston, South Carolina; in quaint neighborhoods like Old Town in Philadelphia and New York's Greenwich Village; or around the plazas of early Spanish-American cities like Albuquerque—grew incrementally along patterns familiar to European settlers. Most American cities grew at a modest pace until the Industrial Revolution took hold after the Civil War.

The new industrial economy powered growth in cities from the Midwest to New England; some cities, like Denver and San Francisco, arose in response to mining booms; others, like St. Louis and Cincinnati, grew from river ports or railroad hubs. More than 25 million immigrants thronged to America's cities in the late nineteenth and early twentieth centuries. Widespread adoption of electric streetcars by 1900 greatly expanded the land area available for development in many cities, further fueling growth.

Neighborhoods built to house this explosive growth experienced dramatic changes over time, but homogeneity remained a constant. For example, East Boston's population grew from a few thousand before the Civil War to more than sixty thousand in the 1920s. Waves of immigrants from Ireland, Europe's Jewish ghettos, Italy, Latin America, and elsewhere washed through its neighborhoods, transforming their ethnic character repeatedly. With each transition, these neighborhoods reemerged as highly homogeneous communities whose residents lived within an interconnected web of shared schools, houses of worship, and cultural organizations.

This period of steady neighborhood development in U.S. cities ground to a halt with the Depression and World War II. America emerged from the war into a dramatically different constellation of conditions. A century of explosive industrial expansion began to slow at the same time that automobiles came into much broader use, meaning that people no longer needed to live close to their jobs. On a smaller scale, developers built some urban neighborhoods that emulated earlier models into the 1960s, but the era of large-scale urban neighborhood development within central cities had passed.

The impact of the rapid decline of urban industry and equally rapid rise of suburbia was apparent around the country. Between 1950 and 1956, the population of America's suburbs increased by almost half. By 1970 more Americans lived in suburbs than in cities or rural settlements. The neighborhoods that formed the building

West Savannah, Georgia. Transforming a declining older neighborhood with a broadened mix of housing choices and a strengthened public realm of parks and tree-lined streets. Courtesy of Goody Clancy.

blocks of America's suburbs, however, were as homogeneous as the urban neighborhoods erstwhile city dwellers had left behind.

From the end of the war to the beginning of the 1990s, American housing patterns followed this template, with the vast bulk of new housing springing up in homogenous, car-oriented suburban neighborhoods. Yet several important changes decisively recast America's housing market during the 1990s, paving the way for a resurgence of older urban neighborhoods. First, rising congestion and mounting frustration with long commutes boosted the desirability of close-in urban neighborhoods. Boston's Metropolitan Area Planning Council reports that during the 1990s, hours lost to traffic congestion in the region increased by more than 50 percent, a pattern repeated elsewhere across the country. In late 2004, 79 percent of respondents to a poll by the National Association of Realtors cited reducing the length of their commute as a "a primary factor in choosing their next house." In a similar vein, *Parade* magazine reported in May 2006 that homebuyers were increasingly choosing shorter commutes over additional square footage when buying new homes.

In recent years, proximity to transit has turned into a powerful market force. In 2004 the Environmental Protection Agency's *Hidden in Plain Sight* report found that regions with well-developed transit systems would need to double the amount of housing located near transit to meet market demand over the subsequent two decades.

The housing industry changed in another important way during the 1990s. For the first time in its history, the United States no longer had a homogeneous, mass housing market. Instead "a nation of niches" had emerged, in the words of the Urban Land Institute. Younger, older, and childless households today control a much larger share of housing spending than was the case historically, and many of these niche markets choose to invest in urban neighborhoods, attracted by and reinforcing their increasingly diverse and heterogeneous character.

Approaches Today

Five recent trends increasingly influence the planning and design of urban neighborhoods:

1. **A much stronger real estate market.** Rapidly shifting demographics and values, as described in Chapter 4, have yielded rising demand for additional housing in urban neighborhoods and a broader, more varied selection of urban housing types. Much new urban housing has taken the form of lofts and apartments in buildings that introduce greater height and density into predominantly row-house neighborhoods.

2. **Historic preservation.** The preservation movement produced many early advocates for urban neighborhoods and continues to shape attitudes to revitalization and development in urban neighborhoods. Savannah established one of the first historic districts in the 1950s in response to activists' efforts to save downtown neighborhoods, planned in the 1730s, from destruction by urban renewal. The campaign to protect the city's historic heritage led to revitalization of the downtown and older urban neighborhoods, and it launched one of America's most notable early urban renaissances.

3. **New Urbanism.** The 1993 charter of the Congress for the New Urbanism—the movement's highest-profile organization—asserts that the design of new development should consciously incorporate the qualities that people love in traditional urban neighborhoods, such as a grid of streets, front porches, and detailed design. New urbanists today advocate using these same measures to restore traditional character in new development within existing neighborhoods.

4. **Sustainability.** The U.S. Green Building Council has introduced a sustainability rating system for neighborhood and community design that follows its LEED® (Leadership in Energy and Environmental Design) program for buildings. The rating system quantifies how urban neighborhoods can achieve sustainability through "smart location" (assuring access to transit, avoiding greenfield sites); traditional patterns of neighborhood design (employing a street grid, assuring compactness); and preservation of historic buildings. At the same time, the ratings make clear that even existing neighborhoods need to meet more rigorous sustainability standards for traffic management, affordable housing generation, and reduction of impervious surfaces like parking lots.

5. **Social equity.** Responding to continued escalation of housing sale prices and rents in urban neighborhoods, organizations representing long-time residents have joined with elected officials and others in calling for greater social equity. They most often voice concern about the need for more affordable housing, followed by more public spaces and Main Streets that reflect the culture and traditions of long-term residents.

6. **Neighborhood activism.** The pace of growth and change in cities has prompted a wave of neighborhood activism. Where rents and sale prices have risen rapidly, organizations representing long-time residents have begun to demand more affordable housing as an act of social equity. Residents in other neighborhoods have demanded greater local control over development in an effort to preserve traditional character.

Case Studies

Taken together, these case studies from across the United States offer a remarkable testament to the resurgence of urban neighborhoods. These initiatives embody a level of aspiration for America's urban centers not seen since before the Depression.

Lafayette Courts

LOCATION: Baltimore, Maryland

URBAN DESIGNER: CHK Architects & Planners

CLIENT: Housing Authority of Baltimore City

STUDY AREA AND PROGRAM: Located between the central business district and a group of middle- and lower-income residential neighborhoods, the 21.5-acre site contained 23 high- and low-rise public housing structures and a community center. The replacement development includes 374 units of housing together with almost 100,000 square feet of community, medical clinic, and recreation facilities in a mix of low- and mid-rise buildings and new public spaces.

YEAR OF AWARD: 1997

STATUS: Redevelopment has been completed.

Critical issues

"We just want to live in the same kind of housing everybody else has," was how one Lafayette Courts resident put the community's problem. The urban designer's "overriding goal…[was] to create a new neighborhood that is visually, socially and economically integrated with the rest of the city." Like public housing in most American cities, the design of the development had isolated it from the surrounding neighborhoods through a combination of superblocks that did not connect to surrounding streets and blocks; barracks-like low-rise structures punctuated by bleak high rises that stood in sharp contrast to the scale and character of areas outside the development; and lack of any shared public space.

Key urban design concepts

The urban design team worked closely with residents, the housing authority, and the developers to create a new neighborhood that overcame the site's isolation. The centerpiece of this effort comprised a series of workshops held over the course of a year. Designed to involve residents integrally in every aspect of planning, the workshops aimed to build a sense of resident responsibility for continuing active engagement in guiding the neighborhood's future once redevelopment was completed. The resulting plan embraces the surrounding neighborhoods by:

- **Replacing superblocks** with a network of traditionally scaled streets, blocks, and public squares connected to the existing city street system.

- **Introducing a mix of row houses and mid-rise buildings** scaled and designed to complement the character of surrounding neighborhoods.

- **Introducing significant new community, recreation, and medical facilities** that serve residents of Lafayette Courts and the surrounding neighborhoods. The development continues to serve residents with low incomes rather than housing a mix of incomes, so

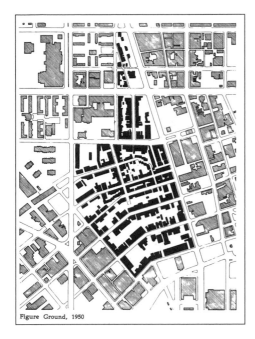

Figure Ground, 1950

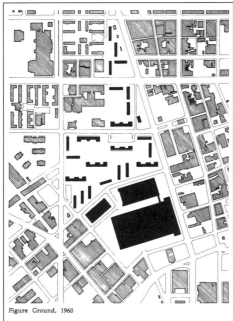

Figure Ground, 1960

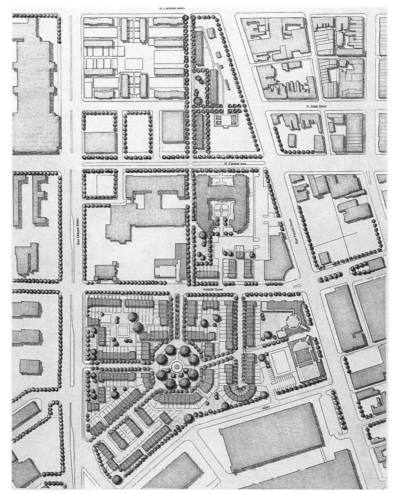

▲ Illustrative plan for the site. Drawings by Torti Gallas and Partners. *See color insert, C-18.*

▼ The site in 1950. Drawings by Torti Gallas and Partners.

◀ The site in 1960. Drawings by Torti Gallas and Partners.

Lafayette Courts, Baltimore, Maryland. CHK Architects & Planners' plan transformed a public housing development from twenty-three buildings, including towers, into a mix of row houses and mid-rise buildings that define streets, blocks, and public squares built to a traditional urban scale. The plan met the goals of public housing residents and nearby neighbors alike "to create a new neighborhood that is visually, socially, and economically integrated with the rest of the city."

nity's ties to the surrounding neighborhood." Copyright Alain Jaramillo.

drawing nonresidents to these new facilities will play a key role in breaking down the development's long-time social isolation.

- **Creating a traditional public park** in the center of Lafayette Courts that includes mature trees, benches, lawns, a fountain, and other amenities that will draw residents both from the development and from surrounding blocks. The park's design offers a sense of safety because the surrounding housing overlooks the park; the community-service facilities also reinforce a sense of security by adding more "eyes on the park" and introducing additional activity.

Diggs Town

Location: Norfolk, Virginia

Urban designer: Urban Design Associates

Client: Norfolk Redevelopment and Housing Authority

Study area and program: Originally developed in the 1950s, Diggs Town comprised 428 units of barracks-type housing isolated from surrounding neighborhoods. Unlike other HOPE VI case studies in this chapter, the housing authority did not envision full-scale redevelopment but rather strategic redevelopment of the site and buildings that would support transformation from an isolated "project" into a vibrant neighborhood. Most of the housing was occupied when the urban designer began working with the community, and the final plan maintains roughly the same number of housing units. Unlike many HOPE VI developments, this project did not seek to address social issues by shifting the community from a low- to a mixed-income profile. It relies instead on a variety of social-support and educational programs, together with improved design, to address such issues.

Year of award: 1999

Status: Redevelopment has been completed.

Critical issues

The Norfolk Redevelopment and Housing Authority (NRHA) commissioned this plan in part to demonstrate that targeted planning and design improvements, enhanced social programs, and active resident participation in planning could together transform a crime-plagued and economically distressed public housing community into "a safe, stable neighborhood." At the same time, by creating a deeper sense of community and a greater degree of personal safety, these improvements would—with enhanced workforce-readiness and education programs—support residents' efforts to improve their economic prospects.

Key urban design concepts

The urban design plan grew out of a collaborative working process with Diggs Town residents and key staff from the NRHA and City of Norfolk. The plan introduced "many traditional elements of successful urbanism" to a site whose superblocks and long rows of buildings bore little resemblance to traditional urban or suburban neighborhoods. Key elements included:

- **At a neighborhood scale,** creating new connections to surrounding streets and "changing the image of buildings to resemble the houses in a 'normal'" neighborhood. These measures represented an effort to erase the most visible distinction between the public housing residents and their neighbors. These changes also convey the sense that the "schools, churches, and institutions in the area are now part of the daily life of residents."

- **At the street-block scale,** redividing each superblock to create multiple blocks of a size similar to those in

▲▲ Diggs Town, Norfolk, Virginia. Urban Design Associates' plan transformed Diggs Town from an isolated public housing "project" into a constituent element of a larger, economically diverse neighborhood. The plan breaks up superblocks with new streets that tie into the surrounding grid; reorients the housing from interior parking lots to new public streets and paths; and gives the barracks-like townhouses individual character by adding porches and other human-scale design elements. Courtesy of Urban Design Associates.

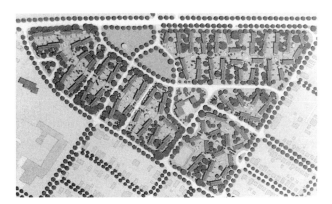

Site plan. Courtesy of Urban Design Associates.

▲ The neighborhood prior to redevelopment. Courtesy of Urban Design Associates.

The addition of front porches more firmly anchors the buildings to new public streets. Courtesy of Urban Design Associates.

each other, be together, so we can come together to solve our problems as a community."

Post-occupancy studies (rare for any type of development) have shown a "dramatic drop in crime and an increase in self-esteem and community pride." Participation in workforce-readiness and education programs has risen, as have employment rates and resident incomes.

Jury Comments

"This project demonstrates so eloquently how a few simple urban design moves integrated with good design principles can transform a public housing wasteland into a wonderful place to live. A true collaboration between governmental authorities and residents, the remarkable transformation of Diggs Town has created a realization of community at one level and a sense of individual ownership at another."

adjacent neighborhoods. New streets built through interior courts meant that most housing now faces tree-lined public streets. Where new streets could not fit, well-lit public walkways form mews connecting to adjacent streets.

- **At the house scale,** erasing the monolithic character of the development's housing by adding porches and other design details to provide each unit with an individual identity and public street address. Common open spaces were subdivided into traditional front and back yards for individual houses, providing places for more than seven hundred resident children to play while assigning informal responsibility for maintenance and security to individual households. Front porches addressed a strongly expressed desire by residents to have a place to "come out of our houses, see

---

Ellen Wilson Neighborhood Redevelopment

LOCATION: Washington, D.C.

URBAN DESIGNER: Weinstein Associates Architects

CLIENT: District of Columbia Housing Authority and Ellen Wilson Neighborhood Community Development Corporation

STUDY AREA AND PROGRAM: Using a HOPE VI grant, redevelopment of a 5.3-acre abandoned public housing site into 154 housing units (an increase of 20 units), a community building, and new public streets. The site sits within the Capitol Hill Historic District and abuts an elevated highway on the south.

YEAR OF AWARD: 1998

STATUS: Construction completed in 1999

Ellen Wilson Neighborhood Redevelopment, Washington, D.C. Weinstein Associates draws on the rich Victorian vocabulary of Capitol Hill architecture to connect this former public housing site physically to the historic neighborhood. To integrate it economically and socially, the plan provides choices that allow residents of widely varying income levels to live in the neighborhood. Courtesy of Weinstein Associates Architects.

Critical issues

From its inception in 1988, the project maintained a three-part mission "to physically, economically, and socially return the Ellen Wilson site to its place as an integral part" of the Capitol Hill community. Integrating the development into the community required the introduction of new connections to existing streets, the creation of architecture visibly inspired by the rich Victorian vernacular that characterizes much of Capitol Hill, and the formation of an economically heterogeneous community that reflected the area in the late 1990s.

To match the income diversity of the surrounding neighborhood, 20 units located throughout the site were sold to families with incomes between 80 and 115 percent of the area median income. To replace the public housing units once located on the site, the project created 134 rental units, reserving at least one-quarter of them for residents whose income fell below 25 percent of the area median. Uniform unit designs provide management flexibility and avoid any visible distinctions that might call attention to residents' differing income levels.

Key urban design concepts

The urban design team built the plan with a focus on interrelated planning, design, and programmatic principles:

- **Developing the site to its maximum allowable density,** yielding the maximum amount of badly needed affordable housing, accommodating a range of economic levels, and providing room for market-rate units that would expand diversity and help subsidize affordable units.

- **Promoting "a sense of community and personal investment"** by developing the replacement housing as a cooperative; the additional twenty units were sold on a fee-simple basis to meet requirements of the market.

- **Aligning income diversity with that of the neighborhood**—roughly 40 percent of households earn less than half of the area median income (AMI), 40 percent earn between half and four-fifths of AMI, and more affluent households account for the rest.

- **Creating a variety of housing sizes, characters, and types** in support of age, life-style, and cultural diversity.

- **Designing all units to one standard,** providing maximum flexibility in mixing income tiers and avoiding stigmatization of low-income residents on the basis of architectural design or quality.

- **Designing all buildings in the Victorian vocabulary of Capitol Hill,** but providing a mix of heights and styles.

- **Providing community support services and facilities.**

▼ The plan introduces two new public streets that reflect the unusual parcel shapes dictated by the Pierre-Charles L'Enfant plan for the District of Columbia. To reinforce the role of the streets as public realm, the architect gave all buildings individual street-facing entrances. Courtesy of Weinstein Associates.

▼ To match the existing context, the development liberally mixes styles and housing types, as shown in all three photos. Courtesy of Weinstein Associates Architects. *See color insert, C-19.*

Bahçesehir

LOCATION: Western outskirts of Istanbul, Turkey

URBAN DESIGNER: Torti Gallas and Partners—
CHK Architects and Planners

CLIENT: Emlak Bankasi

STUDY AREA AND PROGRAM: A 170-acre district
within a new town that lies roughly 40
miles west of Istanbul, along a rail line
and highway that link Istanbul to Europe.
The district will include more than 2,300
housing units, ranging from freestanding
"villas" to apartments, together with roughly
105,000 square feet of retail and office space;
entertainment; schools and other civic uses;
mosques; and parks and neighborhood
squares.

YEAR OF AWARD: 2000

STATUS: Redevelopment has been completed.

Bahçesehir, outside Istanbul, Turkey. In many rapidly growing urban regions outside of the United States, sprawl takes a different form—for example, as clusters of anonymous towers hastily built without regard to creating a cohesive new community. Torti Gallas & Partners devised an alternative approach in its plan for a new mixed-use district outside of Istanbul. The plan translates the densities typically found in these developments into a series of walkable neighborhoods with housing types that range from towers to townhouses organized around neighborhood squares, streets, and a distinctive stairway and terraced fountain that can serve as building blocks of community. Courtesy of Torti Gallas and Partners.

Critical issues

Istanbul's burgeoning population (which grew by more than 1,000 percent between 1950 and 2000) has generated a building boom—primarily rapidly erected suburban towers—that produces sprawl "as environmentally irresponsible as it is aesthetically unattractive." This project grows out of an initiative to produce better models that

Buildings clearly frame streets and parks, and provide clear transitions from public to semi-private to private space. Photo by Ersin Alok, courtesy of Torti Gallas and Partners.

demonstrate how the densities required to accommodate rapid growth can be shaped into cohesive, walkable communities.

Key urban design concepts

The plan focuses on creating a place that conveys the sense of a community rich in civic qualities, drawing on historical examples from Turkey and Europe. The urban designer identified a series of qualities that should shape the new community's form and character:

- **The community accommodates a full range of human activities,** including living, working, shopping, recreation, entertainment, civic life, and religious life.
- **People relate to the community at a neighborhood, quarter, and townwide scale.** Neighborhoods are defined by their walkable centers and small local parks; quarters, by their central squares and larger parks; and the larger town, by its commercial center and central park.
- **At each scale, different transportation systems support appropriate density and character**—walkability defines neighborhoods, a network of local streets defines quarters, and both transit and a freeway link the town center to Istanbul.
- **Buildings frame streets and other public spaces,** and each building, regardless of its design, accommodates a transition from public to semipublic to private spaces.
- **A wide range of housing types and unit sizes** support a diversity of ages, family types, and cultural backgrounds.

Jury Comments
A "livable community."

Village of Park DuValle

Location: Louisville, Kentucky

Urban designer: Urban Design Associates

Client: Housing Authority of Louisville

Study area and program: Funded through HOPE VI and other federal, state, and city programs, Park DuValle replaced 1,100 units of public housing with a neighborhood of more than 1,200 mixed-income housing units, parks, and community facilities. Prior to redevelopment, nearly 80 percent of the development's residents had been unemployed, and median income had fallen below $6,000. More than a third of the housing in the new community is owner-occupied, and household incomes range from less than 30 percent of area median income to well over 100 percent. To the original public housing site the development added adjacent deteriorated and vacant properties, publicly owned land parcels (either parks or unused land), and some vacant retail properties.

Year of award: 2000

Status: Redevelopment has been completed.

The Village of Park DuValle, Louisville, Kentucky. The Urban Design Associates plan replaces 1,100 units of isolated public housing with a mixed-income community of more than 1,200 households that looks and functions like the city's other traditional urban neighborhoods. The plan replaces oversized superblocks with a network of new streets, parkways, and parks that "directly continues the forms established in Louisville by the Olmsteds." Courtesy of Urban Design Associates.

Critical issues

In addition to project-specific challenges—reconnecting to surrounding neighborhoods, replacing barracks-style housing, promoting a greater sense of public safety—Park DuValle posed the challenge of transforming low-income housing into a mixed-income neighborhood, "successfully providing public housing for needy families while simultaneously attracting middle-income homebuyers to the neighborhood. Essentially, prospective homebuyers were being invited to invest their life savings in a house on a site with 40 years of bad newspaper headlines and then to live next to public housing residents—a gutsy move given the condition and reputation of the neighborhood at the outset of the project."

Key urban design concepts

Creating a successful mixed-income neighborhood required building a community of choice, the quality and character of whose housing and public spaces could compete in the marketplace with offerings in more homogeneous (and traditional) areas. While Louisville's housing market had grown increasingly diverse—including an emerging cadre of middle-income and affluent households that favored living in economically and racially mixed communities and that appreciated the new

Although single-family houses predominate, the plan also includes higher-density multifamily buildings. Courtesy of Urban Design Associates.

Illustrative aerial of the site. Courtesy of Urban Design Associates.

neighborhood's proximity to downtown and urban amenities—the urban design strategy had to "instill confidence ... by using the images and forms identified with successful, traditional Louisville neighborhoods, the design strategies [that would] reassure residents, turn their initial skepticism into support, and foster the rebirth of this *area* as a community in which they can take pride." The urban designer worked closely with public housing residents, the housing authority, and the city to create a strategy that consisted of seven basic elements:

- **"Build a neighborhood"** by incorporating adjacent "distressed" areas into the site, connecting new streets to adjacent neighborhood streets, and creating inviting new public parks. This element is meant to link Park

DuValle residents to the schools, churches, playgrounds, and other institutions and locations where the residents of surrounding neighborhoods come together.

- **"Build on Louisville's Olmsted tradition"** by creating a network of new streets, parkways, and parks that "directly continues the forms established in Louisville by the Olmsteds."

- **"Create a mixed-income pattern"** by interpolating rental, ownership, subsidized, and market-rate housing across the new neighborhood. Housing designs offer no visible hint at these distinctions, an achievement made more challenging by the fact that different developers built the rental and ownership housing.

- **"Build good blocks"** by closely spacing the houses that face the streets, giving them street-addressing features like porches, and creating block sizes like those in the neighborhoods around the site.

- **"Build houses not buildings"** by mixing single-family, duplex, triplex, and row houses with small apartment buildings to achieve the number of units needed to fill the neighborhood, attract moderate- and higher-income households, and meet market demand for a wide range of unit types.

- Build **"Louisville architecture"** by creating a "pattern book" to guide the design of houses that embody the "look and feel of a traditional Louisville neighborhood." Larger houses that actually contain two and three units are scattered among smaller single-family houses within the same block.

- **"Mix uses"** by providing recreation medical, community, and convenience retail facilities within walking distance.

Jury Comments

"The rebirth of a Louisville community, linked by a continuous network of streets, homes, and parkways."

▼ Windsor Town Center, Vero Beach, Florida. Merrill and Pastor Architects retrofitted a single-use suburban subdivision with a new town center shaped by "urban" qualities—a mix of different uses; walkability achieved by clustering a post office, stores, and other activities around a landscaped town square; and formal architectural expression that makes direct reference to historically "civic" styles and settings. Courtesy of Merrill, Pastor, and Colgan Architects.

Windsor Town Center

LOCATION: Vero Beach, Florida
URBAN DESIGNER: Merrill and Pastor Architects
CLIENT: Windsor Development
STUDY AREA AND PROGRAM: At the convergence of five roads on the edge of a 300-home village, the project stands as the first visible development upon arrival from the coastal highway. The program calls for a post office, small store, a modest office component, and an unspecified number of apartments. The urban designer added a series of gardens to the program to create a civic space and outdoor spaces for the apartments.
YEAR OF AWARD: 2000
STATUS: The project has been built.

▲ The plan takes advantage of an existing allée of oak trees to create a dramatic approach to the complex from the highway. Courtesy of Merrill, Pastor, and Colgan Architects.

◀ Rendering of the town center, with residential areas behind. The Indian River is at top. Watercolor by Michael Morrissey, courtesy of Windsor Town Center. *See color insert, C-20.*

Critical issues

Traditional New England villages grew up over time and often enjoy a town square or Main Street that originally emerged as the civic and commercial center for the surrounding agricultural region. In contrast, many newer "village" developments and residential communities—despite a tendency to take architectural cues from New England—lack a comparable civic center. Although developers argued for many years that retail malls could serve as the modern equivalent of town squares and Main Streets, such spaces lack the combination of civic spaces and uses, both public and commercial, that draw residents and are essential to creating a vibrant public space. Despite the fact that residents generally report valuing a walkable town center over other amenities, voters often punish local officeholders for investing in public spaces. As a result, most smaller communities lack the financial resources to create a town square.

◀ **Figure C-1** Urban design continues to evolve in response to changing social, economic, cultural, environmental, and other dynamics. Like every work of urban design, Babylon's Ishtar Gate (seventh century BCE) tells many stories about the society that created it. The gate's formal design and rich ornamentation—which, even today place the entry among the world's most arresting gateways—reveal the importance attached to a city that was home to gods as well as mortals.

▶ **Figure C-3** Twenty six centuries later Boston's Prudential Center (Charles Luckman and Associates) was built to protect the city from economic collapse as jobs and residents fled to the suburbs.

Figure C-2 Goody Clancy's 2005 proposal for mixed-use redevelopment of Assembly Square, a former industrial site three miles from downtown Boston, demonstrates the renewed appreciation many Americans now have for vibrant urban places.

▶ **Figure C-4** Moshe Safde Associates' Habitat housing, unveiled at the Montreal world's fair in 1967, helped usher in a new era of visions for rebuilding beleaguered cities.

▼ **Figure C-5** Boston's Faneuil Hall Marketplace, designed by Benjamin Thompson and Associates, America's first urban festival marketplace, melded historic preservation and lively new design to reverse the negative connotations downtowns held for most Americans in the early 1970s.

Two Growth Scenarios for Coyote Valley

This illustration shows how the principal physical elements of the Valley would relate to each other under the sprawl and Smart Growth scenarios.

Coyote Valley as Sprawl

Land Use
Segregated Uses

Single-use districts (housing, shopping, employment, etc.) that are isolated and unrelated to each other, and provide little or no flexibility for future changes. An automobile is necessary for everyday activities.

Circulation
Automobile Oriented

A network of expressways and distributor streets creates a series of isolated enclaves. Discontinuous local streets and cul-de-sacs funnel traffic onto a few key distributor roads, resulting in larger and busier streets with more congestion and pollution.

Open Space
Isolated Parks with Open Space Fragments

Parks and open space are fragmented and isolated as residual elements between the different land uses.

Hydrology
Engineered Solutions

Flood management is seen as an engineering problem to be solved with large, single-use structures. Creeks are turned into drainage channels. Stormwater runoff is sent off-site as quickly as possible.

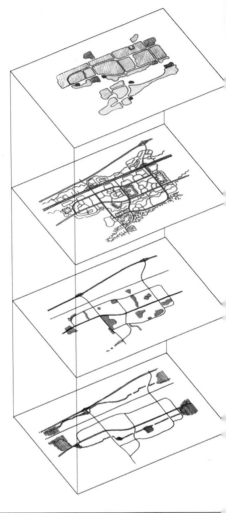

◀ **Figure C-6** "Eastward Ho," Daniel Williams FAIA's vision for redirecting growth from Florida's Everglades back into developed areas stresses core themes—smart growth, well-designed density, livability, social equity, public transportation—that appear in all of the AIA's Regional and Urban Design Honor Award–winning projects that focus on regional development [see Chapter 6: Guiding Regional Growth and Change]. (2000)

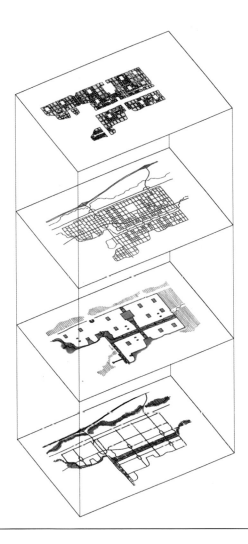

Coyote Valley as a Town

Land Use
Mixed-Use Neighborhoods

A structured and coherent block pattern can accommodate a mixture of land uses in proximity to one another, and provide the flexibility over time to create a compact, pedestrian-friendly, transit-oriented community.

Circulation
Walkable, Bikeable Streets

A hierarchy of interconnected streets and boulevards disperses traffic and creates a network of alternative routes for travel throughout the town. Different modes of travel are safely accommodated, including pedestrians, bicycles, public transit, and the automobile.

Open Space
Network of Parks

Parks and open spaces form an integrated framework that defines neighborhoods and provides for a network of paths linking residential areas to key community destinations. Agricultural lands surround the town, providing an open space buffer and amenity within the context of a working landscape.

Hydrology
Integrated Open Space Solution

Flood management is embraced as natural landscape function and is incorporated into the open space network, maintaining as much of the natural function as possible and integrating improvements as part of a continuous riparian corridor through the town.

▲ **Figure C-7** WRT/Solomon's plan for avoiding sprawl in Coyote Valley near San Jose, California. (2004)

▶ **Figure C-9** Suisman Urban Design's smart-growth vision for the West Bank in Palestine. (2006)

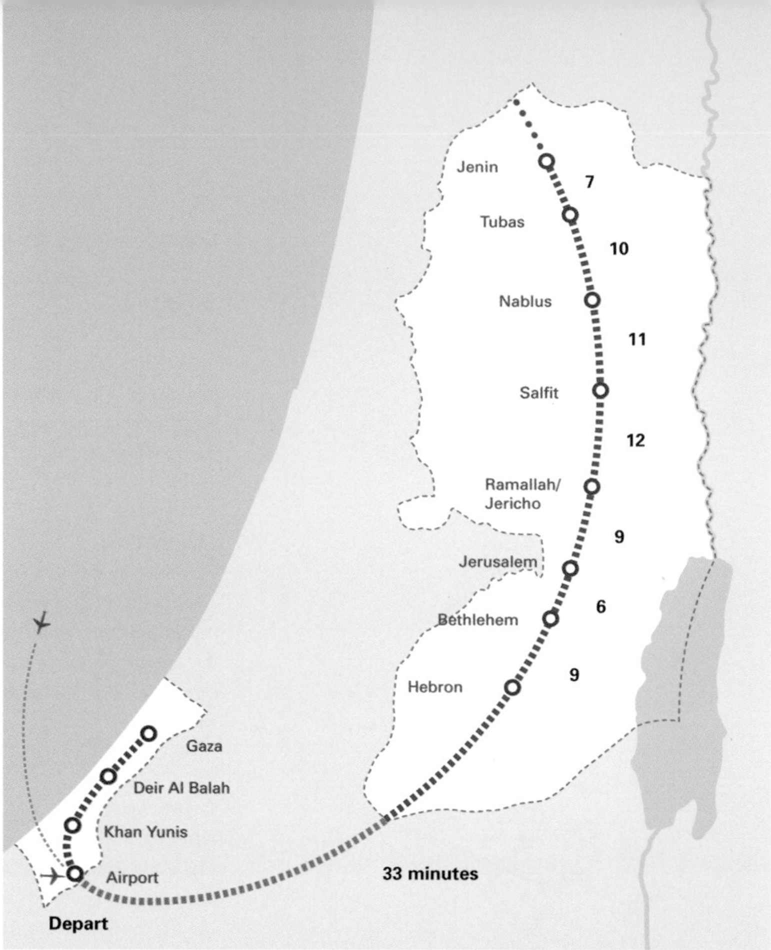

Jenin
7
Tubas
10
Nablus
11
Salfit
12
Ramallah/
Jericho
9
Jerusalem
Bethlehem
6
Hebron
9

Gaza
Deir Al Balah
Khan Yunis
Airport
33 minutes
Depart

▼ **Figure C-8** SOM's proposal for a new city on Chongming Island, near Shanghai. (2005)

Figure C-10 Goody Clancy's strategy for mixed-income and mixed-use development along "Boston's Newest Smart Growth Corridor." (2007)

Figure C-12 SOM's plan re-creates the grandeur of Pennsylvania Station in New York City by redeveloping the nearby Farley Post Office building into a rail hub. (2000)

▶ **Figure C-11** SOM's plan to "restore" Chicago's State Street, along with other Honor Award–winning projects that focus on revitalization of downtowns and Main Streets [see Chapter 7: Rediscovering Downtown and Main Street], symbolizes cities' renewed commitment to reinvigorating urban districts that suffered from decades of disinvestment. (1998)

▼ **Figure C-13** Crandall Arambula's strategy for bringing new life to downtown Racine, Wisconsin. (2001)

Figure C-15 SOM's plan for Lakeshore East, a new urban neighborhood in Chicago. (2002)

◀ **Figure C-14** Zimmer Gunsul Frasca's plan adds a rich array of pedestrian amenities to transform the character of auto-dominated Santa Monica Boulevard in West Hollywood, California. (2001)

▼ **Figure C-16** Torti Gallas and Partners' plan accommodates a new chapter of growth in Charlottesville's (Virginia) older commercial districts. (2003)

▶ **Figure C-19** Weinstein Associates' Ellen Wilson Neighborhood Redevelopment replaced public housing with a new mixed-use neighborhood in Washington, D.C.'s Capitol Hill district. (1998)

▼ **Figure C-17** SOM's Chicago Central Area Plan manages growth in ways that enhance livability. (2004)

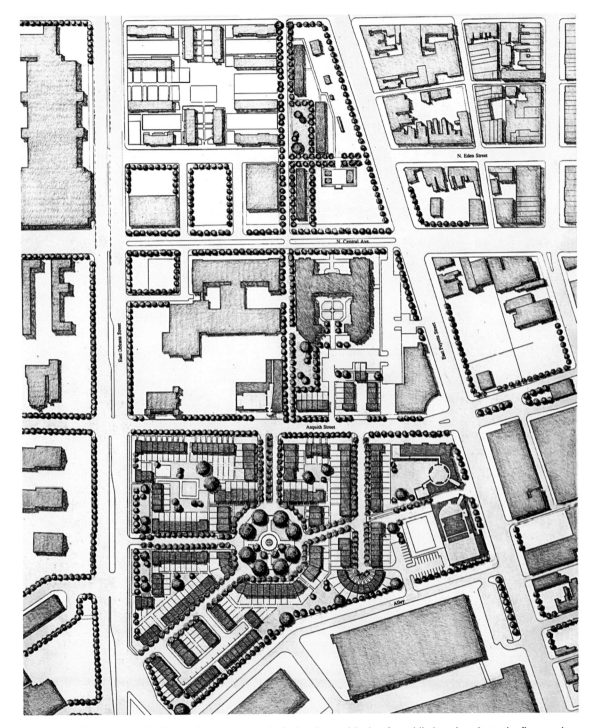

Figure C-18 CHK's plan for Lafayette Courts returns the isolated superblocks of a public housing site to the finer grain that originally existed on the site and restores the kinds of amenities found elsewhere in downtown Baltimore (1997. Like other Honor Award-winning projects that focus on rebuilding older urban districts, the plan demonstrates a new American interest in rebuilding or retrofitting neglected neighborhoods to enhance livability [see Chapter 8: Reinventing Older Neighborhoods].

◀ **Figure C-20** Merrill and Pastor Architects' Windsor Town Center created a central square for a Florida subdivision. (2000)

▼ **Figure C-21** Goody Clancy's Civic Vision for Turnpike Air Rights threads a new generation of high-density growth through eight historic Boston neighborhoods. (2001)

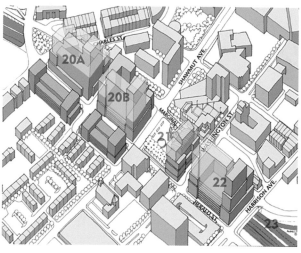

Figure C-22 Torti Gallas and Partners' Flag House Courts builds on the vitality generated by Baltimore's revitalized Inner Harbor to transform public housing into a lively mixed-income neighborhood. (2001)

ACCESSORY DWELLING UNIT PROTOTYPE PLAN SETS

SANTA CRUZ, CALIFORNIA

Office of Planning and Community Development
Housing and Community Development Division
809 Center Street, Room 206
Santa Cruz, CA   95060

telephone: 831-420-5180
email: cityhcd@ci.santa-cruz.ca.us   website: www.ci.santa-cruz.ca.us/pl/hcd/ADU/adu.html

Prototype #1
Detached Single
Story ADU
Prefabricated Wall
Panels

Prototype #2
Detached ADU Over
Existing Garage

Prototype #3
Detached Single
Story Facing Alley

Prototype #4
Detached Single
Story ADU
Alternative Materials
and Techniques

Prototype #5
Attached Garage
ADU Conversion

Prototype #6
Detached
Story-and-a-Half
ADU

Prototype #7
Detached ADU Over
New Garage

Prepared by the City of Santa Cruz • 2003
Funded by the California Pollution Control Financing Authority
Sustainable Communities Grant and Loan Program

Figure C-23 RACESTUDIO worked with the Santa Cruz (California) community to create a plan for infill housing in mature neighborhoods to promote affordability and avoid sprawl. (2005)

Windsor tried a different model, relying on a public-private partnership. The public sector contributed a tenant (post office) and permitted the developers to create a larger project than initially envisioned. In return, the developer took advantage of relatively high housing values in the area and used a portion of the profits from the apartment component to underwrite the cost of public amenities—an amphitheater, the post office, public gardens, and street planting.

Key urban design concepts

This project demonstrates the ability to introduce qualities associated with urban environments—walkability, a mix of public and private uses, a wider range of housing options, shared public spaces—into a suburban or rural development designed on conventional postwar market assumptions that a trip from the local store to the post office would involve driving, that open space would generally consist of private backyards and protected natural areas, and that everyone in the community would share uniform housing needs and aspirations. In the words of the urban designer, "This project, modest in program and scale, and bucolic in setting, is nonetheless urban … [and] it attempts to seamlessly meld architecture, landscape and infrastructure to create the building blocks of urbanism." The project effectively uses several techniques to create a lively town center. Despite the reality that little of the program actually represents public uses and that the entire development relies on surface parking, the design team located all of the buildings to frame a network of public streets and squares. While the designers used a range of styles to convey the distinct character of individual uses ("The gatehouse is a Ledoux-like toll house…. The vehicular gate is a propylea…. The post office is a peripteral temple"), the shared characteristics of a constant focus toward public streets and compatible scale and massing endow the town center with a civic quality. The urban design team also used a palette of landscape elements—"walls, planters, side-walks, trellises, curbs, ramps, bollards, streetlights, street trees, alleys of trees, grass, wooden fences, gravel, steps, hedges and vines"—to support the architecture in creating a strong public realm.

Jury Comments

"A modest program and utilitarian structures, manipulated to create a handsome public space and civic symbol."

A Civic Vision for Turnpike Air Rights in Boston

Location: Boston, Massachusetts

Urban designer: Goody Clancy

Client: Boston Redevelopment Authority, Boston Transportation Department, Massachusetts Turnpike Authority

Study area and program: A vision and framework to guide more than 10 million square feet of mixed-use development on 23 "air rights parcels" above the Massachusetts Turnpike. The study area covered 44 acres in eight distinct neighborhoods along a two-mile section of the turnpike that reaches downtown Boston.

Year of award: 2002

Status: The plan has been approved, and the guidelines function as zoning for these parcels, which, as state property, are exempt from city control.

Critical issues

The Massachusetts Turnpike and adjacent rail lines cut a canyon as wide as 400 feet through the heart of Boston, dividing historic neighborhoods, requiring uninviting block-long bridges, and bringing pollution to the doorsteps of thousands of residents. Two early projects

A Civic Vision for Turnpike Air Rights, Boston, Massachusetts. Goody Clancy worked with public agencies and hundreds of residents to outline a plan for more than 10 million square feet of mixed-use development on air-rights "parcels" above the Massachusetts Turnpike and bordering eight of Boston's oldest neighborhoods. The plan recognizes the scale needed to make air-rights development economically feasible and capitalizes on this greater density to support shops, parks, new connections across the corridor, and other elements that help weave air-rights development into historic neighborhoods while reinforcing their vitality and character. Courtesy of Winn Development.

built above the highway created isolated towers and vast plazas with minimal visual and physical connection to the surrounding fine-grained districts. That history turned nearby residents hostile to the large scale required to make developing air rights economically feasible. Beginning in 1998, a dearth of developable sites in the city and a booming economy joined to push air-rights development onto the public agenda. A proposal for a sixty-story tower between two historic neighborhoods sparked a widespread outcry against the idea of air rights. This backlash prompted the City of Boston to undertake a comprehensive planning initiative to determine if economically feasible air-rights development could also succeed as urban design.

Key urban design concepts

Mayor Thomas Menino charged the urban designer with creating a vision and guidelines that would:

- produce a plan that "adds significant civic value for the whole city and for the neighborhoods located along the Turnpike"
- reflect sufficient agreement on the full range of concerns—political, social, transportation, economic development, neighborhood livability, environmental—represented on a twenty-six-member task force to create "a social compact" that would permit air-rights development

The Civic Vision focused on four equally important principles:

- **Reinforce the vitality and quality of life in adjacent communities** by creating clear guidelines for each of twenty-three air-rights parcels. Balance the scale inherent in air-rights construction with nearby uses, design, and public realm and take into account the planning needs along the corridor—for institutional

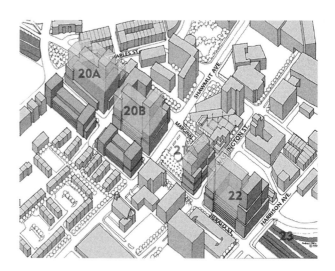

Alternative building massing for four parcels under the Civic Vision guidelines. Courtesy of Goody Clancy. *See color insert, C-21.*

Plan and aerial rendering of the two-mile-long study corridor. Courtesy of Goody Clancy.

growth, diverse housing opportunities, lively public spaces, and the need for a sensitive transition to nearby historic districts.

- **Enhance Boston as a place to live, work, and invest** by accommodating activities that adjacent neighborhoods could not absorb, such as a research campus at Boston University, entertainment near Fenway Park, mixed-income housing in several locations, and new cultural facilities. Development would need to employ design that expresses Boston's current vitality and values.

- **Repair and enrich Boston's public realm** by capturing opportunities to create strong new connections between long-divided neighborhoods, new links to the city's open-space systems, and public realm elements that add to Boston's distinctive character and sense of itself as a community.

- **Foster increased reliance on transit and walking** by locating the highest density close to transit and in locations where it can support retail and other uses that enliven pedestrian access; limit parking to encourage transit access.

Key design guidelines included warning against "automatically reject[ing] towers as somehow alien to Boston"; incorporating street walls that reflect nearby heights; focusing on uses that do not require large floorplates, like housing; honoring the character of "building widths, bay rhythms, and variety in details"; and recognizing the need for above-grade parking but keeping streets active and appealing by building "occupied space in front of parking facing onto public streets."

Jury Comments

"An achievable vision, applicable to the real-world issues that affect air-rights development."

Flag House Courts

LOCATION: Baltimore, Maryland

URBAN DESIGNER: Torti Gallas and Partners—
CHK Architects and Planners

CLIENT: The Integral Group, MidCity Urban,
HJ Russel

STUDY AREA AND PROGRAM: Built on the site of
a series of public housing towers, Flag House
Courts constitutes a new, mixed-income
neighborhood with 338 row houses and small
apartment buildings that line new streets,
squares, and parks. Funding from HOPE VI
and other public and private sources assured
that 40 percent of the new housing will serve
low-income households, with the balance
occupied by middle-income and affluent
households attracted in part by proximity to
downtown Baltimore and the Inner Harbor.

YEAR OF AWARD: 2001

STATUS: Redevelopment has been completed.

Critical issues

Like the other case studies in this chapter that involve
the redevelopment of public housing, the Flag House
Courts plan grew out of a series of intensive working
sessions with residents, city and housing authority staff
members, and other key stakeholders. Residents voiced
concerns similar to those expressed by residents of other
public housing sites facing redevelopment. They ob-
jected to termination of adjacent streets at the development's edges, expressed hope that the nearby commercial street could be revitalized—both to serve their own

▼ Flag House Courts, Baltimore, Maryland. Torti Gallas and
Partners' plan for transforming public housing into a mixed-
income neighborhood focuses on the community's larger
needs. In addition to a mix of new row houses and mid-rise
buildings more in keeping with surrounding blocks, the plan
incorporates redevelopment of vacant and distressed sites
along a nearby Main Street to restore the commercial area
as a community amenity that serves both the new and the
existing neighborhoods. Photo by Steve Hall@Hedrich Blessing. *See color insert, C-22.*

neighborhood and to create a destination that would draw others to the area—and voiced a strong desire to see the development's barren open spaces replaced by safe public parks. Residents also sharply criticized the development's towers, calling them unsuitable for households that included children and characterizing them as tools for reinforcing the site's isolation by their dramatic contrast with the surrounding neighborhoods, primarily filled with row houses.

Key urban design concepts

The urban designer responded to resident concerns and goals by proposing creation of a new neighborhood that would draw directly on the urban design qualities found in many of the neighborhoods around Baltimore's downtown. New streets link directly to the streets of Little Italy, the Inner Harbor, and downtown. The plan expanded the project area beyond the original public housing site by adding vacant land and buildings along nearby Lombard Street, a shopping street, and introducing new small-scale retail with housing above it on those parcels—restoring significant vitality

Drawing on traditional Baltimore housing models, the new neighborhood incorporates rental and ownership housing and a mix of housing types, including apartments and row houses. Photo by Steve Hall@Hedrich Blessing.

to a Main Street that had been in decline for decades. A series of new public spaces honor historic buildings, including the Jewish Museum of Maryland (a complex that includes two historic synagogues) and the Flag House Museum, the house in which the flag that inspired the writing of *The Star-Spangled Banner* was sewn. Flag Courts' architecture builds "on Baltimore row-house typologies. All income levels … have similar plan and facade typologies to avoid identification of the income level of individuals. A wide variety of facade details will be provided to avoid the appearance of mass-produced housing."

Jury Comments

"The transformation of a segregated public housing tower complex and its environs into a diverse mixed-income and mixed-use neighborhood in Baltimore."

Illustrative plan. Courtesy of Torti Gallas and Partners.

Interstate Max Station Area Revitalization Strategy

LOCATION: Portland, Oregon

URBAN DESIGNER: Crandall Arambula, PC

CLIENT: Portland Development Commission

STUDY AREA AND PROGRAM: A revitalization strategy developed to address deficiencies in the design of a three-mile, light-rail transit line along Interstate Avenue, the original road linking Portland and Seattle. A widened right-of-way for the light-rail vehicle (LRV) line would have removed many existing pedestrian-friendly elements, and no plan had been formulated to encourage and guide redevelopment around six new stations.

YEAR OF AWARD: 2003

STATUS: Plan adopted by the Portland City Council in 2002; redevelopment has been completed.

Critical issues

North Portland's lower-income neighborhoods faced escalating housing costs, loss of local retail, and other pressures threatening residents' quality of life. The first plan for the LRV line would have exacerbated these problems and degraded the urban design of the road, adding to the threat to commercial and residential areas and discouraging new investment. Neighborhood activists worked with

▼ Interstate MAX Station Area Revitalization Strategy, Portland, Oregon. In the wake of community criticism of an earlier scheme, Crandall Arambula developed a plan to support revitalization of lower-income neighborhoods along a new light-rail vehicle line. The plan, based on extensive outreach, lays out a strategy for building a context-sensitive, mixed-use neighborhood center around each proposed station. It identifies sites—some created by land acquisition for the line—that could accommodate a total of 3,500 new affordable housing units within walking distance of the stations. Courtesy of Crandall Arambula.

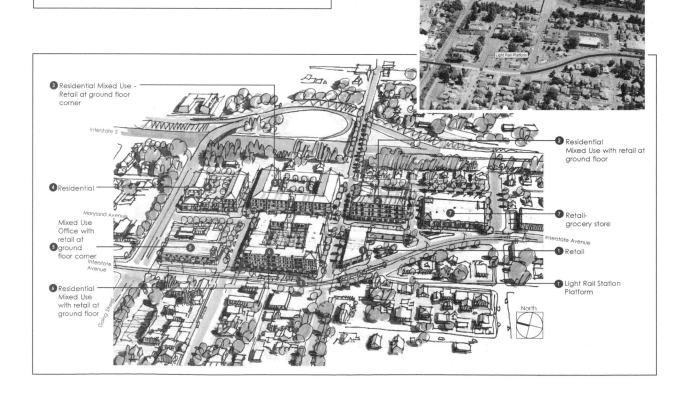

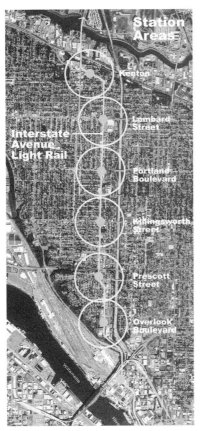

▶ The plan laid out development strategies for six proposed LRV stations. Courtesy of Crandall Arambula.

▶▶ Development theme and approach for each station area. Courtesy of Crandall Arambula.

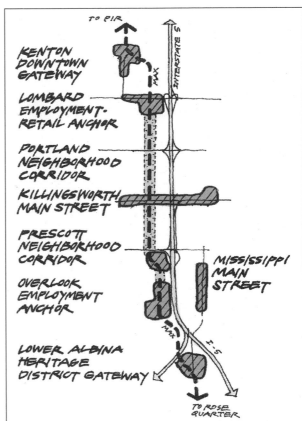

the city and the urban designer to create a new plan that would build neighborhood centers around the new stations; strengthen the pedestrian environment throughout the study area; identify opportunities for affordable housing; and spell out realistic implementation strategies. The design team and residents also sought to create a wide-reaching and inclusive public process for developing and assessing the plan.

Key urban design concepts

The plan focuses on strategies for transforming the LRV line and its stations into a tool for building community and livability:

- **Creating neighborhood centers** by identifying three to four blocks of potential development parcels around

each station. Each center would include varied new development that accommodates larger-floorplate retail uses—particularly grocery stores—and creates an animated, pedestrian-focused streetscape.

- **Creating a strong pedestrian environment around transit stations** by adding curbside parking, planting street trees, widening rather than narrowing sidewalks, and making intersections more pedestrian-friendly.

- **Developing affordable housing opportunities** by identifying sites that can in aggregate support 3,500 units of affordable housing in new buildings, above retail space in neighborhood centers, and on other sites within walking distance of new stations.

- **Creating realistic implementation strategies** by developing public-private partnerships to support a series of strategic development initiatives. Projected private investment around stations nearly quadrupled to $300 million with completion of the plan.

Jury Comments

"This is a buildable, realistic project.... The development around stations will be more predictable and better for each neighborhood than without this plan."

Cady's Alley

LOCATION: Washington, D.C.

URBAN DESIGNER: Sorg & Associates; Frank Schlesinger Associates Architects; McInturff Architects; Martinez & Johnson Architecture, PC; and Shalom Baranes Associates Architects

CLIENT: Eastbanc, Inc.

STUDY AREA AND PROGRAM: Cady's Alley, located in the historic Georgetown district, consists of twelve relatively modest commercial buildings—mainly row structures that face M Street, one of Georgetown's two main commercial streets—and four industrial buildings between the alley behind M Street and the historical C&O Canal. The owner-developer assembled the 2.5-acre site over a five-year period with the idea of creating a "design center" of retail stores and showrooms geared to a professional clientele. The result is a total of 121,000 square feet of primarily home-furnishings retail and office space, six apartments, and a revitalized section of the nation's second-oldest historic district. The facades of the two- and three-story shops along M Street were restored and many have been interconnected, although the original dividing walls remain.

YEAR OF AWARD: 2005

STATUS: Development is complete.

Critical issues

The developer assembled a team of five architects to work collaboratively within the letter and spirit of the complex regulations that govern the historic district to create an environment that honored the vitality of the twenty-first-century community while remaining faithful to its eighteenth- and nineteenth-century historical character. The developer aimed to avoid creating simply "an urbanized version of a suburban 'big box' shopping center" and hoped to capture the diversity of the mix of uses. Each firm designed individual buildings and each was encouraged to respond to the historic context in creative ways that expressed the different character and uses intended for particular buildings. The five firms collaborated on design of the common spaces.

Key urban design concepts

Through a series of design charrettes, the design team created "a mixed-use environment that would appear to be an organic part of Georgetown's evolving urban context" yet would provide patrons and residents with twenty-first-century "shopping and living experiences." The team set as its goal the "combination of two urban design idioms—historic preservation and contemporary design—into a physically complex but visually unified whole." The development introduces a very contemporary mix of retail, housing, and other uses in a way that enriches historic Georgetown's appeal and demonstrates how a historic district can continue to adapt to new retail formats and shifting consumer preferences for different types of retail, housing, and other urban activities.

Jury Comments

"This is a sensitive intervention which breathes new life into a historically significant urban fabric."

▼ View of the development from the Chesapeake & Ohio Canal, which borders Cady's Alley on the south. Courtesy of Suman Sorg, Sorg & Associates, Architects, Washington, D.C.

▲ Cady's Alley, Georgetown, Washington, D.C. Five firms—Sorg & Associates, Frank Schlesinger Associates, McInturff Architects, Martinez & Johnson Architecture, and Shalom Baranes Associates Architects—collaborated to transform a collection of modest buildings in the historic Georgetown neighborhood into a bustling, mixed-use development. The plan demonstrates how careful design and a strong focus on creating a lively pedestrian-oriented public realm can enable larger retailers, usually relegated to suburban locations, to contribute to the character and quality of a historic district. Courtesy of Suman Sorg, Sorg & Associates, Architects, Washington, D.C.

City of Santa Cruz Accessory Dwelling Program

LOCATION: Santa Cruz, California
URBAN DESIGNER: RACESTUDIO
CLIENT: City of Santa Cruz
STUDY AREA AND PROGRAM: A program to provide zoning, design, financing, and other support for adding housing units in the city's residential neighborhoods.
YEAR OF AWARD: 2005
STATUS: The city has adopted the plan.

Critical issues

The city initiated the accessory dwelling unit program in response to a severe housing shortage and a strong commitment to protecting the surrounding natural environment from further development. Santa Cruz had been "ranked as one of the top three least affordable housing markets in the entire country." High housing costs were turning away residents, emptying schools, and raising concerns on the local University of California campus about a potential "brain drain." As residents retired, the city offered few housing options that would permit them to stay in the community as they aged. The only way the city could expand its housing supply—and create a new stock of affordable housing in the process—was to find ways to build new housing within existing neighborhoods.

Key urban design concepts

The urban designer helped the city run a community process—in which four hundred residents participated—to introduce and shape the components of a program for *accessory dwelling units* (ADU) on parcels that already contain a single-family home. The urban design team created a manual that explained the process to homeowners, elaborating on five urban design principles that emerged during the community process:

- **Increase densities within current neighborhoods** rather than locate housing in environmentally sensitive areas outside established neighborhoods.

- **Make the new housing "invisible"** by "blending into existing neighborhoods … behind the host house."

- **Reinforce existing neighborhood character** by using "materials, colors, and other details [that] are similar to the host house."

- **Make sure that each unit is well designed** by providing prototypical designs that homeowners can use and by providing design assistance and review through the city.

- **Involve the community** in the design process.

The plan also addressed a set of very specific challenges. Changing the zoning ordinance to permit homeowners to park in driveways freed up garages for rehabilitation as living space. The urban designer developed a how-to manual and design prototypes, and the city launched a low-interest loan program available to homeowners in return for affordability commitments. The city has hosted ongoing workshops to educate community members about the range of issues involved in adding accessory units within their neighborhoods.

Jury Comments

"An innovative way to increase density while maintaining the scale of the neghborhood."

D2N-PROTOTYPE
DETACHED, TWO-STORY, NEW

68

◀ City of Santa Cruz Accessory Dwelling Program, Santa Cruz, California. RACESTUDIO worked with residents in one of the United States' most expensive housing markets to craft an innovative approach to creating infill housing in existing neighborhoods. The program helps preserve the area's beautiful coastal environment by reducing development pressure at the city's edge, and it adds more affordable options for people who want to remain in or move to the city's diverse neighborhoods. The plan includes design guidelines developed jointly with residents to ensure that infill construction reflects the character of the housing around it. Courtesy of James Herbert © six eight.

▼ Prototype house-plan sets prepared for the program. Courtesy of James Herbert © six eight. *See color insert, C-23.*

▲ Accessory unit built under the program. Courtesy of the City of Santa Cruz, photo by Norm Daly.

Martin Luther King Plaza Revitalization

Location: Philadelphia, Pennsylvania

Urban designer: Torti Gallas and Partners

Client: Uni-Penn, LLC, Philadelphia Housing Authority

Study area and program: A high-rise public housing project located in a predominantly working-class neighborhood just south of downtown Philadelphia. Approximately 700 units of new housing, half on the original site, the balance built as infill development in the surrounding community.

Year of award: 2006

Status: Redevelopment has been completed.

Critical issues

Redevelopment of Martin Luther King Plaza spotlights the importance of addressing the impact of public housing on surrounding areas. As working-class residents left the surrounding neighborhood after World War II, proximity to the site deterred new arrivals; even when people began moving back into the city and nearby neighborhoods thrived, deterioration spread and vacancies proliferated in the blocks around the site.

Key urban design concepts

Redevelopment focused equally on replacing towers that clashed with the historic and traditional character of surrounding blocks and on infill development that helped restore the character of those blocks. As many successful HOPE VI developments have done, the plan

subdivided the public housing superblock, creating a series of smaller blocks lined by buildings compatible in scale and character with nearby row-house blocks. Of particular note, the urban designer paid careful attention to a program of infill development and restoration of existing buildings along adjacent streets that repaired years of damage to the neighborhood's fabric.

Jury Comments

"Exceptional in combining new construction with rehabilitation of viable existing buildings.... Demolition of a housing project in Philadelphia is replaced with a scale of domestic architecture that heals the urban fabric."

▲▲ Martin Luther King Plaza Revitalization, Philadelphia, Pennsylvania. Torti Gallas and Partners builds on the approach used in its Flag House Courts redevelopment in Baltimore, replacing public housing with a new mixed-income community designed to fit comfortably among surrounding row-house neighborhoods. The plan extends the reach of the redevelopment with infill construction on abandoned parcels and renovation of distressed buildings nearby. Photo by Steve Hall@Hedrich Blessing.

▲ Illustrative plan. Courtesy of Torti Gallas and Partners.

The plan locates half of the redevelopment on the site of the demolished high-rise (as new construction) and scatters the remainder in renovated buildings and infill construction on adjacent blocks. Photo by Steve Hall@Hedrich Blessing.

Zoning, Urban Form, and Civic Identity: The Future of Pittsburgh's Hillsides, Pittsburgh, Pennsylvania. Perkins Eastman fashioned a plan to preserve the unique character of the city's undeveloped hillsides—about one-fifth of Pittsburgh's land mass—and to balance environmental concerns against the need to identify buildable sites that promote economic development. The planning team explored ways to incorporate measures into zoning designed to yield certain kinds of urban form traditionally found in the city. The planning team makes a bold assertion, which has yet to receive full exploration in comparable urban design work: " Enhancing urban identity should be a primary goal in planning a city's future. Strengthening and protecting physical characteristics that support identity should be an integral purpose of zoning." Courtesy of Perkins Eastman.

Zoning, Urban Form, and Civic Identity: The Future of Pittsburgh Hillsides

LOCATION: Pittsburgh, Pennsylvania

URBAN DESIGNER: Perkins Eastman

CLIENT: Department of Planning, City of Pittsburgh, Allegheny Land Trust

STUDY AREA AND PROGRAM: The city sought to replace existing hillside guidelines for slopes of greater than 25 percent grade—representing approximately one-quarter of the land area in this hilly city—with enforceable regulations that would control development and preserve open space and green hillsides in highly visible locations.

YEAR OF AWARD: 2007

STATUS: The plan's recommendations have been adopted and translated into new zoning regulations that replace earlier guidelines in governing hillside development.

Critical issues

Like many older industrial cities in the Northeast and Midwest, Pittsburgh has struggled to attract investment in recent decades. In the face of continued erosion of jobs and population regionally, the city has experienced some success in attracting new residents and jobs by capitalizing on its built and natural amenities—proud old neighborhoods and Main Streets, a vibrant downtown, a rich supply of educational and cultural institutions, two riverfronts, and dramatic hillsides. In particular, its hillsides have been viewed as places to create distinctive new urban housing that woos suburbanites with dramatic views and easy walking access to neighborhood commercial districts. The city did not have zoning or other regulatory tools to manage a growing interest in this kind of development.

Key urban design concepts

The plan calls for a targeted set of regulations to govern the unique environmental, development, open

Rooms Created by Geography

River Valley Rooms

Plateau Rooms

Stream Hallways

space, civic, and other aspects of hillside development. The plan underscores the contributions that the highly visible hillsides make to the city's character and recommends development and open space patterns based on the each hillside's unique context. Recommendations for each hillside were shaped and tested at citywide, neighborhood, and site-specific scales. One of the plan's signal contributions is the assertion that "enhancing urban identity should be a primary goal in planning a city's future. Strengthening and protecting physical characteristics that support identity should be an integral purpose of zoning."

How the Projects Illustrate the Principles

1. **Build community in an increasingly diverse society.** The HOPE VI case studies focus directly on one of the most challenging dimensions of diversity—transforming isolated pockets of low-income public housing into mixed-income communities woven into the neighborhoods around them. While several introduce a new park or other central green space, all of the HOPE VI plans focus on making neighborhood streets work as good public spaces—adding trees, framing and enlivening streets, and taking similar steps to make streets inviting both to residents of these developments and to their neighbors. For the HOPE VI case studies, new parks, like community facilities (and in one instance a health center), support diversity by drawing residents from the surrounding community into the respective developments. In a sense, Santa Cruz's innovative ADU program achieves diversity by inserting it—scattering affordable housing units throughout an existing community that had seen dramatic housing-price inflation. In very different ways Windsor Town Center and A Civic Vision for Turnpike Air Rights offer dramatic examples of retrofitting existing neighborhoods to promote a sense of community. Windsor Town Center, located in a growing suburb,

gives a subdivision the town center it never had. This project combines civic uses, stores, and well-designed public space to draw people together and offer them a place to build and enjoy a sense of community. The Air Rights case study asserts that the primary reason to develop buildings over the Massachusetts Turnpike is not to encourage economic development but to create buildings that can pay for, and enliven, a walkable public realm that reconnects neighborhoods separated by this transportation corridor for more than a century.

2. **Advance environmental sustainability.** The HOPE VI case studies and Turnpike Air Rights add another dimension to the case for smart growth by demonstrating not only that established urban communities can accommodate significant growth and change but also that good design and added amenities can equip urban neighborhoods to attract middle- and upper-income residents. The Santa Cruz initiative makes the case from the opposite perspective—established neighborhoods with rapidly appreciating land values can nevertheless accommodate economic diversity in communities that choose to contain sprawl. Santa Cruz residents, offered a planning process that was broadly inclusive and that addressed a wide range of concerns, chose to increase density in existing neighborhoods in part to discourage further encroachment into natural areas outside the city. Cady's Alley teaches a similar lesson: good design makes it possible to introduce substantial new uses into a densely built area, enabling growth to occur where infrastructure already exists.

3. **Expand individual choices.** The Bahçeşehir, HOPE VI, Interstate MAX, and Santa Cruz case studies introduce an entire new generation of housing choice. In place of one-size-fits-all housing, they offer a range of housing types that enable people of different ages, household types, cultural backgrounds—and, in most cases, incomes—to choose housing that suits their varying needs and aspirations yet allows them to become part of a larger community. By addressing both

social and design problems that have plagued public housing, the HOPE VI developments have not only improved quality of life for public housing residents but have also helped transform their neighborhoods into places that welcome more affluent people looking for urban living options. The Santa Cruz plan opens up new choices with a similarly dramatic impact: older residents in search of a smaller house can now remain in their neighborhoods, families can create apartments for aging relatives, and younger people can find less costly housing in a closer-in neighborhood or in the neighborhood where they grew up. The other case studies also represent a flowering of the notion of individual choice. The Bahçeşehir and Pittsburgh Hillside projects provide opportunities to enjoy nature within walking distance of the heart of the city. Many of these case studies, even in widely divergent contexts, also recognize the value people place on walkable Main Streets and commercial centers. The Interstate MAX plan came about in part because neighborhood activists insisted that design of a light-rail connection should work to breathe life back into struggling old-neighborhood centers. Windsor Town Center provides residents of a growing subdivision an alternative to malls and the chance to enjoy a town square—a public space rarely found in newer suburbs. Cady's Alley does the reverse: it brings the suburbs to downtown by skillfully integrating larger retailers into a historic neighborhood and giving residents an alternative to driving to a far-flung mall.

4. **Enhance personal health.** The Future of Pittsburgh Hillsides represents a new generation of urban design plans that carves walking trails into the hearts of cities, providing access to riverfronts, woodlands, and other natural features—and new opportunities for exercise. Each of the case studies acknowledges the increased value that people place on walkability, most notably by rebuilding superblocks at the scale of traditional, more walkable urban grids. For Windsor Town Center and Cady's Alley, a new mix of added uses—and, in Windsor, a new sense of community—turns walking into an appealing choice. Turnpike Air Rights adds more than two miles of sidewalks and requires that development line these sidewalks with stores (or other pedestrian-friendly uses) and street trees to ensure that they are inviting.

5. **Make places for people.** Virtually all of these plans represent reactions to the urban renewal mistakes of previous decades. Each succeeds at placemaking by focusing on creating a public realm that enhances human experience. In place of superblocks, the HOPE VI and the Turnpike Air Rights case studies create—or create anew—grids of pleasant tree-lined streets. In place of blank walls or buildings that turn their backs to the street, these plans line their new streets with human-scaled buildings and introduce new shops and other activities to increase activity in the street. Public parks incorporate fountains and mature trees to invite people to enjoy them. These case studies demonstrate how new buildings, even multistory towers, can be welcome neighbors in historic and traditional districts when they pay careful attention to transitions in scale. The Ellen Wilson redevelopment plan also makes the case that mixing heights and styles can help new development blend into the variety found nearby. In the heart of a nationally prominent historic district, Cady's Alley demonstrates that even the historic context of Georgetown can accommodate larger retailers and innovative design that is carefully integrated into its distinctive setting and that takes advantage of market opportunities created by a dense, mixed-use urban district to avoid adding significant on-site parking. Windsor Town Center succeeds by breaking many of the tenets of suburban shopping design to create a place that is organized around people and human sensibilities, not cars. The Pittsburgh Hillsides plan makes a strong argument for honoring the past when it asserts that an entire city has the right to legislate preservation of its identity.

CHAPTER 9

Inventing New Neighborhoods

Former Oklahoma City mayor Kirk Humphreys and his son Grant are developing the city's first new urban neighborhood in more than sixty years. After years of successful development projects in the suburbs, their firm has turned its attention to the city's new frontier—downtown. As mayor, Humphreys oversaw a revival that brought downtown a new art museum, housing and restaurants, and an influx of jobs and entertainment—all of which opened new development opportunities in the city's urban neighborhoods. "Instead of building just another project," says Grant Humphreys, "we wanted to create an entire neighborhood that responded to the new appetite for urban living. We also wanted to create a real community where a diverse mix of people could live, work, shop, and have fun. The only place to do this right was in the city, close to downtown."

Nearly all new neighborhoods built in the United States after World War II followed an auto-focused, subdivision model that emerged in the 1940s. Beginning in the 1990s, and accelerating with the founding of the Congress for the New Urbanism in 1993, urban designers began to challenge this model. This pushback took two forms: exploring alternate designs for suburban neighborhoods that accommodated changes taking place in demographics, living styles, and market preferences; and addressing rising demand for new urban development in reviving central cities across the United States.

Today, urban designers focus on introducing walkable town centers into existing suburbs—giving places with no "there" a there—providing models for infill development and creating the first new urban neighborhoods since the Depression. Much of this work is sponsored by the public sector, although the private sector has played an increasingly active role by hiring urban designers to create entire new town centers and new neighborhoods.

Roots

Historically, new neighborhoods have evolved in tandem with changes in transportation technology. The rapid adoption of electric streetcars in the 1890s encouraged

201

development of larger-scale new neighborhoods outside of the densely urbanized (and still relatively compact) centers of American cities. Horse-drawn streetcars, which had been in use since the 1820s, already carried more than 180 million passengers annually in the United States by the time the electrified version appeared. Residential neighborhoods served by horse-drawn streetcars developed after the Civil War and established a model of leapfrogging poorer, older neighborhoods with new construction intended for wealthier residents at the city's edge.

Three factors fueled the creation of new neighborhoods as electric streetcar service spread at end of the nineteenth century:

- Rapid industrial growth, concentrated in urban areas, attracted large numbers of people to live and work in cities. In the 1850 census, New York was the only American city with more than 200,000 residents. By 1920, more than thirty cities had passed that mark (New York itself had reached 5.6 million). Industrial development fueled most of this population growth.

- Intensifying noise, pollution, and other negative impacts of industrializing cities induced increasing numbers of affluent and middle-class residents to decamp to outlying new neighborhoods suddenly accessible by electric streetcars.

- Growing diversity in cities—as new residents poured in from around the world and from rural America—and an industrial-era custom of separating managers' housing from workers' housing evolved into a wide-spread practice of creating homogeneous neighborhoods for people of similar incomes, ethnic roots, and cultural backgrounds.

The first popularized vision for creating new neighborhoods arose in England with the garden cities movement, also called the Town and Country movement, which founder Ebenezer Howard described in his 1898 book *To-morrow: A Peaceful Path to Real Reform* (reissued in 1902 as *Garden Cities of Tomorrow*).[220] Howard described these new suburban communities—a blend of the best attributes of city and country—as self-contained towns surrounded by a permanent "green belt" of agricultural land. Howard's model separated the residential from shopping and from industrial districts.

But Howard's suburban vision did not survive a trans-Atlantic crossing unaltered. Even as new neighborhoods proliferated at the edges of U.S. cities, most jobs stayed in the core, a pattern that encouraged construction of bedroom communities rather than self-sufficient garden cities. The spread of automobile ownership in the 1920s encouraged this suburbanizing tendency.

After World War II, a series of mutually reinforcing changes spurred the growth of suburban neighborhoods, among them widespread adoption of single-use zoning; an increase in exclusionary mortgage practices like redlining of urban neighborhoods; the growth of large residential home builders and the rise of a mass housing market; and an exodus of jobs from urban centers to suburbs. From the 1950s through the mid-1990s, the terms "new neighborhood" and "subdivision" were synonymous to most Americans—single-use, bedroom communities built in a short period by a single development company.

The New Urbanism movement in the 1990s deserves much credit for sharpening the critique of the subdivision model and for exploring alternative design approaches—often reaching back for precedents that predated postwar subdivisions—to creating new neighborhoods and

Norfolk, Virginia. Redevelopment creates a vibrant, new mixed-use neighborhood that strengthens downtown and serves every income level. Courtesy of Goody Clancy.

> In the 21st century, the province of urban design is no longer the spaces between buildings or the decoration of streetscapes. Rather, the meaning and role of urban design is to recognize and enhance the fundamental relationship between physical form and the social life of our communities.
>
> Jean Marie Gath, principal, Pfeiffer Partners Architects and Planners, New York

rebuilding existing ones. In addition to these traditional approaches, urban designers increasingly used concepts like planned-unit developments and other mechanisms for introducing mixed uses, street grids, concentrated development that preserves open space; and techniques to enhance design quality and overall livability.

By the time the American Institute of Architects (AIA) launched its Regional and Urban Design Honor Awards program in the 1990s, urban designers were working across the country to retrofit subdivisions with new town centers and create new mixed-use, denser suburban neighborhoods. By the late 1990s—as noted in Chapter 4—rapid shifts in demographics and values, together with metastasizing congestion and growing support for sustainability, stoked a resurgent interest in urban living not seen since the Depression. As a result, urban designers have begun working on planning and designing new urban neighborhoods for the first time since José Luis Sert gave the profession a name at a 1956 conference on urban design at the Harvard Graduate School of Design.

Approaches Today

The AIA's Center for Communities by Design offers a set of fundaments, described in *Ten Principles for Livable Communities* (available at http://www.aia.org/liv_principles), that reflect the aspirations many urban designers bring to the design of new neighborhoods:

1. **Design on a human scale.** Compact, pedestrian-friendly communities allow residents to walk to shops, services, cultural resources, and jobs and can reduce traffic congestion and benefit people's health.

2. **Provide choices.** People want variety in housing, shopping, recreation, transportation, and employment. Variety creates lively neighborhoods and accommodates residents in different stages of their lives.

3. **Encourage mixed-use development.** Integrating different land uses and varied building types creates vibrant, pedestrian-friendly, diverse communities.

4. **Preserve urban centers.** Restoring, revitalizing, and infilling urban centers take advantage of existing streets, services, and buildings and avoid the need for new infrastructure. This helps to curb sprawl and promote stability for city neighborhoods.

5. **Vary transportation options.** Giving people the option of walking, biking, and using public transit, in addition to driving, reduces traffic congestion, protects the environment, and encourages physical activity.

6. **Build vibrant public spaces.** Citizens need welcoming, well-defined public places to stimulate face-to-face interaction, collectively celebrate and mourn, encourage civic participation, admire public art, and gather for public events.

7. **Create a neighborhood identity.** A "sense of place" gives neighborhoods a unique character, enhances the walking environment, and creates pride in the community.

8. **Protect environmental resources.** A well-designed balance of nature and development preserves natural systems, protects waterways from pollution, reduces air pollution, and protects property values.

9. **Conserve landscapes.** Open space, farms, and wildlife habitat are essential for environmental, recreational, and cultural reasons.

10. **Design matters.** Design excellence is the foundation of successful and healthy communities.

Case Studies

These case studies illustrate the growing focus on the importance of community in larger-scale developments. Most represent a type of project not seen since before the Depression, the creation of new urban neighborhoods.

Kaka`ako Makai Area Development Strategy

LOCATION: Beachfront between downtown Honolulu and Waikiki

URBAN DESIGNER: ELS/Elbasani & Logan Associates

CLIENT: Hawaii Community Development Authority

STUDY AREA AND PROGRAM: A mostly flat, 220-acre peninsula that is home to light industry and a narrow waterfront park. Approximately 7,500,000 square feet of development will be phased in following the framework this plan establishes. The first phase includes an expanded waterfront park, roughly 1,200,000 square feet of mixed-use development, a 700-seat theater, an amphitheater, and a children's museum.

YEAR OF AWARD: 1997

STATUS: The plan was adopted and redevelopment is underway.

Critical issues

Low-quality, high-density development, largely along the "towers in the park" model, had propelled widespread public opposition to development; the public had come to view growth "as paradise lost, rather than urbanity gained." Density reductions in response to this resistance had forced growth to the edge of the metropolitan area, where it claimed growing amounts of undeveloped land. Growth requires new alternatives, and this project was intended to serve as "a model for tropical urbanism" that could reestablish "the city's physical and psychological links to its waterfront" while providing "new options for urban living."

Key urban design concepts

The plan "superimposes a close-knit urban pattern over a system of interconnected, open-air spaces at the ground plane.... [A]s the distinction between outdoors and indoors is blurred, the continuous open ground plane becomes the forum for public life as well as a link to nature for tropical city dwellers." The plan weaves together a series of components:

- **A stronger linkage of the waterfront park to the city,** achieved by expanding the park, "a key link in a continuous 'lei of green' extending from Waikiki to the airport."

- **A unified open space network** formed by "a continuous system of broad, shady walkways, arcades, passages and courtyards linked to the park."

- **A broad range of park environments** achieved by introducing a variety of uses—from basic open spaces to lively retail-lined squares that "draw a much broader spectrum of the population to...Kaka`ako Makai."

- **A more finely grained urban pattern** that contrasts with much recent Honolulu development. The plan calls for smaller blocks, narrower streets, and a much stronger emphasis on lining streets and public spaces with retail and other uses that promote walkability. When paired with walkability, high densities will help deepen the pool of residents and workers who can support pedestrian-level restaurants and stores.

- **Better form and definition of public spaces** by orienting all buildings to enliven and frame streets and public spaces and confer "personality" on these spaces.

Kaka`ako Makai Area Development Strategy, Honolulu, Hawaii. ELS/Elbasani & Logan Associates offer a "a model for tropical urbanism" that departs from unpopular earlier approaches to development that had led Honolulu residents to reject growth "as paradise lost, rather than urbanity gained." The plan proposes a high-density mixed-use district shaped around a fine grain of narrow walkable streets lined with shops and lushly landscaped squares and parks that connect to a new oceanfront park. Courtesy of Hawaii Community Development Authority.

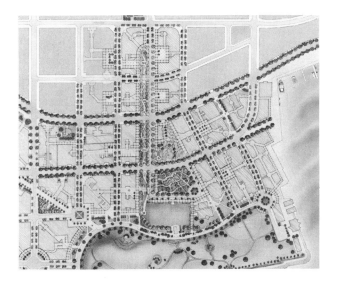

- **A reconfigured roadway network** with narrower existing and proposed waterfront boulevards.

- **Integration of autos and pedestrians** by relying heavily on curbside parking to reduce dependence on garages and by designing all roadways to focus on the needs of pedestrians, not just automobiles, with wide, tree-lined sidewalks.

▶ Illustrative plan. Courtesy of ELS Architecture and Urban Design.

▲ Potential massing of buildings under the plan. Courtesy of ELS Architecture and Urban Design. *See color insert, C-24.*

Saigon South Master Plan

LOCATION: Ho Chi Minh City (formerly Saigon), Vietnam

URBAN DESIGNER: Skidmore, Owings & Merrill

CLIENT: A joint venture between Central Trading & Development Corporation of Taipei and Ho Chi Minh City's municipal government

STUDY AREA AND PROGRAM: A city for 1,000,000 people located on 6,400 acres (at the time predominantly agricultural land), south of the existing core of Ho Chi Minh City along a proposed new highway

YEAR OF AWARD: 1997

STATUS: Approved by the Ho Chi Minh City municipal government in 1994; first phase construction (roadway and utility infrastructure) began in 1997.

Critical issues

Anticipating a doubling of its early 1990s population to more than 10 million residents by the year 2010, the municipality of Ho Chi Minh City had grown deeply concerned about accommodating such rapid growth. How would it affect the environment and quality of life? Could the city's existing infrastructure support it? The municipality committed to creating a new city, just south of the existing city core, as an alternative to sprawling across the region's natural environment and destruction of existing lower-scaled historic neighborhoods.

▼ Saigon South Master Plan, Ho Chi Minh City, Vietnam. Developers proposed the new city built under this plan by Skidmore, Owings & Merrill as an alternative to sprawl. The plan lays the framework for a "city of islands" for one million residents on a tidal delta south of Ho Chi Minh City's core. Organized into high-density, mixed-use districts, the plan preserves the larger city's lively, walkable urban culture but establishes its own distinctive sense of place. Courtesy of Skidmore, Owings & Merrill LLP. *See color insert, C-25.*

Aerial view of one of the island districts proposed in the plan (outlined areas on the plan diagram are shown in figure at right). Courtesy of Skidmore, Owings & Merrill LLP.

Key urban design concepts

The master plan was designed to function as "a comprehensive planning tool intended to help Ho Chi Minh City manage the physical expansion generated by extensive economic growth while safeguarding its significant cultural and natural assets." The plan follows existing topography to create a "city of islands" for which natural waterways (in fact, channels of the Mekong River delta) establish the boundaries of each neighborhood. These neighborhoods are planned as "high-density...mixed-use" districts to preserve Ho Chi Minh City's lively, walkable urban culture. Five core goals address conditions in a rapidly developing country, but they have clear applicability to and resonance in the United States:

- **Enhancing quality of life** by integrating cultural, recreational, educational, and similar facilities into the new city's neighborhoods to ensure that they have a civic dimension.

- **Maintaining "a sustainable ecology"** through creation of an environmental "framework" that helps manage the region's hydrology, water quality, flood system, and shoreline ecosystems—in part by using

Canals and existing watercourses in the river delta shape the development plan. Courtesy of Skidmore, Owings & Merrill LLP.

waterways as a defining design element and by avoiding engineered manipulation of them.

- **Managing sustainable accessibility** by creating a new pedestrian and transit-oriented transportation network that reduces the need for acquiring or using an automobile.

- **Creating a sense of place** by introducing the concept of a "city of islands" to confer a distinctive character on a series of walkable neighborhoods.

- **Creating an adaptable framework** that establishes essential qualities but permits the community to grow and evolve in response to shifting market conditions.

Critical issues

This plan addressed a wide range of urban design issues inherent in transforming one of the city's poorest neighborhoods into a mixed-use, mixed-income district. Most but not all of these issues concern physical design:

- Revitalizing surrounding neighborhoods, including relocation, new housing, and public realm improvements.

- Creation of a new system of public spaces for a community that lacked public parks.

- Creating a variety of housing densities to accommodate a range of ages and household types and to form an appropriate transition from larger research buildings to the neighborhood's traditional row-house scale.

- Introducing new stores, community spaces, a school, and other facilities that support community life.

- Creating a state-of-the-art research center adjacent to the Johns Hopkins Medical Center.

- Addressing educational, public health, child care, job training, and other issues that will arise in the course of a transition from a predominantly low-income community to one with a mixed-income profile.

Key urban design concepts

The plan builds on the area's traditional character, but it also integrates significant new elements to enhance livability and make the neighborhood competitive both as a mixed-income community and as a location for scientific research. Principal elements for the 215-acre area include a new street grid and block pattern to create interconnected landscaped blocks that can accommodate off-street parking (the area's small house lots, platted before the automobile era, have no room for parking spaces). A new park system takes advantage of a rail right-of-way to fashion a series of connected parks and public spaces. New mixed-income housing includes a variety of unit types, from single-family row houses to mid-rise multifamily

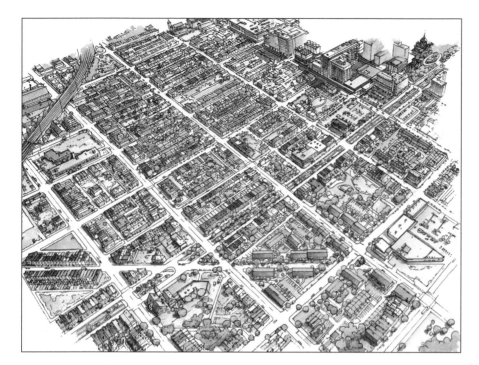

View of proposed residential street. Courtesy of Urban Design Associates; copyright Urban Design Associates.

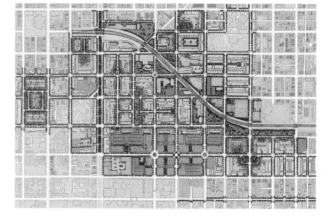

Illustrative plan. Courtesy of Urban Design Associates; copyright Urban Design Associates.

buildings. Planning for the new East Baltimore Biotechnology Center reflects three "must haves" identified in an earlier feasibility study: a planning process that builds a strong commitment from all stakeholders—residents, city and state officials, and Hopkins itself; a location close enough to the Hopkins Medical Center to allow easy access on foot; and "a bold re-development vision."

Jury Comments

"This is an extremely complex project with sensitive solutions for 40 suffering neighborhoods."

Mission Bay Redevelopment

Location: San Francisco, California

Urban designer: Johnson Fain

Client: Cotellus Development Corporation

Study area and program: A plan for the largest undeveloped site in San Francisco. Previous development proposals for the 303 acres of bayside land had failed due to lack of economic viability or neighbors' resistance to large-scale development. Four factors helped make this initiative feasible: a rapid increase in the cost of housing citywide, a new San Francisco Giants baseball stadium immediately adjacent, plans for a new University of California medical research campus on the site, and extensive outreach to surrounding communities. The development program includes 6,000 units of housing (1,700 of them affordable); 800,000 square feet of regional and neighborhood-serving retail and entertainment; a 500-room hotel; 5 million square feet of office, multimedia, and biotech research and development; and 2,650,000 square feet for the research campus.

Year of award: 2004

Status: The plan has been approved.

Mission Bay Redevelopment, San Francisco, California. Johnson Fain's plan for roughly 20 million square feet of mixed-use growth on the largest undeveloped site in San Francisco focuses on extending the city's "'genetic' structure" by recreating its historic block pattern, providing for a mix of incomes, emphasizing walkability, and creating a new open-space system that brings views of the bay and downtown skyline into the heart of the site. Courtesy of Johnson Fain. *See color insert, C-26.*

Critical issues

Created in the wake of the 1906 earthquake as a landfill and depository for much of the city's wastes, the site had more recently held industrial and distribution uses but remained cut off from the rest of the city by highway ramps and railroad tracks. In a city with soaring real estate values and a dearth of available land—never mind land with extensive frontage on San Francisco Bay— "changing economic, social and cultural values now dictate that the image of an industrial wasteland be reversed, in order to integrate Mission Bay into the rest of the city."

Key urban design concepts

The plan weaves "Mission Bay seamlessly into the 'genetic' structure of San Francisco, so that it extends the physical, economic, aesthetic and cultural life of the City." Blending basic elements of "the DNA of San Francisco's urban form," the plan:

- **Makes extensive use of a historic block structure** that dates to at least 1840 and **deploys buildings to frame and reinforce the character of public streets.**

- **Designs open space to create pedestrian corridors connecting the new neighborhood—and adjacent neighborhoods—to the water,** providing views across the bay to the city's iconic downtown skyline, and offering opportunities for recreation.

- **Assures a mix of uses in every area,** even as the mix varies from one area to the next.

- **Makes the new district walkable and links it to the larger region** by public transit.

Jury Comments

"This plan has a nice mix of public spaces that accommodate lots of public activities.... Urbanistically, it relates to San Francisco as a whole and establishes its own grid in a straightforward manner."

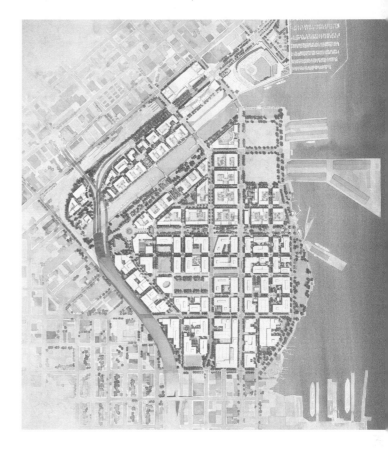

▶ District plan. Courtesy of ProehlStudios.com.

Mission Creek Park. Courtesy of Johnson Fain.

Jackson Meadow

LOCATION: Marine on St. Croix, Minnesota

URBAN DESIGNER: Salmela Architect

CLIENT: Jackson Meadow Company

STUDY AREA AND PROGRAM: Located within the oldest settlement in Minnesota, this new residential development adjoins 191 acres of permanently protected open land. The development sits on 145 acres of meadows and wooded hills overlooking the St. Croix River.

YEAR OF AWARD: 2005

STATUS: The plan was approved and development is complete.

Critical issues

The site's pristine beauty and natural state represented both an asset and a challenge. At the same time, the developer wanted to create a unique identity for this project, located at the edge of an historic town.

▲▲ Jackson Meadow, Marine on St. Croix, Minnesota. Salmela Architect's plan for a new residential development adjacent to Minnesota's oldest settlement "complements the existing town and preserves the site's rural character and open space" by clustering houses in a traditional village form. Project architect Salmela Architect. Photo courtesy of Peter Bastianelli Kerze.

▲ Concentrated development leaves the great majority of the land under conservation restrictions or for agriculture. Photography courtesy of Peter Bastianelli Kerze.

Key urban design concepts

The plan created a residential development that "complements the existing town and preserves the site's rural character and open space" by clustering houses into a "traditional village form." More than two-thirds of the site remains as protected conservation land. The forms, materials, and character of the houses reflect qualities found in the adjacent historic town.

Jury Comments

"The jury appreciated the sensitive and respectful approach taken in this project. We were impressed with the elegance and balance of the solution. The architecture is at once both familiar, as it relates to the vernacular of the region, and yet beautifully and elegantly modern in its detailing and restrained use of color."

Ramsey Town Center

LOCATION: Ramsey, Minnesota

URBAN DESIGNER: Elness Swenson Graham Architects, Inc., in collaboration with Close Landscape Architects

CLIENT: Ramsey Town Center

STUDY AREA AND PROGRAM: Ramsey Town Center grew on a "smart growth opportunity site" designated by the Metropolitan Council, a regional body that governs regional growth issues in the Twin Cities. The site, located in a "third ring suburb," was identified as a potential transit station along the proposed Northstar commuter-rail line through a lengthy public process involving the surrounding community. The town center incorporates 320 acres of new growth, including roughly 2,500 units of mid- to high-density housing, 700,000 square feet of retail and entertainment, and 460,000 square feet of office, medical, and civic uses, including town offices.

YEAR OF AWARD: 2005

STATUS: The town has approved the plan; as of 2005, groundbreaking had occurred on the roads, parks, utilities, a school, and a transit station.

Critical issues

The Town Center is intended to offer a new, mixed-use, and walkable regional model for growth in contrast to the auto-oriented and predominantly single-use development that has dominated suburban development along the Route 10 corridor and elsewhere around the Twin Cities.

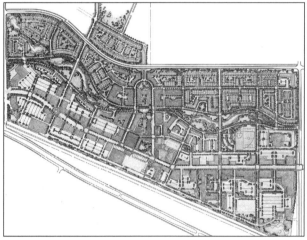

▲▲ Ramsey Town Center, Ramsey, Minnesota. Elness Swenson Graham Architects collaborated with Close Landscape Architects to transform 320 acres with access to a proposed commuter rail station into a regional smart-growth model. The plan creates an "authentic … downtown" in a third-ring surburb of Minneapolis. "Not just a main street or outdoor shopping mall, but instead a compact district of streets and blocks lined with houses, stores, offices, restaurants, cinema and many other uses, … the Town Center will be a crossroads and gathering place." Courtesy of ESG Architects.

▲ Illustrative plan. Courtesy of ESG Architects.

Key urban design concepts

Ramsey Town Center does not transform Ramsey from a third-ring suburb into an urban district. The community's suburban residential streets remain intact. However, the Town Center does offer the community "an authentic... downtown, characterized by a mix of goods and services that meet the needs of local residents and promote Ramsey as a regional destination. Not just a main street or outdoor shopping mall, but instead a compact district of streets and blocks lined with houses, stores, offices, restaurants, cinema and many other uses,... the Town Center will be a crossroads and gathering place." While the Town Center will in reality be largely a private mixed-use development, the presence of town offices, a cinema, and performing arts faculties will draw "residents and visitors of all ages to live, shop, work, dine, play, and stay." In addition, the urban designer emphasized the Town Center's public character by focusing on creation of a lively and varied public realm. In addition to a series of "strolling streets" enlivened by retail and other uses that engage pedestrians, the plan includes three signature public spaces in which "to be seen and to celebrate community":

- A **"busy urban marketplace,** surrounded by shops, restaurants, entertainment, and mixed uses above."

- A **"quiet respite from the marketplace,"** a park that links to the larger park system crossing the Town Center.

- An **indoor winter garden** "that provides the heart and soul of the community through winter."

Jury Comments

"This eminently livable plan is in the best tradition of town planning where home and work and civic spaces are more closely related and a sense of place is created."

Lloyd Crossing Sustainable Urban Design Plan

LOCATION: Portland, Oregon
URBAN DESIGNER: Mithun Architects + Designers + Planners
CLIENT: Portland Development Commission
STUDY AREA AND PROGRAM: A plan for redeveloping a 60-acre, 35-block district that yields "a five-fold increase in the area's population and built space"
YEAR OF AWARD: 2006
STATUS: The plan has been approved.

Critical issues

Embracing the spirit as well as the letter of Portland's growth boundary requires "transforming an underused inner-city neighborhood into a vibrant, attractive, and highly desirable place to live and work" while restoring the site's ecosystem to mimic the behavior of a pristine forest and match predevelopment environmental impact levels in key areas.

Key urban design concepts

Woven into the fabric of this plan are initiatives for streetscape design, green building, tree planting, use of solar energy, and other measures that give the district an extremely high level of environmental performance. When completed in 2050, Lloyd Crossing will produce environmental impacts similar to an equivalent area of virgin forest as measured by groundwater recharge, carbon footprint, and other key metrics. Just as noteworthy, the urban designer achieves these sustainability benefits in the context of a vision for a district distinguished by a lively public realm in which retail space and animated public squares assure a significant level of human activity. A critical element in achieving both sets of goals has been to demonstrate how well-designed, higher-density development can fit smoothly into a lower-density context. The plan includes a mix of towers, one rising past 300 feet, that meet the matrix of street and squares with active uses and that step down to the scale of surrounding blocks.

Lloyd Crossing Sustainable Urban Design Plan, Portland, Oregon. By increasing density in a 35-block section of Portland by 500 percent, this plan from Mithun Architects + Designers + Planners generates significant sustainability benefits. The plan applies a wide range of tools, including green building, solar-energy-capture, and groundwater-recharge techniques, to transform "an underused inner-city neighborhood into a vibrant, attractive, and highly desirable place to live and work." The plan yields a net environmental impact, as measured by carbon footprint and other key metrics, comparable to an equivalent area of virgin forest. Courtesy of Mithun Architects + Designers.

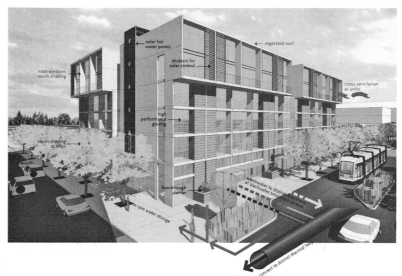

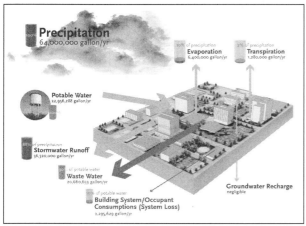

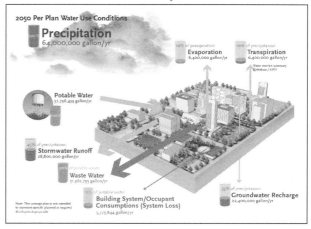

Current levels of storm water runoff are compared to those projected under the plan. Courtesy of Mithun Architects + Designers + Planners.

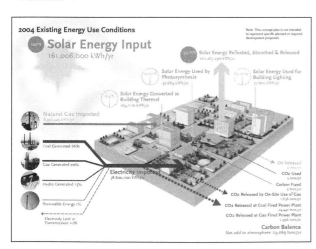

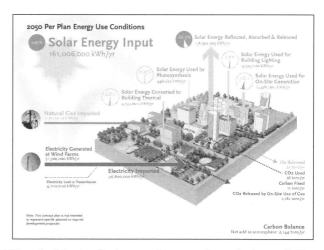

Current solar energy use is compared to projected use. Courtesy of Mithun Architects + Designers + Planners. *See color insert, C-27.*

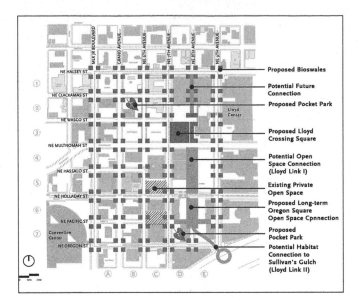

Diagram of the plan's open-space scheme. Courtesy of Mithun Architects + Designers + Planners.

Jury Comments

"A brilliant technical analysis of urban ecosystems.... Ecological analysis provided unique perspective, which we hope will be more broadly adopted in future urban design and planning.... Density done in sustainable way needs to be taken in the context of Portland's growth boundary."

North Point

LOCATION: Cambridge, Massachusetts

URBAN DESIGNER: CBT Architects and Greenberg Consultants, Inc.

CLIENT: Spaulding & Slye Colliers

STUDY AREA AND PROGRAM: Redevelopment of a 45-acre former rail yard, less than two miles from both MIT and downtown Boston, into a transit-oriented development that provides 2,700 residential units, 2,200,000 square feet of office space, and 150,000 square feet of retail space

YEAR OF AWARD: 2006

STATUS: The plan has been approved and development is under way.

Critical issues

Isolated by railroad tracks and a major arterial roadway, North Point had remained one of the largest undeveloped sites in the core of the Boston region. Previous development efforts foundered on aggressive community opposition. In response, the City of Cambridge commissioned a planning study that addressed community concerns and ultimately built support for intensive transit-oriented development. The city required that more than 10 percent of the development's housing units qualify as affordable.

Key urban design concepts

The plan unlocks the value of the site by creating a 10-acre public park (which exceeds zoning requirements). It creates "a vibrant mixed community" organized into twenty new blocks built around the park, which connects to a regional bike trail. The density required to support the costs of public improvements and amenities—which approaches a floor-area ratio of 4.0 after subtracting streets and public spaces from the site's total area—is significantly higher than in nearby neighborhoods. This higher density takes advantage of access to transit (including a new station at the terminus of a light-rail line), supports new retail spaces, and creates a sense of vitality on an otherwise isolated site.

Jury Comments

"Represents a beautiful plan and incorporates three jurisdictions combining a range of housing types, public transportation, and commercial development on a brownfield site.... Exemplar of how good density through high-quality urban development will remake 21st-century American cities."

North Point, Cambridge, Massachusetts. Taking advantage of direct transit access to downtown Boston, CBT and Greenberg Consultants fashioned a plan to transform this former rail yard into a lively mixed-use district that uses higher densities—called for in an earlier municipal plan—to support new stores, a wide variety of housing choices, and a sense of vitality on an otherwise isolated site. Courtesy of CBT Architects.

▲ Aerial rendering of North Point *(lower left)* looking toward downtown Boston. Courtesy of CBT Architects.

▲▲ The plan lays out a grid of inviting, walkable streets. Courtesy of CBT Architects. *See color insert, C-28.*

The Carneros Inn

LOCATION: Napa, California

URBAN DESIGNER: William Rawn Associates, Architects

CLIENT: Carneros Partners

STUDY AREA AND PROGRAM: A 27-acre inn and town center in California's Carneros Valley, planned and designed to integrate into the surrounding community and natural setting

YEAR OF AWARD: 2006

STATUS: The plan has been approved.

Critical issues

The development is intended to serve both as a "base camp" for visitors exploring the surrounding areas and as a new center for the surrounding community.

Key urban design concepts

The plan creates an "agrarian village" that comprises four neighborhoods and includes a town center, guest cottages, ownership courtyard houses, a restaurant, reception building, and a spa complex set atop a hillside with a commanding view. The town center will serve

◀ The Carneros Inn, Napa, California. William Rawn Associates created an "agrarian village" and a new town square that provide a focus for an agricultural district and complement its rural character. The plan demonstrates how development can enhance environmental character with a series of integral steps—such as collecting rainwater for use by neighboring vineyards—intended to tie the new community directly into its existing agricultural surroundings. Courtesy of Hundleyphoto.com.

▲ The inn and related structures adopt the community's vernacular architecture. Courtesy of Hundleyphoto.com.

▶ Site plan. Courtesy of William Rawn Associates, Architects.

the larger existing community and includes a town square surrounded by retail and public uses. The project is 100 percent geothermally heated, and all of the site's stormwater is processed and reused for on-site irrigation. Stormwater is also stored for use by neighboring vineyards, integrating the new community directly into its existing agricultural context.

Jury Comments

"The clear design carries through very consistently from the site plan, through the architecture into the landscaping design and details…. It is regionally contextual in its relationship to its site topography, spatial hierarchies and the scale of its architectural and landscape elements…. This exceptionally clean, compact village plan is centered around nature and natural systems and creates a quality of life which embodies a respect for nature and contemplation…. A well designed project."

▶ Crown Properties, Gaithersburg, Maryland. The plan from Ehrenkrantz Eckstut & Kuhn Architects provides a model for suburban growth that respects the environment and promotes urban qualities. The plan concentrates growth in relatively compact, higher-density, walkable villages along a planned transit line and offers a wide range of housing options. Courtesy of Ehrenkrantz Eckstut & Kuhn Architects, © 2006.

◢ Illustrative plan. Courtesy of Ehrenkrantz Eckstut & Kuhn Architects, © 2006.

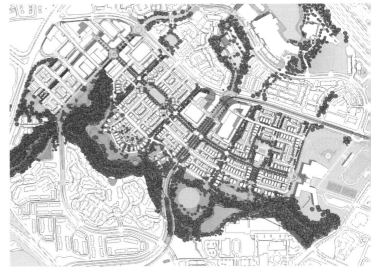

Crown Properties

LOCATION: Gaithersburg, Maryland

URBAN DESIGNER: Ehrenkrantz Eckstut & Kuhn Architects

CLIENT: KB Homes

STUDY AREA AND PROGRAM: Located on 180 acres of land, the program calls for 2,500 units of various housing types, 350,000 square feet of retail space, community facilities, a 30-acre biotechnology high school campus, parks, and more than 70 acres of open space.

YEAR OF AWARD: 2007

STATUS: The plan has been approved.

Critical issues

Provide a model for suburban growth that respects the environment and promotes urban qualities such as walkability, compact development transit use, and broader housing-type choices.

Key urban design concepts

The plan seeks to create "a sustainable, financially-feasible, vibrant, and healthy suburban development" by concentrating growth in a series of relatively compact, walkable suburban villages along a planned transit line. A portion of the site remains undisturbed as protected open space.

▲▲ Commercial center. Courtesy of Ehrenkrantz Eckstut & Kuhn Architects, © 2006. *See color insert, C-29.*

▲ Central green. Courtesy of Ehrenkrantz Eckstut & Kuhn Architects, © 2006.

Jury Comments

"A comprehensive proposal that identifies key urban design principles and strategies for the creation of the 21st-century sustainable city and attempts to deal with the environmental, economic, and public benefits of each idea.... It is an excellent model to be used for the redevelopment of worn suburban sprawl.... Uses 'green' strategies in combination with urban place-making to create high-density neighborhoods with a rich hierarchy of public spaces.... Expresses contemporary architecture—an architectural approach that stresses building design based on environmental principles."

How the Projects Illustrate the Principles

1. **Build community in an increasingly diverse society.** The five urban case studies include mixed-income housing that is generally funded through additional density or other development incentives. Of this group, the East Baltimore Development Initiative resembles the HOPE VI program but goes further by redeveloping an entire lower-income neighborhood into a mixed-income and mixed-use community; supportive services help current residents negotiate the transition. Three plans—Kaka`ako Makai, Mission Bay, and North Point—create distinctive new public parks consciously designed and programmed to attract people of varying backgrounds and thus help promote a sense of community in diverse new neighborhoods. All of the urban case studies deploy retail uses to enliven principal streets and public spaces. The Carneros Inn plan consciously incorporates a town square that will serve the surrounding rural community and draw residents to its mix of stores and civic spaces.

2. **Advance environmental sustainability.** Green site planning and building design stand as a high-prior-

ity goal in each case study. In addition to specific (and frequently imaginative) features designed to promote sustainability, the urban projects embody an additional advantage: they locate millions of square feet at the core of their respective regions, taking advantage of a fundamental principle of smart growth—accommodating growth and new development in existing urban areas. The Kaka`ako Makai plan makes an explicit case that new models of denser urban development represent a credible and necessary alternative to continued sprawl—and it makes this case by weaving buildings, public spaces, and nature together in a new high-density, urban district. The Lloyd Crossing plan goes beyond the other urban examples, boldly proposing through remediation mechanisms to approach, over time, the environmental footprint of undisturbed natural wilds. The Crown Properties plan represents classic suburban smart growth: densely built development within a matrix of walkable streets and blocks focused on a new transit station.

3. **Expand individual choices.** Each of these case studies responds to growing market demand for a greater array of lifestyle choices. The urban case studies open opportunities for residents to choose from an array of housing options that provide direct walking access to shopping, jobs, parks, recreation, and transit. Located close to the regional core, these new districts also offer an opportunity to choose short commutes and more personal time. Although suburban, Ramsey Town Center and Crown Properties present similar options. Kaka`ako Makai makes the case that people can choose urban living and still enjoy nature. Lloyd Crossing adds to this list an unusual option—although one likely to become more common over the next decade—the chance to live and participate in a green community. Jackson Meadow and Carneros Inn also broaden housing choices, offering the chance to live or spend time in the modern equivalent of a rural vil-

lage, a place close to nature but without the isolation such a setting often entails.

4. **Enhance personal health.** All of the case studies emphasize walkability and most—including both urban and rural case studies—incorporate connections to regional path systems that offer residents convenient opportunities for biking, jogging, running, and hiking. By offering alternatives to auto use, the urban case studies also reduce the otherwise significant risk of auto-related accidents. Each of the urban case studies builds in explicit measures that reduce air and water pollution, but Lloyd Crossing presents an ambitious, far-reaching model for sustainable development that consumes large volumes of water yet scarcely alters its quality.

5. **Make places for people.** All of the case studies share a strong emphasis on the public realm—making streets, squares, and parks their visible focus, not individual buildings. Each underlines the importance of creating a conscious identity that conveys its spirit, but each explores a distinctive path toward achieving that identity. East Baltimore builds on the traditional forms, street patterns, and architecture of surrounding neighborhoods in a conscious effort to restore them. North Point uses dramatic new architecture to accomplish the opposite goal of setting itself apart as a symbol of twenty-first-century vitality. Lloyd Crossing uses a similarly modern idiom, but draws its character from the highly visible integration of natural functions and features into its urban context. Kaka`ako Makai and Mission Bay stress connection to their settings: Kaka`ako Makai weaves development through a tropical waterfront; Mission Bay sites development along open space corridors that open views to the bay and San Francisco's skyline. Jackson Meadow and the Carneros Inn come closest to a shared approach—each conveying a village-like sense of a community of buildings coexisting with rather than dominating a natural setting.

CHAPTER 10

Reclaiming the Waterfront

Cities on very different bodies of water—from the James River in Richmond, Virginia, to Lake Erie in Cleveland, to Elliot Bay in Seattle—have transformed underutilized waterfronts into lively, walkable, mixed-use districts. Some redevelopment efforts target individual parcels and some focus on expanding all public access to the water's edge. In cities where a waterfront adjoins a dense urban center—such as Boston, Seattle, and New York City—urban designers have worked to expand water transit and create new opportunities for development of water-oriented cultural and recreational venues in harbors and shipping channels. As more cities—including San Antonio; Louisville, Kentucky; Pittsburgh; and Washington—target investment toward waterfront redevelopment, demand increases for design and planning professionals with special expertise in urban waterfront design and development.

Roots

With their proximity to shipping and trading corridors along coastlines and rivers, city waterfronts once formed the industrial hubs of many urban economies. Some early American ports, such as Boston, New York, and San Francisco, grew by filling parts of their waterfronts to accommodate shipping and water-related industry.

Many forces contributed to the demise of marine industries in historic urban centers—primarily trucking's displacement of rail as the preferred means of shipping goods, but also the growth of mechanized, modular shipping facilities that effectively pushed heavy industries to less-developed locations inland with more and cheaper land. Migrating industries left behind vast tracts of underused and abandoned waterfronts, and following a worldwide trend, U.S. cities that once turned away from their industrial origins began to reorient themselves to the water. As part of this reevaluation, many cities have removed railroad tracks, rail yards, and elevated freeways that once severed their waterfronts from city centers—and many others face citizen pressure to do so.

Redeveloped waterfronts have begun to reclaim the importance to city economies that they held a century ago. A secondary goal of Boston's well-publicized Big Dig (a fifteen-year-long project that replaced an elevated freeway with an underground road along the city's harbor) was strengthening of the visual and physical connections between downtown and the waterfront, seen as a frontier for new growth. Even before the project got fully under way, the city steered new investment toward the waterfront.

Transformed from utility to amenity, reinvented urban waterfronts perform vastly different functions than before. Since the mid-1980s, waterfront redevelopment has played a central role in renewing downtown vitality for cities such as Boston; Providence, Rhode Island; Philadelphia; Baltimore; Richmond, Virginia; Chattanooga, Tennessee; Cleveland; Indianapolis; Chicago; Milwaukee; Seattle; and both Portlands (Oregon and Maine).

Many currents fed this new regard for waterfronts as amenities, beginning with the environmental movement. Urban harbor clean-ups, mandated under tough new environmental laws in the 1970s and 1980s, played a critical role in unlocking the appeal of waterfronts for residential development, tourism, and recreation. The environmental movement drew interest to improving and expanding urban park systems. Vast tracts of recently abandoned waterside land opened new opportunities for downtown waterfront parks, harbor walks, and esplanades that often tied into regional open-space networks.

The historic preservation movement also generated new appreciation for older historic fabric and signature building types found in early industrial centers. Mills, warehouses, and other industrial buildings that line many urban waterfronts acquired new cultural meaning, reinterpreted not as failures but as picturesque reminders of industrial heritage in a postindustrial age. People looked for ways to preserve these structures, newly imbued with cachet, and adapt them to new uses.

The growing importance of tourism in urban economies also spurred interest in revitalizing waterfronts, and attracted new visitors—often from the immediate region—to downtown (regional visitors represent the largest segment of tourism for most cities, even well-known destinations like Boston and San Francisco).

Finally, important shifts in demographics created a more amenity-based urban housing market, fueling residential building in cities around the nation. Waterfronts frequently emerged as the first urban areas to attract new and affluent residents—including substantial numbers of suburbanites, many discovering downtown for the first time. New shopping districts that boast a mix of restaurants, entertainment, art creation, recreational activities, and other amenities have drawn many new urban dwellers to redeveloped waterfront areas.

For several decades, the growth of these new waterfront uses created significant conflicts with more traditional marine industries. Cities moved to protect fishing, fish processing, shipping, and other industries that needed waterfront locations but could not afford the rising land values that often accompanied the arrival of nonmarine activities. Most of these tensions had been

Fort Point Channel, Boston. Waterfront revival can extend to the surface of the water itself with programming, public art, and boating that introduces unique ways to experience urban space. Rendering by David Curran, courtesy of Goody Clancy.

resolved by 2000, but even these industries followed the now well-worn trail to industrial parks with the help of refrigerated trucking.

The vast range of waterfront projects along coasts, rivers, and other waterways in cities large and small shows the value of rediscovered waterfronts in a variety of places with very different economies. Some of the best-known models of transformed waterfronts include:

- **Portland, Oregon.** Despite an early recommendation by the Olmsted office to build parks along the Willamette River, which bisects downtown, Portland largely turned away from the river in the early twentieth century. In 1976 the city relocated the I-5 corridor to make way for Waterfront Park. Known as "Portland's front yard," it provides pedestrian and bike access to riverwalks, accommodates special events like a well-established blues festival, and offers views of the eastern side of downtown and Mount Hood. More recently, expansion of the park toward the new South Waterfront District has encouraged transformation of industrial land once occupied by warehouses and shipyards into a new mixed-use neighborhood. Following the model of the city's now-established Pearl District, development on the south waterfront will include an extension of the city's streetcar line, parks, and a riverside trail.

- **San Antonio, Texas.** San Antonio's Riverwalk has evolved from its beginnings as a flood-control project in the late 1930s into a tourist attraction that rivals the Alamo and serves as a lushly planted amenity for everyone who works in and uses downtown. Restaurants, shops, and hotels line the parklike walk, which follows the river on both sides for 2.5 miles, helping generate an estimated $800 million annually for the area's economy.

- **Chattanooga, Tennessee.** Over twenty years, Chattanooga has wielded strategic public investments in its riverfront to attract significant private investment.

The two funding streams have transformed 20 acres along the banks of the Tennessee River at the center of the city from abandoned industrial parcels into a tourist mecca that includes a high-profile aquarium, two museums, an emerging arts district, iconic bridges, and parks. The connective tissue for these components is a pedestrian-oriented network of public spaces and paths that includes a new pier, new mooring space for boats, a riverside esplanade, and a walking path that connects downtown with the Chickamauga Dam eleven miles upstream. The Chamber of Commerce counts $60 million in new private development downtown, including housing and five hotels, and sees that figure doubling by 2015—a significant total for a city of 170,000.

- **Baltimore, Maryland.** Beginning in the 1960s, city-led redevelopment of a derelict industrial waterfront has turned Baltimore Inner Harbor into the force behind a dramatic revival that has spread into the city's downtown and along the waterfront to the east and west. In the late 1970s a string of major projects debuted on the harbor, including a science museum, festival marketplace, concert pavilion, and an aquarium. Hotels, offices, and residential development followed. The Inner Harbor attracts nearly 14 million visitors annually, yet a 2003 report on developing a unified management structure for the area noted that it "also provides enjoyment and a meeting ground for Baltimoreans of diverse economic and cultural backgrounds."

- **Providence, Rhode Island.** A plan first outlined in the 1970s—when Providence had decked over its downtown river to create a vast parking lot—began producing striking results in the 1990s: an elegantly detailed riverside promenade; new parks and squares; and a waterfront amphitheater in the Old Cove Basin. The restored riverfront inspired the striking WaterFire installation, which mixes music and performance art and draws thousands of people to the river's banks on warm summer and fall evenings. New hotels, offices, restaurants, and a shopping complex have filled in around the uncovered river.

Approaches Today

The Waterfront Center has established itself as an active advocate of the idea that waterfronts represent unique opportunities to enrich community life. In 1999 the center issued an *Urban Waterfront Manifesto*, which set out basic tenets—in the judgment of its advocate authors—of waterfront redevelopment. The *Manifesto* incorporates many of the values that urban designers bring to planning and designing waterfronts:

1. **The public sector should act as the "steward" of waterfronts** and stand ready to implement waterfront plans in partnership with the private sector.

2. **All urban waterfront projects should provide public access** to and along the water.

3. **One size does not fit all.** Waterfront redevelopment projects should flow from the nature of each site and reflect its essential spirit.

4. **Waterfronts should accommodate a variety of uses,** from passive open space to active uses, be welcoming both day and night, and incorporate places and activities that attract people of all ages, races, and incomes.

5. **Waterfront projects should preserve and interpret "the tangible aspects of the history" of a site** as a way of enhancing its character and telling the larger waterfront's story.

6. **Water-dependent uses should receive preference in the redevelopment programs,** "even if they are unsightly."

Case Studies

These case studies demonstrate the steadily increasing importance that cities of all sizes place on bringing new life to their waterfronts, many of which no longer serve the industrial and maritime roles that defined them from their earliest days.

Parco San Giuliano

LOCATION: Venice, Italy

URBAN DESIGNER: Comunitas, Inc.

CLIENT: City of Venice

STUDY AREA AND PROGRAM: Transportation and infrastructure improvements; reforestation and land reclamation; and the development of 2.2 million square feet of cultural, recreational, sports, commerce, and transportation facilities at thirteen strategic sites across 1,500 acres of land, water, and marshes. Separating the twin cities of Venice and Mestre, the former marshland had become over time "an isolated toxic waste dump with physical degradation, traffic problems, and visual pollution. Yet a place full of opportunities."

YEAR OF AWARD: 1997

STATUS: The plan received unanimous approval by the Venice City Council.

Critical issues

Parco San Giuliano represents "the most important public works undertaken by the City of Venice" in a century and is the largest metropolitan park planned in Italy. In addition to remediating several centuries of environmental degradation and transforming an industrial landfill into actively used public open space and new development, the plan had to resolve four issues:

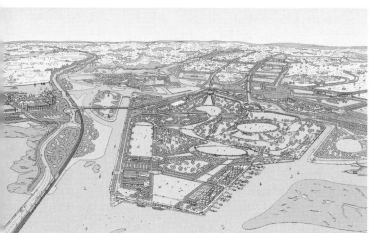

Aerial perspective of the park. Courtesy of Antonio Di Mambro + Associates.

- Connect the site to both Mestre and Venice in ways that would make the new park and other facilities inviting and highly accessible.

- Create a new "meeting ground" to draw residents from both cities together.

- Provide a catalyst to attract hundreds of millions of dollars of private investment to the area.

- Establish a new image for this no-man's-land by telling the lagoon's ecological story and providing visible continuity with the culture and history of the cities to either side.

◀ Parco San Giuliano; view of park through North Gateway, Venice, Italy. Venice's mayor described Parco San Giuliano as "the most important public works undertaken by the City of Venice" in the last century. The plan prepared by Antonio Di Mambro + Associates overcomes the historic separation between predominantly working-class Mestre and more affluent Venice by providing a wide range of inventively designed ways to enjoy nature, recreation, and culture. Courtesy of Antonio Di Mambro + Associates, architects; Ing. Giovanni Cocco, structural engineer; photograph © Alberto Bevilacqua.

▲▲ The park's ice-skating rink. Courtesy of Antonio Di Mambro + Associates.

▲ One of a series of modern gateways. Courtesy of Antonio Di Mambro + Associates; photograph © Filippo Leonardi.

Key urban design concepts

The plan for Parco San Giuliano constitutes an "organization framework" shaped around four elements:

- **Regional transportation,** including two major intermodal centers north and south of the park that carry tourist and regional traffic headed to Venice together with a new Mestre-Venice intermodal center that serves residents.

- **Land use,** providing attractive sites for uses that will benefit both cities, draw diverse communities to the park, and stimulate regional investment. These uses include a lagoon biology center; an industrial redevelopment area; university activities; a cultural center comprising two museums and an aquarium; exhibition and performance facilities; and recreational and sports facilities.

- **Circulation,** which acknowledges that regional transportation limitations and the park's size require tree-lined "parkways" and well-landscaped parking areas throughout the site; provides parallel systems that link all of the park's facilities; and opens up a variety of active and passive opportunities to enjoy the waterfront.

- **Environmental reclamation,** which influences almost every aspect of the park's form—notably reclaiming the lagoon's ecosystem, restoring historic waterways and salt marshes, launching a reforestation program, capping areas of toxic waste for use as public and natural areas, reintroducing indigenous plant species, and stabilizing embankments.

Robert F. Wagner Jr. Park

LOCATION: New York, New York
URBAN DESIGNER: Machado and Silvetti Associates
CLIENT: Battery Park City Authority
STUDY AREA AND PROGRAM: A park on a spectacular site with dramatic views of the Statue of Liberty and New York Harbor
YEAR OF AWARD: 1998
STATUS: The plan was approved by the Battery Park City Authority and has been built.

▶ Robert F. Wagner Jr. Park, Battery Park City, New York, New York. Machado and Silvetti Associates' lively waterfront park succeeds in the many roles a new park can play: as an amenity for people who live and work near it; as a regional destination that helps weave the new Battery Park City district into the life of the larger city; and as a place of community designed to attract people of all ages, backgrounds, and interests. Courtesy of Goody Clancy.

Dramatic harbor views and open lawns attract visitors from outside of Battery Park City. Copyright © Facundo de Zuviria.

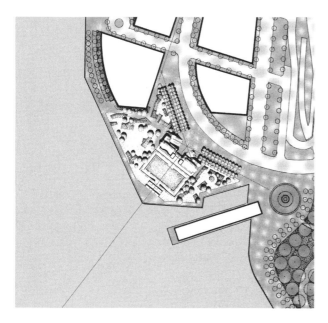

◀ Axis of view from the park to the Statue of Liberty. Copyright Machado and Silvetti Associates.

Key urban design concepts

The park design encourages exploration, beginning with two tree-lined allées that lead pedestrians approaching from the north and the south to the park entrance. Inside, paths and walkways wind through a blend of open lawns and intensively planted gardens. In part as a tactic for drawing people to the park, the design incorporates two pavilions that house a restaurant and a public roof deck from which visitors have sweeping views of New York Harbor and the Statue of Liberty. The balconies and the lawns below provide multiple levels with a mix of grass, stone, and wooden surfaces to encourage uses such as picnics and sitting to contemplate the view. The Museum of Jewish Heritage serves as an additional attraction within the park.

Critical issues

The park is one of a string of waterfront parks and public spaces intended to create a lively public realm that makes Battery Park City appealing as a new urban neighborhood; to forge a stronger sense of connection to the larger city by creating destinations that draw people to the area; and to foster a greater sense of community on the part of the district's increasingly diverse population.

Jury Comments

"Within the changing urban landscape of the world's most densely populated city, a design initiative that recognizes the need for civic order, public spaces, and connection to the natural environment."

Hong Kong Central Waterfront Development

Location: Hong Kong

Urban designer: Skidmore, Owings & Merrill International, Ltd.

Client: Swire Properties, Ltd.

Study area and program: Creation of an iconic green space at the center of the Hong Kong waterfront, covering roughly 40 acres. The plan represents a studied attempt to unify new infrastructure (convention center and high-speed rail connections); better define three important corridors comprising new and planned open spaces and buildings; provide a new "front door" for the densely built heart of the city; and create a landmark open space that will play a central role in the city's civic life and identity.

Year of award: 2000

Status: The plan was approved by the Town Planning Board.

Critical issues

Two sweeping initiatives create a fresh context for charting the next chapter in Hong Kong's growth: development of a new convention center and civic center as a spectacular new gateway to the downtown and construction of a new airport with a high-speed rail link to downtown. The city had originally intended to pursue its traditional policy of filling in along the harborfront to create new development sites—viewed as essential to attracting investment—but the new rail line creates similar opportunities elsewhere in the city. Meanwhile, the city had paid a high price for constantly encroaching on the harbor to invite newer development. Its history of infill had cut off access and views from the downtown core to the harbor, degraded the spectacular urban waterfront, and foreclosed a chance to create one of the world's signature downtown parks. Leaders from the development community stepped forward to sponsor a new waterfront plan based on a sense that the city's competitiveness for growth would increasingly rely on its ability to offer amenity. "New development alone will not secure Hong Kong's place as a leading international city. Hong Kong's ability to take advantage of its unique natural setting will give the city its edge in sustaining economic growth in the years to come."

Hong Kong Central Waterfront Development, China. Hong Kong's business community invited Skidmore, Owings & Merrill to design a new waterfront park out of concern that the city needed to offer more than spectacular new buildings to compete for investment in the global marketplace: "Hong Kong's ability to take advantage of its unique natural setting will give the city its edge in sustaining economic growth." Rendering by Christopher Grubbs, courtesy of Skidmore, Owings & Merrill LLP. *See color insert, C-30.*

View toward the new waterfront convention center. Rendering by Christopher Grubbs, courtesy of Skidmore, Owings & Merrill LLP.

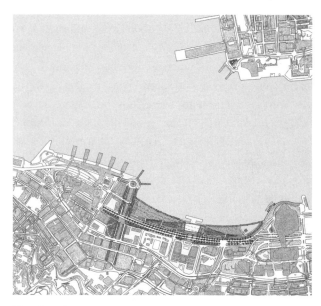

The plan's broad crescent park brings the waterfront into focus and anchors three distinctive corridors into the business district that reinforce the city's distinct sense of place. Courtesy of Skidmore, Owings & Merrill LLP.

Key urban design concepts

The plan is a vision for the city's core that responds to the values that drive twenty-first-century investment. At the same time it introduces the city's most significant civic space. The waterfront park "will provide Hong Kong with a public centerpiece that is found at the heart of all the world's great cities: London, San Francisco,

Shanghai. This grand public open space will provide a ceremonial focus for historic events and celebrations of community pride. Its dedication will commemorate the city's reunification with China and symbolize its continuing evolution as one of Asia's leading centers of business and culture." The plan rests on these elements:

- A "**graceful crescent park and boulevard stretching along 1,000 meters of the water's edge**" serves as the focal point. Designed to serve as a public gathering place, the park functions as a setting for civic and cultural institutions; contributes to a dramatic sense of arrival by air, water, and land; offers prestigious addresses for harbor-view development; accommodates waterfront retail and entertainment in a park setting; and creates a peaceful sanctuary from bustling city life, with spectacular views of the ever-changing harbor.

- **A series of corridors** will connect the park to the larger city:
  - the **Arts Corridor,** whose sequence of new and existing art and cultural sites extends uphill into the heart of the city;
  - the **Historic Corridor,** a more formal passage that leads directly to Statue Square, an important civic landmark; and
  - the **Civic Corridor,** a grand series of public buildings and courtyards that dips below a waterfront boulevard into the heart of the crescent park.

- **Improved access** will benefit the entire Central Waterfront, combining a new pedestrian network and expanded water- and rail-transit service.

Jury Comments

"Within the changing urban landscape of the world's most densely populated city, a design initiative that recognizes the need for civic order, public spaces, and connection to the natural environment."

Shanghai Waterfront Redevelopment, China. Skidmore, Owings & Merrill's plan transforms Shanghai's outmoded port, which is being relocated, and extends the postcard-view character of the historic Bund. It accommodates significant new growth shaped by design guidelines and creates a vibrant new sense of connection between the historic and modern cities that showcases "Shanghai's rich history, culture, and world-class aspirations." Rendering by Christopher Grubbs, courtesy of Skidmore, Owings & Merrill LLP. *See color insert, C-31.*

Shanghai Waterfront Redevelopment

LOCATION: Shanghai, China

URBAN DESIGNER: Skidmore, Owings & Merrill

CLIENT: Shanghai P&K Development Company

STUDY AREA AND PROGRAM: Transform roughly 1,200 acres of the downtown waterfront—former shipping facilities unable to handle the large container vessels now used in maritime trade—into "a place for business, tourism, housing, and recreation." In the process, create new areas to accommodate significant downtown development demand and open broad swaths of the waterfront to the public.

YEAR OF AWARD: 2000

STATUS: The plan was approved by the Town Planning Board.

Critical issues

The plan focuses primarily on extending the "postcard view" character of the historic Bund, a riverfront promenade along 4.5 miles of the Huangpu riverfront in Shanghai, which had long served only shipping and related marine industries, while showcasing "Shanghai's rich history, culture, and world-class aspirations."

Key urban design concepts

The plan sketches a vision of "a modern, vibrant waterfront community" replacing old port uses with a thriving mix of housing, commercial, community, and tourism development. The revitalized waterfront and river will unite the historical grandeur of Puxi (west of the Huangpu River) with the modern vitality of Pudong (east of the river). Working within a Chinese tradition of tightly knit urban fabric and clear hierarchy for open spaces, the plan weaves together a set of core elements:

Development framed by new waterfront parks. Rendering by Christopher Grubbs, courtesy of Skidmore, Owings & Merrill LLP.

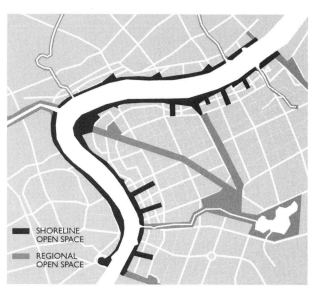

Open space system. Courtesy of Skidmore, Owings & Merrill LLP.

- **Return the Huangpu riverfront to the public** by dedicating the majority of the newly accessible waterfront as public space and locating a variety of civic, cultural, entertainment, recreational, and retail uses at key points to draw a wide variety of people to the riverfront.

- **Improve transit and access to the river** by creating a new network of cross-river ferries and tunnels and extending local streets to the river.

- **Provide a pedestrian-friendly environment** by creating a continuous walkway, narrowing streets along the riverfront, and removing through streets.

- **Create new identity** by introducing a series of civic and cultural nodes along the riverfront and preserving view corridors to landmarks such as the Bund.

- **Preserve linkage to history and culture** by preserving and reusing historic warehouses, office buildings, and other port elements together with cranes and other distinctive elements of the former port economy.

- **Promote water-based activity** by encouraging new development to provide for recreational uses such as sailing, rowing, and floating markets together with river taxis and tours.

- **Acknowledge the river** by devising design guidelines that create visibly unique buildings that step down toward the river; space towers to maximize river views. More specific guidelines that reinforce the distinct character of each district along the river should provide further guidance in specific areas.

- **Devise an economically viable and socially flexible plan** by creating a framework that can respond to evolving market demands and housing needs.

Jury Comments

"A comprehensive vision for the redevelopment of a key portion of Shanghai's urban waterfront."

Riverwalk Gateway

LOCATION: Chicago, Illinois

URBAN DESIGNER: Skidmore, Owings & Merrill

CLIENT: City of Chicago Department of Transportation

STUDY AREA AND PROGRAM: The Chicago River Corridor Development Plan identifies the Chicago River as one of the city's most valuable natural resources and sets improved access to walkways and bicycle paths along the river as a primary goal. This project creates a new gateway between the Chicago lakefront and the Riverwalk system at the point where a two-level bridge carries Lake Shore Drive over the river.

YEAR OF AWARD: 2002

STATUS: The gateway has been built.

Critical issues

A 200-foot wide, steel-frame roadway structure crosses just 15 feet above the original walkway and bicycle path. Rubbish-strewn areas adjacent to and beneath the bridge had become dark and threatening. The combination of a claustrophobic passageway and unmistakable signs of neglect had turned the passage into an urban barrier, a problem the Gateway plan addresses.

Key urban design concepts

The design overcomes by distraction and design, focusing attention away from the low overpass and onto new public art and architectural elements that articulate the passage with visual and historical interest. The plan combines entry pavilions, patterned paving, cast-concrete details, and colorful structural arches that help define a "ceiling" for the walk and frame a public gallery—twenty-eight brightly lit glazed ceramic wall panels

▲▲ Riverwalk Gateway, Chicago, Illinois. Skidmore, Owings & Merrill's design demonstrates the value of collaboration: artists, engineers, lighting designers, planners, urban designers, and others worked together to transform a forbidding underpass into an inviting, widely admired gateway between miles of familiar lakefront jogging and bicycling trails and a newer, multi-use trail along the Chicago River. Photo by Mark Ballogg of Steinkamp Ballogg Photography, courtesy of Skidmore, Owings & Merrill LLP. *See color insert, C-32.*

▲ Ceramic murals focus on key moments in Chicago history. Photo by Mark Ballogg of Steinkamp Ballogg Photography, courtesy of Skidmore, Owings & Merrill LLP.

Lakeshore Drive passes 15 feet overhead. Photo by Mark Ballogg of Steinkamp Ballogg Photography, courtesy of Skidmore, Owings & Merrill LLP.

along both walls of the gateway depicting key events in Chicago history. The axis defined by the entry pavilions is slightly realigned to enhance views of nearby landmarks. At night the entry pavilions become civic-scaled lanterns, clearly marking the connection between the river corridor and the lake.

Jury Comments

"Expresses an economy of means in structure and controlled interface with other systems ... [and] the structural solution is one with the architecture.... [T]he beauty of the plan is in its simplicity and in the clarity of its spatial organization."

Vision Plan for the Pittsburgh Riverfront

LOCATION: Pittsburgh, Pennsylvania

URBAN DESIGNER: Chan Krieger & Associates

CLIENT: Riverlife Task Force

STUDY AREA AND PROGRAM: A plan for creating a new riverfront park downtown that incorporates at least 50 feet of shoreline along 11.5 miles of riverbank at the convergence of the city's three rivers. The plan incorporates bridges, trails, and 590 acres of parkland.

YEAR OF AWARD: 2002

STATUS: The plan has been approved.

Critical issues

The plan addressed a set of fundamental challenges:

- Create a compelling vision for an inviting park that offers high-quality public space on former industrial riverfronts.

- Establish a new level of amenity for a city in a region that continues to lose jobs and investment but whose downtown "renaissance" had successfully deployed entertainment uses and introduced incentives to restore its attractive housing stock and draw a new generation of urban residents. The city believed that significant new amenities would draw new residents, who would in turn contribute to the recovery of neighborhood commercial centers, strengthen the tax base, and lure employers back to downtown.

- Create a framework that balances the potentially conflicting goals for the riverfront—from commerce to recreation, entertainment to living—held by different stakeholders.

Key urban design concepts

Defining the park's edges as bridges that span each of the three rivers, the plan comprises a continuous shoreline strip at least 50 feet deep that circles the edge of downtown and the opposite banks. In a sense the "spine" of the park, this strip ties together existing parks, bridges, trails, green space, and waterfront amenities. A new complement of water-based activities will be launched on the rivers, and the plan adds multiple new pedestrian connections into adjacent neighborhoods, including downtown. New design guidelines govern development abutting the park, with a focus on using new construction to promote and enhance connections to the riverfront. The urban design team identified a set of core principles to guide planning and future development:

- **Organize riverfront investment** in relationship to the shared vision of Three Rivers Park as Pittsburgh's premier public domain.

- **Reinforce the power of place** by revealing and seeking inspiration in history.

- **Enhance the shoreline experience and the range of uses** encouraged to locate along the banks of the rivers.

- **Increase connections to the rivers,** especially from the neighborhoods, and endeavor to create new neighborhoods near the rivers.

- **Activate the watersheet by incorporating diverse uses** while working to mitigate any potential conflicts' among them.

- **Celebrate the City of Bridges through lighting and pedestrian amenities** and by incorporating such amenities into the river trail system.

- **Improve regional connections and the continuity of public green space** along the river's edge.

- **Consolidate transportation and minimize industrial impediments** at the river's edge.

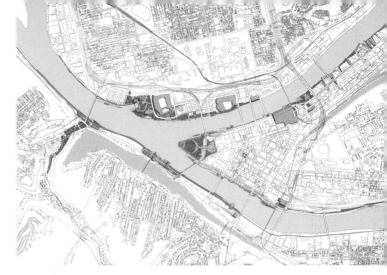

▲▲ Vision Plan for the Pittsburgh Riverfront, Pennsylvania. Chan Krieger's plan for more than 11 miles of riverfront parks and trails represents a critical next step in downtown Pittsburgh's renaissance. It adds significant new amenities—including continuous shoreline open space—to help the city attract a new generation of residents, jobs, and investment. Copyright Chan Krieger Sieniewicz, 2001.

▲ The plan creates a continuous band of paths and parks along both banks of all three rivers. Copyright Chan Krieger Sieniewicz, 2004.

- **Incorporate the values of urban ecology and sustainability** in the implementation of this plan.

Jury Comments

"The plan presents a bold, simple vision in a clear and compelling manner and unequivocally establishes the riverfront as public domain."

UrbanRiver Visions

Location: Seven communities across
   Massachusetts

Urban designer: Goody Clancy

Client: Massachusetts Executive Office of
   Environmental Affairs

Study area and program: A statewide initiative
   to assist cities across Massachusetts in making
   better use of downtown riverfronts. The first
   seven communities to participate in the
   initiative—Athol, Chicopee, Easthampton,
   Fall River, Hudson, Lawrence, and
   Worcester—were small to midsized cities that
   brought a wide range of programmatic goals
   to enhancing their riverfronts.

Year of award: 2004

Status: The plan was adopted by the Office of
   Environmental Affairs and by each of the
   communities.

Critical issues

The state launched this initiative to promote smart growth by spurring revitalization of older urban centers. Increased public ability to use and enjoy these riverfronts offered a powerful tool to draw people to live and work in these older urban centers as a counterpoint to sprawl. Similarly, the state identified riverfront revitalization as an effective way to attract investment, housing, and jobs to communities struggling with a long-term decline in industrial jobs. The state and the urban designer worked together to establish a widely inclusive public process. The process responded to a different set of issues: a need to break down barriers among stakeholders, many with

▼ UrbanRiver Visions, Athol, Chicopee, Easthampton, Fall River, Hudson, Lawrence, and Worcester, Massachusetts. Goody Clancy led a statewide initiative to help small cities devise plans for revitalization of decaying industrial riverfronts with lively parks and mixed-use development. Attracting people to live and work in these older urban centers reinforces other state efforts to counteract sprawl. Courtesy of Goody Clancy. *See color insert, C-33.*

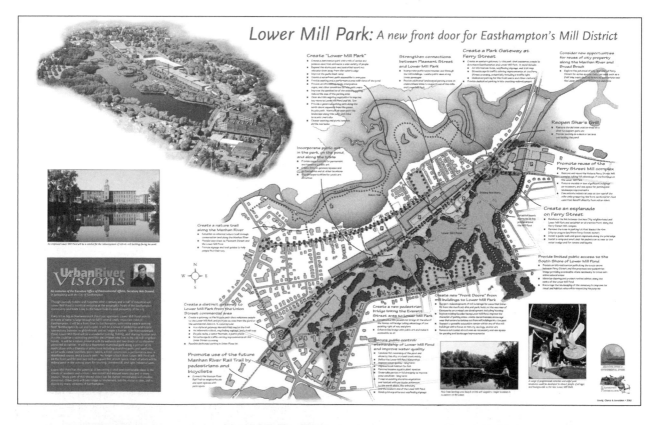

Lower Mill Park: *A new front door for Easthampton's Mill District*

▲ Public charrettes and open houses shaped recommendations for each community. Courtesy of Goody Clancy.

◄ Proposed riverfront park for a former mill town. Courtesy of Goody Clancy.

a history of contentious relationships; a recognition that grassroots political support would emerge only for plans that integrated environmental, economic, and social perspectives; and a desire to involve decision makers from all levels to ensure that public financing and other funding would be available to support implementation. The urban design team tailored the charrettes and resulting plans to each community rather than following a formulaic process or proposing "cookie-cutter" solutions.

Key urban design concepts

The urban design team addressed a broad array of issues in each community, including urban design, environmental concerns, economic development, transportation, infrastructure, recreation, and community participation. The plans envision compact, walkable, mixed-use and mixed-income downtowns and neighborhoods that have direct access to their respective riv-

ers and to new amenities like parks and trail networks. Charrette participants developed strategies for strengthening access to the river and for using changes on the riverfront to enhance the visual image of their city and to support its economy. Examples of key urban design concepts include:

- **Expansion of green space.** By closing a street and reusing a vacant lot, one town could expand a small island of green space between its town hall and train depot. The resulting park would create a new civic focal point downtown—a town common in the New England tradition.

- **Pedestrian access to river.** Providing pedestrian access along the riverbank allowed another town to open up the river, hidden behind fences and buildings, to downtown and the public. A riverwalk promenade will introduce an important new amenity into downtown.

- **Brownfields redevelopment downtown, rather than suburban expansion.** A charrette served to redirect town thinking toward reuse of an existing but largely vacant mill property and away from development of a new industrial park outside downtown.

- **Making brownfields green.** Conversion of vacant industrial sites alongside a river to mixed-use developments with dedicated parkland would turn a brownfields site—literally—green.

Jury Comments

"This plan is an important first step in educating the public about the possibilities of revitalization. It represents a true collaborative process whereby each community has a different asset that is shared along the river.... Fifty years ago, the river was viewed as least desirable, but now it is seen as the center of the community."

▼ Anacostia Waterfront Initiative Framework Plan, Washington, D.C. In an effort to spur revitalization of areas bypassed by Washington's economic resurgence, Chan Krieger created a plan to transform miles of industrial riverfront into new parks and mixed-use development that connect nearby neighborhoods to the river. Copyright Chan Krieger Sieniewicz, 2003. *See color insert, C-34.*

Anacostia Waterfront Initiative Framework Plan

LOCATION: Washington, D.C.

URBAN DESIGNER: Chan Krieger & Associates, Inc.

CLIENT: District of Columbia Office of Planning

STUDY AREA AND PROGRAM: A plan to guide a new generation of growth adjacent to the Anacostia River, including roughly 900 acres of mostly public land. This underutilized riverfront could accommodate 15,000–25,000 new mixed-income households; 20 million square feet of office and retail space; expanded government facilities; and miles of trails and parks.

YEAR OF AWARD: 2005

STATUS: The plan was adopted by the District of Columbia.

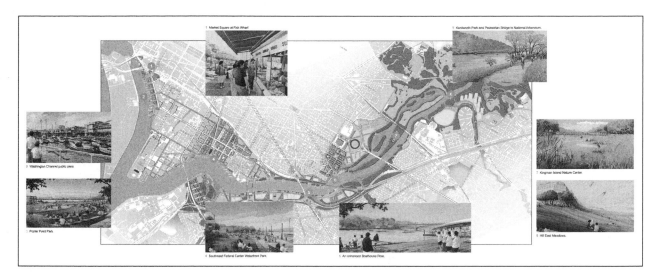

The plan proposed a network of parks. Copyright Chan Krieger Sieniewicz, 2005.

Critical issues

Mayor Anthony W. Williams captured the plan's mission: "Nothing would better symbolize our success than restoring the Anacostia waterfront.... Let the river that once divided us as two cities, unite us as one city. Let it bridge the gap between the haves and have-nots. Let its flow remind each of us to pour out rivers of compassion and justice to all our citizens. Let its currents carry us forward to a new day." As Washington, D.C., continues its recovery from decades of population outflow and disinvestment, the city confronts a novel problem: how to use growing affluence to address deeply rooted problems, one of which is the poverty, environmental degradation, and isolation of the Anacostia riverfront. "Long assumed to be less important to Washington than the Potomac,...the Anacostia steadily declined. It gradually yielded its natural beauty to...[m]ilitary...infrastructure; absorbed too much of the region's surface run-off and pollutants; [and] gave its banks over to highway and railroad corridors." Williams defined a second critical mission: securing agreement from the full range of city and federal agencies with jurisdiction over portions of the river and environmental and other issues affecting redevelopment.

Key urban design concepts

The framework "reintroduces the river into the life of the city and its residents," organizing its recommendations around "five themes for revitalization":

- **A clean and active river,** achieved by eliminating point and nonpoint pollution sources along the length of the river with the goal of supporting rowing and other recreational uses and achieving swimmability by 2025.

- **Breaking down barriers and opening up access,** achieved by bringing transit to the river and replacing existing roadways and bridges, over time, with a new roadway system designed to complement the river and celebrate its enhanced community value.

- **A great riverfront park system,** achieved by creating a network of interconnected and continuous waterfront parks tied together by the Anacostia Riverwalk and Trail.

Riparian Meadows, Mounds, and Rooms: Urban Greenway for Warren, Arkansas. Community leaders, biological engineers, planners, and architects worked with the students of the University of Arkansas's Community Design Center to generate a plan for making Town Branch Creek wilder—in the service of taming it. Stream and wetlands restoration form the basis of flood-control interventions that mimic natural processes, and the new configuration adds recreational opportunities for the community. Courtesy of University of Arkansas Community Design Center.

- **Cultural destinations of distinct character,** achieved by recognizing the Anacostia's enhanced character as a desirable setting for museums, sports venues, and facilities that celebrate its cultural heritage.

- **Building strong waterfront neighborhoods,** achieved by using the lure of waterfront living to attract 15,000–25,000 new households to live on or within walking distance of the river; creating places to shop and enjoy entertainment near the river; and, in the process, reinvigorating nearby neighborhoods and Main Streets.

Jury Comments

"The Anacostia Waterfront Initiative Framework Plan is in the great tradition of 'making no little plans.'"

Riparian Meadows, Mounds, and Rooms: Urban Greenway for Warren, Arkansas

LOCATION: Warren, Arkansas

URBAN DESIGNER: University of Arkansas Community Design Center.

CLIENT: Warren Townscape Committee

STUDY AREA AND PROGRAM: Restore the ecological functioning of Town Branch Creek, while exploring potential park and other improvements made possible by reclaiming areas that now flood and the urban design potential of new walkways and public spaces that play a role in stabilizing the creek's banks.

YEAR OF AWARD: 2005

STATUS: The plan was adopted by the town.

The plan creates a network of outdoor spaces that add new layers of amenity to a small downtown, including a new low-maintenance park with increased biological diversity. Courtesy of University of Arkansas Community Design Center.

Critical issues

This project established a university-based collaboration among biological engineers, planners, and urban designers to explore the ways in which innovative approaches to improved stream design can support community development.

Key urban design concepts

"Riparian Meadows, Mounds, and Rooms is…an extended family of urban conditions generated from the riparian corridor as a community development platform. Floodplains become parks, riparian edges form outdoor rooms and great streets, and landscape mounds remain accessible activity islands even during floods. Improved stream ecology also solves the inflow problem with the city's sewer system. Riparian Meadows, Mounds, and Rooms seeks a balance between infrastructural and ecological solutions, offering solutions for collateral community projects related to aesthetics, health, and recreation." The highly inclusive urban design process produced a series of recommendations that extended far beyond the project's initial scope: enhancement of the existing park featuring a restored riparian corridor and willow stand; conversion of a city maintenance yard to a wet meadow; restoration

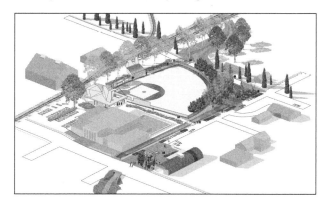

The landscaped stream corridor edges an existing ball field. Courtesy of University of Arkansas Community Design Center.

of the stream's natural floodplain with adjacent refuge mounds to accommodate trails and recreation during high-water periods; and daylighting a stream that empties into the creek through a culvert to create a new, naturally landscaped pedestrian amenity.

Jury Comments

"This project celebrates the potential of a stream to be viewed as an asset to the community. Various architectural events are strategically placed along its course, further serving the community and reinforcing its connection to the stream."

West Harlem Waterfront Park

LOCATION: New York, New York

URBAN DESIGNER: W Architecture & Landscape Architecture, LLC

CLIENT: New York City Economic Development Corporation

STUDY AREA AND PROGRAM: Phase one of a multiphase master plan for revitalization of a 42-acre study area in West Harlem. The two-acre park replaces a surface parking lot.

YEAR OF AWARD: 2005

STATUS: The plan was adopted by the Manhattan Community Board 9.

Critical issues

Mixed-use development linked visually and directly to the river will play a significant role in revitalizing West Harlem. The neighborhood lacks adequate and convenient parks; its increasing diversity underscores the need to build new civic spaces that can attract people from all incomes, ages, and cultural backgrounds.

Key concerns included development of an inclusionary public process and effective advisory group (ultimately comprising forty stakeholders' representatives); strengthening a sense of place; and developing an understanding of environmental forces (tidal patterns and subsurface compositions) and site topography to shape designs that work with, rather than in opposition to, site conditions.

Key urban design concepts

Instead of focusing on uses, the plan recommends creation of the park as an amenity designed to attract development. The master plan, of which this is a subsidiary project, focuses on 42 acres of the surrounding neighborhood, identifying transit improvements that would spur investment, recommending generous tree planting on existing streets to encourage walkability, and proposing other measures intended to spur redevelopment of this former industrial section along the Hudson River. The master-plan framework proposed a mix of higher, denser development paired with lower-scale development that takes advantage of a pronounced drop-off toward the river. The higher-density development would offer both economic development benefits and essen-

West Harlem Waterfront Park, New York, New York. W Architecture & Landscape Architecture created a plan for a park that recognizes a new generation of opportunities for this traditionally lower-income neighborhood. The park functions as an amenity to attract mixed-use development, which for decades has bypassed the area, and creates a place whose varied features and dramatic views will attract new and longtime residents to build a sense of community that to date has proved elusive. Copyright © 2003 W Architecture and Landscape Architecture LLC.

With a restaurant and, potentially, an "adventure store," a pavilion adds more activity and serves as an additional draw to residents and visitors. Copyright © 2003 W Architecture and Landscape Architecture LLC.

tial capital and operations funding for the park. The park itself contains a number of landscaped spaces that take advantage of the site's dramatic views and proximity to the water. A new ferry terminal strengthens the neighborhood's connections to other waterfront destinations.

Jury Comments

"This is a very sustainable design. This very elegant response makes a direct connection between the Harlem community and its riverfront by incorporating and celebrating its existing infrastructure. It establishes elements of connectivity to the riverfront and creates a minimal yet vibrant waterfront infrastructure that encourages activities related to the water."

Historic Third Ward Riverwalk

LOCATION: Milwaukee, Wisconsin

URBAN DESIGNER: Engberg Anderson Design Partnership, Inc.

CLIENT: Historic Third Ward Association and Business Improvement District #2

STUDY AREA AND PROGRAM: A three-quarter mile riverwalk, together with transformation of a three-quarter-acre parking lot into a riverfront park and a new ecology and neighborhood history center in Milwaukee's Third Ward. Listed on the National Register of Historic Places, the Third Ward played an important role as a commercial center in the nineteenth and early twentieth century. The area housed printers, knitting factories, and clothing manufacturers. Largely abandoned after World War II, the Third Ward has reemerged as a lively arts district, and its buildings have been renovated to hold lofts, shops, and offices for creative businesses seeking a "funky" location. Now one of the city's highest-density districts, the Third Ward's renaissance is "anchored by many extraordinary shops, restaurants, art galleries, theatre groups, dance companies, photographers, advertising agencies, and graphic artists." Projections suggest a doubling of population over the coming decade.

YEAR OF AWARD: 2007

STATUS: The plan was adopted by the city and the riverwalk has been built.

Critical issues

While the Third Ward had experienced significant investment, the riverfront remained isolated behind buildings, forming a "ribbon of blight" through the neighborhood. The riverwalk's core mission was to turn the river into a second front door for the neighborhood and

Historic Third Ward Riverwalk, Milwaukee, Wisconsin. The Engberg Anderson Design Partnership created an entirely new sense of connection to the Milwaukee River for the Third Ward, a lively downtown neighborhood that has taken root in former warehouses and factories along the riverfront. The boardwalk offers opportunities to enjoy the river that range from dining to strolling to kayaking, and it opens up a second front for the old industrial buildings that had turned their backs to the river. Courtesy of Ellen Pizer. *See color insert, C-35.*

Cafés spill out of buildings to take advantage of and contribute to the new activity along the river. Courtesy of Ellen Pizer.

Elevated overlook. Courtesy of Ellen Pizer.

transform it into an amenity that enhances quality of life and opens up possibilities for new investment.

Key urban design concepts

The plan converts "a blighted riverfront into a vibrant destination, providing green space and riverfront amenities for residents, visitors and business owners." Of particular interest, the completed riverwalk has "opened up new and desirable opportunities to experience and enjoy the river, by foot, bicycle, while dining or by launching a kayak…[and] has created a three-dimensional second 'front' for buildings along the river."

Together with the park, the riverwalk set the stage for a new public market, now open, which is supported in part by the pedestrian activity that the riverwalk attracts. The walkway itself is a pile-supported wooden boardwalk that connects directly to all local streets and passes in front of balconies and patios that face the river. It makes a conscious effort to "green" the river by introducing plantings native to Wisconsin river environments.

Jury comments

"This project responds to the many different conditions along the urban river's edge.... It captures the rugged, gritty complexity of the historic buildings and the many conditions along the river and features them rather than homogenizes them.... It is unpretentious and well done, not over-designed.... This is a reclamation of the industrial river edge in a downtown that's reinventing itself.... Stimulates redevelopment and in so doing, reclaims the river for the people from the old industrial uses."

A Balanced Plan for the Trinity River Corridor

LOCATION: Dallas, Texas

URBAN DESIGNER: Chan Krieger Sieniewicz, Inc.

CLIENT: The City of Dallas

STUDY AREA AND PROGRAM: A plan for the Trinity River and its floodplain within the city of Dallas, including neighborhoods within one mile of either side of the river. The plan uses flood-control measures as the basis for a transformation of the river into an open-space system that reconnects the city to the river and opens significant new opportunities for development.

YEAR OF AWARD: 2007

STATUS: The plan was adopted by the city.

Critical issues

The central mission of the project was a comprehensive examination of the role that the Trinity could play in the city's life and economy. Recognizing the citywide value of this initiative, which originated in the private sector, the municipality took responsibility for moving beyond its initial phase. In discussing the benefits of the plan, Mayor Laura Miller might well have been describing the growing understanding of the value that well-designed waterfronts have delivered to cities across the United States: "A decade from now, people driving into Dallas will see the city's river not as an obstacle to be overcome, but as a destination to discover. Our changing relationship to the water, I predict, will enliven every aspect of urban life in our city."

Key urban design concepts

The plan introduces a large urban park designed to support a broad range of passive and recreational uses; replaces an artificially straightened channel with a looping course that more closely reflects the river's original path; creates a sensitive design for a multilane parkway that runs along the downtown levee, affords park and city vistas, yet is screened from the view of most park users; offers long-term flood protection through levee improvements, parks, and trails; and opens the possibility of new development on several hundred acres along the river corridor. The plan works to balance the "diverse and potentially conflicting goals of providing":

- **Increased levee protection against flooding** while expanding access and views to the river by designing the levee tops for public uses and by locating public spaces on the river side of the levees.

- **Increased funding from public and private sources** for open space development and management without privatizing the riverfront.

- **Expanded recreation** that accommodates vehicular traffic and periodic flooding and that enlists natural processes to provide simple remediation of stormwater run-off.

- **New economic development opportunities** for adjacent neighborhoods and downtown without compromising the river's ecology and natural setting.

A Balanced Plan for the Trinity River Corridor, Dallas, Texas. Chan Krieger Sieniewicz's plan replaces the Trinity River's artificially straightened channel through downtown Dallas, which many see as an eyesore, with a more naturally winding course. The plan transforms the river's floodplain into a broad new urban park that enhances neighborhoods and downtown, improves flood control, and opens significant new opportunities for development. Copyright 2006 Chan Krieger Sieniewicz.

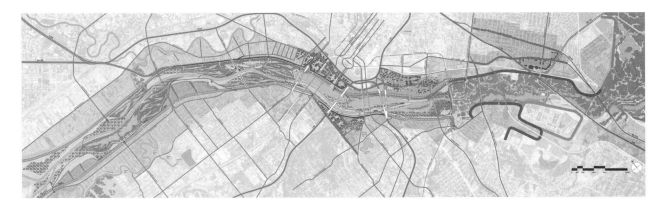

Ilustrative plan. Copyright 2003 Chan Krieger Sieniewicz.

Water-based recreation. Copyright 2006 Chan Krieger Sieniewicz.

Playing fields. Copyright 2006 Chan Krieger Sieniewicz.

Jury Comments

"We were impressed by the vast scale of this proposal.... They've taken a significant physical and environmental barrier and transformed it into a regionally scaled public domain that stitches together the surrounding urban areas and unifies the city.... The design concept returns the river to its innately sinuous state and draws on the natural features of the terrain.... Its emphasis on natural systems and sustainability addresses basic human needs."

How the Projects Illustrate the Principles

1. **Build community in an increasingly diverse society.** Whether for Shanghai, Venice, New York City, or Warren (Arkansas), all of the case studies address the compelling power of water to draw people together to create places that deepen a sense of community. Uniformly, they make the point that public access to the waterfront—in and of itself essential—provides a potent draw for people from every stratum of the city; a power that larger revitalization plans should harness. Attracting a mix of ages, backgrounds, incomes, races, and other distinctions requires the introduction of a rich and complementary mix of retail, cultural, recreational, and other activities. Each of these appeals to some people; all of them, together, help create places of universal appeal. The case studies also share an emphasis on ensuring that these waterfronts remain entirely public and fully accessible—an issue because most of these plans rely on significant private investment or sponsorship as a complement to public funds. The Hong Kong plan specifically calls for creation of an important *civic* space, rather than another round of *private* development, that can provide a new gateway and visual focus for the city's core. The plans for Riparian Meadows, Parco San Giuliano, and the Shanghai riverfront transform bodies of water that have functioned as barriers between parts of a community into seams that unite them. Similarly, the plans for Anacostia, Pittsburgh, Milwaukee, and UrbanRiver Visions address the symbolic value of enhancing deteriorated waterfronts to erase the stigma that disinvestment brings. Parco San Giuliano, Anacostia, West Harlem, and Pittsburgh place an explicit focus on social equity by spelling out ways that waterfront access can spur revitalization of lower-income neighborhoods and commercial centers.

2. **Advance environmental sustainability.** All of these case studies stress the restoration of degraded environments and pay special attention to supporting fragile ecological systems. Most offer substantive strategies

for promoting smart growth—interestingly, a goal that occupies the minds of urban designers working in China and Italy as much as it does those working in the United States. In support of smart growth, plans consciously introduce opportunities to add high-density and high-value development to the core. Parco San Giuliano, Shanghai, Hong Kong, UrbanRiver Visions, Anacostia, Milwaukee's Third Ward, and West Harlem all specifically include this goal as part of their mission.

3. **Expand individual choices.** Across the board these case studies create significant new opportunities to enjoy an unbuilt environment within walking distance of downtowns and urban neighborhoods. Whether creating a new creek-side trail in Warren, Arkansas, or opening possibilities for boating and swimming for central neighborhoods in other cities, the projects focus on programming that ushers a new generation of choices and amenities into urban communities. Interestingly, most of the case studies make a specific point of proposing expanded transit—directly or by inference arguing that the projects add regionally valuable amenities to the regional core, reinforcing the need for transit access into and through the core.

4. **Enhance personal health.** More explicitly than many of the case studies, these promote walkability and other forms of urban recreation, such as biking, through creation of continuous waterfront walks, links to regional trail systems, direct connections to nearby neighborhoods, and a conscious effort to create a system of retail and other destinations that invite walking. Like the public realm case studies in Chapter 11, these introduce new opportunities to jog, bike, kayak, and enjoy other types of exercise into urban settings where such opportunities are scarce.

5. **Make places for people.** These case studies illustrate a principle set out in the Urban Waterfront Manifesto discussed at the start of this chapter: each waterfront boasts a unique combination of natural features, built context, and community values; each plan should reflect the distinct place it addresses. The greatest distinction among the case studies divides those communities that view waterfront parks as integral elements of the urban fabric from those communities that consider their waterfront parks distinct entities—even parks that sit immediately next to urban neighborhoods or downtowns. The plans for Shanghai, Hong Kong, UrbanRiver Visions, the Third Ward Riverwalk, West Harlem, and Warren, Arkansas, create parks integrated into adjacent districts—unique and unlike any streets, parks, or squares but fully part of the larger public realm. In contrast, the plans for Pittsburgh, Anacostia, and Dallas treat their waterfront parks as adjacent to the city but standing apart as open space systems. Not surprisingly, most of the integrative plans propose very urban settings in which buildings directly engage new promenades and other public spaces. In none of these plans does adjacent building height appear as an issue (understandably, this is not an issue in a small community like Warren). In contrast, the parklike approaches treat retail and other uses as pavilions inserted into the park setting and emphasize setbacks and other conscious separations between a waterfront park and the city next door. From a different perspective, the Chicago Riverwalk Gateway shows how public art, lighting, and imaginative design can redefine barriers created by earlier infrastructure into visually exciting invitations to waterfronts and other public spaces.

Figure C-24 ELS/Elbasani & Logan's Kaka`ako Makai Area Development Strategy and similar RUDC Honor Award–winning projects represent a trend that symbolizes the resurgence of cities in America and elsewhere—design of the first new generation of urban neighborhoods since the Depression [see Chapter 9: Inventing New Neighborhoods]. (1997)

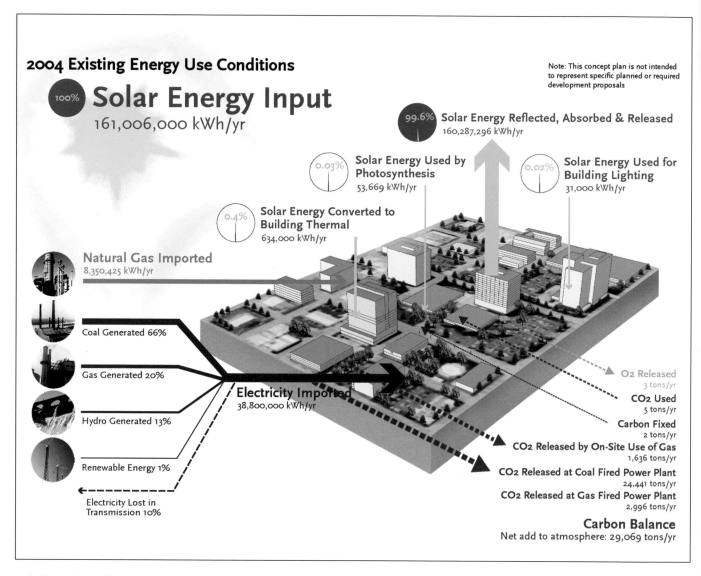

2004 Existing Energy Use Conditions

100% Solar Energy Input
161,006,000 kWh/yr

Note: This concept plan is not intended to represent specific planned or required development proposals

99.6% Solar Energy Reflected, Absorbed & Released
160,287,296 kWh/yr

0.03% Solar Energy Used by Photosynthesis
53,669 kWh/yr

0.02% Solar Energy Used for Building Lighting
31,000 kWh/yr

0.4% Solar Energy Converted to Building Thermal
634,000 kWh/yr

Natural Gas Imported
8,350,425 kWh/yr

Coal Generated 66%

Gas Generated 20%

Electricity Imported
38,800,000 kWh/yr

Hydro Generated 13%

Renewable Energy 1%

Electricity Lost in Transmission 10%

O2 Released
3 tons/yr

CO2 Used
5 tons/yr

Carbon Fixed
2 tons/yr

CO2 Released by On-Site Use of Gas
1,636 tons/yr

CO2 Released at Coal Fired Power Plant
24,441 tons/yr

CO2 Released at Gas Fired Power Plant
2,996 tons/yr

Carbon Balance
Net add to atmosphere: 29,069 tons/yr

▲ ▶ **Figure C-27** Mithun Architects+Designers+Planners' plan for Lloyd Crossing increases the Portland neighborhood's population by five times while reducing its carbon footprint. (2006)

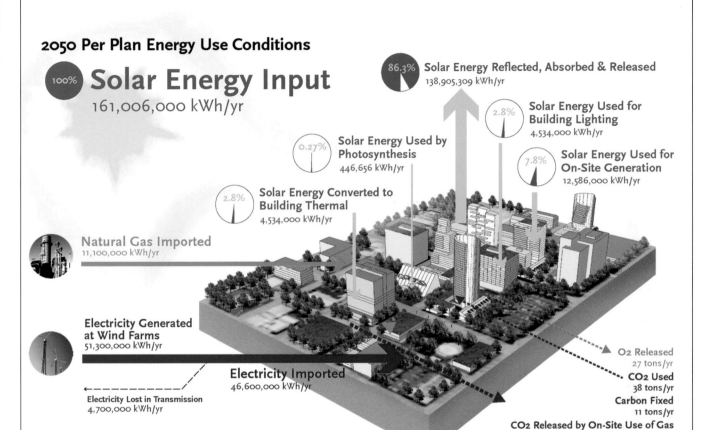

2050 Per Plan Energy Use Conditions

100% Solar Energy Input
161,006,000 kWh/yr

86.3% Solar Energy Reflected, Absorbed & Released
138,905,309 kWh/yr

2.8% Solar Energy Used for Building Lighting
4,534,000 kWh/yr

0.27% Solar Energy Used by Photosynthesis
446,656 kWh/yr

7.8% Solar Energy Used for On-Site Generation
12,586,000 kWh/yr

2.8% Solar Energy Converted to Building Thermal
4,534,000 kWh/yr

Natural Gas Imported
11,100,000 kWh/yr

Electricity Generated at Wind Farms
51,300,000 kWh/yr

Electricity Imported
46,600,000 kWh/yr

Electricity Lost in Transmission
4,700,000 kWh/yr

O2 Released
27 tons/yr

CO2 Used
38 tons/yr

Carbon Fixed
11 tons/yr

CO2 Released by On-Site Use of Gas
2,182 tons/yr

Note: This concept plan is not intended to represent specific planned or required development proposals

Carbon Balance
Net add to atmosphere: 2,144 tons/yr

Figure C-25 SOM's Saigon South Master Plan envisions an alternative to sprawl in a developing country. (1997)

Figure C-26 Johnson/Fain's plan for Mission Bay creates an entirely new mixed-use neighborhood in San Francisco. (2004)

▲ **Figure C-28** CBT and Greenberg Consultants translate ambitious new zoning into a high-density urban neighborhood in Cambridge, Massachusetts. (2006)

◀ **Figure C-29** Ehrenkrantz Eckstut & Kuhn Architects creates an urban alternative to suburban subdivisions for Crown Properties in Gaithersburg, Maryland. (2007)

Figure C-30 SOM's plan for Hong Kong's Central Waterfront Development, along with other Honor Award–winning waterfront projects, focuses on the ways in which waterfronts can attract diverse people to enjoy a sense of community and enhance both civic and economic value [see Chapter 10: Reclaiming the Waterfront]. (2000)

Figure C-31 SOM's plan redevelops Shanghai's outmoded port into an extension of the city's historic Bund waterfront. (2000)

◀ **Figure C-32** SOM's design turns a forbidding Chicago underpass into a handsome pedestrian and bicycle gateway to the lakefront. (2002)

▼ **Figure C-33** Goody Clancy's UrbanRiver Visions created customized public processes to help residents and public officials in eight Massachusetts communities craft revitalization plans for their urban waterfronts. (2004)

▲ **Figure C-34** Chan Krieger's plan enhances Washington, D.C.'s Anacostia Waterfront as a tool for helping revitalize nearby urban neighborhoods. (2005)

▶ **Figure C-35** The Engberg Anderson Design Partnership's Historic Third Ward Riverwalk in Milwaukee, Wisconsin, creates a new public face for a warehouse district that had turned its back to the river. (2007)

Figure C-36 SOM's Tribeca Bridge, a distinctive pedestrian connection between Lower Manhattan and Battery Park City, joins other Honor Award–winning public-realm projects in demonstrating the broad new interest in well-designed streets, squares, and parks to forge new connections, create a greater sense of community, and instill increased public pride [see Chapter 11: Creating the Public Realm]. (1997)

Figure C-37 The Jerde Partnership's design for the Beursplein creates a lively new pedestrian street to reconnect two halves of Rotterdam's principal downtown retail district. (1998)

Figure C-38 Rogers Marvel Architects' design for post-9/11 security measures makes Battery Park City more inviting to pedestrians. (2005)

Figute C-39 Urban designers, architects, artists, landscape architects, and others collabo-rated to create a garden of wonders that draws people from every walk of life to enjoy this downtown Chicago park located partially on the roof of a large parking facility. (2006)

◀ **Figure C-40** Lee + Mundwiler Architects' design for the Swiss Government Piazza uses a simple modernist design to invite people to enjoy a large formal square in Bern. (2006)

▼ **Figure C-41** Rogers Marvel Architects' design to increase post-9/11 protection for the New York Stock Exchange creates lively public spaces and supports a transition from an office district to a mixed-use neighborhood. (2007)

Figure C-42 Lee Meyer & Company's plan for the Savannah College of Art and Design's downtown campus demonstrates a quality shared by the other Honor Award–winning campus planning projects—an emphasis on transforming the ivory tower into a community of learning in which campus and community blend and support each other [see Chapter 12: Transforming Campus into Community]. (1998)

COLORED BY DESIGN LEE/2002

▲ **Figure C-44** Goody Clancy's North Allston Strategic Framework, created by a partnership among the city, Harvard University, and North Allston community, guides the university's growth in Boston. (2005)

▶ **Figure C-43** Sasaki Associates' Schuylkill Gateway forges new physical and economic synergies between Philadelphia's Center City and major universities across the Schuylkill River. (2003)

© Anderson Illustration Associates, Inc. 2002

Figure C-45 William Rawn Associates' plan connects Boston's Northeastern University to surrounding neighborhoods. (2005)

CHAPTER 11

Creating the
Public Realm

In *Privately Owned Public Space: The New York City Experience* (New York: John Wiley & Sons, 2000), author Jerold S. Kayden documents a rising appreciation for the public realm and the benefits that accrue from well-designed public spaces. "As cities...seek new ways to improve their physical, social, and economic environments, they are paying greater attention to the value of public space. Provision of new plazas and parks, reclamation of existing waterfronts, and beautification of public streets are all increasingly viewed as important strategies for enhancing the quality of urban living."

In an era of scarce public dollars, cities can barely keep up with basic sidewalk repaving and light repair. Instead, as Kayden observes, they "are teaming with the private sector in innovative public-private partnerships" to finance a new generation of public spaces. Some of these spaces capture the monumental visual appeal of the City Beautiful movement. Others offer interactive experiences (such as computer-driven fountains), mix public and private activities (cafés operating inside a public park), and create new venues for performance and art displays. Some

offer dramatic new views to the public by opening access to once-isolated waterfronts.

Urban designers play an active role in planning many of these new spaces, helping bring the public and private sectors together in collaborative partnerships, and designing the spaces themselves. Urban designers may work for either public- or private-sector clients or for business-improvement districts, park conservancies, and other partnerships formed by communities to revitalize and manage Main Streets and public spaces.

Roots

As discussed in Chapters 1 and 2, urban squares and spaces took on a new role in the Renaissance and Baroque periods as contributors to communities' distinctive identities. Boston Common in Boston; Central Park in New York City; the squares of Philadelphia and Savannah, Georgia; San Antonio's Riverwalk; and San Francisco's Golden Gate Park represent well known and highly influential urban public spaces in the United States that help define

A Vision for a Grand Waterfront Park of Parks

Museum Park should celebrate arts, nature, and city life, on land and water.

Connect the waterfront across the boat slip.

Connect the waterfront from the arena to the marina.

Connect the waterfront by water taxi.

A redesigned Bayfront Park for residents, downtown workers, and visitors.

Connect the riverfront and the bayfront.

Proposed Baywalk
Future Riverwalk

CITY OF MIAMI PARKS & PUBLIC SPACES MASTER PLAN

Miami, Florida. Knitting a collection of existing parks into a cohesive system with a plan to provide green space within a quarter mile of every household and a new downtown "park of parks" designed as common ground to bring residents together downtown. Courtesy of Goody Clancy.

the character of these cities. During the decades of urban decline that followed the Depression, regard for these public spaces plummeted. The Boston Common abutted the city's infamous Combat Zone. Washington Square in Philadelphia became a place given over to panhandling, as Jane Jacobs noted. Savannah filled more than one of its squares with parking garages; large parts of Central Park and Golden Gate Park were considered dangerous; and San Antonio came close to paving over its river.

A relatively small group of planners, designers, and urbanists deserve special credit for rekindling interest in spaces like these in the two decades after World War II.

They offered fresh planning and design prescriptions for refashioning the public realm to respond to changing social, economic, cultural, and other dynamics. Three seminal books in the early 1960s helped revive the idea of public spaces that delight people and enhance the quality of communities, a revival that has gained momentum in recent decades:

- Gordon Cullen's *The Concise Townscape* (New York: Van Nostrand Reinhold Co., 1961) awoke a generation of designers schooled in modernism and influenced by urban renewal to the aspirations of the City Beautiful movement and the joys of artfully designed public spaces.

- In *The Death and Life of Great American Cities: The Failure of Town Planning* (New York: Random House), which also appeared in 1961, Jane Jacobs described the critical role that streets and squares play in shaping and enriching the urban experience. Although Jacobs is now judged one of the most influential leaders of the reaction to modernist planning—in particular, the "towers in the park" model that informed the urban renewal movement—her contention that public streets functioned as important places of civic interaction initially provoked powerful resistance.

- In *The Image of the City* (Cambridge, Massachusetts: MIT Press, 1960), Kevin Lynch returned to a traditional notion that public spaces should be planned and designed in the context of the surrounding community. Lynch described cities as a unified system of paths, districts, edges, nodes, and landmarks, and he understood the public realm as part of this system. His concept of streets, squares, parks, and other public spaces that together constitute a public-realm matrix for any neighborhood or district has influenced many urban designers.

More recently, the environmental movement and growing public interest in sustainability have added

> Cities are more than sculptures to be seen only from bird's eye views and figure ground diagrams. They are constantly changing entities with unique physical and social landscapes made vibrant by the people who live, work and celebrate in them. The chemistry of that interaction between people and environment gives value and identity to the places where we live. Urban design continues to be a vital discipline because the care and shaping of our cities are too complex and too important to be left to those who see them only as objets d'art.
>
> M. David Lee, FAIA, vice president, Stull and Lee, Architects and Planners, Boston

critical new dimensions to the way urban designers think about and work with the public realm. These include:

- Spreading interest in comprehensive tree planting and other landscaping programs that, beyond providing visual amenity, cool streets and improve urban air quality.

- Interconnected and continuous systems of parks, greenways, and other green elements that help capture and naturally filter pollutants out of rainwater before it reaches rivers and aquifers.

- Zoning initiatives that ensure the availability of sunlight and natural ventilation in densely built areas.

- New technologies that bring light and water to public spaces. In 2007, for example, photovoltaic panels mounted atop a tower at Rockefeller Center provided electricity to light the complex's outsize Christmas tree for the first time.

Growing hunger for a sense of community and for measures that can draw together increasingly diverse urban populations has focused attention on the design of public spaces and on their benefits. Initiatives in cities as diverse as Oklahoma City, St. Louis, and Milwaukee are reviving and redesigning former industrial waterfronts, long cut off from their cities. A long-range environmental vision and plan for New York, PlanNYC 2030 sets a goal of providing a public park within a ten-minute walk of every residence in the city. Miami recently completed a citywide parks and public spaces master plan to make public parks available to residents in every neighborhood and to program the city's parks to respond better to the needs and aspirations of the city's extremely diverse neighborhoods.

Many cities are discovering opportunities for new public spaces in older industrial areas, from old railroad rights-of-way converted into bikeways—as in Minneapolis and Indianapolis—to parks developed from industrial sites like Seattle's Gas Works Park or Gantry Plaza State Park on the Queens waterfront in Long Island City, New York.

Finally, new financing and operating strategies have unlocked opportunities for reclaiming neglected areas and transforming them into exciting new public realms. Private donations support WaterFire, an award-winning art and music installation that draws tens of thousands of people to the heart of downtown Providence, Rhode Island, on weekends from late spring through the fall. The Bryant Park Restoration Corporation—a business-improvement district supported by nearby landowners—has transformed a derelict park into a public space that teems with people day and night. In his *Guide to Great American Public Places* (New York: Urban Initiatives, 1996), author Gianni Longo describes the reborn park as "one of the most sensual, graceful open spaces in New York City." Columbus Center, a high-rise, mixed-use air rights development sandwiched between Boston's historic Back Bay and South End neighborhoods, won approval for additional height in return for the developer's agreement to fund creation of a new neighborhood park.

Approaches Today

An editorial in the March 2006 issue of the *Urban Land*, the journal of the Urban Land Institute (ULI), addresses fundamental issues that shape planning and design of the public realm today. Editor Kristina Kessler opens by underscoring the growing importance—and value—of the public realm. She reminds readers that ULI's 2005 World Cities Forum called the public realm "the defining characteristic signifying the extent to which a city values all its residents." She examines the increasing importance that cities place on the public realm as they compete in a global marketplace and discusses ways in which globalization has made many cities far more aware of diversity and "encourag[es] the development of public spaces for increasingly diverse cultures."

The second half of Kessler's editorial is more challenging. Noting that the World Cities Forum had declared that the public realm "must be designed to foster an atmosphere of inclusivity, of classlessness that gives all residents a sense of ownership and a shared stake in their cities," she reminds us that the increased diversity in the United States' cities brings "new sets of values" and that "defining new public space can arouse intense debate over its use, the users it will serve, the public message it will send." She locates an even greater concern, however, in the reality that private investment—an increasingly crucial source of funding for public spaces that are lively and inviting—threatens to privatize these spaces. Kessler notes that:

> Privatization of the public realm raises questions of access and identity, and the very notion of democracy and the public good.... [N]ew public spaces are being developed as spaces for consumerism.... In their intent to attract an upscale clientele, these projects divide and exclude.... The privatization of public space is facilitated by various enclosures: the "captured" public street with limited access; the indoor venue with arbitrary closing times. The essential quality of public space is that it is open to everyone to use.... [O]therwise, it represents a limited sense of citizenship.[221]

Case Studies

These case studies illustrate the growing importance that cities have placed over the past decade on investing in the quality and character of the public realm, both to promote a stronger sense of community and to cultivate the amenities that draw people to live, work, and invest in downtowns and urban neighborhoods.

Tribeca Bridge–West Side Highway at Chambers Street

LOCATION: New York, New York
URBAN DESIGNER: Skidmore, Owings & Merrill
CLIENT: Battery Park City Authority
STUDY AREA AND PROGRAM: A pedestrian bridge to connect Battery Park City to adjacent neighborhoods
YEAR OF AWARD: 1997
STATUS: The bridge has been built.

Critical issues

Create a unique pedestrian gateway that represents a work of public art while reinforcing the character of a larger grid of streets and sidewalks.

Key urban design concepts

With its integration of architecture, engineering, and urban design, this project boasts a stronger focus on pure design than later projects in this category. This approach contrasts with a more recent tendency of urban designers to work closely with planners, real estate consultants, and others who bring a more economic and social focus to their work. The bridge employs towers and a dramatic arched silhouette to form a highly visible and inviting pedestrian gateway that celebrates Battery Park City's walkable nature. By broadcasting the continuation of the existing street grid as it crosses the West Side Highway, the bridge suggests that Battery Park City forms an organic extension of the city.

Tribeca Bridge-West Side Highway at Chambers Street, New York, New York. Skidmore, Owings & Merrill's distinctive design for this pedestrian gateway yields a work of public art while serving a second, urbanistic function: It reinforces the character of New York's grid of streets and sidewalks, signaling Battery Park City's connection to the larger city. ©Edward Hueber/archphoto .com. *See color insert, C-36.*

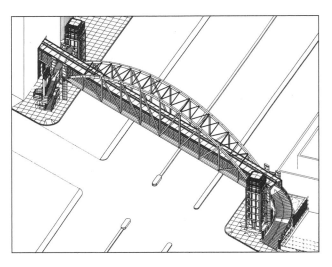

▲ Perspective. Courtesy of Skidmore, Owings & Merrill LLP.

◀ Detail. Courtesy of Skidmore, Owings & Merrill LLP.

Beursplein

LOCATION: Rotterdam, Netherlands

URBAN DESIGNER: The Jerde Partnership International, Inc.

CLIENT: Multi Vastgoed b.v.

STUDY AREA AND PROGRAM: Higher-density, mixed-use development in the heart of Rotterdam in conjunction with a new below-grade shopping street that connects two important downtown shopping districts separated by an arterial roadway

YEAR OF AWARD: 1998

STATUS: The city adopted the plan and construction is complete.

Lower-level shopping street. Photo by Christian Richter, courtesy of The Jerde Partnership.

Critical issues

Concerned that stores and housing were leaving the city for suburban locations, a city plan called for intensive re-development to reinforce the existing core with higher-density housing and a new retail connection that would repair the damage caused by postwar reconstruction, which ran a highway through the middle of a popular downtown shopping district.

Key urban design concepts

The new Beursplein recreates "the heart of an inner city which had been bombed and destroyed during World War II." It inventively reunites the two halves of the downtown retail core by building a broad and inviting street underneath a six-lane arterial roadway. The plan deploys lively public art, inviting new public spaces, dramatic glass canopies, ramps, and escalators to create a gradual transition as the Beursplein descends beneath the highway from both sides. Imaginatively lit and designed, the below-grade section of the plaza contains a series of high-value retail shops, ensuring that it forms a destination in its own right. The plan includes a new subway station and a 116-unit housing tower built after completion of the retail street. More than two million people visited the new street the day after its opening in 1996.

Beursplein, Rotterdam, Netherlands. The Jerde Partnership's plan reconnects two halves of Rotterdam's downtown shopping district separated by an arterial road built during postwar reconstruction. Based on lively new public spaces that descend on each side of the road to a new pedestrian retail street, the plan has helped slow the flow of retail businesses to the city's suburbs. Photo by Christian Richter, courtesy of The Jerde Partnership. *See color insert, C-37.*

▲ Aerial view of both levels. Photo by Christian Richter, courtesy of The Jerde Partnership.

▶ Theater District Streetscape Master Plan, Boston, Massachusetts. Kennedy & Violich Architecture's plan focuses on bringing life back to Boston's Theater District, which, at the time the plan was prepared in the mid-1990s, had not yet recovered from a decades-long decline. The plan deploys inexpensive elements, such as lighting, public art, banners, and restored marquees, to support private initiatives to rehabilitate theaters and reopen restaurants. Copyright © 2004 Kennedy & Violich Architecture, LTD.

Theater District Streetscape Master Plan

LOCATION: Boston, Massachusetts
URBAN DESIGNER: Kennedy & Violich Architecture
CLIENT: City of Boston Public Works Department; Boston Redevelopment Authority
STUDY AREA AND PROGRAM: Reconstruction of streets and sidewalks, together with streetscape improvements, for a twelve-block area in Boston's Theater District
YEAR OF AWARD: 1999
STATUS: The city adopted the plan.

Critical issues

For more than thirty years following the Great Depression, Boston endured a seemingly bottomless economic decline. Even after the city began to reemerge as a financial and research center in the 1980s, its Theater District showed the impact of years of private disinvestment and public neglect. Although some theaters had undergone renovation, peep shows more than Broadway shows set the tone. Streets and sidewalks showed visible deterioration

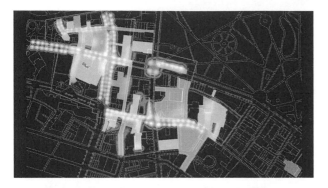

▲▲ Night plan. Copyright 2004 Kennedy & Violich Architecture, LTD.

▲ Nighttime projection on blank building wall in an alley. Copyright 2004 Kennedy & Violich Architecture, LTD.

and lacked trees and adequate lighting. Nearby "mega-developments" from the urban renewal era towered over theaters and shadowed streets. Parking lots took up prime corner parcels. An ambitious program of streetscape upgrades and ambitious redevelopment proposals proved unfeasible by the mid-1990s. Although the city anticipated that development spillover from more prosperous adjacent neighborhoods and downtown itself would ultimately rescue the district, it sought an interim solution that the city could afford to implement and maintain until the private sector stepped forward.

Key urban design concepts

The urban design plan employed four affordable but highly visible tactics:

- Using **lighting** to capture the district's spirit at night: a public art initiative attracted private-sector funding for lighting still-spectacular theater facades—even those awaiting restoration.

- Using **murals** and similar large-scale art installations to tell the theater world's stories.

- Creating **safe and inviting pedestrian access to theaters** by adding lights, streetscape enhancements, and other improvements to strengthen pedestrian connections from parking and transit.

- Concentrating **visible public investment** in a new public square, strategic tree planting, and other improvements that could produce maximum impact in exchange for scarce public funds.

Jury Comments

"This subtle, modest, and ephemeral disposition of streetscape elements and lighting is a powerful response to both the existing uses and leftover spaces of a city. Daring and creative, this project is an alternative to the typical capital-intensive top-down commercial strategies that guide too many urban redevelopment projects, and as such should become the standard rather than the exception."

Mid-Embarcadero Open Space and Ferry Terminal

Location: San Francisco, California

Urban designer: ROMA Design Group

Client: Public Works, City and County of San Francisco

Study area and program: After the 1989 Loma Prieta earthquake closed the elevated Embarcadero Freeway — a 1950s highway that had cut downtown off from the waterfront — the City of San Francisco determined to replace the structure with a waterside recreational corridor. The planning team prepared an urban design concept and design plans for improvement of the streetscape, including a major plaza at the foot of Market Street; a station for a new light-rail line; introduction of new open space development of exterior spaces around the landmark Ferry Building; and shoreline promenade and access areas. The goal of the effort was to create a grand civic space that would embrace the waterfront rather than turning away from it.

Year of award: 2000

Status: The city adopted the plan. Major components have been completed, including streetscape improvements, the new plaza, the light-rail vehicle stop, new park space, and waterside access along the Ferry Building.

Mid-Embarcadero Open Space and Ferry Terminal, San Francisco, California. The City of San Francisco's decision to tear down the elevated Embarcadero Freeway reunited downtown with the waterfront. The ROMA Design Group's plan for the newly freed land in front of the iconic Ferry Building lays out a series of grand civic spaces that showcase the building and the waterfront. A farmers' market, skateboard park, and spaces for festivals and other programming ensure that active uses clearly mark the area as "belonging to everyone." Photo by Kim Steele, courtesy of ROMA Design Group.

Critical issues

The loss of the Embarcadero Freeway "created the once-in-a-lifetime opportunity to reconceive" what is in some senses the heart of San Francisco—for more than a century the main point of entry for visitors and commuters, the site of perhaps its most iconic building, and a terminus for its main street. The new public spaces presented the opportunity to open up signficant new access to San Francisco Bay and showcase the renovation of the historic Ferry Building, but it posed the challenge of melding and extending the traditional walkable scale of the city's downtown streets and public spaces.

Key urban design concepts

The urban design plans weaves together a series of elements to create a rich and lively public realm:

- **Embarcadero Plaza,** a one-acre public space immediately in front of the Ferry Building at the foot of Market Street, is designed to accommodate a range of

Aerial view of the Ferry Building before demolition of the freeway. Photo by Boris Dramov, courtesy of ROMA Design Group.

The plan included design of a station in front of the Ferry Building to serve a new trolley line. Photo by Boris Dramov, courtesy of ROMA Design Group.

activities, including the light-rail track (with historic trolleys), festival areas, a farmers' market, and places to sit and people watch. Two light cannons shoot beams of light 600 feet into the night sky to announce special events.

- **Cityside Park,** conceived as "a grand civic room" and defined on one side by a wall of symmetrically planted palm trees, offers a lively mix of uses, including an amphitheater and a skateboard feature. It connects the plaza and the Financial District with a green corridor.

- **Ferry Terminals** include two ferry basins to accommodate expanded ferry service together with a new public access pier, which extends dramatically into the bay.

- **The historic Ferry Building,** with historically sensitive renovation, becomes a retail arcade mixing non-chain restaurants and vendors of locally produced specialty foods.

Battery Park City Streetscapes

LOCATION: New York, New York

URBAN DESIGNER: Rogers Marvel Architects

CLIENT: Battery Park City Authority

STUDY AREA AND PROGRAM: Urban design plan to improve the streetscapes, parks connections, and perimeter security for the World Financial Center

YEAR OF AWARD: 2005

STATUS: The Battery Park City Authority adopted the plan.

Critical issues

Many perimeter-security initiatives launched in response to the September 11, 2001, attacks undercut the character and civic quality of important public spaces by isolating adjacent buildings. In some cases, public spaces—particularly lively streets and squares—were closed completely; in other instances, they were cut off from the buildings that helped animate them. Faithful to its mission, which includes creation of a walkable

▶ Battery Park City Streetscapes, New York, New York. Rogers Marvel Architects created a plan for fortifying security around buildings in Battery Park City after the destruction of the World Trade Center, with the hope that "the funds invested in physical security measures will never be called to service." The planning team paid equal attention to enhancing the day-to-day experience of using the public realm by adding mature street trees and handsome street furniture, providing strong pedestrian connections, and recommending measures—such as eliminating truck queues from residential streets—that serve to improve both security and the quality of the public realm. Copyright Rogers Marvel Architects.

▶ Street furniture addresses security concerns and enhances the public realm. Copyright © Rogers Marvel Architects.

district with a distinctive public realm, the Battery Park City Authority determined that this project needed to chart a different course and aimed to demonstrate that considerable investment in building security could at the same time enhance the quality and character of the public realm. The plan explored opportunities to satisfy goals that appeared mutually exclusive: protect buildings in a dense urban environment from vehicles carrying explosives and similar threats while keeping sidewalks open; provide street furniture and other essential public realm improvements; and improve the regime that governs the way commercial vehicles, residents, visitors, and others share Battery Park City's streets.

Key urban design concepts

Noting that everyone hoped that "the funds invested in physical security measures will never be called to service," the urban design plan points out that such measures should also enhance the public's day-to-day ability to use and enjoy the public realm. The plan applies this spirit to the design of the landscaping, bus

Strong pedestrian connections. Courtesy of RMA Photos. Copyright Rogers Marvel Architects. *See color insert, C-38.*

shelters, benches, and other elements that play dual roles as protective devices and public amenities. The same approach governed efforts to improve pedestrian access to parks and other public spaces, both by creating more direct routes and by improving the quality of street crossings. Similarly, the plan resolves "public realm management" problems—for example, commercial trucks' queuing in front of residential blocks and in other areas, which constituted both a nuisance and a potential risk. This nuanced approach helped reinforce the district's sense of community at a time when this quality felt particularly important for people living in the shadow cast by 9/11.

Jury Comments

"This design resolves two seemingly contradictory goals.... First, to provide security in our public spaces, and second, in doing so, to allow for public spaces that are still open and inviting—not dependent upon the more typical barrier response."

Millennium Park

Location: Chicago, Illinois

Urban designer: Skidmore, Owings & Merrill (master planner); with McDonough Associates; Teng & Associates; Frank O. Gehry & Associates; Harley Ellis Devereaux; Gustafson Guthrie Nichol; Muller & Muller, Ltd.; Hammond Beeby Rupert and Ainge; Krueck & Sexton Architects; OWP/P; Renzo Piano; and City of Chicago staff

Client: City of Chicago

Study area and program: A 24.5-acre area that completes Chicago's 100-year-old vision for Grant Park, located on air rights over a parking garage and multimodal transit center

Year of award: 2006

Status: The city adopted the plan and has completed construction of the park.

Critical issues

The rail yards (later used as surface parking) that occupied this site from the middle of the nineteenth century onward had blocked completion of the 100-year-old vision for Grant Park. Responding to a proposal floated by civic groups for "lakefront gardens for the performing arts," Mayor Richard M. Daley announced in 1997 that the city would transform the site into a parking structure and transit center topped by the world's largest "green roof"—a new park. Sensing that a landmark park would justify its cost by attracting significant private investment to the area, the mayor committed to a plan that would include a series of important attractions and would draw on the services of world-renowned designers. The city's investment has already paid off—the area around Millennium Park represented Chicago's "hottest real estate market" by the time the park opened in 2004.

Millennium Park, Chicago, Illinois. Skidmore, Owings & Merrill submitted the design for Millennium Park to the Honor Awards judging on behalf of an interdisciplinary collaboration of architects, artists, engineers, landscape architects, urban designers, and others. The park forgoes a formal design in favor of creating a garden of wonders in the form of innovative and interactive public art, spectacular fountains, seductive cafés, and other sensual delights that have quickly made it one of the city's best-loved places. The awards jury called the park the "most beautifully executed new urban public space in America." Copyright Skidmore, Owings & Merrill LLP and Steinkamp Ballogg Photography.

Key urban design concepts

The plan drew inspiration from an interdisciplinary collaboration of architects, artists, engineers, landscape architects, planners, urban designers, and others. It created a park setting for pavilions, performance spaces, and sculpture, each of which constituted an important work of art or destination in its own right. Strategically sitting cafés and other park activities to disguise elevation changes required to provide clearance for the parking and transit functions below, the park is integrated into the adjacent downtown and lakefront through its design and its programming. The blending of traditional park uses, such as places to eat and to enjoy well-designed landscaping, with internationally recognized landmarks such as Frank Gehry's Jay Pritzker Pavilion, Jaume Plens's interactive Crown Fountain, and Anish Kapoor's Cloud Gate produced a park that quickly became one of the best loved—and most talked-about—places in Chicago.

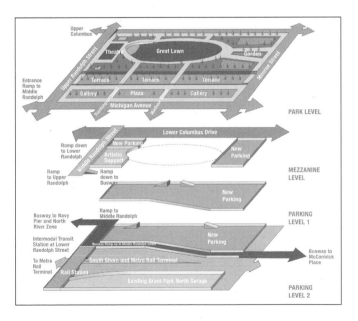

Diagram of the park as a green roof for transit infrastructure. Copyright Skidmore, Owings & Merrill LLP.

▲▲ Cloud Gate. Photo © 2006, found at D. Dima/wikimedi-commons in 2007. *See color insert, C-39.*

▲ Millennium Fountain. Copyright © iStockphoto.com/DLewis33.

Jury Comments

"The most beautifully executed new urban public space in America.... It's a masterpiece of urban ingenuity and creativity.... The plan reflected the desire to foster collaboration with designers and as a result elevated the role of public art in the city."

Swiss Government Piazza

LOCATION: Bern, Switzerland

URBAN DESIGNER: Lee + Mundwiler Architects

CLIENT: City of Bern/Tiefbauamt

STUDY AREA AND PROGRAM: Redesign of the Federal Plaza in front of the Swiss Bundeshaus (parliament building). Although the plaza is historically significant, no urban design plan had ever been prepared for the area, which was in use as a parking lot. Chosen in an international design competition, the plan transforms the plaza into a public space that can play a more active role in the city's daily life—as a public space for markets, political demonstrations, orienting visitors and telling the city's story, and similar activities.

YEAR OF AWARD: 2006

STATUS: The city adopted the plan, and construction is complete. The new plaza was dedicated in 2004.

Critical issues

The piazza lies at the center of Swiss civic life—as a forecourt to the country's parliament and other important federal buildings—and at the heart of medieval Berne, a UNESCO World Heritage Site. That location meant that its design had to achieve a timeless quality and avoid competing visually with the important public and historic buildings surrounding it. At the same time, the design needed to animate the large plaza and transform it from a vast expanse of pavement into a valued public space in its own right.

Key urban design concepts

The urban design plan "survived 12 years of scrutiny and emerged with the architect's initial vision intact." While

◀ Swiss Government Piazza, Bern, Switzerland. Lee + Mundwiler Architects' redesign of the Federal Piazza, which fronts Switzerland's parliament building, relies on elegant details to define a spare, modernist space. The plan reinforces the piazza's civic, symbolic, and historic roles while inviting the public to enjoy a series of simple yet innovative fountains that animate a once-lifeless expanse of paving. Photo courtesy of Ruedi Walti. *See color insert, C-40.*

its details and craftsmanship are superbly elegant, the plan's urban design merit lies in its ability to use highly imaginative fountains and night lighting to transform a featureless sweep of pavement into a lively public space that draws and engages people—in a way that deepens the piazza's civic, symbolic, and historic meanings. In the process, the design demonstrates persuasively that terms like "spare" and "modernist" need not mean detachment from the way people experience and enjoy public spaces.

Jury Comments

"A successful Modern intervention in an historic setting that is sublime.... Demonstrates impressive design restraint.... Allowed traditional civic activities of the plaza to continue."

▲▲ Aerial view of the piazza. Courtesy of Lee + Mundwiler Architects.

▲ View across the piazza's long axis, with the parliament building at right. The 26 fountains represent Switzerland's 26 cantons. Photo courtesy of Ruedi Walti.

▲ New York Stock Exchange Financial District Streetscapes—Security, New York, New York. On the strength of its Battery Park City plan, Rogers Marvel Architects won a similar assignment for the area around the New York Stock Exchange—planning perimeter security for "iconic institutions while improving the quality of public spaces ... [and avoiding] making the area appear under siege." Little of the new security is evident to passersby, taking the form of new landscaped squares, security barriers that look like public art, street furniture, and other public-realm amenities. Rendering © Michael McCann, courtesy of Rogers Marvel Architects. *See color insert, C-41.*

▶ Rogers Marvel designed the faceted "NOGO" security barriers installed throughout the plan area. Copyright Rogers Marvel Architects.

Critical issues

This case study addressed the same issues posed by the Battery Park City Streetscapes project in a far denser context. Like the Battery Park City Authority, the City of New York insisted that critical measures to protect the stock exchange not compromise the district's openness and walkability—in essence, it sought to "harden" the site without destroying the existing urban fabric. In another development that echoed the Battery Park City experience, the project evolved into an effort to use investment in security measures as a way to enhance the quality and character of the sidewalks and the public realm around the stock exchange. Because of its older and denser context, this project presented issues even more complex than those raised by Battery Park City: the physical constraints of narrow streets and sidewalks; a complicated filigree of underground utilities just beneath the site surface; and the presence of National Historic Landmark properties. Additionally, the enhanced public spaces needed to support Wall Street's emerging residential community, which

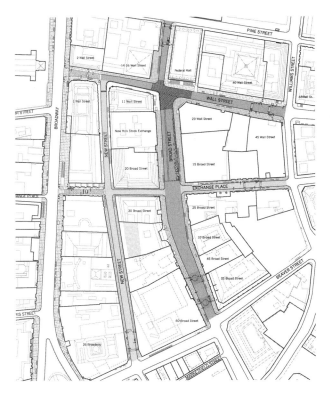

District plan. Copyright Rogers Marvel Architects.

The plan's broader focus on pedestrian-friendly street amenities makes its security measures virtually unnoticeable to passersby. Copyright Rogers Marvel Architects.

reflects a new interest in living in parts of New York City that had never before attracted residential development.

Key urban design concepts

"We believe that security is an urban design problem," said the urban design team. "Not only does this make for more effective protection, but more importantly creates the opportunity to use this funding to simultaneously sponsor a better urban realm." This attitude informed the plan's recommendations at every scale. The urban designer devised a barrier system to prevent vehicle-borne attacks from reaching likely target buildings. The system "reduces the amount of space devoted to vehicle barriers by half, . . . is shaped to provide surfaces for sitting . . . or leaning, . . . is inviting to touch," and in other ways enriches the character of streets without sacrificing efficacy. By reorienting traffic, the plan also created new public squares and other spaces that accommodate cafés and similar enlivening uses. New street trees and street furniture, together with these new public spaces, will help make Wall Street a more livable neighborhood for close to 40,000 new residents projected in the area by 2012.

Jury Comments

"This is an elegant solution to a thorny contemporary problem. . . . The approach addresses security as a neighborhood-wide design matter rather than as a building perimeter issue and in doing so, contributes to the creation of a pedestrian-friendly, high-quality public realm while taking a very full environmental approach to the problem. . . . Much of the security becomes invisible by transforming security devices into amenities . . . . The solution also recognizes the need for implementing short-term emergency measures that might later evolve into longer-term permanent solutions."

How the Projects Illustrate the Principles

1. **Build community in an increasingly diverse society.** The spaces in these case studies almost universally have as a core mission the fostering of a greater sense of community. That mission stands in contrast to squares and other urban spaces—built until quite recently—that generally functioned to meet aesthetic goals, such as making cities more beautiful, setting off civic buildings, or creating vistas. Some of the case studies explore the most challenging aspects of creating community in an increasingly diverse society. Above almost any other recent public space, Millennium Park shows how a well-programmed park can draw people from across every urban division—age, ethnicity, income—without resorting to attractions that reduce citizens to consumers. Although the park relied on millions of dollars of private contributions—memorialized in the names of such features as AT&T Plaza, Jay Pritzker Pavilion, and Crown Fountain—all of these elements have remained genuinely public in nature. Perhaps the park's most popular attraction is Anish Kapoor's Cloud Gate—an elongated silver orb that could have dropped from a Georgia O'Keefe painting—which provides viewers with unique perspectives on themselves and the city around them. Swiss Government Piazza was for centuries an uninspiring, utilitarian space, but now it exemplifies the new urban agenda for public spaces. Also skirting consumerism, the Piazza relies on an astonishingly simple device—allowing people to interact with water—to attract a broad cross section of residents and visitors. Plans for Boston's Theater District and San Francisco's Embarcadero also recognize a new level of responsibility to reach out and attract the full

spectrum of society; each focuses on retail, theater, and other private uses to spin off an inviting vitality, but both strive to avoid creating privatized environments. Approaching public space with a different and more focused charge, the Battery Park City and New York Stock Exchange plans reveal a tenacious will not just to hold on to but to reinforce the role of public streets as center stage for community in the wake of 9/11.

2. **Advance environmental sustainability.** Like many of the previous case studies, these plans enrich the quality and vitality of downtowns, where density reduces per-capita energy use and carbon outputs. The plan for the Beursplein in Rotterdam makes a direct case for smart growth, describing its mission as preserving downtown's retail preeminence and reversing the flow of shopping and housing out of the city's core. The streetscape plans for Battery Park City and the New York Stock Exchange make the case that sprawl is the unavoidable price of closing urban streets and barricading major buildings, as such measures will force people and important buildings to leave urban centers. As the world's largest green roof, Millennium Park serves as a model of environmental thinking, and it builds in environmentally friendly features such as a bicycle "garage" and changing facility that signal a serious commitment to one of the most environmentally benign modes of transit.

3. **Enhance personal health.** All of these public spaces emphasize walkability, in contrast to public spaces of the 1960s and 1970s that sat atop or adjacent to large parking structures. Notably, the plans for the Battery Park City and New York Stock Exchange streetscapes, Beursplein, Boston's Theater District, and the Tribeca Bridge all focus directly on streets and sidewalks—and new ways to connect them—suggesting how much more importance is attached to walkable environments today than in a previous era, when planners and public officials had yet to begin thinking of streets as "public spaces."

4. **Expand individual choices.** Most of the case studies describe public spaces that offer a broad set of choices as the principal tool for reaching diverse audiences. Only Swiss Government Piazza relies primarily on the strength of its design to draw people—and even here it offers multiple ways to interact with the space, from fountains to twice-weekly markets. The Mid-Embarcadero Open Space plan represents an emerging approach to designing public spaces, common to many of these case studies. It combines an array of physical features with rich programming that appeals to a range of individual choices and preferences as a way of drawing people. In effect, the case studies challenge a long-held assumption that public spaces should appeal to universal aspirations—sunlight, seating, people-watching—a list that assumes a homogeneous set of values among all users. The planning and design for these projects intentionally appeal to the broad aspirational landscape of a heterogeneous society.

5. **Make places for people.** Of all these case studies, only the Swiss Government Piazza takes a traditional, formal approach to design—and it leavens its refinement with the light-hearted pleasure of splashing water. Most of the plans work to create experiences that people will love, rather than simply designs they will admire. Probably the best-loved new public space of the last decade, Millennium Park, lacks a formal overall design. Instead, it gathers together a collection of unique, brilliantly conceived experiences, not least of them being its connections to downtown Chicago and the lakefront. None of these spaces is dull or designed as a backdrop for other activities. They succeed because imaginative planning has woven them into the lives and characters of the surrounding communities, and because they celebrate and delight the people who use them.

CHAPTER 12

Transforming Campus into Community

Four dynamics have begun to transform academic institutions into integrated communities for learning, driving new urban design approaches on campuses around the United States and prompting colleges and universities to redefine their functions.

- A more **diverse student population** has indelibly reshaped the landscape of learning. Institutions of higher education have identified design that fosters greater academic interaction and social exchange among students, faculty, and staff as a key to success. Urban designers have responded by creating public areas and spaces on campus that promote spontaneous interaction and by designing urban-style, mixed-use environments, with more opportunities for walking to class or work and a greater choice of living and transportation options.

- Current design of academic facilities and campuses also reflects an understanding that some of the least traditional spaces—public spots like a campus coffee shop, a library corridor, or an outdoor bench—may

yield some of the best thinking. **A growing focus on interdisciplinary and collaborative learning and teaching** calls for greater visibility, proximity, and connectivity among different disciplines. Chance encounters between people from different disciplines can frequently provoke novel ideas and foster new learning opportunities. As a result, colleges and universities have worked to break down the walls among departments and between campuses and surrounding communities.

- The decline of manufacturing across the United States has left **educational institutions,** especially health-care and research facilities, **as major regional economic engines,** particularly in older industrial cities. Planning for economic development today consciously seeks to take advantage of and encourage concentrations of research and teaching in anticipation of spin-off economic benefits.

- Increasingly, **faculty and students view the community as their campus.** Universities understand that competition for top faculty, students, and staff requires them to pay as much attention to the vitality and character of the district and city around them as they do to the campus proper.

These four dynamics have pushed campus planning well beyond the traditional siting studies for a single building or public space toward an ambitious, holistic, community-building approach. Once organized largely around separate zones of activity, campuses have reconstituted themselves as interconnected and interdisciplinary centers of learning. A growing demand for more housing for students, faculty, and staff—from these groups and, in some cases, from nearby neighbors—has prompted many urban institutions to take an active role in the planning and design of adjacent neighborhoods.

These changes in higher education have motivated different types of client groups to hire urban designers to plan campuses and the surrounding communities. In addition to educational institutions, cities and public agencies have sponsored urban design initiatives to guide growth and change on campuses and in the districts around them.

Roots

The earliest thinking about campus design in the United States focused on the idea of enclaves that would insulate students from sinful external influences (of the nine colleges chartered before the American Revolution, only one began with no religious affiliation). Suspicion of the secular world colored thinking about campuses, their form, and their relationship to the communities around them well into the nineteenth century. Among the more than 4,300 institutions of higher learning in the United States, a few influential models of campus development predominate:

- The **urban model,** borrowed from English universities like Oxford and Cambridge, which organized themselves as a series of academic communites next to but walled off from surrounding towns. Founded in the seventeenth and early eighteenth centuries, Harvard and Yale universities and the College of William and Mary in Virginia adopted this insular model and continue to follow it today.

- The **rural "idealized" campus,** conceived of as a self-sufficient community independent from city life and commerce. Along with academic facilities and residences, Thomas Jefferson included vegetable gardens—and slave quarters—in his celebrated 1817 plan for the University of Virginia.

- The **natural campus,** integrated with the surrounding landscape and influenced to some extent by a romantic view of nature and a desire to escape industrial urban centers. Frederick Law Olmsted designed many university campuses on this model, beautifully exemplified in his plan for Stanford University, which dates from the late 1880s.

- The **City Beautiful model,** which traces to Daniel Burnham's plan for the World's Columbian Exposition in Chicago in 1893, has shaped some urban universities. The campus plan for the Massachusetts Institute of Technology, dedicated in 1916, and other urban institutions incorporated imposing facades intended to impress and stand as beacons of tranquility and learning in their urban settings.

- An emerging **integrated model.** In the last decade of the twentieth century, colleges and universities began to develop an urban model that integrated the campus with the adjacent community, as exemplified

Emory University in Atlanta leads a collaborative effort with residents and other institutions to turn an auto-dominated suburban setting into a mixed-used community with multiple options for living, working, walking, and experiencing nature. Courtesy of Goody Clancy.

by the New York University (NYU) campus. With facilities scattered across Greenwich Village, NYU has been one of the few academic institutions to engage fully with its surrounding neighborhood.

In recent years, increasing numbers of colleges and universities have turned toward this integrated campus and community model. Trinity College, for example, renewed ailing urban areas adjacent to its Hartford, Connecticut, campus, and in the process greatly improved the neighborhood for both students and longtime residents. In the 1990s The Ohio State University reversed a decades-old policy of "walling off" surrounding neighborhoods in Columbus and created Campus Partners for Community Development to invest in lively mixed-use development intended to revitalize High Street along the eastern edge of its campus. Campus Partners also sponsored housing development to attract students, faculty, and staff, as well as city residents to this long-neglected neighborhood. The University of Cincinnati joined with a group of medical institutions and the Cincinnati Zoo to form the Uptown Consortium, which has led to revitalization of the neighborhoods, commercial districts, institutional campuses, residential neighborhoods, and parks around the university's campus.

Approaches Today

In a similar vein, Atlanta's Emory University established the Clifton Community Partnership to collaborate with the surrounding older-suburban community and institutions such as the U.S. Centers for Disease Control and Prevention on an initiative that integrates walkable, mixed-use development with preservation of historic neighborhoods, restoration of natural areas, and development of infill retail. Although no organizations have drawn up principles for integrating campuses and communities, the guidelines that Emory has developed—in consultation with the community—reflect an emerging consensus around goals that urban designers seek to achieve.

1. **"Create places of greater civic value"** by focusing development in ways that protect natural areas and established neighborhoods, that have a mix of uses, that draw diverse people together, and that strengthen quality of life for the entire community.

2. **"Promote environmental sustainability"** by restoring and connecting degraded natural habitats, reducing the need to drive (by adding more housing and by increasing walkability), linking development

rights to natural-area enhancement, and promoting green construction and building-operations techniques.

3. **"Expand choices"** in housing, transportation, recreation, culture, and shopping. Make it easier for residents of adjacent neighborhoods to shop and work in the area, and make it easier for workers to shop and consider moving to the area.

4. **"Improve accessibility and connectivity"** with development that creates "transit-ready" centers to support future transit expansion, and with networks that connect all the area's functions, support cyclists and pedestrians, and serve all age groups and mobility levels.

5. **"Enhance personal well-being"** by working to bring the built and natural environments into balance, improve environmental design in ways that promote health, reduce auto-related injuries, and increase options for lifelong learning.

6. **"Foster community-wide engagement"** through continuing education of all stakeholders and creation of a permanent forum for discussion of decisions about growth and change. Make a commitment to use development as a way of increasing quality of life for all members of the community.

Case Studies

These case studies illustrate a dramatic transition in planning for communities of learning. Moving away from a traditional focus on campuses in physical and social isolation from their surroundings, planning now integrates the campus and its neighborhood, particularly in cities, where institutions have traded ivory towers for full participation in vibrant urban communities.

The City Campus of the Savannah College of Art and Design

LOCATION: Savannah, Georgia

URBAN DESIGNER: The Savannah College of Art and Design; Lee Meyer & Company, Architects

CLIENT: The Savannah College of Art and Design

STUDY AREA AND PROGRAM: The Savannah College of Art and Design (SCAD) decided to expand its campus in the midst of the city's declining downtown, buying and finding new uses for former department stores, office buildings, cinemas, and other older structures. As a college of applied arts, SCAD needed a wide variety of facilities, including student housing, classroom and studio spaces, galleries, performance spaces, retail spaces, and places that brought students, faculty, and staff together.

YEAR OF AWARD: 1998

STATUS: SCAD continues to develop its downtown campus.

Critical issues

The college wanted to create a cohesive community of learning in which students, faculty, and staff lived, worked, and studied with each other. But it consciously chose to place equal emphasis on a second goal, revitalization of downtown Savannah. This represented both a commitment to producing a broad civic benefit and a way of creating a lively environment that would strengthen SCAD's ability to attract students, faculty, and staff and draw them all together.

City Campus of Savannah College of Art & Design, Georgia. This plan turns downtown Savannah into the campus for Savannah College of Art and Design, which offers in exchange its presence as a force for energizing the city center. Lee Meyer & Company, Architects created a plan that breathes new life into department stores, office buildings, cinemas, and other older buildings by converting upper floors into classrooms, studio spaces, offices, and other academic and administrative spaces while filling ground floors with performance venues, galleries, shops, cafés, and other uses that help animate surrounding streets. Courtesy of Savannah College of Art and Design.

▲ Student population adds to downtown activity and appeal. Courtesy of Savannah College of Art and Design.

▶ New use for a shuttered theater. Courtesy of Savannah College of Art and Design. *See color insert, C-42.*

Key urban design concepts

SCAD launched its downtown strategy more than a decade before the award submission. By the time of the award, SCAD had located most of its 4,000 students and 700-plus faculty and staff in fifty downtown buildings. This growth has been shaped around a commitment to integrate the institution into downtown in ways that add vitality and erase barriers between community and institution. The college has used the phrase "the campus as the city, the city as the campus" to describe its goals and convey its intention that its students become active citizens in the larger community and that the larger community benefit in tangible ways from SCAD's growth. In furthering its goals, the college made a critical commitment to program the street level of its buildings as galleries, stores, cafés, and other uses that build on the college's vitality to animate downtown streets.

University of Washington Tacoma Master Plan

LOCATION: Tacoma, Washington

URBAN DESIGNER: Moore Ruble Yudell Architects & Planners

CLIENT: University of Washington Tacoma

STUDY AREA AND PROGRAM: The 46-acre campus occupies a major portion of Tacoma's historic warehouse district, together with a partially abandoned residential neighborhood to the west. The master plan calls for some 500,000 gross square feet of facilities to serve an initial student population of 1,200 by 2010. The campus would continue to grow over several decades, ultimately accommodating a student population of up to 25,000 and occupying several million square feet in the heart of downtown.

YEAR OF AWARD: 1999

STATUS: The university adopted the plan and has proceeded with development.

Critical issues

The University of Washington adopted two central goals for its new campus: to make higher education accessible to a diverse "place-bound" population, including many employed adults well beyond traditional college age, and to combine preservation and revitalization of a decaying downtown district.

Key urban design concepts

The plan celebrates its commitment to preservation and revitalization by rehabilitating historic warehouses to create dramatic settings for classrooms, labs, gathering places, administrative offices, and a range of other uses. The campus is connected to the larger community along three axes. Nineteenth Street serves as the campus's Main Street and its connection to the existing downtown. A former railway line creates a second axis that connects the university to an emerging open space system. A view corridor that extends through the warehouse district to Mount Rainier provides a sense of connection to the larger region. Nothing bet-

▼ University of Washington Tacoma Master Plan, Tacoma, Washington. Preserving and revitalizing an important part of Tacoma's industrial legacy, Moore Ruble Yudell Architects & Planners developed a plan to integrate a 46-acre campus into an area of historic warehouses. The campus's arrival—and the promise of future expansion—has brought new vitality to a struggling part of downtown while providing a dramatic setting for the university and responding to student desires to enjoy city life. Courtesy of Werner Huthmacher Photography.

▲ The plan mixes adaptive reuse and new construction. Courtesy of Werner Huthmacher.

▶ The plan shapes the campus around trucking and rail corridors established in the early twentieth century. Courtesy of Moore Ruble Yudell Architects & Planners.

ter symbolizes the synergies between the city's history and its future, represented by the university as a newly central institution, than the transformation of a former power substation. Designed as a Greek Revival temple in the early twentieth century, the building has become the campus library's main reading room and connects to state-of-the-art facilities that house library collections and staff spaces. The library has become a landmark on campus and has played a key role in a "budding synergistic relationship between campus life and that of the surrounding community." The university's decision to locate its campus here instead of on Tacoma's edge has been credited with sparking a broad downtown revival.

Jury Comments

"This large-scale development, fully integrated into the city fabric, establishes its own campus atmosphere and introduces vitality, activity, and a sense of place in a formerly down-at-the-heels neighborhood. Reflecting a sensitive adaptation of existing warehouse blocks, the plan successfully transforms uses while maintaining the distinctive urban character and form. A significant new public environment is created to serve both school and city."

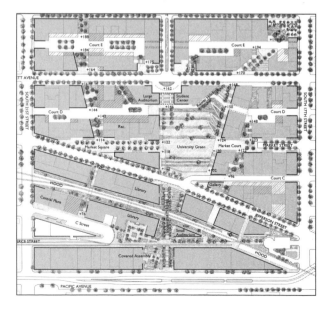

▶ Howard University—LeDroit Park Revitalization Initiative, Washington, D.C. Sorg and Associates worked with Howard University to build a neighborhood-revitalization model that avoids gentrification and the displacement of long-term residents. The plan celebrates the neighborhood's African American history, provides affordable housing options for long-term residents, and introduces new stores, jobs, and public spaces designed to enhance quality of life and attract new residents. Courtesy of Sorg and Associates, P.C.

◀ Illustrative plan. Courtesy of Sorg and Associates, P.C.

Howard University—LeDroit Park Revitalization Initiative

LOCATION: Washington, D.C.

URBAN DESIGNER: Sorg and Associates

CLIENT: Howard University

STUDY AREA AND PROGRAM: A revitalization plan for 150 blocks around the university. The plan focuses on streetscape improvements; land-use initiatives designed to promote economic opportunity, community-serving stores, and other investment that can take advantage of proximity to a nationally important university; and creation of new and renovated mixed-income housing.

YEAR OF AWARD: 2003

STATUS: The District of Columbia government provided "public affirmation" of the plan by incorporating its findings into the city's comprehensive plan. By the time of the award submission, initial improvements had already transformed LeDroit Park into one of the district's "hot residential markets."

Critical issues

In deciding to put the the university's resources to work on improving LeDroit Park's quality of life and physical character, Howard University sought to avoid the familiar fall-out from revitalization: widespread gentrification that would force out longtime residents. The university also sought to build on the substantial cultural, social, and architectural heritage of one of America's first African American national historic districts.

Key urban design concepts

The plan included specific recommendations for the public realm—economic development, cultural resources, housing, transportation, and other aspects of the neighborhood—but it carefully applied to each a uniform filter: honoring and building on the community's substantial African American heritage. "Located in an area rich in African-American culture, historical figures and historical events, the Revitalization Initiative took the threads of the past and reworked them to create a newly revitalized community fabric to celebrate the pioneering, visionary, and heroic spirit of its past and, at the same time, created a solid foundation for its future development." The design team organized its recommendations into three interrelated strategies:

- **The Streetscape Plan** extends beyond needed sidewalk and street repairs to a series of interpretive elements—for example, "sidewalk paving embodying famous quotations and local anecdotes by and about residents, and the introduction of 'contemplation' sidewalk offsets that honor illustrious former residents."

- **The Land Use Plan** includes a series of cultural and commercial development projects together with open space and other community amenities. Prominent examples include the first national African American museum, located on axis with the National Archives, and restoration of the historic Howard Theater.

- **The Housing Initiative** begins with "a seed project to spur revitalization of the broader area" by renovating and building forty-five houses for moderate-income households. The comprehensive program incorporates financing to support existing and new residents in restoration of historic houses and to encourage in-fill development on vacant parcels.

Jury Comments

"[The Initiative] really centered on a cultural notion... [and represents] history turned into the physical."

Schuylkill Gateway

LOCATION: Philadelphia, Pennsylvania
URBAN DESIGNER: Sasaki Associates
CLIENT: Philadelphia Industrial Development Corporation
STUDY AREA AND PROGRAM: A $2 billion revitalization of largely abandoned industrial land designed to link downtown (known locally as Center City) to University City, a redevelopment program well into its third decade around the University of Pennsylvania and Drexel University. The 170-acre site straddles the Schuylkill River and can accommodate more than 8 million square feet of mixed-use development. Housing would comprise roughly three-quarters of the new development, which would rise from a matrix of new tree-lined streets, squares, and parks. Completion will require at least twenty years.
YEAR OF AWARD: 2003
STATUS: In 2007 the University of Pennsylvania purchased a key section of the study area, 27 acres of former U.S. Postal Service land on the west bank of the Schuylkill and immediately east of the Penn campus.

Critical issues

The study describes a combination of assets that "are striking when considered at the regional level—the amount of available land, the convenient access, and the proximity to Center City, universities, and residential neighborhoods" and challenges that "seem almost insurmountable when viewed at the local level—the difficult development sites, the lack of good vehicular and pedestrian circulation, and the separation and perceived distance from Center City, the universities, and the residential neighborhoods." Four goals define the response to these conditions:

Schuylkill Gateway, Philadelphia, Pennsylvania. Sasaki Associates' plan takes advantage of economic engines on both sides of Philadelphia's Schuylkill River—Center City to the east and growing academic and health-care activity around the University of Pennsylvania and Drexel University—to transform industrial lands and rail yards into a lively mixed-use district framed around a grid of new streets and continuous riverfront parks. Courtesy of Sasaki Associates, Inc. *See color insert, C-43.*

- **Transformation** of the river itself from a barrier into a seam.
- **Accommodation** of residential growth and expansion of research and other activities spun off by the nearby universities.
- **Integration** of the study area with nearby transit, roadways, and pedestrian connections.
- **Creation** of "a unified regional center that joins Center City and University City."

Key urban design concepts

The plan, which envisions entire city blocks of development running along both sides of the river, gains significant power from two trends benefiting downtowns—new residential demand and the growth of urban universities and medical centers and the economic activities that they spin off. The development provides a setting for new riverfront parks and weaves itself into existing Center City and University City fabric along major streets. At the same time, the plan seeks design inspiration in the area's industrial history. The main urban design elements include:

- **A public realm shaped by the area's industrial heritage,** including a linear park whose green lawn "will

flow beneath the stone piers and iron frame structure" that support a railbed 60 feet above the ground. Streets elevated on viaducts above the rail lines serving the area's industry will be preserved, accommodating parking below with less visual impact than is customary for surface lots.

- A new **open-space framework** that links a series of parks, landscaped streets, and squares to create a new sense of connection among the universities, the nearby medical district, Center City, both sides of the river, and adjacent neighborhoods. Street-level promenades will add pedestrian-oriented overlooks on river bridges, opening vistas of the district's new parks.

- A new **street network** that builds on Philadelphia's tradition of quiet side streets "to create a sense of place" for new residential neighborhoods. Construction of new north-south thoroughfares will restore the city's street grid on the river's western ("left") bank, connect the heavily used arterials that cross the project area (which themselves will be rebuilt as more appealing urban boulevards), and rebalance the twentieth-century emphasis on vehicular traffic by adding significant amenities for bicyclists and pedestrians.

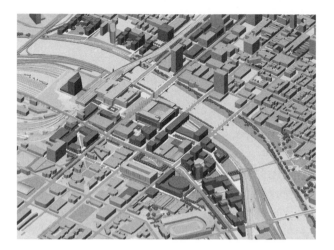

▲ Aerial model of potential new buildings on both sides of the river. Courtesy of Sasaki Associates, Inc.

◥ Aerial view across the Schuylkill River toward University City. Courtesy of Sasaki Associates, Inc.

- A **framework for development** that draws characteristics from the two flanking districts and supports a variety of uses—housing, research, academic, retail, and office—in a mix determined by market opportunities. Right-bank scale will be low, consistent with adjacent historic residential neighborhoods. On the left bank, taller buildings will define a continuous street wall along existing major streets, but lower-scale, mid-rise construction along the side streets will preserve views to the downtown skyline.

- In addition to tree-lined sidewalks and parks, "vibrant uses" that draw people to the area and reinforce new **connections** between Center City and University City.

Jury Comments

"The project made positive elements of what might be seen as negative, incorporating industrial aspects of the existing site.... This project offers a creative solution to the intractable problem of university expansion in a dense urban context."

Strategic Framework for Harvard University's North Allston Campus

LOCATION: Boston, Massachusetts

URBAN DESIGNER: Goody Clancy

CLIENT: The City of Boston (in collaboration with Harvard University and the North Allston community)

STUDY AREA AND PROGRAM: In 2000 Harvard University announced its intention to develop more than 10 million square feet of academic, research, and residential space on approximately 100 acres of land it had acquired in a traditionally blue-collar Boston neighborhood. In response, Mayor Thomas M. Menino commissioned a study designed to produce a planning framework that would accommodate the university's need to grow; equip the city to manage growth in ways that benefit citizens; and protect the neighborhood's traditional residential character.

YEAR OF AWARD: 2005

STATUS: The city adopted the plan, the community endorsed it, and Menino described it as "the mayor's plan for North Allston."

▲▲ North Allston Strategic Framework, Boston, Massachusetts. Goody Clancy worked with the City of Boston, the North Allston community, and Harvard University to create a framework to guide the university's expansion in this diverse neighborhood located across the Charles River from Harvard's existing campus. The plan focuses on ways in which university growth can enhance neighborhood character for residents and the campus community—preserving existing residential areas and transforming former industrial sites and strip retail into a new, walkable Main Street and neighborhood square, mixed-income housing for both populations, and new connections to the river. Courtesy of Goody Clancy. *See color insert, C-44.*

▲ District plan, with new construction shown in dark red. Representative buildings at right indicate Harvard's planned campus. Courtesy of Goody Clancy.

Critical issues

- **Preservation** of North Allston's stable residential areas while addressing their limited ability to generate jobs and economic growth.

- **Parking lots and industrial uses dominate** a degraded and pedestrian-hostile streetscape. Poor transition from large-scale uses like big-box stores to nearby residential areas.

- **Strong resident suspicion of Harvard's intentions and size** reinforce the university's instinct to close campus off from its neighbors.

Key urban design concepts

The urban designers built a framework on three major elements:

- **Treating growth and change as engines** that could generate visible improvements for residents: increased livability in the existing residential neighborhood; revitalization of the weak commercial corridor; creation of a new town square as a meeting ground for campus and neighborhood; rebuilding of the neglected streetscape; introduction of new cultural facilities; and opening of access to new jobs.

- **Avoiding the prevalent buffering of town from gown,** creating instead an integrated community in which neighborhood and campus are permeable, welcoming, and blend in ways that draw together residents, students, faculty, and staff.

- **Recognizing the benefits of "civic density" by creating transitions in scale that respect the traditional neighborhood** and encouraging height and building types in strategic locations that allow the university to accommodate the people and activity needed to support new commercial activity and public elements, including revitalized public parks and better access to nearby natural assets like the Charles River.

Jury Comments

"Democracy at its best. There was a tenacity of all parties…to reach a comprehensive plan…. Edges and connections between 'town and gown' are made with great skill."

Northeastern University West Campus Master Plan

LOCATION: Boston, Massachusetts
URBAN DESIGNER: William Rawn Associates Architects, Inc.
CLIENT: Northeastern University
STUDY AREA AND PROGRAM: A plan to extend the existing campus to a 10-acre parcel. Dormitory space for 2,000 students occupies most of the 1.2 million square feet of development.
YEAR OF AWARD: 2005
STATUS: The plan has been approved and Northeastern has completed development of the campus.

Critical issues

In the early 1990s, Northeastern faced a choice. As it made a conscious transition from commuter school to large residential university, it could extend its traditional

Northeastern University West Campus Master Plan, Boston, Massachusetts. William Rawn Associates helped Northeastern University reach back to its roots as an institution that embraced the city. The plan introduces a new generation of buildings and spaces that "welcome the city onto the campus" with large, formal arches and other elements that lead visitors into the heart of the university. Aerial photo Alex S. MacLean/Landslides—www.landslides.com. *See color insert, C-45.*

pattern of inward-focused development or return to its roots as an institution whose form and character reached out to embrace the city around it. Choosing the latter course, the university asked the urban designer to create a campus plan that demonstrated its commitment to being "Boston's urban university," an institution that takes advantage of its urban setting by creating a series of open spaces and buildings that connect to surrounding public streets and demonstrate the institution's strong ties to the city.

Key urban design concepts

Working with an advisory committee with representatives from community and civic organizations, elected officials, representation from the mayor's office, and other key stakeholders, the urban design team created a plan over two years that combined "a strong civic presence ... [and] a strong sense of engagement and openness to the city." The plan's core elements included:

- **A new generation of buildings that convey an urban character** by "facing the city and contributing to the public realm."

- **Shaping building designs to "welcome the city onto the campus"** with large, formal arches and other elements that lead visitors into the heart of the campus.

- **Creation of campus open spaces that connect directly to the street grid** and visibly relate to buildings and spaces surrounding the campus.

- Mixed-use **buildings that integrate university and community-serving uses** and locate them along public streets.

Jury Comments

"Through the skillful, strategic placement and shaping of a handful of new buildings, powerful, memorable spaces are created for this urban campus that relate to and engage the surrounding urban context."

University Square, University of British Columbia

LOCATION: Vancouver, British Columbia
URBAN DESIGNER: Moore Ruble Yudell Architects & Planners
CLIENT: UBC Properties Trust
STUDY AREA AND PROGRAM: The 18-acre project accommodates 415,000 square feet of mixed-use development that will form a new gateway to the university area.
YEAR OF AWARD: 2006
STATUS: The plan has been approved.

Critical issues

After years of working to create an "ivory tower" distinct from the surrounding community, a university may find it difficult to change course and begin trying to build stronger physical, social, cultural, and economic connections to surrounding neighborhoods. This project

The heart of Northeastern's new West Campus. Architect: William Rawn Associates. Copyright 1999 Steve Rosenthal.

University Square, University of British Columbia, Vancouver. Under Moore Ruble Yudell Architects & Planners' design, what might have been a fairly straightforward development emerges as a vibrant public square, animated by adjacent uses, celebratory architecture, and its function as the physical connection between the university and its surrounding neighborhood. Courtesy of Moore Ruble Yudell Architects & Planners with Hugh Condon Marler, architects; Olin Partnership, landscape architect.

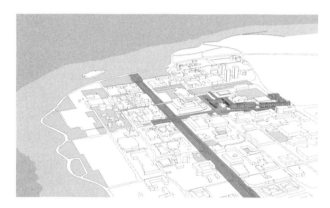

Connections to the larger neighborhood. Courtesy of Moore Ruble Yudell Architects & Planners with Hugh Condon Marler, architects; Olin Partnership, landscape architect.

directly acknowledges the need to forge a sense of connection for UBC, and it locates connection as much in the vitality it injects into its new gateway as in the physical linkage the gateway creates.

Key urban design concepts

The plan transforms what could have been a fairly straightforward development into a vibrant "University Square" animated by surrounding uses, celebratory architecture, and its physical connection between the university and adjacent neighborhood.

How the Projects Illustrate the Principles

1. **Build community in an increasingly diverse society.** All of these case studies stress the key role a mix of uses and spaces can play in strengthening community. Notably, not one of the projects reflects a desire to insulate the campus in question from its host community; instead, each aims to integrate a campus into its surrounding neighborhood. The most striking examples include the Savannah Collage of Art and Design, which uses downtown Savannah as its campus, and Harvard's North Allston framework, which seeks to rethink the university's tradition of cloistered "yards" and deploy campus facilities in collaboration with the community to create a rich, lively public realm. The master plan for the University of Washington Tacoma embraces its urban location with a plan that inserts new

educational uses into outmoded industrial buildings and warehouses, bringing new life to a section of the city's downtown. Northeastern University's West Campus plan dramatically opens the campus to the surrounding city. The plans for revitalizing LeDroit Park in Washington, D.C., Schuylkill Gateway in Philadelphia, and University Square at the University of British Columbia reflect a new level of commitment to building social, cultural, and physical connections to adjacent communities. The Howard University, Harvard, and Schuylkill plans focus on social equity with the incorporation of significant mixed-income housing and other community benefits.

2. **Advance environmental sustainability.** Spanning a decade, these case studies chart a steadily emerging focus on the constituent elements of sustainability. In addition to commitments to state-of-the-art green building and site design, they place increasingly explicit emphasis on public transit and the ability of students, faculty, and staff to live near the campus to reduce their need for automobiles. Among the more recent case studies, the urban designers challenge client institutions—and surrounding neighborhoods—to grow with only minimal new parking by adding housing, increasing walk-to-work options, reviving walkable commercial districts, and similar steps.

3. **Expand individual choices.** The once-uniform vision of campuses as outposts of learning buffered from the larger world has faded. Many institutions have reversed course and now strive to break down barriers between campus and community, in part because the students, faculty, and staff they seek to recruit prefer integration to cosseted isolation. Rather than a respite from urban excitement, these groups tend to find value in the housing, shopping, dining, entertainment, recreation, and other opportunities that urban life offers. With the breaking down of campus and community

barriers (both physical and metaphorical), surrounding communities have gained their own access to new choices. Savannah residents now head downtown to enjoy SCAD's cultural offerings, and the densely built North Allston community voiced strong interest in access to the green spaces that Harvard will create as it builds its new facilities.

4. **Enhance personal health.** Far more than previous campus-related planning, as noted earlier, these case studies focus on walkability. More recent plans acknowledge a growing responsibility to create housing and other uses within walking distance of campus—to serve both institutional and surrounding communities—as a significant step toward promoting a culture of healthier lifestyles.

5. **Make places for people.** Like the public realm case studies, most of these plans do not rely solely on a formal design to achieve excellence. Rather than an act of physical design, the urban design teams approached these plans as an exercise in community building. Northeastern's West Campus Master Plan comes closest to the traditionally formulated site plan, but even it functions more as a policy document. Each of the plans commits its institution to seek distinction in how it animates streets, squares, and other public spaces around the campus rather than in the placement and design of individual buildings. These plans acknowledge that each institution will continue to modify the details of its plan to adapt to emerging opportunities—SCAD will buy downtown buildings that meet its requirements at some point in the future, and Harvard will build new research buildings as fields of knowledge evolve—but all of these institutions will continue to shape their campuses with an eye firmly on how growth can enrich their relationship to the larger community.

Conclusion

For a book that looks to the future of urban design, there is no more fitting conclusion than New Orleans.

Two months after Hurricane Katrina, Louisiana's governor organized a Conference on Recovery and Rebuilding. Despite nonstop media coverage, the sight and stillness of a New Orleans with more than 300,000 residents missing stunned outsiders arriving for the conference. The staggering losses of the city (and region) told two distinct stories. The first suggested a devastation impossible to comprehend fully—even with direct experience of it. A second story, however, offered a measure of hope equal to the first story's despair. Well over three-quarters of the seven hundred conference participants were local leaders from every walk of life, every race, and every economic level. All had weathered profound personal misfortune, and most—like their fellow residents—had lost their jobs as the city's economy ground to a halt. Still, they exhibited compassion, humor, and hope.

Over three days these participants crafted a vision as humane as it was beautiful and as bold as it was realistic. It suggests how America can build its cities in the twenty-first century. The vision, to which New Orleanians have returned again and again as reconstruction planning has made its slow progress (inevitable after destruction at this scale), spoke explicitly to the principles that inform this book—community, sustainability, health, choice, and the kinds of places people love. Participants talked about the rich sense of community that music, history, food, and festivals had given the city. Yet they talked just as often about their hope for new places animated by these qualities that, finally, could bring people together, erasing the racial and class lines that had long divided New Orleans. They dreamed of a region that could reverse the impetus for sprawl, which had chewed away at the city's natural protections against flooding, by focusing on renewed respect for nature and a commitment to attracting people back to older neighborhoods by enhancing quality of life there.

One community member after another rose to lament what they saw as the city's greatest loss in the years preceding Hurricane Katrina: a long, slow surrender of Main Streets to suburban malls. They asked how they could rebuild a walkable city in ways that would improve both their own health and the social health of their communities. Throughout the conference, participants made clear that they wanted transportation choices that freed them from their cars; housing choices that helped them stay in familiar locales, accommodated lifestyle differences, and allowed them to grow old in the neighborhoods they loved; and development choices that let them walk to work, to stores, to schools, and to parks. Asking how the two-thirds of New Orleans that must be rebuilt should look yielded a startling yet reassuring response: Residents, participants said, love the city's historic neighborhoods for their scale and connections to the past. Yet they also yearn for new models in other districts whose character (and, surprisingly, density) can support community, sustainability, walkability, and choices that they defined as integral aspects of beauty.

We might consider this a utopian vision had it not come from the people whose hands will build it. Across the United States, more than half the structures in which Americans will live, work, and play in 2030 have yet to be built. This country will embark on a massive rebuilding—New Orleans writ large—over these next decades. The principles behind this post-Katrina vision could form a remarkable template for that rebuilding—a gift to every American community from the beleaguered citizens of New Orleans.

Endnotes

Part I

1 Jane Jacobs, *Death and Life of Great American Cities* (New York: Random House, 1961); Kevin Lynch, *The Image of the City* (Cambridge, Mass.: MIT Press, 1960); Christopher Alexander, Sara Ishikawa, Murray Silverstein, et al., *A Pattern Language: Towns, Buildings, Construction* (New York: Oxford University Press, 1977).

2 William Manchester, *A World Lit Only by Fire: The Medieval Mind and the Renaissance; Portrait of an Age* (London: Little, Brown and Company, 1992).

3 David Owen, "Why New York Is the Greenest City in America," *New Yorker*, October 18, 2004, 111. "Carbon footprint" refers to the cumulative amount of specific gases—carbon dioxide being the most commonly measured—produced by the activities of a person or a group of people (e.g., a business, a community, a country, all of humanity). These gases trap heat in the earth's atmosphere, and the resulting worldwide rise in temperatures has begun to produce large-scale climatic change. Efforts to curtail production of these so-called "greenhouse gases" and mitigate their impacts over the twenty-first century have emerged as the focus of political debate since the year 2000.

4 Interview with Rebecca Barnes, 2008.

5 See the American Institute of Architects (AIA) Web site for more information: http://develop2.aia.org/press_facts&defPr=1 (accessed August 21, 2007).

6 Interview with Terry Foegler, 2008.

7 José Luis Sert, in an address to the Harvard University Graduate School of Design Invitation Conference on Urban Design, April 9, 1956.

8 Roger K. Lewis, speaking in "Density: The New American Dream," panel discussion at "Density: Myth and Reality", conference sponsored by the Boston Society of Architects, American Institute of Architects, and Civic Initiative for a Livable New England, Boston, September 14, 2003.

9 Christopher B. Leinberger, "The Next Slum?" *Atlantic* 301, no. 2 (March 2008): 74.

10 Ibid., 71.

11 Spiro Kostoff, *The City Shaped: Urban Patterns and Meanings Through History* (New York: Bullfinch Press, 1991), 43ff.

12 Ibid., 102–103; Lewis Mumford, *The City in History: Its Transformations and Its Prospects* (New York: Harcourt Brace & Company, 1961), 61–63; see also http://en.wikipedia.org/wiki/Hippodamus_of_Miletus (accessed July 21, 2008).

13 Mumford, *The City in History*, 87.

14 Mumford, *The City in History*, 192.

15 Mumford, *The City in History*, 191–192; also, Kostoff, *The City Shaped*, 104–105.

16 Kostoff, *The City Shaped*, 108.

17 Kostoff, *The City Shaped*, 108–111. See also *bastide*, Wikipedia, http://en.wikipedia.org/wiki/bastide (accessed April 29, 2007); Adrian Randolph, "The Bastides of Southwest France," *Art Bulletin* 77, no. 2 (June 1995): 290–307; and Horst De La Croix, *Military Considerations in City Planning: Fortifications* (New York: George Braziller, 1972), 33, 36.

18 Kostoff, *The City Shaped*, 108–111; Nancy Volkman and Phillip Pregill, *Landscapes in History: Design and Planning in Eastern and Western Traditions* (New York: John Wiley & Sons, 1999), 194.

19 "Historic Centre of the City of Pienza," *UNESCO World Heritage List*, April 30, 2007, http://whc.unesco.org/pg.cfm?cid=31&id_site=789 (accessed July 13, 2008).

20 Mumford, *The City in History*, 386–395; De La Croix, *Military Considerations in City Planning*, 48–52.

21 Edmund N. Bacon, *Design of Cities*, rev. ed. (New York: Viking Press, 1974), 217; Kostoff, *The City Shaped*, 143–145.

22 Mumford, *The City in History*, 387.

23 Ibid., 387.

24 Kostoff, *The City Shaped*, 215.

25 Ibid., 216; Bacon, *Design of Cities*, 140ff.

26 Ibid., 143.

27 Ibid., 134; Niklaus Pevsner, *An Outline of European Architecture* (Baltimore: Penguin Books, 1966), 251.

28 The Architecture Working Group, *Architecture and the Built Environment: A Consultation Document* (Belfast: Arts Council of Northern Ireland, 2002), http://www.artscouncil-ni.org/departs/creative/architect/architect.pdf (accessed July 13, 2008).

29 Mumford, *The City in History*, 439ff.; Kostoff, *The City Shaped*, 136 and 252.

30 Mumford, *The City in History*, 442.

31 Edwin G. Burrows and Mike Wallace, *Gotham: A History of New York City to 1898* (New York: Oxford University Press, 1999), 23ff.

32 Ibid., 23–74.

33 Ibid., 43.

34 Bacon, *Design of Cities*, 217–219; Kostoff, *The City Shaped*, 144–146.

35 Bacon, *Design of Cities*, 217–221; Kostoff, *The City Shaped*, 96, 146.

36 Andro Linklater and David McCullough, *Measuring America: How the United States Was Shaped by the Greatest Land Sale in History* (New York: Plume Books, 2003), 70–73.

37 Kostoff, *The City Shaped*, 99–101.

38 Burrows and Wallace, *Gotham*, 421.

39 Kostoff, *The City Shaped*, 209.

40 Mumford, *The City in History*, 422.

41 Mumford, *The City in History*, 446–449.

42 Oliver Gillham, *The Limitless City: A Primer on the Urban Sprawl Debate* (Washington, D.C.: Island Press, 2002), 25–26.

43 Campbell Gibson, *Population of the 100 Largest Cities and Other Urban Places in the United States: 1790 to 1990* (Washington, D.C.: U.S. Census Bureau, 1998), http://www.census.gov/population/www/documentation/twps0027.html (accessed July 13, 2008).

44 Leo Marx, *The Machine in the Garden: Technology and the Pastoral Ideal in America* (New York: Oxford, 1964), 26.

45 For example, Catherine Beecher's *Treatise on Domestic Economy, for the Use of Young Ladies at Home, and at School* (Boston: Marsh, Capen, Lyon, and Webb, 1841), which offers plans for two-story cottage dwellings, and Andrew Jackson Downing's *Architecture of Country Houses, including Designs for Cottages, Farm-houses, and Villas* (New York: D. Appleton & Co., 1850).

46 Gillham, *The Limitless City*, 26–27.

47 Ibid., 27–28.

48 Ibid., 29; Louis P. Cain, "Annexation," *The Electronic Encyclopedia of Chicago* (2005), http://www.encyclopedia.chicagohistory.org/pages/53.html (accessed July 13, 2008).

49 Kenneth T. Jackson, *The Crabgrass Frontier: The Suburbanization of the United States* (New York: Oxford, 1985), 136. "Sanitary" refers to the extension of sewer lines, as well as to the changeover from horse to electric traction power.

50 Gillham, *The Limitless City*, 179–180; Mumford, *The City in History*, 515–516.

51 R. Stephen Sennott, *Encyclopedia of 20th Century Architecture* (London: Taylor & Francis, 2003), 364.

52 Gillham, *The Limitless City*, 179–180.

53 John A. Kouwenhoven, *The Columbia Historical Portrait of New York* (New York: Harper & Row, 1972), 243–244. See also "James Bogardus," *Encyclopædia Britannica Online*, http://www.britannica.com/eb/article-9080396 (accessed May 13, 2007).

54 "American Architecture," *Microsoft Encarta Encyclopedia* (Redmond, WA: Microsoft Corporation, 2003); Melissa Matlins, "Singer Building, Tallest Building in the World 1908–1909," NYC-Architecture.com (2005), http://www.nyc-architecture.com/GON/GON003.htm (accessed May 14, 2007); Christopher Gray, "Once the Tallest Building, but Since 1967 a Ghost," NYC-*Architecture.com* (2004), http://www.nyc-architecture.com/ GON/GON003.htm (accessed May 14, 2007).

55 Gray, "Once the Tallest Building."

56 Gillham, *The Limitless City*, 26.

57 Jane Jacobs, *The Death and Life of Great American Cities* (New York: Vintage Books, 1961), 235ff.

58 Gillham, *The Limitless City*, 26.

59 Marx, *The Machine in the Garden*, 227ff.

60 "Central Park," *Wikipedia*, http://en.wikipedia.org/wiki/Central_Park (accessed May 14, 2007).

61 Kostoff, *The City Shaped*, 82.

62 Camillo Sitte, *City Planning According to Artistic Principles*, trans. George R. Collins and Christiane Crasemann Collins (New York: Random House, 1965).

63 Kostoff, *The City Shaped*, 82.

64 Ibid., 235.

65 Ibid., 217.

66 Kostoff, *The City Assembled*, 160, 237; see also Rai Y. Okamoto and Frank E. Williams, Regional Plan Association, *Urban Design Manhattan* (New York: Viking, 1969), 45.

67 Jackson, *The Crabgrass Frontier*, 157.

68 Ibid., 161.

69 Gillham, *The Limitless City*, 32–33.

70 Ibid., 29–30; Mumford, *The City in History*, Plate 51; Richard Moe and Carter Wilkie, *Changing Places: Rebuilding Community in the Age of Sprawl* (New York: Henry Holt, 1997), 42–43.

71 Gillham, *The Limitless City*, 29–30.

72 Ibid., 30; Jackson, *The Crabgrass Frontier*, 175–185.

73 Gillham, *The Limitless City*, 30; Jackson, *The Crabgrass Frontier*, 175–185.

74 Frank Lloyd Wright, *Modern Architecture, Being the Kahn Lectures for 1930* (Princeton, N.J.: 1931), 101.

75 Frank Lloyd Wright, *The Living City* (New York: Horizon Press, 1958), 22.

76 Gillham, *The Limitless City*, 30–31.

77 As quoted in Moe and Wilkie, *Changing Places*, 45.

78 Kenneth Frampton, *Modern Architecture: A Critical History* (New York: Thames and Hudson, 1992), 156; Alan Colquhoun, *Modern Architecture* (New York: Oxford University Press, 2002), 140–142.

79 Gillham, *The Limitless City*, 42; Frampton, *Modern Architecture*, 155–156.

80 Frampton, *Modern Architecture*, 154–156.

81 Robert Furneaux Jordan, *Le Corbusier* (New York: Lawrence Hill & Company, 1972), 34.

82 Frampton, *Modern Architecture*, 101–102.

83 Ibid., 102.

84 Anatole Kopp, *Town and Revolution: Soviet Architecture and City Planning 1917–1935* (New York: George Braziller, 1970), 60–63.

85 Eric Mumford, *The CIAM Discourse on Urbanism, 1928–1960* (Cambridge, Mass.: MIT Press, 2000), 27.

86 Ibid., 19–22.

87 Kopp, *Town and Revolution*, 168.

88 Ibid., 171–172.

89 Ibid., 181ff.; Mumford, *The CIAM Discourse on Urbanism*, 45.

90 Ibid., 1.

91 Ibid., 12–16.

92 Ibid., 15.

93 Nikolai Miliutin charged that skyscrapers were "the last cry of capitalism" in his criticism of Le Corbusier's 1930 recommendations for Moscow. See Mumford, *The CIAM Discourse on Urbanism*, 47.

94 José Luis Sert, *Can Our Cities Survive? An ABC of Urban Problems, Their Analysis, Their Solutions* (Cambridge, Mass.: Harvard University Press; London: H. Milford, Oxford University Press, 1942).

95 Mumford, *The CIAM Discourse on Urbanism*, 90.

96 Sigfried Giedion, *Space, Time and Architecture: The Growth of a New Tradition* (Cambridge, Mass.: Harvard University Press, 1966), 833.

97 Mumford, *The CIAM Discourse on Urbanism*, 79.

98 Ibid., 79.

99 From a 1929 article written by Le Corbusier in *L'intransigeant* and quoted in Mumford, *The CIAM Discourse on Urbanism*, 56.

100 Giedion, *Space, Time and Architecture*, 822.

101 Ibid., 833.

102 Mumford, *The CIAM Discourse on Urbanism*, 49.

103 William L. C. Wheaton, "Federal Action Toward a National Dispersal Policy," *Bulletin of the Atomic Scientists* 7, no. 9 (September 1951): 274.

104 Goodhue Livingston Jr., "The Blight of Our Cities," *Bulletin of the Atomic Scientists* 7, no. 9 (September 1951): 262.

105 Giedion, *Space, Time and Architecture*, 821.

106 Gillham, *The Limitless City*, 44.

107 Eric Mumford, "The Emergence of Urban Design in the Breakup of CIAM," *Harvard Design Magazine* 24 (Spring/Summer 2006): 10–20.

108 Giedion, *Space, Time and Architecture*, 818.

109 Richard Marshall, "The Elusiveness of Urban Design," *Harvard Design Magazine Harvard Design Magazine* 24 (Spring/Summer 2006): 25.

110 Mumford, "The Emergence of Urban Design in the Breakup of CIAM," 11.

111 Ibid., 12.

112 Ibid., 11.

113 "'Urban Design': Extracts from the 1956 First Urban Design Conference at the GSD," *Harvard Design Magazine* 24 (Spring/Summer 2006), 5.

114 Ibid., 12.

115 Ibid., 13.

116 Ibid., 5.

117 Ibid., 5.

118 Mumford, "The Emergence of Urban Design in the Breakup of CIAM," 16.

119 "'Urban Design': Extracts from the 1956 First Urban Design Conference at the GSD," 6.

120 Ibid., 9.

121 David Gosling, *The Evolution of American Urban Design: A Chronological Anthology* (Chichester, UK: John Wiley & Sons, 2003), 36, 38.

122 Among other, earlier attempts was that of Gruen's ex-partner, Morris Ketchum, who designed Shopper's World in Framingham, Massachusetts. There, stores were organized around an outdoor "village green" and surrounded by surface parking. See Alex Wall, *Victor Gruen: From Urban Shop to New City* (Barcelona: Actar, 2005), 65–67, 81–87, 92–100.

123 Wall, *Victor Gruen*, 122–138.

124 Alex Krieger and Lisa J. Green, *Past Futures: Two Centuries of Imagining Boston* (Cambridge, Mass.: Harvard University Graduate School of Design, 1985), 72–73.

125 Victoria Newhouse, *Wallace K. Harrison, Architect* (New York: Rizzoli, 1989), 245.

126 Gosling, *The Evolution of American Urban Design*, 89.

127 Colquhoun, *Modern Architecture*, 223–229.

128 Ada Louise Huxtable, *Will They Ever Finish Bruckner Boulevard?* (New York: Macmillan, 1970), 44.

129 Jane Holtz Kay, *Asphalt Nation: How the Automobile Took Over America and How We Can Take It Back* (New York: Crown, 1997), 249.

130 "'Urban Design': Extracts from the 1956 First Urban Design Conference at the GSD," 8.

131 Jacobs, *The Death and Life of Great American Cities*, 187.

132 Ibid., 153.

133 Gillham, *The Limitless City*, 57–58.

134 Ibid., 58.

135 National Trust for Historic Preservation, Main Street Center, http://www.mainstreet.org/content.aspx?page=1807&section=1 (accessed June 28, 2007).

136 Peter Katz, *The New Urbanism: Toward an Architecture of Community* (New York: McGraw-Hill, 1994), xxxvii–xli.

137 Andrés Duany, Elizabeth Plater-Zyberk, and Jeff Speck, *Suburban Nation: The Rise of Sprawl and the Decline of the American Dream* (New York: North Point Press, 2000), 27–31; see also http://www.ci.boca-raton.fl.us/dev/pdf/CRA/MiznerParkHandout.pdf (accessed June 30, 2007) and http://www.epa.gov/smartgrowth/case/mizner.htm (accessed June 30, 2007).

138 James Howard Kunstler, *The Geography of Nowhere: The Rise and Decline of America's Man-Made Landscape* (New York: Simon & Schuster, 1993).

139 Gillham, *The Limitless City*, 180–184.

140 Interview with Constance Bodurow, 2007.

141 Rodger Doyle, "Deindustrialization: Why Manufacturing Continues to Decline," *Scientific American*, May 2002, http://www.sciam.com/print_version.cfm?articleID=00094F4E-11F8-1CD4B4A8809EC588EEDF (accessed August 22, 2007).

142 Richard Florida, "The Rise of the Creative Class," *Washington Monthly*, May 2002, http://www.washingtonmonthly.com/features/2001/0205.florida.html#byline (accessed August 21, 2007).

143 Maureen MacAvey, presentation to *Reinventing the Urban Village* symposium sponsored by the Boston Society of Architects and AIA Center for Communities by Design, May 14, 2005, Boston.

144 Laurie Volk, "Making Density Work: Dollars, Design, and the Environment," panel discussion at the American Institute of Architects annual meeting, Boston, May 15, 2008.

145 Ibid.

146 Kemba J. Dunham and Ray A. Smith, "Behind Zooming Condo Prices: New Demographics or a Bubble?" *Wall Street Journal*, August 18, 2005, A1.

147 USA Today article in 2006.

148 Christine Quinn, "The Cooperator," *Co-op and Condo Monthly* 27, no. 6 (June 2007): 23. http://cooperator.com/articles/1456/1/City-Council-Speaker-Christine-Quinn/Page1.html (accessed August 5, 2008).

149 Gillham, *The Limitless City*, 62.

150 Gillham, *The Limitless City*, 39–40.

151 Mumford, *The City in History*, 472.

152 Louis Uchitelle, "Rebuilt City Starts to Feel the Effects of the Slowdown," *New York Times*, April 9, 2001.

153 Edward McMahon, "Stopping Sprawl by Growing Smarter," *Planning Commissioners Journal* 26 (Spring 1997): 4.

154 Gillham, *The Limitless City*, 105.

155 U.S. Department of Transportation, *Transportation Statistics Annual Report 1999*, 106–110.

156 Ibid., 110. See also U.S. Department of Energy, Energy Information Administration, *Petroleum Overview 1949–2006*, http://www.eia.doe.gov/emeu/aer/petro.html (August 30, 2007).

157 "Gas Prices Send Surge of Riders to Mass Transit," *New York Times*, May 10, 2008. http://www.nytimes.com/2008/05/10/business/10transit.html (accessed August 20, 2008).

158 "Gas Prices Apply Brakes to Suburban Migration," *Washington Post*, August 5, 2008, A1. A New Jersey appraiser's analysis of suburban real estate patterns in the fall of 2007 suggested that closer suburbs on commuter-rail lines had levels of unsold homes normally found in rising real estate markets. Otherwise similar communities located away from commuter-rail lines more commonly had unsold inventory levels typically seen in falling markets. See "Where the Deals Are," *New York Times*, September 16, 2007. http://www.nytimes.com/2007/09/16/realestate/16cov.html?pagewanted=1&sq=monclair%20%20%20maplewood (accessed August 7, 2008).

159 Peter Newman and Jeffrey Kenworthy, *Sustainability and Cities: Overcoming Automobile Dependence* (Washington, D.C.: Island Press, 1999), 49–51.

160 Colin J. Campbell and Jean H. Laherrere, "The End of Cheap Oil," *Scientific American*, March 1998, 78–83.

161 Gillham, *The Limitless City*, 108.

162 IPPC estimate from http://www.cop.noaa.gov/stressors/climatechange/current/sea_level_rise.html (accessed August 6, 2008); report on research at the Proudman Oceanographic Laboratory, UK, from http://environment.newscientist.com/channel/earth/climate-change/dn13721-sea-levels-will-rise-15-metres-by-2100.html (accessed August 6, 2008).

163 Gillham, *The Limitless City*, 113–114; see also Julian Borger, "Half of Global Car Exhaust Produced by U.S. Vehicles," *The Guardian*, June 29, 2006, http://www.guardian.co.uk/environment/2006/jun/29/travelandtransport/usnews (accessed September 26, 2008).

164 Gillham, *The Limitless City*, 12.

165 U.S. Department of Transportation, Bureau of Transportation Statistics, *Transportation Statistics Annual Report 1999*, BTS99-03 (Washington, D.C.: U.S. Department of Transportation, Bureau of Transportation Statistics, 1999), 54–56, http://www.bts.gov/publications/transportation_statistics_annual_report/1999/pdf/entire.pdf (accessed July 13, 2008); see also Texas Transportation Institute, *2001 Urban Mobility Report* (College Station: Texas A&M University Sys-

tem, 2001), Table A-7, http://tti.tamu.edu/documents/ums/mobility_report_2001.pdf (accessed July 13, 2008).

166 Comment from unidentified audience member, "Density: The New American Dream," panel discussion at "Density: Myth and Reality," conference sponsored by the Boston Society of Architects, American Institute of Architects, and Civic Initiative for a Livable New England, Boston, September 14, 2003.

167 Wendell Cox, "Coping with Traffic Congestion," in *A Guide to Smart Growth*, ed. Jane Shaw and Roger Utt (Washington, D.C.: The Heritage Foundation, 2000), 39.

168 Donald Chen, *Greetings from Smart Growth America* (Washington, D.C.: Smart Growth America, 2000), 7.

169 Steven E. Polzin, *The Case for Moderate Growth in Vehicle Miles of Travel: A Critical Juncture in U.S. Travel Behavior Trends* (Washington, D.C.: U.S. Department of Transportation, 2006), 26. Polzin uses data from the 2001 National Household Travel Survey/Nationwide Personal Transportation Survey, the most recent available.

170 Gillham, *The Limitless City*, 93.

171 http://www.publictransportation.org/facts/080731_transit_savings.asp (accessed August 7, 2008).

172 American Public Transportation Association, *Public Transportation Facts*, http://www.apta.com/media/facts.cfm (accessed August 29, 2007).

173 American Public Transportation Association, *Transit Scores Wins in States, Regions Throughout U.S.*, http://www.apta.com/passenger_transport/thisweek/061113_1.cfm (accessed August 29, 2007).

174 Center for Transit-Oriented Development, *Hidden in Plain Sight: Capturing the Demand for Housing near Transit* (Washington, D.C.: Federal Transportation Administration, 2004). Currently, roughly 6.0 million households are located within a half mile of the stations along 27 existing rail and light-rail transit systems. The Center's 2004 report concluded that by 2025, an additional 8.6 million households would seek housing in those half-mile zones and near stations on 15 other transit systems now in planning or under construction. In 2008, the Center updated its demand estimate to 15.2 million (9.2 million new) households seeking these locations by 2030. http://www.reconnectingamerica.org/public/reports (accessed August 7, 2008).

175 Christopher B. Leinberger in a panel discussion on "Density by Design" at the National Building Museum, February 1, 2007, Washington, D.C.

176 Gillham, *The Limitless City*, 204.

177 Portland Tri-Met Web site, http://www.trimet.org/about/history/maxoverview.htm and http://www.trimet.org/projects/index.htm (accessed September 1, 2007).

178 *Transit Friendly Development: Newsletter of Transit-Oriented Development and Land Use in New Jersey* vol. 2, no. 2 (November 2006), http://policy.rutgers.edu/vtc/tod/newsletter/vol2-num2/ (accessed September 1, 2007). Details about the program are available at http://www.state.nj.us/transportation/community/village/faq.shtm (accessed August 7, 2008).

179 U.S. Environmental Protection Agency, Office of Air Quality Planning and Standards, *Latest Findings on National Air Quality: 1999 Status and Trends* (Research Park Triangle, N.C.: USEAA, 2000), 20.

180 Andrew C. Revkin, "Tiny Bits of Soot Tied to Illnesses," *New York Times*, April 21, 2001.

181 U.S. Environmental Protection Agency, Office of Transportation and Air Quality, *Air Toxics from Motor Vehicles*, Environmental Fact Sheet, EPA400-F-92-004 (Washington, D.C.: U.S. Environmental Protection Agency, 2004), http://www.epa.gov/OMSWWW/f02004.pdf (accessed July 13, 2008).

182 Lawrence Frank, Peter Engleke, Thomas Schmid, Richard Killingsworth, and Centers for Disease Control, *How Land Use and Transportation Systems Affect Public Health: A Literature Review of the Relationship Between Physical Activity and Built Form* (Atlanta, GA: Centers for Disease Control and Prevention, 2001), 11; see http://www.cdc.gov/nccdphp/dnpa/pdf/aces-workingpaper1.pdf (accessed July 13, 2008).

183 Gillham, *The Limitless City*, 118.

184 U.S. Department of Transportation, Bureau of Transportation Statistics, *National Transportation Statistics 2007* (Washington, D.C.: U.S. Department of Transportation, 2007), http://www.bts.gov/publications/national_transportation_statistics/html/table_02_17.html (accessed August 30, 2007). See also: U.S. Census Bureau, *Population Estimates for Cities with Populations of 10,000 and Greater: July 1, 1999* (Washington, D.C.: Population Estimates Program, Population Division, U.S. Census Bureau (accessed October 20, 2000), http://www.census.gov/population/estimates/metro-city/SC10K-T3.txt.

185 U.S. Department of Transportation, Bureau of Transportation Statistics, *Transportation Statistics Annual Report 1997* (Washington, D.C.: U.S. Department of Transportation, 1997), 54–55.

186 U.S. Department of Agriculture, Economic Research Service, *Major Uses of Land in the United States, 2002*, http://www.ers.nrcs.usda.gov/publications/EIB14/eib14j.pdf (accessed August 6, 2008).

187 U.S. Department of Agriculture, Natural Resources Conservation Service, *State Rankings by Acreage and Rate of Non-Federal Land Developed* (Washington, D.C.: U.S. Department of Agriculture, 2000), http://www.nrcs.usda.gov/technical/NRI/maps/tables/t5845.html (accessed July 13, 2008). Note that the rate of development increased from 1.4 million acres per year in the ten-year period 1982–1992 to 3.2 million acres per year in the five-year period 1992–1997. An average number has been used for the entire fifteen-year period.

188 Peter J. Howe, "EPA Takes On Sprawl in Region," *Boston Globe*, February 2, 1999, http://www.search.boston.com/local/Search.do?s.sm.query=%22EPA+takes+on+Sprawl%22&S.tab=. Also see http://www.epa.gov/region1/pr/1999/020299.html.

189 William Fulton, et al. "Who Sprawls Most?" *The Brookings Institution Survey Series*, July 2001, 9.

190 Jonathan Glater, "Telecommuting's Big Experiment," *New York Times*, May 9, 2001.

191 Joel Kotkin, *The New Geography: How the Digital Revolution is Reshaping the American Landscape* (New York: Random House, 2001), 61.

192 Thomas A. Horan, *Digital Places: Building Our City of Bits* (Washington, D.C.: Urban Land Institute, 2000), 53.

193 Ibid., 61–62.

194 Richard Florida, *The Rise of the Creative Class: And How It's Transforming Work, Leisure, Community and Everyday Life* (New York: Basic Books, 2004).

195 Harriet Tregoning, "Making Density Work: Dollars, Design and the Environment," panel discussion at the American Institute of Architects annual meeting, Boston, May 15, 2008.

196 William S. Saunders, "Cappuccino Urbanism and Beyond," *Harvard Design Magazine* 25 (Fall 2006/Winter 2007), 3. Elsewhere in the same issue, architect and author Michael Sorkin uses the term "Starbucks urbanism."

197 Gillham, *The Limitless City*, 157.

198 "Designing to inspire, touch the heart, elevate the spirit, and restore a degraded environment," interview by Robert Gilman from *In Context* 35 (Spring 1993): 9.

199 U.S. Environmental Protection Agency, "Marylanders Confront Sprawl," *Nonpoint Source News-Notes* 47 (January/February 1997), http://www.epa.gov/NewsNotes/issue47/nne47.htm (accessed September 3, 2007).

200 Peter Calthorpe, *The Next American Metropolis: Ecology, Community and the American Dream* (New York: Princeton Architectural Press, 1993), 56–57.

201 Michael Bernick and Robert Cervero, *Transit Villages in the 21st Century* (New York: McGraw-Hill, 1997), 84.

202 Ibid., 5.

203 See "Urban Villages," http://www.urbanvillages.com/pages/829276/index.htm (accessed September 3, 2007).

204 Congress for the New Urbanism, "Canons of Sustainable Architecture and Urbanism," 7, http://www.cnu.org/canons (accessed September 29, 2008).

205 Gillham, *The Limitless City*, 181.

206 See the Congress for the New Urbanism Web site, "Principles of New Urbanism," http://www.newurbanism.org/newurbanism/principles.html (accessed September 3, 2007).

207 See John Ray Holke Jr., FAIA, ed., *Architectural Graphic Standards*, 10th ed. (New York: John Wiley & Sons, 2000), 81ff.

208 Michael Sorkin, "The End(s) of Urban Design," *Harvard Design Magazine* 25 (Fall 2006/Winter 2007), 17. See also the Michigan Debates on Urbanism series edited by Douglas Kelbaugh, *Everyday Urbanism; New Urbanism; Post Urbanism and ReUrbanism* (Ann Arbor: University of Michigan Press, 2005).

209 Nicolai Ouroussoff, "Streetwise: Critic's Notebook; Outgrowing Jane Jacobs," *New York Times*, April 30, 2006. http://www.nytimes.com/2006/04/30/weekinreview/30/Jacobs.html?partner=rssnyt&emc=rss (accessed July 6, 2008).

210 From a review of Rem Koolhaas' *S, M, L, XL* by Herbert Muschamp, "Architecture View: Rem Koolhaas Sizes Up the Future," *New York Times*, March 3, 1996.

211 Michael Sorkin, "The End(s) of Urban Design," *Harvard Design Magazine* 25 (Fall 2006/Winter 2007): 17. See also the Michigan Debates on Urbanism series edited by Douglas Kelbaugh, *Everyday Urbanism; New Urbanism; Post Urbanism and ReUrbanism.*

212 Tim Love, "Urban Design after Battery Park City," *Harvard Design Magazine* 25 (Fall 2006/Winter 2007), 60–70.

213 Ouroussoff, "Streetwise: Critic's Notebook; Outgrowing Jane Jacobs."

214 Sorkin, "The End(s) of Urban Design," 18.

Part II

215 Cache Valley (Utah) SDAT, *A Report by the Sustainable Design Assessment Team* (Washington, D.C.: American Institute of Architects, 2005), http://www.aia.org/liv_sdat_cities (accessed August 12, 2008).

216 See the AIA/RUDC Web site: http://www.aia.org/rudc2_template.cfm?pagename=rudc%5Fabout (accessed July 25, 2007).

217 "Testimony of Gladys W. Mack Before the Council of the District of Columbia's Committee on Finance and Revenue," January 23, 2006, www.wmata.com/about/MET_NEWS/pressroom/testimony/docs/Mack testimony 1-23-06.pdf (accessed August 15, 2008).

218 Christopher B. Leinberger in a panel discussion on "Density by Design" at the National Building Museum, February 1, 2007, Washington, D.C.

219 Smart Growth America, "What Is Smart Growth?" http://www.smartgrowthamerica.org/whatissg.html (accessed August 12, 2008).

220 Ebenezer Howard, *Tomorrow: A Peaceful Path to Real Reform* (London, 1898); reissued as *Garden Cities of Tomorrow* (London: S. Sonnenschein & Co., Ltd., 1902).

221 Kristina Kessler, "Defining the Public Realm," *Urban Land* (March 2006).

222 Christopher Hill and David Nagahiro, "Town and Gown Seek Common Ground," *Urban Land* (March 2008): 93.

Index